THE MULTILEVEL POLITICS OF TRADE

The Multilevel Politics of Trade presents a timely comparative analysis of eight federations (plus the European Union) to explore why some sub-federal actors have become more active in trade politics in recent years. As the contributing authors find, there is considerable variation in the intensity and modes of sub-federal participation. This they attribute to three key factors: the distinctive institutional features of federal systems; the nature and scope of trade policy and trade agreements; and the extent of social mobilization that accompanies a particular trade policy conversation.

As a whole, *The Multilevel Politics of Trade* argues that sub-federal actors' interests (jurisdictional, political, and economic) are what motivate them to participate in trade debates. However, institutional configurations, coupled with the influence of civil society actors, political parties, and others, determine the nature and scope of that participation. Informed by a deep knowledge of federal dynamics, this volume provides extensive comparative analyses of all of the North American and European federations and represents a significant intervention into the study of both federalism and political economy.

JÖRG BROSCHEK is an associate professor and Canada Research Chair (Tier 2) in comparative federalism and multilevel governance in the Department of Political Science at Wilfrid Laurier University.

PATRICIA M. GOFF is an associate professor of political science at Wilfrid Laurier University and Senior Fellow at the Centre for International Governance Innovation.

Studies in Comparative Political Economy and Public Policy

Editors: MICHAEL HOWLETT, DAVID LAYCOCK (Simon Fraser University), and STEPHEN MCBRIDE (McMaster University)

Studies in Comparative Political Economy and Public Policy is designed to showcase innovative approaches to political economy and public policy from a comparative perspective. While originating in Canada, the series provides attractive offerings to a wide international audience, featuring studies with local, subnational, cross-national, and international empirical bases and theoretical frameworks.

Editorial Advisory Board

Jeffrey Ayres, St Michael's College, Vermont
Neil Bradford, Western University
Janine Brodie, University of Alberta
William Carroll, University of Victoria
William Coleman, University of Waterloo
Rodney Haddow, University of Toronto
Jane Jenson, Université de Montréal
Laura Macdonald, Carleton University
Rianne Mahon, Wilfrid Laurier University
Michael Mintrom, Monash University
Grace Skogstad, University of Toronto
Leah Vosko, York University
Kent Weaver, Georgetown University
Linda White, University of Toronto

For a list of books published in the series, see page 383.

The Multilevel Politics of Trade

EDITED BY JÖRG BROSCHEK
AND PATRICIA GOFF

UNIVERSITY OF TORONTO PRESS
Toronto Buffalo London

© University of Toronto Press 2020
Toronto Buffalo London
utorontopress.com
Printed in Canada

ISBN 978-1-4875-0674-2 (cloth)   ISBN 978-1-4875-3477-6 (EPUB)
ISBN 978-1-4875-2452-4 (paper)   ISBN 978-1-4875-3476-9 (PDF)

Library and Archives Canada Cataloguing in Publication

Title: The multilevel politics of trade / edited by Jörg Broschek and
    Patricia Goff.
Names: Broschek, Jörg, editor. | Goff, Patricia M., editor.
Series: Studies in comparative political economy and public policy ; 59.
Description: Series statement: Studies in comparative political economy and
    public policy ; 59.
Identifiers: Canadiana (print) 20200156446 | Canadiana (ebook)
    20200156551 | ISBN 9781487524524 (paper) | ISBN 9781487506742
    (cloth) | ISBN 9781487534776 (EPUB) | ISBN 9781487534769 (PDF)
Subjects: LCSH: Commercial policy. | LCSH: Federal government.
Classification: LCC HF1411.M85 2020 | DDC 382/.3–dc23

University of Toronto Press acknowledges the financial assistance to its
publishing program of the Canada Council for the Arts and the Ontario Arts
Council, an agency of the Government of Ontario.

Canada Council   **Conseil des Arts**
for the Arts   **du Canada**

ONTARIO ARTS COUNCIL
CONSEIL DES ARTS DE L'ONTARIO
an Ontario government agency
un organisme du gouvernement de l'Ontario

Funded by the   Financé par le
Government   gouvernement
of Canada   du Canada

Canadä

MIX
Paper from
responsible sources
FSC® C016245

Contents

Acknowledgments

A little over four years ago we met on the way to get coffee. We chatted about the news and our work. The subject soon turned to the Canada-European Union Comprehensive Economic and Trade Agreement (CETA), and we were both intrigued by the role of sub-federal actors in those negotiations. Little did we know it at the time, but a research partnership was born.

This book emerged from a workshop that we held at the Balsillie School of International Affairs in October 2016, which was funded by a Connection Grant of the Social Sciences and Humanities Research Council of Canada, with support from the school and the Forum of Federations, Ottawa. During the first day of our workshop, on 14 October, the Regional Parliament of Wallonia's resolution against CETA made headlines – a coincidence demonstrating vividly and in real time the relevance of our emerging project.

We gratefully acknowledge all of the participants at that workshop. We were fortunate to have a number of practitioners present to engage with the academic perspective, and the exchange was enormously fruitful. Our sincere thanks go to Hugo Cameron, Terry Collins-Williams, Markus Gehring, Daryl Hanak, Laurence Marquis, Catherine Moureaux, Jean-François Raymond, Werner Schempp, Yvonne Stinson Ortíz, and Kay Wilkie for generously sharing their time and expertise. We would also like to thank John Light from the Forum of Federations for his support and Christian Freudlsperger for enriching our discussion.

John Ravenhill was at that workshop and served as a discussant on a later International Studies Association panel (San Francisco, 2018) where we presented some of this work. He has kindly read a good portion of this manuscript, and we thank him for his excellent comments, support, and insight. We would also like to thank the anonymous reviewers for their constructive and thoughtful suggestions, which contributed to improvements in the manuscript.

A number of research assistants helped with the preparation of the manuscript. Our thanks go to Jake Gorenkoff, Josh Mechler, Mike Piaseczny, Rachel Suffern, and Neven Vincic.

We are very grateful to Daniel Quinlan at University of Toronto Press for his enthusiastic support of this book project from the very beginning and for his guidance and advice throughout the process. Finally, we thank all our fabulous contributors for their patience, cordial engagement, and excellent work.

Jörg Broschek and Patricia Goff
Waterloo, Ontario

Abbreviations

11.11.11	Centre national de coopération au développement
AFL-CIO	American Federation of Labor and Congress of Industrial Organizations
AGP	Agreement on Government Procurement (Canada-US)
AIT	Agreement on Internal Trade
ANZCERTA	Australia-New Zealand Closer Economic Relations Trade Agreement
ATTAC	Association for the Taxation of Financial Transactions and Citizen's Action
AUSFTA	Australia-United States Free Trade Agreement
BGMK	Federal Law on the Participation of the Cantons in the Foreign Policy of the Swiss Confederation
BPUK	Bau-, Planungs- und Umweltdirektoren-Konferenz
B-VG	Bundes-Verfassungsgesetz
CAD	Canadian dollar
CCPA	Canadian Centre for Policy Alternatives
CDU	Christlich Demokratische Union Deutschlands
CE marking	Conformité Européenne
CER	Comprehensive Economic Relations Trade Agreement
CETA	European Union-Canada Comprehensive Economic and Trade Agreement
CFTA	Canadian Free Trade Agreement
COAG	Council of Australian Governments
COC	Council of Canadians
CoF	Council of the Federation
CPTPP	Comprehensive and Progressive Agreement for Trans-Pacific Partnership
CSOs	civil-society organizations
CSU	Christlich Soziale Union in Bayern

CTC	Citizens Trade Campaign
CTM	Mexican Confederation of Labour
CUSFTA	Canada-United States Free Trade Agreement
DFAT	Department of Foreign Affairs and Trade
EC	European Commission
ECJ	European Court of Justice
EFTA	European Free Trade Association
EP	European Parliament
EU	European Union
EUSFTA	European Union-Singapore Free Trade Agreement
FDI	foreign direct investment
FDP	Freie Demokratische Partei
FIT	Feed-In Tariff Program
FPÖ	Freiheitliche Partei Österreichs
FTA	Free Trade Agreement
FTAA	Free Trade Area of the Americas
FTQ	Fonds de solidarité
GATS	General Agreement on Trade in Services
GATT	General Agreement on Tariffs and Trade
GIs	geographic indications
GPA	Government Procurement Agreement (WTO)
IGPAC	Intergovernmental Policy Advisory Committee
IIAs	inter-institutional agreements
ISDS	investor-state dispute settlement
JCPC	Judicial Committee of the Privy Council
JEFTA	Japan-EU Free Trade Agreement
JSCOT	Joint Standing Committee on Treaties
KAFTA	Korea-Australia Free Trade Agreement
KdK	Konferenz der Kantonsregierungen
LAEIT	Law on the Approval of Economic International Treaties
LCT	Law on Celebration of Treaties
LHK	Landeshauptleutekonferenz
MAI	Multilateral Agreement on Investment
MEDT	Ministry of Economic Development and Trade
MEPs	Members of the European Parliament
MPs	Members of Parliament
MRA	mutual recognition agreement
MRA Committee	Joint Committee on Mutual Recognition of Professional Qualifications
MXN	Mexican peso
NAFTA	North American Free Trade Agreement

NCSL	National Conference of State Legislators
NDP	New Democratic Party
NGA	National Governors' Association
NGO	non-governmental organization
NWPTA	New West Partnership Trade Agreement
OAS	Organization of American States
OECD	Organisation for Economic Co-operation and Development
OMC	open method of coordination
ÖVP	Österreichische Volkspartei
PAN	Partido Acción Nacional
PQ	Parti Québécois
PRD	Partido de la Revolución Democrática
PRI	Partido Revolucionario Institucional
PROCEI	Programa de Competitividad e Innovación
PS	Parti socialiste
RCF	Regulatory Cooperation Forum
S&D	Progressive Alliance of Socialists and Democrats (aka Socialists and Democrats Group)
SCO	Standing Committee of Officials
SCOT	Commonwealth-States Standing Committee on Treaties
SEA	Single European Act
SMOs	social movement organizations
SPD	Sozialdemokratische Partei Deutschlands
SPÖ	Sozialdemokratische Partei Österreichs
SRE	Secretaría de Relaciones Exteriores
STOG	Senior Trade Officials Group
TFEU	Treaty on the Functioning of the European Union
TIEA	Trade and Investment Enhancement Agreement
TILMA	Trade, Investment, and Labour Mobility Agreement
TiSA	Trade in Services Agreement
TJN	Trade Justice Network
TPA	Trade Promotion Authority
TPP	Trans-Pacific Partnership
TTIP	Transatlantic Trade and Investment Partnership
US	United States
USMCA	United States-Mexico-Canada Agreement
USTR	United States Trade Representative
WTO	World Trade Organization

THE MULTILEVEL POLITICS OF TRADE

Introduction: The Evolution of Multilevel Trade Politics

JÖRG BROSCHEK AND PATRICIA GOFF

Capitalist economies have a built-in dynamic to expand markets, transcending the boundaries of regional, national, and supranational political entities. At the same time, however, sub-federal entities can play a pivotal role in facilitating or impeding economic integration as political authorities from different territorial scales shape aggregating markets (Wallner and Boychuk 2014; Weingast 1995; Wibbels 2005). For example, the Canadian provinces have emerged as important stakeholders in international trade policy since the 1980s. Intergovernmental relations in trade policy have remained informal, but most observers agree that ongoing interaction between the federal level and the provinces and territories has helped to foster a cooperative spirit (Kukucha 2016; Paquin 2013; Skogstad 2012). Recent developments surrounding the negotiation of the Canada-European Union Comprehensive Economic and Trade Agreement (CETA) or the new United States-Mexico-Canada Agreement (USMCA) bear this out. But as incentives to deepen economic integration are increasingly met with resistance, sub-federal units can also jeopardize trade liberalization, as exemplified through the refusal of three Belgian sub-federal parliaments to ratify CETA in October 2016. Likewise, ongoing debates about internal trade barriers, which are often connected to international-trade-agreement obligations, further signify the importance of sub-federal actors to processes of economic integration (Anderson 2012; Brown 2003; Kukucha 2015b; Mann and Smith 2015; Painter 1998). It is clear, for example, that replacement of the Agreement on Internal Trade with the more ambitious Canadian Free Trade Agreement (CFTA) in 2017 does not signify the end of internal-trade-policy reform in Canada. Rather, it represents an episode of institutional change in an ongoing process (CFTA 2017).

A border effect, therefore, remains in place unless economic integration culminates in the complete dissolution of previously existing political boundaries. In the case of trade-policy debates, which represent an important domain of economic integration, the presence of sub-level actors is somewhat puzzling. In order to facilitate the creation of markets, the central level in virtually all federal systems formally enjoys exclusive jurisdiction over most important matters related to trade policy. Constitutions usually furnish the federal level with the authority to establish and maintain a domestic economic union and to negotiate external trade agreements.[1]

Contrary to the intentions reflected in most constitutional designs, however, trade policy today, de facto, tends to take place in multilevel settings. This does not mean that sub-federal entities seek to obstruct new trade agreements per se. The constructive partnership between the federal level and the provinces in Canada is a case in point. Nor do we posit a unidirectional trend towards sub-federal engagement across all federal systems. Nonetheless, recent developments indicate that sub-federal units in many federations are taking on a new role in trade policy, displaying considerable variation regarding the intensity and modes of participation. Accordingly, some sub-federal units are becoming more active on the trade file in some instances. Moreover, in some federations – like Canada or Switzerland – sub-federal participation in trade policy has evolved incrementally since the 1980s or 1990s, while in others – like Germany or Austria – this is a relatively new phenomenon. In some federations constituent units seek to oppose trade agreements, and in other cases they are more inclined to shape the contents of trade agreements.

These differences point to three key sets of questions that lie at the heart of this volume:

1. What are the patterns of sub-federal engagement in trade policy? *How* do sub-federal units participate in different stages of the policy process?
2. What are the key factors that account for different patterns of sub-federal engagement? *Why* are sub-federal units taking on a new role in trade policy (or not)?
3. *What* are the consequences of increased sub-federal activity in trade policy? More specifically, are we witnessing a major transformative process towards a "new" multilevel trade order in which sub-federal units (and, possibly regional entities in unitary states or municipalities) emerge as key stakeholders? Regarding the policy level, what are possible consequences for the legitimacy and effectiveness of trade policy in the future?

The first set of questions has descriptive answers. They require us to map the forms and modes of sub-federal engagement and to detect if regularities exist in how they seek to influence trade policy. The questions in the second area are causal. They are the springboard to our explanation of pattern variation. The questions in the third area have prescriptive answers. Considering that recent developments in trade politics have unfolded at a rapid pace, our answers will remain necessarily speculative. We do not wish to make audacious claims concerning the future of trade policy, but our concluding chapter will speculate, based on the findings from our case studies, about the possible consequences of the changing nature of sub-federal participation.

Aim and Scope of the Volume

Sub-federal units play an increasingly important role in trade policy, a classical domain of "high politics" (Tatham 2018), as evident in the two weeks of cliff-hanger negotiations between Wallonia, the federal government of Belgium, the EU, and Canada on CETA's provisional application in the fall of 2016; the Land governments in Germany threatening to block ratification of CETA through the second chamber, the Bundesrat; and Ontario's Liberal government introducing legislation that would allow it to adopt retaliation measures in response to New York's and Texas's protectionist "Buy American" provisions.

On a general level, these events point to a fundamental question that underpins multilevel politics generally: who should have the right to make politically binding decisions and on what scales (Benz 2016; Hooghe and Marks 2016)? Functional theories suggest allocating jurisdictions among governmental tiers in a way that reflects the comparative advantage of each level. Accordingly, public goods should be provided by the level most capable of delivering a certain policy (see also Peterson 1995). A functional allocation of regulatory authority among different jurisdictions in an increasingly interdependent world, however, often collides with the aspirations of the socio-political communities that constitute these jurisdictions. The result is an ongoing tension between the need to address functional requirements and the need to reach agreement over which political unit should have the "right to act" and the "right to decide" (Braun 2000) over the provision of public goods.

Developments in recent trade policy and trade-agreement negotiations increasingly reflect such tensions inherent in multilevel politics. Most federal constitutions adhere to the functional model in so far as they assign authority over external and internal trade, along with other economic competencies such as commerce, currency, and inter-regional infrastructure, exclusively to the federal level (Watts 2008, 90). This holds, in particular, for the so-called coming-together federations (Stepan 1999) that emerged from modern state-building processes between the eighteenth and mid-twentieth centuries, including the European Union (EU). The creation of an integrated market was a main driving force behind modern state formation, a process that has been replicated on a larger scale through European integration since the 1950s (Bartolini 2005; Fabbrini 2010). In this context the centralization of trade policy was, for the most part, undisputed. But the historical context has been changing, and sub-federal units increasingly seek to participate in trade-policy development, albeit in very different ways. Exclusive federal-level control over all aspects of trade policy is no longer taken for granted, and sub-federal ambitions to shape the direction of trade policy generate tensions that have the potential to transform established governance structures through formal or informal institutional change.

This volume sets out to examine such tensions and corresponding dynamics. While there is ample preliminary evidence that trade-policy governance is in flux, perhaps even undergoing a major transformation, we lack a deeper understanding of the extent, patterns, causes, and consequences of these trends. Research on internal and external trade policy is divided between scholars of federalism and those of international political economy. Moreover, comparative scholarship on the multilevel architecture of trade policy – that is, variation in actor configurations and their dynamic evolution and consequences – is almost non-existent (for a notable exception see Kukucha 2015a). The lack of systematic knowledge on the changing nature of multilevel trade is particularly problematic in light of growing concerns about policy legitimacy and efficacy, as well as the high degree of variation in sub-federal participation across time and space. A comparative approach that acknowledges the multilevel nature of trade policymaking and the interconnectedness of internal and external trade policy is thus warranted.

In order to address the three broad questions underlying this volume – how, why, and with what effect do sub-federal units engage in trade policy? – we distinguish three constitutive dimensions that help us gain insight into multilevel trade politics from different, yet interrelated perspectives: the *policy dimension*, the *institutional dimension*, and the *state-society dimension*. We suggest that these three dimensions contribute to identifying the key factors that mobilize (or do not mobilize) sub-federal units in the field of trade policy.

The *policy dimension* refers to the changing scope and content of trade agreements themselves. We assume that these changes in trade-agreement provisions, and the goals and instruments of trade policy generally, prompt the activity of sub-federal units because they variously affect the interests of the units. The policy dimension alone, however, cannot explain pattern variation. Federal institutional architectures differ considerably and furnish sub-federal units with distinct institutional resources to react to policy changes emanating from higher territorial scales. We therefore expect that differences in the *institutional dimension* matter as well for the way and the reasons sub-federal units take on a role in trade policy. Finally, a third source of variation is the larger political environment surrounding multilevel trade politics. The *state-society dimension* connects the institutional and policy dimensions as it directs our attention to political and social actors that affect the trade-policy agenda of sub-federal governments, the actors being most notably political parties, business interests, unions, and non-governmental organizations. In the following sections we unpack each dimension and indicate potential interaction effects among them.

The Changing Nature of Trade Policy and Agreements

The goals and instruments of trade policy are in flux. The Washington Consensus no longer represents the dominant transnational policy paradigm. The emergence of a progressive trade agenda, for example, indicates that traditional trade-policy goals are enmeshed increasingly with policy goals emanating from other, cross-cutting sectors like the environment or human rights. What is more, the nature of trade agreements as one particular element of trade policy has been changing. New, often more encompassing and "deeper" regional trade agreements are layered upon the established global multilateral trade order, with important consequences for domestic politics.

We suspect that two significant developments in particular have increasingly affected the interests of sub-federal actors and, therefore, mobilized them as stakeholders in trade policy. The first is the proliferation of free trade agreements (Trebilcock, Howse, and Eliason 2013). Between 2005 and 2015 alone, their number doubled from 132 to 260 (Mattoo, Mulabdic, and Ruta 2017). As of 2016, every World Trade Organization member was a party to at least one free trade agreement, and some had inked as many as twenty (WTO 2017). This increase denotes a major shift from multilateral approaches to trade governance, favoured in the period after the Second World War, towards a more fragmented, regional or preferential trade regime. This fragmentation can have profound consequences for the constellation of actors involved in different stages of the external-trade-policy process, creating many more opportunities for influence.

The second development concerns the fact that emerging free trade agreements are often "comprehensive," "second generation," or "deep" treaties that move beyond the liberalization of goods trade to services, intellectual property, and government procurement, among other issues. Priorities have been shifting from tariff reduction and market access to regulatory cooperation through instruments such as mutual recognition or even harmonization (Dür and Elsig 2015; Goff 2014; Hofmann, Osnago, and Ruta 2017; Kim 2015). Accordingly, enhancing access to foreign markets for domestic exporters is no longer simply a matter of removing border measures. It increasingly requires a change in so-called behind-the-border policies (Young 2016). Many of these policies and regulations fall within the jurisdiction of sublevel entities, not only prompting increased sub-federal activity in the realm of external trade policy but also necessitating the removal of internal trade barriers in many federations (for Canada see, for example, Berdahl 2013).

This observation leads us to link the increased demand for the participation of sub-federal actors to those trade agreements that impinge to a greater degree on sublevel jurisdiction and, accordingly, their interests. Trade-policy-related preferences emerge from three types of interests, which, in various combinations, mobilize the engagement of sub-federal units: *jurisdictional*, *economic*, and *political interests*.

First, trade agreements often entail provisions that have the potential to constrain the capacity of sub-federal units to formulate and implement political decisions within their jurisdictions. As scholars of new institutionalism have argued, political and bureaucratic actors have an intrinsic motivation to shield their institutional domain from developments threatening their policymaking capacity (Cairns 1986; Evans, Rueschemeyer, and Skocpol 1985; Lecours 2005). Trade policy thus may activate jurisdictional interests of sub-federal units as they seek to protect their institutional integrity. When trade policy has focused on the removal of tariffs and quantitative restrictions, sub-federal actors have felt the impact, especially those with import-competing or export-oriented sectors. However, deeper agreements can affect sub-federal actors in fundamental ways linked to politics and governance, sometimes threatening to limit significantly their room for manoeuvre. CETA's intellectual-property provisions are a case in point. Had the Canadian government agreed to extend pharmaceutical-patent life in conformity with EU requests, the consequences would have fallen squarely on provincial governments whose role it was to fund and provide health care. Indeed, in subsequent renegotiations of the North American Free Trade Agreement (NAFTA), leading to USMCA, this was the outcome in that Canada agreed to patent-term extensions to compensate for delays in approvals processes. Another example is investor-state dispute settlement (ISDS), which is highly contested in Europe because it is perceived as a potential threat to the institutional integrity of sub-federal units. The German and Austrian Länder and the Belgian French-speaking regions and communities all vehemently oppose the creation of ISDS mechanisms, a main rationale for them to agree to provisional application of most of CETA, but not to ISDS provisions.

Second, political economy scholarship highlights the importance of economic interests for political behaviour. Trade agreements variously affect regional political economies, depending on their size, dominant sectors, or degree of integration with other markets through supply chains. As a consequence, sub-federal units may also develop an interest in shaping trade policy because they need to promote and protect their regional economy. Especially in federations characterized by an open and highly diversified economy such as Canada, economic interests have always been an important mobilizing force behind the prominence of sub-federal units in the trade policy field. In addition, trade agreements can also confront them with contradictory imperatives. In the NAFTA renegotiation process, for example, provincial governments had to cope with very different challenges. The province of Ontario had to champion open markets in the automobile sector and, at the same time, ward off demands for abolishing supply management in the agricultural sector. In a similar vein, the Swiss cantons of Vaud and Thurgau sought to prevent the liberalization of market access for palm oil in the free trade agreement with Malaysia in 2016 in order to protect their agricultural sector (see Ziegler in this volume).

Finally, political interests have spurred European sub-federal units to take on a role in trade policy. This type of interest is an expression of neither jurisdictional self-interest nor regional economic motives. Rather, it reflects a concern over the direction of trade-policy goals in general and the content of trade agreements in particular. Mass mobilization against recent trade agreements like the Transatlantic Trade and Investment Partnership (TTIP) and CETA indicates an increasing politicization of trade policy in Europe with profound consequences for federal politics. In particular, coalition governments with centre-left or left-wing political parties seek to oppose, or at least modify, trade agreements because they are concerned with the implications of trade liberalization for environmental and food standards or human and animal rights. In its 2013 TTIP resolution, for example, the German Bundesrat demanded import restrictions for products not meeting the Conformité Européenne marking, for genetically modified products, and for meat from animals treated with hormones and steroids, as well as from cloned animals. In a similar vein, the Council of Ministers for Consumer Protection flagged issues concerning food safety, and the Council of Ministers for the Environment pointed to problems related to safety standards in areas such as genetic engineering, the regulation of chemicals, and any new technologies that carry a certain risk like fracking (see Broschek, Bußjäger, and Schramek in this volume).

Accordingly, while in some federations such as Australia or Switzerland sub-federal units have played a role in trade policy for quite some time, it is the emergence of new trade agreements in recent years that has driven this trend broadly. We suspect that the trend results from the changing nature of trade agreements themselves. They contain provisions that trigger a wide range of concerns. Table 0.1 showcases trade agreements in which sub-federal units have directly or indirectly participated. As our case studies detail, the degree and frequency of involvement varies greatly. For example, in the United States and Mexico sub-federal governments have so far only played a limited role. In Germany and Austria sub-federal involvement is also a more recent development, but the Länder – in Germany more so than in Austria – seem to have leverage to consolidate further their emerging role. In other federations, like Australia, Canada, and Belgium, new trade agreements have amplified an already existing pattern. The emergence of new encompassing trade agreements, therefore, offers a useful starting point to understand this trend. In order to explain variation, however, we need to analyse how policy dynamics interact with institutional and societal factors.

The Institutional Configuration of Federalism

Wallonia's attempt to block CETA offered a powerful demonstration of how relatively small sublevel entities can jeopardize the ratification of trade agreements. The Austrian Länder have recently flexed their muscles in a similar way, but to no avail. Despite several joint resolutions through which they called upon the federal government not to ratify CETA in its current form, Austria eventually ratified the agreement in June 2018 (see Broschek, Bußjäger, and Schramek in this volume).

Accordingly, sub-federal units have different institutional resources to influence the content and scope of trade agreements at various stages of the policy cycle. Competencies that provide sub-federal units with

0.1 Examples of Sub-federal Involvement in Trade Agreements (External and Internal without the European Union)

Case	External trade agreements	Internal trade agreements
Australia	• Australia-New Zealand Closer Economic Relations Trade Agreement, 1983 • Australia-United States Free Trade Agreement, 2005 • Korea-Australia Free Trade Agreement, 2014	• Mutual Recognition Act, 1992 • National Competition Policy, 1997–2005 • National Reform Agenda, 2006
Canada	• Canada-United States Free Trade Agreement, 1989 • North American Free Trade Agreement (NAFTA), 1994 • Canada-European Union Comprehensive and Economic Free Trade Agreement (CETA), 2017 • Trans-Pacific Partnership, signed 2016 • NAFTA 2.0 / United States-Mexico-Canada Agreement (USMCA)	• Agreement on Internal Trade, 1995 • New West Partnership Trade Agreement, 2010 • Canadian Free Trade Agreement, 2017
United States	• Transatlantic Trade and Investment Partnership (TTIP), not concluded • NAFTA 2.0 / USMCA	
Mexico	• European Union-Mexico Global Agreement, modernization and update since 2016 • NAFTA 2.0 / USMCA	
Austria	• TTIP, not concluded • CETA, 2017 (provisional)	
Germany	• European Union-Colombia/ Peru Trade Agreement, 2013 (provisional) • TTIP, not concluded • CETA, 2017 (provisional)	
Switzerland	• European Economic Area, 1994 (but rejected through referendum) • European Free Trade Association (EFTA)-Hong Kong Free Trade Agreement, 2012 • EFTA-Ukraine Free Trade Agreement, 2012	• Bundesgesetz über die technischen Handelshemmnisse THG [Federal Act on Technical Barriers to Trade], 1995 • Binnenmarktgesetz BGBM [Internal Market Act], 1995
Belgium	• TTIP, not concluded • CETA, 2017 (provisional)	

direct and formal capacity to participate in trade policy, however, are the exception. Among the cases examined in this volume, only the Belgian regions and communities, along with the Swiss cantons, enjoy such institutional privileges. More often, then, sub-federal units can mobilize institutional resources whenever trade-agreement provisions have the potential to affect their legislative or administrative competencies. Either way, we posit that the institutional configuration of federalism offers a second point of entry into the investigation of the emerging multilevel politics of trade (Broschek and Goff 2018; see also Freudlsperger 2017).

Federal institutional architectures display significant variation. The most prominent indicator for measuring differences in federal systems is the degree of centralization. This measure essentially captures the number and weight of competencies that one level has vis-à-vis the other (Riker 1964). An exclusive focus on centralization and decentralization tends to neglect the point, however, that federalism is more than just an allegedly clear-cut allocation of competencies between two levels of government. Recent scholarship seems to acknowledge more readily the limits of this dichotomy and uses the distinction between self-rule and shared rule to capture differences in the institutional relationships between and among constituent units and the federal level (Behnke and Mueller 2017; Broschek 2015b; Hooghe, Marks, and Schakel 2010). Accordingly, federal systems variously combine self-rule (or the separation of powers) and shared rule (or power-sharing) to balance the desire of territorial units (including the federal level) to act autonomously with the need to work together. The relative weight of self-rule and shared rule in federal systems depends on how three key components are organized:

- The allocation of competencies can be primarily dual – featuring an exclusive allocation of legislative and administrative competences (self-rule) – or integrated; that is, one level implements legislation of the other level (shared rule).
- The degree of institutionalization of the system of intergovernmental relations can be low (self-rule) or high (shared rule).
- The second chamber can be weak (self-rule) or strong (shared rule).

No federal system exhibits exclusively either self-rule or shared rule. Rather, it is possible to situate federations on a continuum between a hypothesized ideal model of self-rule federalism on the one hand and a shared-rule model on the other hand. While the Canadian case, for example, epitomizes the logic of self-rule federalism, the German case represents the empirical manifestation of shared-rule federalism. Other federations are more mixed in character and tend to blend variously self-rule and shared rule. How does the relative weight of self-rule and shared rule, then, empower sub-federal entities in trade politics?

First, trade agreements affect different types of competencies. In shared-rule federations that exhibit an integrated allocation of competencies, trade-policy changes have the potential to indirectly constrain the authority of sub-federal units to implement higher-level legislation. In addition, another concern may arise from the fact that trade policy has the potential to further limit their authority in the few remaining areas where they hold exclusive legislative competencies. In contrast, in self-rule federations trade policy is more likely to impinge directly on the exclusive legislative and administrative competencies of sub-federal units. Put simply, trade-policy changes have the potential to affect broadly the different types of sub-federal competencies.

CETA provisions, for example, touch on a wide range of exclusive provincial jurisdictions, ranging from labour mobility to municipal procurement. In addition, CETA, which represents one of the most ambitious trade initiatives in history, has profound implications for areas under shared jurisdiction, like agriculture and financial services. It is far from clear, however, if and to what extent the agreement has a direct impact on the competencies of the German or Austrian Länder. Regarding Germany, this question has sparked an interesting debate among legal scholars. From a legal perspective it is important to determine how CETA provisions will affect Länder jurisdictions because the question has implications for their involvement in the domestic ratification process via the second chamber, the Bundesrat.

Moreover, a dual allocation of competencies often makes it difficult to determine exactly where "exclusive" jurisdictions held by one governmental level begin and where they end (Broschek 2015a). To be sure, federations featuring an integrated allocation of competencies are certainly not immune from rival interpretations over the boundaries of political authority, but the distribution of legislative and administrative functions – rather than policy competencies – tends to be less ambiguous. Although the drafters of dual federal constitutions, like in Canada, the United States, and Australia, sought to tailor exclusive jurisdictions in order to avoid mutual interference, such "watertight compartments" have turned out to be an illusion in light of de facto interdependencies, externalities, and new social challenges. This not only offers more opportunities for contestation between governmental tiers but also empowers constitutional courts as "external" actors with the authority to shape the multilevel politics of trade.

Constitutional courts often have the authority to determine the scope of competencies. The Australian High Court, for example, has always been more inclined to strike down state law that created internal trade barriers than has the Judicial Committee of the Privy Council, which acted as the final court of appeal in matters related to the division of competencies in Canada until 1949 (Brown 2003; Smith and Mann 2015). Regarding external trade, the committee ruled that the federal government's competence covers the negotiation and implementation of international treaties but not the implementation of provisions that fall under exclusive provincial jurisdiction. More recently, the German constitutional court, the Bundesverfassungsgericht, and the European Court of Justice had to decide whether or not more recent trade agreements like CETA and the European Union-Singapore Free Trade Agreement needed to be concluded as "mixed" agreements.

Second, an integrated allocation of competencies often goes hand in hand with a strongly institutionalized system of intergovernmental relations (Thorlakson 2003). Intergovernmental relations capture the forms and modes of interaction between and among the federal level and the sub-federal units (vertically), as well as among sub-federal units themselves (horizontally). An integrated allocation of competencies creates strong policy interdependencies and, therefore, requires close collaboration among governments. By contrast, a dual allocation of competencies often correlates with a moderate or low degree of institutionalization. While there certainly is a considerable degree of variation not only among different dual federations but also across policy sectors within individual federations, intergovernmental relations are less formalized and often more volatile. For example, the frequency of meetings is more contingent on the willingness of governments to meet rather than on institutionalized routines, and outcomes – often taking the form of communiqués – tend to be less binding. The new generation of deeper and more encompassing trade agreements, however, has prompted a greater demand for intergovernmental coordination of trade policy and trade-agreement negotiations as they often affect federal and sub-federal jurisdictions.

Variation in the degree of institutionalization is also important to understand how sub-federal units and the federal level interact through different modes (see also Bakvis and Skogstad 2012; Scharpf 2001, 2011) (fig. 0.1).

A low degree of institutionalization allows the federal government or constituent units to act unilaterally. *Unilateralism* can take different

0.1 Modes of Interaction in Intergovernmental Relations

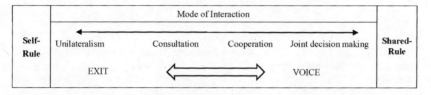

forms, ranging from antagonistic "thrust and riposte" behaviour to competition to mutual adjustment. Regardless of the form, collective actors fully rely on their self-rule capacity to interact. In the case of *consultation*, the degree of reciprocity between governmental actors is higher, but they still act independently from each other. Interaction through consultation is sporadic and not binding. *Cooperation*, in contrast, expresses a commitment to work together to reach an agreement on viable policy solutions. This interaction mode, therefore, leans more towards the shared-rule pole. Unlike *joint decision making*, however, cooperation presupposes voluntary negotiations. No actor is forced to participate in this mode of policymaking, while in arrangements of joint decision making, negotiations are compulsory. Actors have no exit option, and unless an agreement is reached, the status quo remains in place.

We expect that the ways in which federal institutional architectures are institutionally "pre-set" matters for how actors working within these settings perceive and respond to new developments in trade policy. Federal systems that lean towards self-rule tend to provide sub-federal units with a wider array of strategic choices. The sub-federal units can attempt to deploy unilateral "exit" strategies, for example by deliberately disregarding or by-passing trade-agreement provisions that fall into their jurisdictions and which require active implementation on their part. Alternatively, they can embark on cooperative or collaborative "voice" strategies to actively shape policy outcomes and to claim concessions from the federal government in return for their compliance. In contrast, sub-federal actors in shared-rule federations tend to be more restricted with respect to the repertoire of strategies available to them. As they enjoy a lesser degree of legislative autonomy, unilateral action is usually not a viable option, and exit threats are barely credible. The most powerful strategy for these sub-federal actors, therefore, is to further institutionalize voice through cooperation or even compulsory joint decision making.

Finally, profound differences in the composition and strength of the second chamber are likely to affect the mode of interaction as well. Comparative federalism scholarship distinguishes broadly between two models, the senate model and the council model. The senate approach allows for only indirect representation of regional interests through elected or appointed senators, with no formal role for sub-federal governments who remain confined to the system of intergovernmental relations. Regional concerns may be expressed in the legislative process in committees, but in practice they are often superimposed on partisan interests (Hueglin and Fenna 2015, 55). By contrast, in the council model sub-federal executives – and not senators – directly represent regional interests at the federal level. Although executives are not entirely immune from partisan politics, the council model tends to promote a more genuine articulation of regional interests in federal legislation. Most case studies assembled in this volume feature a second chamber that follows the senate model, with two important exceptions: the German Bundesrat and the Council of the European Union. This has afforded the Länder and the EU member states an additional institutional avenue to participate in trade policy under certain circumstances. For example, through the second chamber they requested information on the progress of trade-negotiation processes through the European Commission and the federal government and responded through opinions and resolutions, most notably on the European Union-Colombia/Peru Trade Agreement in 2013, on TTIP in 2013 and 2014, and on CETA in 2015 (see the chapter by Broschek, Bußjäger, and Schramek and by Garcia for the case of member states in the European Union).

Table 0.2 summarizes key institutional characteristics of the case studies examined in this volume. First, federal institutional architectures vary considerably, but the distinction between self-rule and shared-rule components is a useful tool to map institutional complexity and to compare commonalities and differences among our case studies. The three Anglo-Saxon federations, along with Mexico and Belgium, are organized around a dual allocation of authority. In addition, their system of intergovernmental relations tends to feature a rather low degree of institutionalization. By contrast, Austria, Germany, Switzerland, and the European Union tend to split legislative and executive functions between governmental tiers, with sub-federal units implementing federal law, albeit with varying degrees of autonomy. At the same time, these federations all exhibit a highly institutionalized system of intergovernmental relations. The type and strength of the second chamber also vary considerably. Whether a federation tends to lean towards the

0.2 Overview of Institutional Characteristics of Case Studies

Case	Allocation of competencies	Degree of insti-tutionalization of intergovernmental relations	Second chamber: type and strength	Self-rule/shared-rule balance
Australia	Dual	Medium	Senate, medium	Leans towards self-rule favouring the federal level, with shared-rule elements
Canada	Dual	Low	Senate (modified: appointed senators from four main regions plus territories and Newfoundland), de jure strong, de facto weak	Leans heavily towards self-rule favouring provinces, weak shared rule
United States	Dual	Low	Senate, strong	Leans towards self-rule favouring the federal level with shared-rule elements
Mexico	Dual	Low	Senate (modified: state-level senators and national senators), medium	Leans towards self-rule favouring the federal level with shared-rule elements
Austria	Integrated	High	Hybrid: delegates from Land parliaments, between three and twelve per Land, weak	Leans towards shared rule with self-rule elements strongly favouring the federal level
Germany	Integrated	High	Council, strong	Leans heavily towards shared rule, with some self-rule elements for the Lander and the federal level

(*Continued*)

0.2 Continued

Case	Allocation of competencies	Degree of insti-tutionalization of intergovernmental relations	Second chamber: type and strength	Self-rule/shared-rule balance
Switzerland	Integrated and dual features	High	Senate, strong	Leans towards shared rule with important self-rule elements favouring the cantons
Belgium	Dual	Low	Senate (modified: appointed delegates from community and regional parliaments plus co-opted senators), medium	Leans heavily towards self-rule favouring regions and communities with shared-rule elements
European Union	Integrated and dual features	High	Council, strong	Leans towards shared rule with important self-rule elements favouring the member states

self-rule or shared-rule pole is largely a consequence of the ways in which the allocation of competencies and the system of intergovernmental relations are organized, while the power of the second chamber mitigates or reinforces these characteristics.

Second, disaggregating federalism this way also helps to identify the main institutional arenas within which sub-federal units can participate in multilevel trade politics. While the allocation of competencies may directly or indirectly situate sub-federal units in multilevel trade politics, modes of interaction between and among governmental tiers – vertically between the federal level and constituent units, or horizontally among constituent units – are shaped through different arenas of the federal architecture, most notably the system of intergovernmental relations or the second chamber. Regarding the latter, sub-federal governments are only represented in the German Bundesrat and the Council of the European Union. Most other federations, however, feature second chambers that are more in line with the senate model, providing regional interest representation through appointed or elected senators.

State-Society Linkages: Party Politics and Societal Mobilization

As E.E. Schattschneider (1935) demonstrated in his study of American trade politics, the structure of policies affects the mobilization of organized interests and the forms of political contestation and, ultimately, constitutes a polity's "institutional terrain" (Hacker and Pierson 2014, 645). Likewise, comparative federalism scholarship highlights the importance of intermediary collective actors for understanding the direction and scope of institutional and policy dynamics in federal systems (Benz and Broschek 2013; Detterbeck 2012). This literature reveals complex interaction effects between federal institutions and the organizations that represent a federal society. Such effects are contingent upon the degree of societal homogeneity (e.g., mono-national versus multinational federations), the institutional architecture of federalism (self-rule versus shared-rule federations), and the organizational features of political parties and party systems (e.g., integrated versus bifurcated political parties). On a more general level, it is important that federal institutions offer multiple access points for political parties and interest groups to shape political decisions. Indeed, the emerging multilevel politics of trade have activated and mobilized various types of collective actors, not only institutional stakeholders such as subfederal governments and parliaments but also political parties, business interests, and civil-society organizations that can target different arenas on different governmental tiers. An encompassing understanding of multilevel trade politics thus requires examination of the broader socio-political environment.

Irrespective of the importance of societal mobilization and party politics, however, we assume that these factors are highly contingent. For example, the EU has negotiated a number of recent trade agreements without much public attention or significant opposition (see Garcia in this volume). This changed with the successful linking of CETA and TTIP in the public debate by activists. Their campaign created an opportunity structure, making it possible for trade opponents to gain considerable momentum. In Canada the question of the direction of external trade policy had been one of the most divisive issues in the country's politics for decades, culminating in the historic 1988 free-trade election. Since then, surprisingly, trade policy disputes have been almost non-existent. Another example is the November 2016 United States presidential election when strongly anti-trade sentiment emerged in the campaign and policy of Donald Trump. This event marked a highly contingent historical turning point for American trade politics, which will very likely give way to a new approach to trade policy with important international and domestic consequences.

In short, while crucial, these factors have waxed and waned and are extremely difficult to predict. This does not mean, however, that they are less important. Most notably, political parties respond to increased civil-society mobilization (see in this volume: Bollen, De Ville, and Gheyle; and Gistelinck). As a consequence, political interests, in addition to jurisdictional self-interests and regional economic interests for sub-federal governments to participate in trade policy, have gained importance. This, in turn, impinges on the mode of interaction in intergovernmental relations. In Germany and the European Union, for example, joint decision making is a dominant mode of interaction. As long as political mobilization is low, joint decision making can lead to productive solutions or even open up institutional escape routes (Falkner 2011). By contrast, in a highly politicized environment this mode of interaction may result in the "joint decision trap" (Scharpf 1988) in which free-trade opponents successfully mobilize the public and political parties. The outcome, then, is the lowest common denominator at best, or deadlock at worst.

Generally we expect that a moderate or even high degree of social mobilization reinforces evolving multilevel trade structures for at least two reasons. First, the sub-federal arena affords interest groups additional targets for influence, which enhances their strategic options (see in this volume: Kukucha; Siles-Brügge and Strange). In Germany, for example, a broad alliance of trade-policy opponents has increasingly turned its attention to the sub-federal level since 2013. They began to push Land governments both to insist that new European trade agreements should be considered "mixed agreements" and to block their ratification in the Bundesrat (Broschek, Bußjäger, and Schramek in this volume). Second, the politicization of trade further complicates the negotiation, ratification, and, possibly, implementation of trade agreements, making them even more contentious. In the absence of polarization, sub-federal engagement in trade politics is primarily motivated by jurisdictional self-interest and regional economic concerns. Sub-federal units may anticipate a loss of their ability to control the regulation of important aspects of the regional economy, for example through subsidies or soft rules for procurement. Such concerns, however, become reinforced and amplified if political parties – in government or opposition – frame trade-related issues in a more political way, often in

response to demands by civil-society groups. In addition, the politicization of trade can create substantial problems for coalition governments,
as well as for interest aggregation within individual political parties, as
Myriam Gistelinck's case study in this volume on the German Social
Democratic Party demonstrates.

Table 0.3 summarizes the degree of social mobilization concerning
trade policy, as well as the degree of polarization among political parties.
Not surprisingly, the indicators correlate. If actors representing social
interests – such as environmental groups, anti-globalization movements,
trade unions, and religious groups – oppose liberalization of trade, political parties have strong incentives to take these issues into the electoral
or legislative arena. This holds, in particular, for parties with strong linkages to interest groups and movements, like western European social
democrats or Green parties. Likewise, mobilization against trade liberalization, in turn, mobilizes pro-trade actors, most notably corporate interests that expect advantages from the removal of trade barriers.

Taken together, the studies in this volume point to a nascent theory
of sub-federal participation in trade policy and trade-agreement negotiations, grounded in the three factors we have identified: the changing
nature of trade policy and trade agreements; the institutional configuration of individual federations; and state-society linkages. In the case
studies that follow, some constellation of these three factors explains
an increase (or lack) of sub-federal activity with regard to trade. No
one case is identical to another. Nonetheless, as we develop in greater
detail in the conclusion, understanding the distinctive ways that these
factors interact in each case contributes greatly to a coherent account of
the outcomes observed.

0.3 State-Society Linkages and Trade Policy Mobilization

Case	Degree of societal mobilization	Degree of polarization among political parties
Australia	Low	Low
Canada	Low	Low
United States	Moderate	Moderate
Mexico	Moderate	Moderate
Austria	High	High
Germany	High	High
Switzerland	Low	Low
Belgium	High	High

The Book at a Glance

The Multilevel Politics of Trade assembles case studies from North America, Europe, and Australia to investigate how the interaction of the three factors identified – trade policy, federal institutions, and state-society linkages – generate different patterns of sub-federal engagement in trade policy. In doing so, our volume seeks to open up an exciting research agenda. Although research on different aspects of trade policy and federalism exists, we have little knowledge about the changing nature of multilevel trade governance grounded in systematic comparative analysis.

The ensuing chapters explore sub-federal actor participation in trade policy in the three North American federations (Canada, Mexico, and the United States), the four European federations (Austria, Belgium, Germany, and Switzerland), Australia, and the European Union. The book therefore covers, first of all, the six "classic" federations that emerged from modern state building in Europe and the Anglo-Saxon settler societies. In its modern form, federalism was first established with the United States constitution of 1789, followed by Switzerland (1848), Canada (1867), Germany (1871), Australia (1901), and Austria (1920). In addition, we include Mexico, which is not only geographically part of North America but also part of the free trade area established through NAFTA in 1994 and USMCA in 2018. For a similar reason we invited chapters dedicated exclusively to the EU as the supranational entity that has far-reaching jurisdiction for both external and internal trade policy. Finally, we include Belgium as the fourth formal federal system in Europe, which was established in 1993 after a long transformation from a decentralized unitary state.

In order to examine systematically how the three dimensions interact to produce different patterns and dynamics of sub-federal engagement in trade policy, we organize our cases in broadly geographic sections. At first, slightly more emphasis is placed on the Canadian case. Indeed, Canadian scholars like Chris Kukucha, Grace Skogstad, Stéphane Paquin, and Patrick Leblond pioneered the study of federalism and trade policy. In addition, the enhanced role of the Canadian provinces in CETA (and later of Wallonia in the same agreement) brought this phenomenon to the fore. Our research builds on insights from the Canadian case and seeks to situate them in a larger comparative context. The three opening chapters showcase different aspects gleaned from the Canadian experience. From here, we present developments in other North American federations. The focus then shifts to the European federations and Australia, as well as three analyses of the distinctive federation that is the European Union. Our main findings are summarized in the conclusion.

Stéphane Paquin opens the section on North America with his analysis of the role of the Canadian provinces. Their direct participation in CETA negotiations sparked much of the recent interest in the subfederal role in trade conversations. Yet Paquin argues that the provinces' seat at the CETA negotiating table was less a clear break from past practice and more a logical progression. He traces the evolution in intergovernmental consultation mechanisms, arguing that CETA does not exemplify a "new normal" for Canadian provinces in trade negotiations. The provinces reverted to prior modes of consultation in the Trans-Pacific Partnership (TPP) negotiations. Nonetheless, provincial voices have become progressively louder as trade agreements intrude further into the terrain of their constitutionally defined areas of jurisdiction.

While Paquin focuses on the earlier negotiating stage, Christian Hederer and Patrick Leblond complement this analysis by emphasizing the later trade-agreement-implementation stage as a key moment for sub-federal action in Canada. Although Canadian intergovernmental relations have been relatively collaborative, the authors argue that comprehensive agreements that move into provincial jurisdiction require "more elaborate" institutional arrangements for successful implementation. Conflict has been avoided to date, but the prospect of new deep agreements, as well as ongoing efforts to reconcile the regulation of interprovincial trade with international trade commitments, warrants attention to implementation.

Sophie Schram hones in on the perspective of a specific Canadian sub-federal actor, exploring the puzzling move by the Government of Quebec to volunteer to open up provincial procurement markets as part of CETA talks with the EU. Not surprisingly, such opening had been resisted previously by all provinces, and particularly by Quebec because it linked the promotion of domestic companies to both provincial economic development and the Quebec nation-building project. As procurement became more prominent in trade agreements – and as access to Canadian sub-federal procurement became a critical EU objective in CETA – Schram argues that Quebec saw a unique opportunity to modify its "logic of provincial development." Shifting focus away from protecting against competition in domestic procurement markets towards competing in European ones could promote economic development at a time when opportunities in the United States appeared to be waning. It could simultaneously consolidate Quebec's political autonomy. In so doing, Quebec was instrumental in moving CETA talks forward. By slicing into the Canadian case from three distinctive angles, these opening chapters clear the comparative terrain for those that follow.

Michelle Egan picks up on the interface between internal and external trade in the American context. She outlines the various mechanisms through which US states can use their voice in trade policy, including advocacy and lobbying by state associations and participation in the Intergovernmental Policy Advisory Committee. She also notes the heightened interest of sub-federal actors in "the new generation of 'deeper' trade agreements." She argues that the internal market in the United States is relatively fragmented, even going so far as to suggest that it is "less integrated than the EU internal market." The diversity of regulatory approaches across the fifty states, some of which can be quite protectionist in nature, can limit federal trade-liberalization efforts and prevent deeper integration with trading partners. Unlike Canadian provinces, which can refuse to implement domestic legislation to give effect to trade agreements, or Belgian regions, which can refuse to approve federal signature to a trade agreement, American states interrupt the trade-liberalization process very early on by clinging to favoured state-level regulatory, procurement, and other policies.

Rounding out the striking variation across North American federal systems, Jorge Schiavon and Marcela López-Vallejo provide an important comparison in their study of Mexico, pointing out that not all sub-federal actors are enjoying greater influence over trade policy. They combine comprehensive statistics with a case study of the state of Jalisco to show that Mexican states are empowered to enter into some international agreements; however, they participate minimally in trade-agreement negotiation. As the authors point out, even if there were a "more inclusive legal framework," most Mexican states lack the institutional capacity and resources to participate in the trade-policy process. This theme recurs in several of the contributions to this volume.

Christopher Kukucha's comparative study of all three North American federations sheds light on the interaction between the institutional and state-society dimensions. He argues that the institutional make-up of North American federal systems influences patterns of civil-society involvement in the conversation about trade policy. Where federal structures empower sub-federal governments, civil-society mobilization can be diminished, or the interests of non-governmental actors can be channelled through political parties or unions. Of course, federal structures are not the only determinant of civil-society impact on trade policy, but attention to this aspect can deepen our understanding. Kukucha also notes that civil-society groups are often transnational in nature.

The next four chapters examine the remaining "classic" federations (Switzerland, Germany, Austria, and Australia), plus Belgium. In Andreas Ziegler's contribution, he tracks the evolving trade-policy role of Swiss cantons since the 1990s. The Swiss federation is a complex one with four official languages and one quarter of the population lacking the right to vote. Recent constitutional reforms clarified the cantonal role, but discussion continues about the appropriate role for sub-federal actors in Swiss foreign affairs, including trade policy. Ziegler echoes Paquin and Schiavon and López-Vallejo in underlining how the diversity of sub-federal actors within a federation can affect their relative influence over trade policy. He also shows that a federal government can move beyond what is constitutionally mandated when political circumstances seem to demand it, as they did when Switzerland negotiated its bilateral arrangements with the EU. That agreement was subject to a referendum and to cantonal approval.

Jörg Broschek, Peter Bußjäger, and Christoph Schramek examine the increasing salience of trade agreements at the sub-federal level in Austria and Germany. In response to the new generation of EU trade agreements, like TTIP, CETA, and the Japan-EU Free Trade Agreement, the Austrian Länder have sponsored a growing number of parliamentary debates, motions, and resolutions. In 2016 Austrian Land governors declared their opposition to CETA and TTIP, barring fulfilment of certain conditions. For their part, German Länder have been similarly active – and activist – though in ways that reflect the distinctive political and institutional features of the German federation. The authors locate the explanation for this Land-based activity in three factors: the institutional capacity of Länder in both countries to give voice to their concerns; political mobilization around second-generation trade agreements perceived to threaten the European ability to regulate critical policy domains; and the ongoing process of Europeanization that has progressively whittled away at Land-level competencies in both countries.

Annmarie Elijah asks whether intergovernmental cooperation and consultation mechanisms are fit for purpose as Australia negotiates deeper trade agreements that target "behind the border" issues. She outlines Australian institutional processes for involving six states and two territories in trade policy and then shows the variation in their use and application across three recent agreements – the Australia-New Zealand Closer Economic Relations Trade Agreement, the Australia-United States Free Trade Agreement, and the Korea-Australia Free Trade Agreement. The different institutional paths taken by sub-federal actors in each instance are due to the nature of the bilateral relationship, the complexity of the agreements, and the relative activism of some jurisdictions in using their voice, among other factors.

Yelter Bollen, Ferdi De Ville, and Niels Gheyle confirm the paradox that the Lisbon Treaty was supposed to centralize and streamline the EU trade-policy process. Instead, not only national but also sub-federal parliaments seem to have been empowered (see also Garcia in this volume). Two decisive factors intervened in this process. Bollen, De Ville, and Gheyle show that the changing nature of trade agreements themselves, combined with civil-society activity, led Wallonia, Flanders, and Brussels to take action. As trade agreements became more intrusive and as European civil society succeeded in politicizing TTIP and CETA, Belgian sub-federal actors responded by flexing their institutional powers to scuttle federal action. The Belgian case is especially informative given Wallonia's eleventh-hour bid to prevent the Belgian government from signing CETA.

The final three chapters explore unique developments in the context of the EU. In fact, the EU constitutes a quasi-federal system in its own right, comprising the sub-federal entities presented in the previous chapters. Our volume acknowledges the complexity of multilevel trade governance in Europe in the chapter by Maria Garcia. As she asserts, the EU is akin to a federal state in many ways despite its sui generis nature. She analyses it from this angle, exploring the multilevel aspects of EU trade policy that implicate the supranational bodies, including the commission, council, and parliament, as well as national, member-state governance mechanisms. Garcia points to the "principal-agent" relationship that developed after the Lisbon Treaty, which sought to shift the power over trade and investment towards EU institutions. Ironically, although the Lisbon effort intended to consolidate EU power, the effect has been an escalation in non-ratification threats and the designation of key trade agreements as "mixed competence," requiring member-state approval. In an already complex multilevel environment the politicization of trade, especially around the inclusion of controversial provisions like investor-state dispute settlement, has complicated matters even further.

Myriam Gistelinck complements this analysis by focusing on party politics in the European Parliament (EP). The Lisbon Treaty expanded the EP's role as it shifted trade-policy competency away from national parliaments. Gistelinck maintains that this move intensified the multilevel dynamics between parties in national parliaments and their counterparts in the EP. She tracks relations between the German Social Democratic Party and the EP's Socialist and Democrat Group before and during TTIP and CETA negotiations. As the scope of the trade agreements broadened and civil-society groups mobilized, the

EP became more vocal. EP resolutions on trade often belied a vertical alliance between like-minded political party groups in the EP and key national parliaments. Likewise, EP resolutions evolved as a site where national party officials could influence EU trade policy.

Gabriel Siles-Brügge and Michael Strange round out this section with a rare study of municipal-level trade contestation. The role of the Canadian provinces and of Wallonia in CETA drew our attention to provinces, states, Länder, regions, and communities in the trade-policy conversation, adding a third layer to the multilevel politics of trade beyond the supranational and the national. Siles-Brügge and Strange add a fourth – the municipal – by confronting two key questions: why do civil-society groups target municipalities in their campaigns around trade agreements, and why do municipalities play along? The authors map municipal-level trade contestation in half a dozen campaigns targeting the Multilateral Agreement on Investment, the General Agreement on Trade in Services, the Trade in Services Agreement, TTIP, CETA, and TPP. They argue that activist groups make a considered choice to use their resources to mobilize municipal governments. Joint action at the local level can amplify their message about a global phenomenon. At the same time, municipal governments can benefit; as they have typically fewer opportunities for voice and exit where trade policy is concerned, their participation in a social-movement campaign can afford them a rare channel for communicating their concerns.

The concluding chapter summarizes the overall findings of the volume. Based on the insights provided by our broad array of case studies, we synthesize the findings to develop an account of multilevel trade politics. The chapter assesses the relative weight of institutional, policy-based, and social factors and determines how they interact to explain the dynamics and consequences of multilevel trade politics. In so doing, we seek to unravel the complex relationship among the three dimensions of multilevel trade politics. Building on this discussion, we hope to offer a theoretically informed account that will inspire further research in the field. Our hope is that this volume will transcend the usual silos to interest scholars of federalism and trade at a time when sub-federal activity confirms the multilevel nature of trade politics.

NOTE

1 Even in the case of the European Union, where federalization is an ongoing, slow-moving process, the supranational level's exclusive competencies to regulate the internal market and to develop an external-trade-policy agenda have been gradually expanded over the last decades.

REFERENCES

Anderson, George, ed. 2012. *Internal Markets and Multi-Level Governance: The Experience of the European Union, Australia, Canada, Switzerland, and the United States.* Don Mills, ON: Oxford University Press.
Bakvis, Herman, and Grace Skogstad, eds. 2012. *Canadian Federalism: Performance, Effectiveness, and Legitimacy.* 3rd ed. Don Mills, ON: Oxford University Press.
Bartolini, Stefano. 2005. *Restructuring Europe: Centre Formation, System-Building and Political Structuring between the Nation-State and the European Union.* Oxford: Oxford University Press.
Behnke, Nathalie, and Sean Mueller. 2017. "The Purpose of Intergovernmental Councils: A Framework for Analysis and Comparison." *Regional and Federal Studies* 27 (5): 507–27.
Benz, Arthur. 2016. *Constitutional Policy in Multilevel Government: The Art of Keeping the Balance.* Oxford: Oxford University Press.
Benz, Arthur, and Jorg Broschek, eds. 2013. *Federal Dynamics: Continuity, Change, and the Varieties of Federalism.* Oxford: Oxford University Press.
Berdahl, Loleen. 2013. "(Sub)National Economic Union: Institutions, Ideas, and Internal Trade Policy in Canada." *Publius* 43 (2): 251–74.
Braun, Dietmar. 2000. "The Territorial Division of Power in Comparative Public Policy Research: An Assessment." In *Public Policy and Federalism*, edited by D. Braun, 362–93. Aldershot, UK: Ashgate.
Broschek, Jörg. 2015a. "Authority Migration in Multilevel Architectures: A Historical-Institutionalist Framework." *Comparative European Politics* 13: 656–81.
– 2015b. "Pathways of Federal Reform: Australia, Canada, Germany, and Switzerland." *Publius* 45: 51–76.
Broschek, Jörg, and Patricia Goff. 2018. *Federalism and International Trade Policy. The Canadian Provinces in Comparative Perspective.* IRPP Insight 23. Montreal: Institute for Research on Public Policy.
Brown, Douglas. 2003. *Market Rules: Economic Union Reform and Intergovernmental Policy-Making in Australia and Canada.* Montreal: McGill-Queens University Press.
Cairns, Alan. 1986. "The Embedded State: State-Society Relations in Canada." In *State and Society: Canada in Comparative Perspective*, edited by K. Banting, 53–86. Toronto: University of Toronto Press / Royal Commission on the Economic Union and Development Prospects for Canada.
CFTA (Canadian Free Trade Agreement). 2017. *Backgrounder: Highlights of Canada's New Free Trade Agreement.* 7 April.
Detterbeck, Klaus. 2012. *Multi-Level Party Politics in Western Europe.* New York: Palgrave.

Dür, Andreas, and Manfred Elsig. 2015. "Introduction: The Purpose, Design, and Effects of Preferential Trade Agreements." In *Trade Cooperation: The Purpose, Design, and Effects of Preferential Trade Agreements*, edited by A. Dür and M. Elsig, 1–23. Cambridge: Cambridge University Press.

Evans, Peter, D. Rueschemeyer, and T. Skocpol, eds. 1985. *Bringing the State Back In*. Cambridge: Cambridge University Press.

Fabbrini, Sergio. 2010. *Compound Democracies: Why the United States and Europe Are Becoming Similar*. Oxford: Oxford University Press.

Falkner, Gerda, ed. 2011. *The EU's Decision Traps: Comparing Policies*. Oxford: Oxford University Press.

Freudlsperger, Christian. 2017. "More Voice, Less Exit: Sub-federal Resistance to International Procurement Liberalization in the European Union, the United States and Canada." *Journal of European Public Policy* 25 (11): 1686–1705.

Goff, Patricia. 2014. *Transatlantic Economic Agreements: Parsing CETA and TTIP*. Centre for International Governance Innovation, paper no. 35. Accessed 17 February 2017. https://www.cigionline.org/publications /transatlantic-economic-agreements-parsing-ceta-and-ttip.

Hacker, Jacob S., and Paul Pierson. 2014. "After the 'Master Theory': Downs, Schattschneider, and the Rebirth of Policy-Focused Analysis." *Perspectives on Politics* 12 (3): 643–62.

Hofmann, Claudia, A. Osnago, and M. Ruta. 2017. "Horizontal Depth: A New Database on the Content of Preferential Trade Agreements." Policy Research Working Paper WPS 7981. Washington, DC: World Bank Group.

Hooghe, Liesbet, and Gary Marks. 2016. *Community, Scale and Regional Governance*. Oxford: Oxford University Press.

Hooge, Liesbet, Gary Marks, and Arjan H. Schakel. 2010. *The Rise of Regional Authority: A Comparative Study of 42 Democracies*. New York: Routledge.

Hueglin, Thomas, and Alan Fenna. 2015. *Comparative Federalism: A Systematic Inquiry*. 2nd ed. Toronto: University of Toronto Press.

Kim, Soo Yeon. 2015. "Deep Integration and Regional Trade Agreements." In *The Oxford Handbook of the Political Economy of International Trade*, edited by L.L. Martin, 360–79. Oxford: Oxford University Press.

Kukucha, Christopher. 2015a. "Federalism Matters: Evaluating the Impact of Sub-federal Governments in Canadian and American Foreign Trade Policy." *Canadian Foreign Policy Journal* 21 (3): 224–37.

– 2015b. "Internal Trade Agreements in Canada: Progress, Complexity, and Challenges." *Canadian Journal of Political Science* 48 (1): 195–218.

– 2016. *Provincial/Territorial Governments and the Negotiation of International Trade Agreements*. IRPP Insight 10. Montreal: Institute for Research on Public Policy.

Lecours, André, ed. 2005. *New Institutionalism: Theory and Analysis*. Toronto: University of Toronto Press.

Mattoo, Aaditya, A. Mulabdic, and M. Ruta. 2017. "Trade Creation and Trade Diversion in Deep Agreements." Policy Research Working Paper WPS 8206. Washington, DC: World Bank Group.

Painter, Martin. 1998. *Collaborative Federalism: Economic Reform in Australia in the 1990s.* Cambridge: Cambridge University Press.

Paquin, Stéphane. 2013. "Federalism and the Governance of International Trade Negotiations in Canada: Comparing CUSFTA with CETA." *International Journal* 68 (4): 545–52.

Peterson, Paul. 1995. *The Price of Federalism.* Washington DC: Brookings.

Riker, William. 1964. *Federalism: Origin, Operation, Significance.* Boston: Little, Brown.

Scharpf, Fritz W. 1988. "The Joint-Decision Trap: Lessons from German Federalism and European Integration." *Public Administration* 66 (3): 239–78.

– 2001. "Notes toward a Theory of Multilevel Governing in Europe." *Scandinavian Political Studies* 24 (1): 1–26.

– 2011. "The JDT Model: Context and Extensions." In *The EU's Decision Traps,* edited by G. Falkner, 217–36. Oxford: Oxford University Press.

Schattschneider, E.E. 1935. *Politics, Pressures and the Tariff.* New York: Prentice Hall.

Skogstad, Grace. 2012. "International Trade Policy and the Evolution of Canadian Federalism." In *Canadian Federalism: Performance, Effectiveness, and Legitimacy,* edited by H. Bakvis and G. Skogstad, 203–22. Oxford: Oxford University Press.

Smith, Andrew, and Jatinder Mann. 2015. "Federalism and Sub-national Protectionism: A Comparison of the Internal Trade Regimes of Canada and Australia." Institute of Intergovernmental Relations Working Paper. Accessed 17 February 2017. https://www.queensu.ca/iigr/sites /webpublish.queensu.ca.iigrwww/files/files/WorkingPapers /NewWorkingPapersSeries/SmithAndrewWorkingPaper2015.pdf.

Stepan, Alfred. 1999. "Federalism and Democracy: Beyond the US Model." *Journal of Democracy* 10 (4): 19–34.

Tatham, Michael. 2018. "The Rise of Regional Influence in the EU: From Soft Policy Lobbying to Hard Vetoing."Journal of Common Market Studies 56 (3): 672–86.

Thorlakson, Lori. 2003. "Comparing Federal Institutions: Power and Representation in Six Federations." *West European Politics* 26 (2): 1–22.

Trebilcock, Michael, R. Howse, and A. Eliason. 2013. *The Regulation of International Trade.* New York: Routledge Publishing.

Wallner, Jennifer, and Gerard Boychuk. 2014. "Comparing Federations: Testing the Model of Market-Preserving Federalism on Canada, Australia, and the United States." In *Comparing Canada: Methods and Perspectives on Canadian Politics,* edited by L. Turgeon, M. Papillon, J. Wallner, and S. White, 198–221. Vancouver: University of British Columbia Press.

Watts, Ronald. 2008. *Comparing Federal Systems*. 3rd ed. Montreal and
   Kingston: McGill-Queen's University Press.
Weingast, Barry. 1995. "The Economic Role of Political Institutions: Market-
   Preserving Federalism and Economic Development." *Journal of Law,
   Economics, and Organization* 11 (1): 1–31.
Wibbels, Eric. 2005. *Federalism and the Market: Intergovernmental Conflict and
   Economic Reform in the Developing World*. Cambridge: Cambridge University
   Press.
World Trade Organization (WTO). 2017. *Regional Trade Agreements: Facts
   and Figures*. Accessed 17 February 2017. www.wto.org/english/tratop_e
   /region_e/regfac_e.htm.
Young, Alasdair. 2016. "Not Your Parents' Trade Politics: The Transatlantic
   Trade and Investment Partnership Negotiations." *Review of International
   Political Economy* 23 (3): 345–78.

SECTION ONE

Canada in North America

1 Federalism and Trade Negotiations in Canada: CUSFTA, CETA, and TPP Compared

STÉPHANE PAQUIN

Provinces (and even Canadian territories) have become increasingly important players in Canadian trade negotiations (Fafard and Leblond 2013; Kukucha 2005, 2008, 2013, 2016; Ouellet and Beaumier 2016; Paquin 2006, 2010, 2013, 2014, 2018; VanDuzer 2013). Although the federal government holds, under the Constitution, full powers over the conclusion of treaties and has sole responsibility for international trade, Grace Skogstad has gone so far as to describe the process of trade negotiations as a "de facto shared jurisdiction" (Skogstad 2012, 204).

There are two reasons for provincial involvement in trade negotiations. First, at a constitutional level, although the federal government has responsibility for international trade and can negotiate in areas of exclusive provincial jurisdiction, it cannot compel the provinces to implement ratified trade agreements (Cyr 2009; Kukucha 2008, 2013; Paquin 2006, 2010, 2013, 2018; Skogstad 2012; VanDuzer 2013; see also Hederer and Leblond in this volume). Since treaties do not have a direct effect on domestic law, they must be implemented at either the federal or the provincial level. Provincial action is essential. Second, commercial treaties, particularly those of the "new generation," increasingly involve areas of provincial jurisdiction, be they public procurement, labour mobility, public monopolies and state corporations, investment, or sustainable development. Owing to the evolution of trade agreements, provincial involvement has become more critical. This chapter will thus emphasize the interaction between the Canadian federal system and the evolving trade agreements.

Negotiations with the European Union (EU) are of particular importance as they created a significant precedent. Indeed, for the first time in the history of Canadian trade negotiations, the provinces were represented in the Canadian delegation and even participated directly in negotiations on several subjects (Fafard and Leblond 2013; Kukucha

2013, 2016; Paquin 2013, 2018; VanDuzer 2013). While the precedent is important, it neither represents a paradigm shift in the management of trade negotiations in Canada nor indicates how future negotiations will proceed. The real sustainable change lies in the increasing institutional-ization of intergovernmental mechanisms related to international trade negotiations. This phenomenon is also evident in other fields such as human rights and education (Paquin 2006).

This chapter explains why provinces have become increasingly important players in Canada's trade negotiations. It begins by exam-ining the evolution of treaty-making in Canada in general, which goes beyond trade issues. In the second part it focuses on the negotia-tion of three trade agreements: the Canada-United States Free Trade Agreement (CUSFTA), the Canada-European Union Comprehensive Economic and Trade Agreement (CETA), and the Trans-Pacific Part-nership (TPP). The conclusion argues that the increasing influence of the provinces in trade negotiations is not a radical change on the part of the Canadian government but rather the logical continuation of an evolution in trade negotiations that began in the 1970s.

Federalism and International Negotiations

The treaty-making process in Canada, when it affects provincial juris-dictions, involves two basic steps that are not necessarily sequential: the conclusion of a treaty (i.e., negotiation, signature, and ratification) and its implementation. The federal executive has a monopoly on the first step. This monopoly was contested by the Ontario government in 1936 and has been contested by the Quebec government since the 1965 Gérin-Lajoie doctrine, which basically states that when provisions lie in the field of jurisdiction of Quebec, it is the Government of Quebec that should negotiate the agreements (Paquin 2006, 2018; Paquin and Chaloux 2016). The second step of adopting the legislative measures required to implement a treaty falls to the legislature at either the fed-eral or the provincial level. In Canada there is a need for legislative intervention at the appropriate level to incorporate treaties into domes-tic law (de Mestral and Fox-Decent 2008).

In Canada a treaty does not automatically supersede existing laws. Judges rely on Canadian laws and not on treaties to render judgments, although some judgments refer to pertinent treaties. This is a sizeable challenge in Canada because "roughly 40 percent of federal statutes implement international rules in whole or in part" (de Mestral and Fox-Decent 2008, 578). At the federal level an executive order (an instru-ment of full powers that designates the person or persons vested with the power to sign the treaty on behalf of Canada) is first required before the signature. A second decree is then necessary before ratification (a decree prepared by Cabinet authorizing the minister of foreign affairs to sign an instrument of ratification). Certain multilateral treaties, however, only require a decree for ratification. After it has been signed, the treaty is tabled in federal parliament for a period of twenty-one days unless it is considered an emergency.[1] Once this delay has passed, legislation for implementation at the federal level can be adopted. The Directorate of Treaty Law publishes the Canada Treaty Series, which offers an updated list of treaties in Canada.

As regards the second step, implementation, it must generally be incorporated into domestic law by a law of incorporation or a change of regulation at the competent level (Barnett 2012; Scherrer 2000). If the law is compatible with the treaty, there is no need for new legislation. This is often the case, as the provinces and the federal government have frequently already enacted laws that are stricter than some international standards. When domestic law is incompatible with the treaty, an implementing law is necessary and can take various forms, ranging from a legislative text appended to the treaty that gives it the force of law, to a distinct law that more or less faithfully reproduces the provisions of the treaty. de Mestral and Fox-Decent have identified more than thirteen ways to integrate treaties into domestic law at the federal level (de Mestral and Fox-Decent 2008, 617–22).

In the case of a treaty dealing with Quebec jurisdictions, the National Assembly of Quebec must approve the treaty before the Quebec government gives its assent. This approval is not necessary at the federal level or in any other provinces. Thus, the National Assembly is the only provincial legislature in Canada to intervene in the "approval" of treaties. The law of the Quebec Ministry of International Relations has, since 2002, involved the legislature in the process of approving major international commitments. When an international commitment is described as "important" – meaning that it requires the adoption of a law, the creation of a regulation, the imposition of a tax, or government acceptance of a financial obligation, or it concerns human rights or international trade – it must be approved by the National Assembly (LeDuc 2009, 550–1). Daniel Turp (2016) has identified twenty-seven treaties concluded since 2002 by the federal government that were considered important and were therefore tabled for approval by the National Assembly of Quebec. Thus, Quebec goes further than the federal government and any province because the federal parliament does not have to "approve" a treaty, although it must, as in Quebec, adopt legislation to assure its implementation.

In Quebec the minister of international relations deposits the treaty, along with explanatory notes on its effects, at the National Assembly. The minister can introduce a motion for approval or rejection (there are two precedents for rejection), and debate must last two hours. In an emergency the government may "ratify," in the words of the Government of Quebec, an agreement or approve a treaty before it is tabled in the National Assembly (LeDuc 2009, 550–1). Precedents include the Softwood Lumber Agreement between Canada and the United States (Turp 2016, 23).

It should be noted that the debate and the vote in the National Assembly occur after the Government of Canada has signed the treaty. Quebec parliamentarians therefore have few means to influence the content of the treaty at this stage; they can only adopt or reject it (Turp 2016, 24–5). That said, there is nothing to prevent members from sending signals to their federal counterparts on the mood of Quebec parliamentarians during the negotiations. During CETA negotiations, parliamentarians twice invited Pierre-Marc Johnson, the chief negotiator for Quebec, to a parliamentary commission. This mechanism enabled parliamentarians to raise their concerns.

In the event that the National Assembly refuses to give its approval, the Quebec executive can argue that the treaty is urgent, and pass a decree. However, it would be difficult to adopt implementing legislation in this context (see Hederer and Leblond in this volume). Thus, unlike Wallonia that was able, for a time, to block the signing of CETA, the provinces' only recourse is to refuse to implement a treaty in its areas of jurisdiction. This situation is incongruous because it is the federal government that would need to defend the position of the Quebec government in the event of a denunciation (Ouellet and Beaumier 2016, 76).

There are precedents for Canada having to compensate companies because of measures taken by the provinces. For example, due to measures taken by Newfoundland and Labrador, the Government of Canada had to pay AbitibiBowater CAD 130 million (Lévesque 2015). As a result of this incident the prime minister of Canada asked the federal Department of Foreign Affairs to find a mechanism that would make provinces responsible for their own actions (Côté 2015). A majority of provinces are opposed to this idea, including Ontario, although the Government of Quebec is in favour.

This situation has created many problems. According to de Mestral and Fox-Decent (2008, 644), "from the federal perspective there are many frustrations and pitfalls. The federal government can commit Canada to a treaty, but it cannot guarantee that the treaty will be properly implemented if the subject matter falls within provincial jurisdiction. This fact can be a serious impediment to the rapid consolidation of a treaty relationship with other states."

Given these difficulties, the federal government must be careful when it commits Canada on the international stage, because it risks being undermined by provincial actions. Various strategies have been used historically to avoid such a situation. The first is to limit international negotiations to areas of federal competence. For example, in its trade treaties with Colombia and Peru, the Government of Canada excluded all provincial measures that had predated their conclusion in areas of services and investment obligations (VanDuzer 2013). Another strategy is to use federal clauses to limit the scope of international treaties, and yet another is to create intergovernmental mechanisms for trade negotiations that enable provinces to collaborate in the negotiating process.

Federal Clauses

Since the Government of Canada does not have the power in areas of provincial jurisdiction to impose the treaties it ratifies, it has been forced to use different mechanisms to make sure that they will not be denounced. Federalism and the rights of the provinces in international relations have an important bearing on the conclusion of treaties in Canada. The problem is even more striking when it comes to Canada's involvement in the work of international organizations in areas that fall under provincial jurisdiction, such as UNESCO, the World Health Organization, and the International Labour Organization (Patry 2003, 6; Paquin 2006, 2018).

In order to avoid problems, the federal government has used different strategies in the past. It undertook the entire process to arrive at the signing of a convention or treaty in an international organization but inserted a federal clause in the final treaty. The federal clause (sometimes referred to as the Canada clause) subjects the implementation of the treaty to constitutional imperatives and states that the federal government can only respect the treaty to the extent of its constitutional jurisdiction. The first federal clause of the International Labour Organization of 1946 states: "In the case of a federal state, the power of which to enter into conventions on labour matters is subject to limitations, it shall be in the discretion of that Government to treat a draft convention to which such limitations apply as a recommendation only, and the provisions of this Article with respect to recommendations shall apply in such case" (ILO 1946, 226; see also Dehousse 1991, 187). Federal clauses are also used in Canada's bilateral treaties. The double-taxation agreement between Canada and Australia of 1957, for example, contains a federal clause.

Federal clauses, however, have proved unacceptable to some countries with which Canada enters into agreements. Indeed, when Canada ratifies a convention with a unitary state like France, it has to respect the entire treaty, despite the fact that the federal government can only ensure respect for the treaty in areas under its jurisdiction. The federal clause is unacceptable to unitary countries because its wording is not binding and does not contain any obligation regarding means. Moreover, in some cases, countries, particularly the United States, have used federal clauses even though they had the constitutional capacity to impose the treaty on states. The clause is thus contested, and some authors went so far as to advance, in the 1970s, that federal clauses were "an idea whose time [had] passed" (Patry 2003, 33).

In practice it is difficult not to resort to such clauses because the limitations faced by countries like Canada are very real. Without a federal clause Canada risks marginalization because it would not be able to participate in activities of international organizations that touched on provincial jurisdictions. The federal clause has therefore persisted and evolved in two ways: the first involved limiting the scope of an international convention to certain provinces, and the second required the federal government to take reasonable steps to ensure that provinces enforced the agreement. In this way federal clauses have begun to impose certain obligations on the federal government.

An example of the first evolution comes from the Hague Conference on Private International Law, an international organization. Under the conventions adopted by the conference, the Canadian government supported a provision that allowed federal states to limit the territorial scope of ratification. The federal government could thus limit the scope of the agreement to only a few provinces. The advantage of this practice is that it circumvents the rule of unanimity. Upon ratification of its accession to the Convention Providing a Uniform Law on the Form of an International Will of 1973, the federal government indicated that this convention applied only to Manitoba and Newfoundland and Labrador. A few months later, the scope of the convention was extended to Ontario and Alberta. In another example, the federal government supported the 1980 Hague Convention on the Civil Aspects of International Child Abduction. When the convention was ratified in 1983, it applied to only four provinces. It was gradually extended to other provinces and is now in force across the country (Paquin 2006).

The second evolution of the federal clause stems from treaties such as the General Agreement on Tariffs and Trade (GATT) and, more recently, the North American Free Trade Agreement (NAFTA). According to article XXIV:12.13 of the GATT text, "each Member is fully responsible under GATT 1994 for the observance of all provisions of GATT 1994, and shall take such reasonable measures as may be available to it to ensure such observance by regional and local governments and authorities within its territory." This clause obliges signatory countries to adopt "reasonable measures" to ensure that regional and local governments apply the GATT 1994 treaty.[2] The nature of Canada's federal government obligations to the provinces was clarified by the dispute-settlement body of the organization. In *Canada: Import, Distribution and Sale of Certain Alcoholic Drinks by Provincial Marketing Agencies*, the United States argued that the Canadian government could force the provinces to adopt GATT regulations. The provinces were in fact breaking certain commitments that had been made by Canada. The GATT panel's report did not define what it meant for the federal government to take "reasonable measures" but found that the Canadian government must be able to demonstrate "that it had made serious, persistent and convincing efforts" (WTO 1992, 52). In short, the GATT experts, and today the World Trade Organization (WTO), recognize that the federal government does not have the constitutional authority to impose its treaties on the provinces. This reservation is reflected in the text of article 105 of NAFTA on the scope of obligations. Like article XXIV:12.13 of the GATT text, this article states: "The Parties shall ensure that all necessary measures are taken in order to give effect to the provisions of this Agreement, including their observance, except as otherwise provided in this Agreement, by state and provincial governments."[3]

The federal government became increasingly aware of its limitations and, during the 1970s and 1980s, developed a number of consultation mechanisms to operate between federal and provincial governments. With regard to trade negotiations, the most recent intergovernmental mechanism is known as the C-Trade Forum (Kukucha 2016; Paquin 2006).

Intergovernmental Mechanisms

In theory a typical trade negotiation in Canada is led by the federal government, even when it deals with an area that falls under exclusively provincial jurisdiction. There are many precedents, however, where provincial governments have participated in discussions. In almost every case intergovernmental negotiations between senior officials, and sometimes between ministers, will take place. de Mestral and Fox-Decent (2008, 592) therefore conclude that "the policy-formation process relating to treaty negotiation is entirely in the hands of the federal public service, subject to political direction from the federal cabinet and other elected members of the federal government. In formal terms, provincial, territorial, and First Nations governments are not part of this process. They can be invited to participate, but the invitation is entirely subject to the discretion of the federal government and public service."

Changes to the federal clauses forced the federal government to consult the provinces when international treaties touched on their jurisdictions. Aware of its limitations, the federal government set up mechanisms for consultation with the provinces (Paquin 2006; Turp 2002; Zeigel 1988). In Canada there is no comprehensive framework agreement for federal-provincial consultations related to international negotiations, and there is very little consistency in approaches (de Mestral 2005; Paquin 2006; VanDuzer 2013). Agreements on education, private international law, or human rights are more institutionalized than those on the environment or trade, but on the whole they do not cover all the international treaties that fall within the jurisdiction of the provinces. Rather, they are federal-provincial sectoral agreements. In other words, the mechanisms do not cover all the international negotiations that affect the areas of jurisdiction of the provinces. Moreover, they are often ad hoc, most of the time weakly institutionalized, hardly binding on the federal government, and leave much room for federal arbitrariness. As Renaud Dehousse pointed out in 1991, "generally [Ottawa] tends to downplay the importance of the consultation process by presenting it as an initiative dictated by practical considerations rather than by legal requirements" (136–7). As well, these mechanisms almost never include provincial participation in the negotiations themselves, and provincial officials regularly complain about the difficulty of accessing information.

According to the Canadian government, the ratification of an international treaty strictly concerns the federal executive. This body can commit Canada to agreements on the international stage without any form of provincial consent, even if a treaty requires substantial changes in laws or regulations at all levels. Some authors claim that, in order to avoid foreseeable objections, the federal government does not ratify international treaties requiring provincial legislative changes before the provinces have approved these legislative amendments. Thus, according to de Mestral and Fox-Decent (2008, 624), "generally, the federal government will not ratify a treaty until it is confident that Canada's domestic law is consistent with the treaty and that there are sufficient legal powers in place to comply with its obligations. If legislation is necessary, it is usually passed before the treaty is ratified. The same considerations apply when a treaty relates to matters falling within both federal and provincial jurisdiction, and a fortiori when the treaty relates to matters exclusively within provincial jurisdiction."

In fact, a detailed examination of the steps leading to the conclusion of a treaty shows that the process can be relatively long and is often not completed by the time Canada ratifies the treaty (Paquin 2010; Turp 2016). Looking at the Canada-Costa Rica Free Trade Agreement, we see that Canada signed the treaty on 23 April 2001, the implementation act was passed on 20 September 2001, and the agreement received royal assent on 18 December 2001. The National Assembly of Quebec only approved the treaty on 2 June 2004, over a year after it had come into effect on 1 November 2002. A similar situation arose with the Canada-Chile Free Trade Agreement. The Government of Canada signed the agreement on 5 December 1996, and the House of Commons passed the implementation act on 5 July 1997. The treaty was only approved on 3 June 2004, seven years after its entry into force. This situation is not exclusive to trade agreements (see also the summary table in Turp 2016, 26).

The Canada-United States Free Trade Agreement

After the Second World War Canada's trade policy was essentially structured around its participation in GATT negotiations. Prior to the 1970s, negotiations focused on matters that were exclusively federal, including tariff reduction. With the Kennedy Round (1964–7), and even more clearly with the Tokyo Round (1973–9), multilateral trade negotiations began to have an increasing impact on provincial jurisdictions, notably on non-tariff trade barriers. It was in this context that the Canadian government introduced consultative mechanisms on federal initiatives that affected international trade. As later cycles also involved areas of provincial jurisdiction, these consultation mechanisms were maintained (Winham 1979). With the Uruguay Round, for example, GATT discussions addressed issues such as subsidies, dumping, and phytosanitary measures, as well as agriculture, intellectual property, and services.

Initially, federal-provincial consultations on Canada's trade negotiations in GATT took place within the Canadian Committee on Tariffs and Trade, a new intergovernmental structure. A few years later, this institution was replaced by the Canadian Coordinator of Trade Negotiations (Kukucha 2016). During this phase of negotiations Ottawa was concerned about GATT implementation in provincial jurisdictions. Indeed, in the 1980s the European Economic Community and the United States opposed practices around the sale and distribution of alcohol, notably beer, by the Government of Ontario.

These consultations have gained importance as international negotiations focus increasingly on domestic policies, including business grants and provincial or local regulations, which distort or obstruct international trade. Policies on the pricing of natural resources and on support for agriculture are just two examples of issues falling under the constitutional jurisdiction of the provinces that are beginning to be addressed at international economic conferences. In 1980 this modus operandi was institutionalized through the creation of periodic federal-provincial consultations on trade policy (Winham 1979, 64–89).

During negotiations for CUSFTA in the 1980s and NAFTA in the early 1990s the provinces were actively involved in discussions about the potential impact of these agreements on their economies and jurisdictions. CUSFTA and then NAFTA include areas important to provinces such as rules of origin, technical standards, sanitary and phytosanitary standards, energy, financial services, and certification.

When Brian Mulroney's Progressive Conservative government began discussions on free trade in 1985, the provinces were not formally consulted at the stage of defining the mandate or for the selection of the chief negotiator and the heads of negotiating tables. Nevertheless, they were able to make their positions known, not just at First Ministers' Conferences but also by sending representatives to the preparatory committee for trade negotiations launched by Canada's chief negotiator. During the negotiation of CUSFTA the premiers of the provinces met with the prime minister of Canada fourteen times in eighteen months at federal-provincial meetings (Doern and Tomlin 1991, 126–51).

In order to make their positions clear and to increase their influence in negotiations, Quebec and Ontario retained the services of advisers with experience in this type of exercise. The Ontario government hired Bob Latimer, a former federal official with the Ministry of Foreign Affairs and International Trade, and the Quebec government recruited Jake Warren, who would serve as the Canadian negotiator during the Tokyo Round (Hart, Dymond, and Robertson 1994, 139). However, when the premiers sought to invite themselves to the negotiating table alongside Canada and the United States, the Mulroney government objected.

An intergovernmental mechanism, the Committee on Trade Negotiations, was established to manage relations between the provinces and the federal government during this important negotiation. The ten provinces were represented on the committee. The Canadian government also set up consultative committees on specific issues to be discussed with the provinces, and then it systematized meetings with the provinces to seek technical advice and prepare arguments for the negotiation.

NAFTA negotiations saw the establishment of another forum: the Committee for North American Trade Negotiations. It enabled the provinces to read negotiation documents and obtain information on specific issues (Abelson and Lusztig 1996, 681–98).

These intergovernmental negotiation practices have been perpetuated through the C-Trade Forum. Federal, provincial, and territorial officials meet quarterly to share information and define Canada's position on a range of issues related to trade policy, including trade negotiations. The most important difference between C-Trade Forum meetings and the previous forum is the scope and frequency of meetings.

During negotiations of the NAFTA parallel agreements, which were imposed by the US government following Bill Clinton's election, provincial participation increased. These agreements relate, on the one hand, to labour, which is an exclusively provincial competency, and, on the other hand, to the environment, which is a sphere of shared jurisdiction. Most provinces wished to participate in the negotiation of these side agreements, while the federal government preferred to act alone. In the end the provinces were privy to the strategic positions of Mexico and the United States and participated in drafting Canadian positions. Provincial representatives were invited to a meeting in Washington in August 1993 for the final stage of negotiations. Six provinces were represented during the entire period (Kukucha 2016; 2008, 182–4). In the end the Government of Canada included a specific clause in the side agreements that allowed provinces to withdraw (Kukucha 2003). Only three provinces signed the environmental agreement: Alberta in 1995, Quebec in 1996, and Manitoba in 1997 (Canada 2002). Five provinces signed the agreement on labour: Alberta, Quebec, Manitoba, Prince Edward Island, and Nova Scotia (Canada 2018).

The Canada-European Union Comprehensive Economic and Trade Agreement

In May 2009 the European Union and the Canadian government announced the launch of trade negotiations to conclude a next-generation free trade agreement and decided that, for the first time in Canadian history, the provinces would be represented on the negotiating team (Kukucha 2013; Paquin 2013; VanDuzer 2013).

Provincial participation in CETA trade negotiations stemmed from an EU requirement and was a condition for launching negotiations. The EU considered, based on the failure of prior negotiations, that provincial representatives needed to be present in order for negotiations to have a chance at success. This stipulation was prompted by EU interest in public procurement, an area that in part falls under provincial jurisdiction and is not covered in commercial treaties or by the WTO's Agreement on Government Procurement.

By comparison to previous negotiations on trade liberalization, including with the United States, the provinces saw their role increased at virtually all stages of negotiation. Although they were not consulted about the selection of the chief negotiator, Steve Verheul, they were involved in the critical stages of drafting the joint report and formulating the negotiating mandate. During preparation the provinces were also consulted about issues related to their fields of expertise. In addition, they had access to the negotiation documents and were extensively consulted throughout the process. Quebec, for example, presented over 150 position papers or strategic position briefs.[4] In addition, more "than 275 meetings between federal negotiators and their provincial and territorial counterparts, many meetings involving provinces and territories with common interests, and bilateral meetings in camera between a province or territory and federal negotiators" were held (Johnson, Muzzi, and Bastien 2015, 30). In the case of Ontario, for reasons of confidentiality, interactions with the federal government regarding provincial positions were undertaken verbally. On occasion, Ontario's chief negotiator sent letters to the federal chief negotiator outlining specific areas of interest or concern to the province. No formal record of the number of interactions exists, but one senior official has a rough estimate of around twenty. However, these were supplemented by hundreds of emails at the staff level, which would have addressed more technical and less confidential issues (Anonymous interview in Toronto, June 2017).

The provinces, however, did not have access to all negotiating areas (see table 1.1). They participated actively in discussions on technical barriers to trade, regulatory cooperation, investment (including investor-state dispute settlement mechanisms), cross-border trade in services, mutual recognition of professional qualifications, public procurement, public monopolies and state corporations, sustainable development (labour and environment), wine and spirits, and cooperation (raw materials and innovation, and research in science and technology). However, they were largely excluded from discussions related to agriculture, customs procedures and trade facilitation (rules of origin and procedures of

1.1 Distribution of Subjects of Negotiation between Federal and Provincial Governments in CETA

Federal government	Provincial governments
Trade in goods (agricultural and non-agricultural)	Trade in services
Sanitary and phytosanitary measures	Technical trade barriers
Customs procedures and trade facilitation	Labour mobility
Intellectual property and geographical names	Investment and investor-state dispute settlement mechanisms
Institutional arrangements	Public procurement
	Competition policy and Crown corporations
	Cooperation and collaboration (sustainable development, environment, labour, research, and innovation)

origin), sanitary and phytosanitary measures, trade remedies, subsidies, maritime transport and temporary records, financial services, telecommunications, electronic commerce, intellectual property (geographical indications and patent names), competition policy, institutional issues, and bilateral cooperation on biotechnology (Paquin 2013).

This distribution of subjects in negotiations raises some questions because the provinces were excluded from discussion of areas in which they have shared constitutional jurisdiction, such as agriculture and financial services (regulation of securities), or significant interest, such as intellectual property. In practice, however, while the provinces were excluded from actual negotiations, they were extensively consulted on specific issues (Ontario on the automotive sector, and Alberta on beef, for example). In addition, some issues, such as the diversity of cultural expressions, were not subject to formal negotiations but were discussed as particular areas of interest to Quebec, for example.

During negotiations provincial representatives sat in the room alongside Canadian negotiators. This was somewhat awkward, given that two or three people represented the EU while the Canadian delegation numbered between twenty and thirty. The provinces could not intervene directly during the actual negotiations but could pass notes to Canadian negotiators. They were also able to request a pause in negotiations to allow Canadian negotiators to arrive at a position that satisfied all concerns. Provincial participation was therefore limited during formal negotiating sessions: provincial officials were only able to speak if invited to do so by a federal representative. In addition, provincial officials were not consulted during final arbitration.

Throughout the negotiations provincial representatives maintained informal relations not only with Canadian negotiators but also with European negotiators. The chief negotiator of the Government of Quebec, Pierre-Marc Johnson, for example, had over twelve bilateral meetings with the chief EU negotiator, Mauro Petriccionne (Johnson, Muzzi, and Bastien 2015, 30). One representative from Ontario did not recall any bilateral meetings being held between Ontario's chief negotiator and Mauro Petriccionne. At a January 2010 session in Brussels the Canadian delegation numbered fifty people, including twenty-eight representatives from all Canadian provinces.

During the process Canada's chief negotiator, Steve Verheul, repeatedly recognized the invaluable contribution of the provinces, notably of Quebec. Quebec greatly influenced negotiations on certification issues, labour mobility, and recognition of the diversity of cultural expressions or the cultural exemption. Thus, the role of the provinces became increasingly important and even, in the opinion of the European negotiators, had a decisive impact on the success of the negotiations.[5] Without a clear commitment from the largest provinces (i.e., Quebec, Ontario, Alberta, and British Columbia) the chances of concluding this agreement would have been very low.

The important role of the provinces, and of Quebec in particular, has been recognized and encouraged by the federal government of Justin Trudeau. The Quebec premier, Phillipe Couillard, and Jean Charest and Pierre-Marc Johnson were even invited to travel to Belgium alongside the Canadian prime minister for the formal signing of the agreement.[6] The Government of Canada also coordinated with Pierre Marc Johnson to convince the French and Walloon members of parliament not to block the process. Pierre Marc Johnson met with members in Quebec and abroad who were against the agreement, and continues discussions to assist with the implementation of CETA. No other province has played a similar role. Pierre Marc Johnson has provided a follow-up to negotiations, reporting progress to both provincial and federal levels. He has also produced strategic position papers that have been distributed within the Canadian government. In the case of Ontario the premier released a public statement outlining the province's support of CETA, once a final agreement was reached, and he has been publicly supportive of the positive impact of CETA on the Ontario economy. A number of provinces, including Ontario, have undertaken or are undertaking reforms to bring their measures into compliance with CETA on the implementation front.[7]

The Trans-Pacific Partnership

The TPP negotiations proceeded differently. Canada only joined them in 2012 and was not the only latecomer. For this reason the scoping exercise, and especially the drafting of the negotiating mandate, took place in a very different context. Countries participating in TPP negotiations, in contrast with those of CETA, never broached the question of provincial involvement. Indeed, Canada joined negotiations as a defensive move to ensure that such an agreement was not concluded without it; this contrasts with the proactive role that Canada had played in both NAFTA and CETA.

When we compare negotiations of CUSFTA, CETA, and TPP, many similarities appear between the features of the CUSFTA and the TPP negotiations (see table 1.2). CETA stands as a case apart. According to representatives of the governments of Quebec and Ontario who were

1.2 Summary of Provincial Roles in Trade Negotiations

	CUSFTA	CETA	TPP
Definition of the mandate	Federal only	In consultation with provinces	Federal only
Selection of chief negotiator	Federal only	Federal only	Federal only
Selection of heads of negotiating tables	Federal only	Federal only	Federal only
Provincial presence at the negotiating table	No	Yes, but with limitations	No
Mechanisms for federal-provincial consultation	Premiers' Conferences (14 meetings between the premiers and the prime minister of Canada); Committee on Trade Negotiations	C-Trade Meeting	C-Trade Meeting
Effect on provincial jurisdiction	Minor	Very important	Minor
Approval mechanism	No	Approval by Parliament of Quebec, but not other provinces	Approval by Parliament of Quebec, but not other provinces

close to events, the active participation of the provinces in CETA was not duplicated in TPP and is not anticipated for future negotiations.[8]

Under TPP the provinces were not consulted on the definition of the negotiating mandate, the selection of the chief negotiator, the heads of the negotiating tables, and discussion topics. They did not have access to the negotiating table, and federal-provincial consultation was restricted to the C-Trade Committee. In contrast to trade negotiations between Canada and the United States, no meeting between the prime minister and the premiers took place.

As in CUSFTA, the preferred mechanism to inform provincial representatives was the C-Trade Committee. Some meetings of the committee focused on specific issues such as public procurement, environment, and agriculture. According to a representative of the Government of Quebec, intervention by the provinces during these meetings was limited. In addition, during the rounds of negotiation a specific briefing for the provinces was offered quite late in the day. According to an Ontario representative, the briefing meetings were used as an "information dump" or a sort of "check list."[9] According to one provincial representative, the mechanism was rather unidirectional. A representative of the federal government highlighted, however, that the C-Trade committees were currently much better organized and had more routinized practices than before. Federal officials seem to consider that these meetings have optimized provincial participation.[10]

According to a representative of the Government of Quebec, no province appointed a chief negotiator for TPP. Instead, each province was represented by a high-level public administrator. The Government of Quebec adopted a two-pronged strategy. The first involved having a physical presence at the scene of negotiations in order to attend debriefing sessions, communicate the government's positions, and address certain aspects of the text. Secondly, the Government of Quebec regularly transmitted its own positions, defensive and offensive, along with comments on available texts and Canada's negotiating positions. However, according to a representative of the Quebec government, although the federal government shared negotiating texts and instructions with the provinces during CETA discussions, this practice was not continued during TPP negotiations, where texts were often released to the provinces at the last minute. Comments were requested, but no real reaction was permitted, and there was too little time for analysis. A representative of the Ontario government confirmed that the model employed during CETA was not used in TPP negotiations. According to him, things were done in a very different way, with texts being sent at the last minute for comment, and no real opportunity to participate. A similar approach was employed in briefings following each round of negotiations on site and in meetings of the C-Trade Committee. One Ontario representative thought that the lack of access to the big strategy session was a problem.[11]

Another representative of the Government of Quebec saw things somewhat differently again. This person specified that there was significant provincial participation in TPP negotiations because of the work that had been done under CETA. That work by the provinces was used in TPP, but without allowing the provinces a similarly important level of actual participation.[12]

According to a representative of the Government of Quebec, the provinces did not exercise the same type of leadership in TPP negotiations as they had in CETA. He attributed this to the absence of a clear policy initiative by the Quebec government, explained in part by the departure of Jean Charest as the premier of Quebec. His successors had neither the same level of interest nor the influence and political connections needed (Jeyabalaratnam and Paquin 2016).

Informal coordination between federal and provincial representatives was observed during TPP negotiations. For example, during a negotiating session in Atlanta in October 2015, Quebec ministers Daoust and Paradis wrote to their federal counterparts to ensure coordination during meetings, knowing that agriculture, a delicate subject for Canada, would be discussed. Provincial representatives were also present in rounds held in Singapore and Hawaii.[13]

Conclusion

Provincial participation in Canada's trade negotiations is a progressive phenomenon related to the fact that trade agreements have been evolving since the 1970s and becoming more intrusive for Canadian provinces. The same trend is evident in provincial participation in international negotiations on issues that fall under provincial jurisdiction. While inclusion of provincial representatives within the Canadian delegation at negotiations of the next-generation free trade agreement between Canada and the EU set an important precedent, it is difficult to see it as a fundamental change because this model has not been reproduced in later trade negotiations.

During CETA negotiations the Government of Canada also concluded an agreement with the United States on the issue of "Buy America," which touched on procurement by American states. Canada also initiated trade talks with India, concluded a trade agreement with South Korea, and joined the TPP negotiations. Since then, the renegotiation of

NAFTA, culminating in the United States–Mexico–Canada Agreement, has taken place. In none of these negotiations was the CETA model of provincial involvement employed. Provincial participation was minimal in the "Buy America" agreement with the United States. The Indian government refused to allow federated states to be involved in negotiations, likely for domestic political reasons. As one federal official familiar with the matter stated, "the conversation on this topic was short with the Indians."[14] A similar situation arose in negotiations with South Korea and TPP. In each case, it was through federal-provincial mechanisms that provinces were informed of the progress of discussions. In the case of the renegotiation of NAFTA, provinces were asked by the Trudeau government to intervene with US state governors and different interest groups in order to build consensus to save NAFTA. But no provinces had a similar role to that in the CETA negotiations (Paquin 2017, 2018).

If the Canadian government had wanted to transform radically Canadian federalism and the practice of trade negotiations in order to give more room to the provinces, it likely would have chosen to negotiate a comprehensive framework agreement on provincial participation in trade negotiations. This was not the case. Canadian government officials argue, however, that the C-Trade Committee has become more effective and that federal-provincial collaboration can work well without altering institutions.

NOTES

1 For more details see http://www.treaty-accord.gc.ca.
2 https://www.wto.org/english/tratop_e/region_e/region_art24_e.htm.
3 http://international.gc.ca.
4 Anonymous interview, June 2014.
5 Anonymous interview in Brussels, January 2011 and 2016.
6 http://ici.radio-canada.ca.
7 Anonymous interview in Toronto, June 2017.
8 Anonymous interview in Quebec City, April 2016, and Toronto, June 2017.
9 Anonymous interview in Toronto, June 2017.
10 Anonymous interview in Montreal, August 2016.
11 Anonymous interview in Toronto, June 2017.
12 Anonymous interview in Quebec City, April 2016.
13 Anonymous interview in Quebec City, April 2016, and in Toronto, June 2017.
14 Anonymous interview in Montreal, August 2016.

REFERENCES

Abelson, Donald E., and Michael Lusztig. 1996. "The Consistency of Inconsistency: Tracing Ontario's Opposition to the NAFTA." *Revue canadienne de science politique* 29 (4): 681–98.

Barnett, Laura. 2012. *Le processus de conclusion de traités au Canada*. Ottawa: Bibliothèque du Parlement.

Canada. 2018. "North American Agreement on Labour Cooperation." Web page consulted on 17 September 2018. https://www.canada.ca.

– 2002. *The Canadian Intergovernmental Agreement (CIA) Regarding the North American Agreement on Environmental Cooperation (NAAEC)*. Accessed 15 June 2013. http://naaec.gc.ca.

Côté, Charles-Emmanuel. 2015. "Toward Arbitration between Subnational Units and Foreign Investors?" *Columbia FDI Perspectives* 145: 1–3.

Cyr, Hugo. 2009. *Canadian Federalism and Treaty Powers: Organic Constitutionalism at Work*. New York: Peter Lang.

de Mestral, Armand. 2005. "The Provinces and International Relations in Canada." In *The States and Moods of Federalism: Governance, Identity and Methodology*, edited by J.-F. Gaudrault-Desbiens and F. Gelinas, 319–22. Cowansville, QC: Editions Yvon Blais.

de Mestral, Armand, and Evan Fox-Decent. 2008. "Rethinking the Relationship between International and Domestic Law." *McGill Law Journal* 53 (4): 573–648.

Dehousse, Renaud. 1991. *Fédéralisme et relations internationales*. Brussels: Bruylant.

Doern, Bruce, and Brian W. Tomlin. 1991. *Faith and Fear: The Free Trade Story*. Toronto: Stoddart.

Fafard, Patrick, and Patrick Leblond. 2013. "Closing the Deal: What Role for the Provinces in the Final Stages of the CETA Negotiations?" *International Journal* 68 (4): 553–9.

Hart, Michael, Bill Dymond, and Colin Robertson. 1994. *Decision at Midnight: Inside the Canada-US Free-Trade Negotiations*. Vancouver: UBC Press.

ILO (International Labour Organization). 1946. "Instrument of Amendment Adopted by the International Labour Conference at Its 29th Session." *Official Bulletin* 29 (4): 204–53. https://www.ilo.org.

Jeyabalaratnam, Gopinath, and Stéphane Paquin. 2016. "La politique internationale du Québec sous Jean Charest: L'influence d'un premier ministre." *Revue québécoise de droit international* H-S 2: 165–83.

Johnson, Pierre Marc, Patrick Muzzi, and Véronique Bastien. 2015. "Le Québec et l'AECG." In *Un nouveau pont sur l'Atlantique: L'accord économique et commercial global entre l'Union européenne et le Canada*, edited by C. Deblock, J. Lebullenger and S. Paquin, 27–40. Québec: Presses de l'Université du Québec.

Kukucha, Christopher. 2003. "Domestic Politics and Canadian Foreign Trade Policy: Intrusive Interdependence, the WTO, and NAFTA." *Canadian Foreign Policy Journal* 10 (2): 59–86.

– 2005. "From Kyoto to the WTO: Evaluating the Constitutional Legitimacy of the Provinces in Canadian Foreign Trade and Environmental Policy." *Revue canadienne de science politique* 31 (1): 129–52.

– 2008. *The Provinces and Canadian Foreign Trade Policy.* Vancouver: UBC Press.

– 2013. "Canadian Sub-federal Governments and CETA: Overarching Themes and Future Trends." *International Journal* 68 (4): 528–35.

– 2016. "Provincial/Territorial Governments and the Negotiations of International Trade Agreements." *IRPP Insight* 10: 1–16.

LeDuc, François. 2009. *Guide de la pratique de relations internationales du Québec.* Quebec City: Les publications du Québec.

Lévesque, Céline. 2015. "Les rôles et responsabilités des provinces canadiennes dans le cadre de procédures d'arbitrage entre investisseurs et États fondées sur des traités économiques." *Revue québécoise de droit international* 28 (1): 107–55.

Ouellet, Richard, and Guillaume Beaumier. 2016. "L'activité du Québec en matière de commerce international: De l'énonciation de la doctrine Gérin-Lajoie à la négociation de l'AECH." *Revue québécoise de droit international* H-S 2: 67–79.

Paquin, Stéphane. 2006. "Le fédéralisme et les relations internationales du Canada depuis le jugement de 1937 sur les conventions de travail." In *Les relations internationales du Québec depuis la Doctrine Gérin-Lajoie (1965–2005): Le prolongement externe des compétences internes*, 7–24. Ste-Foy, QC: Presses de l'Université Laval.

– 2010. "Federalism and Compliance with International Agreements: Belgium and Canada Compared." *The Hague Journal of Diplomacy* 5 (1–2): 173–97.

– 2013. "Federalism and the Governance of International Trade Negotiations in Canada: Comparing CUSFTA with CETA." *International Journal* 68 (4): 545–52.

– 2014. "Le fédéralisme d'ouverture et la place du Québec (et des autre provinces) dans le négociations internationales: Rupture dans la continuité?" *Canadian Foreign Policy Journal* 20 (1): 28–37.

– 2017. "Le role de provinces dans la renégociation de l'ALENA." *Options politiques.* http://policyoptions.irpp.org.

– 2018. "Fédéralisme et négociations commerciales au Canada: L'ALE, l'AECG et le PTP compares." *Études internationales* 48 (3–4): 347–69.

Paquin, Stéphane, and Annie Chaloux. 2016. "La doctrine Gérin-Lajoie: 50 ans d'actions internationales du Québec." *Revue québécoise de droit international* H-S 2. https://www.sqdi.org.

Patry, André. 2003. *La compétence internationale des provinces canadiennes.* Montreal: André R. Dorais.

Scherrer, Sylvia. 2000. "L'effet des traités dans l'ordre juridique interne canadien à la lumière de la jurisprudence récente, dans Barreau du Québec." In *Développements récents en droit administratif,* 57–84. Cowansville, QC: Éditions Yvon Blais.

Skogstad, Grace. 2012. "International Trade Policy and the Evolution of Canadian Federalism." In *Canadian Federalism,* 3rd ed., edited by H. Bakvis and G. Skogstad, 203–22. Don Mills, ON: Oxford University Press.

Turp, Daniel. 2002. *Pour une intensification des relations du Québec avec les institutions internationales.* Quebec City: Ministére de Relations internationales.

– 2016. "L'approbation des engagements internationaux importants du Québec: La nouvelle dimension parlementaire à la doctrine Gérin-Lajoie." *Revue québécoise de droit international* H-S 2: 9–40.

VanDuzer, Anthony. 2013. "Could an Intergovernmental Agreement Make Canadian Treaty Commitments in Areas within Provincial Jurisdiction More Credible?" *International Journal* 68 (4): 536–44.

Winham, Gilbert R. 1979. "Bureaucratic Politics and Canadian Trade Negotiations." *International Journal* 34 (1): 65–89.

WTO (World Trade Organization). 1992. "Canada: Import, Distribution and Sale of Certain Alcoholic Drinks by Provincial Marketing Agencies." Report by the Panel adopted on 18 February 1992 (DS17/R - 39S/27). https://www.wto.org.

Zeigel, Jacob. 1988. "Treaty Making and Implementation Powers in Canada: The Continuing Dilemma." In *Contemporary Problems of International Law: Essays in Honour of Georg Schwarzenberger on His Eightieth Birthday,* edited by B. Cheng and E.D. Brown, 338–59. Agincourt, ON: Carswell.

2 Implementation of Twenty-First-Century Trade Agreements in Canada: CETA and Intergovernmental Cooperation

CHRISTIAN HEDERER AND PATRICK LEBLOND

In September 2017 the Canada-European Union Comprehensive Economic and Trade Agreement (CETA) came into force provisionally.[1] Afterwards, Canada became a member of the Comprehensive and Progressive Agreement for Trans-Pacific Partnership (CPTPP), which entered into force at the beginning of 2019. It also agreed to the United States-Mexico-Canada Agreement (USMCA), which modernized the North American Free Trade Agreement (NAFTA) and was meant to replace it. The CPTPP significantly inspired the USMCA. Canada has now concluded three major so-called next-generation free trade agreements (FTAs). As mentioned in the introduction to this volume, such comprehensive trade agreements are considered to be next generation because, to varying degrees, they seek to remove not only trade barriers at the border but also obstacles found beyond the border; they include, for example, chapters on investment, labour, the environment, sustainable development, digital trade, and public procurement.

For instance, CETA will reduce the trading costs arising from technical barriers to trade (e.g., technical regulations or testing and certification requirements). It will do so by specifying the steps necessary to have regulations recognized as equivalent by the other party to the agreement, thereby avoiding the costly need for goods to be produced using different standards depending on whether they are meant to be exported or sold at home. Furthermore, CETA will make it possible for testing and certification bodies to be recognized in both jurisdictions, thereby eliminating duplication in the certification of both product and process. Finally, the agreement establishes mechanisms to encourage regulators and standard setters from Canada and Europe to cooperate on the development of future technical regulations.

The fact that an agreement like CETA addresses a wide range of issues with a view to increasing trade, labour, and investment flows between Canada and the European Union (EU) implies that considerable implementation work needs to be done once the agreement comes into force. The term *implementation* herein is not limited to the adoption of implementing legislation to make existing laws conform with CETA's provisions, which is how the legal literature tends to define implementation.[2] It means much more. It implies the adoption of concrete (i.e., practical) rules, standards, and procedures so that businesses can take advantage of provisions such as the one that aims to facilitate the mobility of professionals, technicians, and businesspeople between Canada and the EU within CETA.

Steger (2012, 109) defines implementation of next-generation FTA issues as follows: "harmonization of standards and development of joint standards codes as well as mutual recognition of technical regulations, standards, and occupational qualifications." This kind of implementation requires a high degree of cooperation between the parties to an FTA. It also demands close cooperation between the various levels of government in each jurisdiction. In Canada this means that the federal government must collaborate with its provincial and territorial counterparts. It also means that provincial governments and their agencies must cooperate with each other across the country long after an international trade agreement has come into force, and not just during the negotiations (for details see the chapter by Paquin in this volume). In other words, multilevel government collaboration must be both vertical and horizontal in order to be effective.

In this context, the chapter addresses the following questions: what is the role of Canadian provinces in the implementation of international trade agreements and how could it be improved? Within the book's framework the current situation in terms of relations between federal and provincial governments on trade matters can best be characterized as one of "consultation" on the continuum of self-rule and shared rule. This has been true mostly with respect to trade negotiations (see the chapter by Paquin in this volume). In terms of implementing trade agreements the provinces have traditionally had little or no role to play in trade agreements because the latter did not typically touch on their areas of competence. Where parts of earlier trade agreements touched on the provinces' competencies, the governance mode was closer to self-rule than to consultation (e.g., NAFTA's labour side agreement).

This chapter argues that, given the extensive scope and depth of next-generation trade agreements such as CETA, intergovernmental relations between the government of Canada and the provinces need to move to the "cooperation" mode of interaction so that these agreements may be implemented effectively. The ideal objective would be a joint decision-making mode; however, given Canada's decentralized model of federalism, such an approach appears to be politically unfeasible in the foreseeable future. This is because Canada's intergovernmental institutions have not evolved to deal with the scope and depth of the next-generation trade agreements of which Canada is now a part. Such an evolution could conceivably happen as a result of significant and sustained pressures from the business community wishing to maximize the benefits derived from trade agreements such as CETA and CPTPP; however, for the time being, there is no indication that such pressure exists.

The chapter is organized into three main sections. The first section provides context with respect to both the implementation of existing Canadian trade agreements on the provincial level and intra-Canadian trade relations between the provinces based on Canadian federalism. The second section focuses on select CETA implementation issues. Building on this, the third section discusses several avenues to improve the implementation of second-generation trade agreements in Canada.

The Context: Trade and the Canadian Provinces

Analysing the role of Canadian provinces in CETA's implementation requires a comprehensive view of the relevant existing institutional framework, thereby providing the basis for an assessment and the development of possible improvements on the way ahead. That is the subject of this section, which is organized in three parts. First, we focus on the implementation of existing international trade agreements in Canada, taking into account the legal framework as well as factual experience. Second, we provide a brief outline of the core institutions and procedures of Canadian federalism generally and on this basis focus on the 2017 Canadian Free Trade Agreement (CFTA) for interprovincial trade as an example that appears to be relevant for the implementation of CETA in both procedural and substantive terms. Finally, we take a broader look at regulatory cooperation as the most important mode of "soft" governance in implementing next-generation international trade agreements, which plays a key role in the Canadian context where federal-provincial cooperation is necessary for an effective implementation of CETA and other similar agreements.

Historically, Canadian federalism and federal-provincial relations have gone through complex transformations, accompanied by an even more complex academic debate (Bickerton 2010). While a full analysis of related issues is beyond the scope of this chapter, a core point is that patterns of interaction both between the federal and provincial levels and between provinces have generally developed from the federally dominated cooperative federalism of the 1950s and 1960s to a collaborative style with a more equal role for the provinces. Concomitantly, a core characteristic that has remained relatively unchanged over the last decades is a strong focus on intergovernmental cooperation, that is, the collaboration of the executive bodies, or executive federalism.[3] The institutional structure of Canadian executive federalism is peculiar in so far as it is relatively elaborate and at the same time only weakly grounded in formal rules (on the levels of both constitutional and ordinary law).

Based on this, we can distinguish procedural institutions and substantive rules constituted by intergovernmental agreements. On the procedural side, the most traditional high-level institution is the First Ministers' Conference, which has been convoked by the prime minister at intervals ranging from a few months to several years. The Annual Premiers' Conference, in contrast, includes provinces only. It was transformed into the Council of the Federation (CoF) in 2003. The council is tasked with strengthening interprovincial cooperation and coordinating policies vis-à-vis the federal government. Building on a relatively dense meeting schedule, it has developed significant activity in some policy areas, including domestic as well as international trade (Collins 2017). This has increased its political importance at the First Ministers' Conference. Below the top procedural level, a key role is played by a diversity of ministerial councils, which by now focus on many policy areas. They sometimes comprise both federal and provincial members and sometimes provincial only and often are central to the respective policy processes (e.g., Minaeva 2012, 15). The ministerial councils are supported by a dense network of semi-formal institutions that regularize executive interaction. The outcomes of these processes are regularly enshrined in intergovernmental agreements. Similar to their procedural counterparts, they lack a clear legislative basis, and their legally binding nature and "justiciability" (Poirier 2004) appear to be ambiguous.

Implementing Trade Agreements in Canada before CETA

The fact that Canada is a federal country implies that legislative powers are distributed between the (federal) Parliament of Canada and the provincial legislatures.[4] A similar distribution exists with respect to executive powers; parts of provincial executive activity take place at the municipal level (e.g., local public procurement).

As a consequence the implementation of Canada's international obligations also lies within the competence of the provinces with respect to the legislative (and executive) powers allocated to them by the Constitution. There is no federal-level legal device that can "force" provinces to comply with international agreements made by the federal government (see Paquin in this volume). Canada can therefore be in a situation where it is held liable for a breach of international law due to a treaty violation by a province. In the trade context this can be particularly problematic in so far as retaliation by a treaty partner as a consequence of non-compliance by a province can generate negative economic effects that go beyond that province (Fafard and Leblond 2012; VanDuzer and Mallet 2016, 101).

Further complicating implementation, the delineation of federal and provincial competences in the Constitution is normally not congruent with the areas subject to trade and investment agreements; some areas may touch upon both federal and provincial competences (e.g., public procurement, environment, digital trade) (de Beer 2012). Moreover, the attribution to either federal or provincial legislation may not be straightforward, because the division of competences is itself not clear-cut. For example, the exact delineation of the provincial power to legislate in property and civil rights from the federal trade and commerce power remains potentially controversial.[5]

Paquin (in this volume) provides a general discussion of the Canadian federal government's strategies to address the issue of provincial non-compliance. Here we focus on the way and extent to which these issues have had an impact on the implementation of the most important Canadian trade agreements before CETA, namely the General Agreement on Tariffs and Trade (GATT) / World Trade Organization (WTO) and NAFTA.

Both NAFTA (article 105) and GATT 1994 (article XXIV:12) enshrine the treaty parties' responsibility for compliance on the sub-national level. On the Canadian federal level, then, both the NAFTA and the GATT/WTO agreements were implemented by omnibus statutes drafted in two parts: (1) a general approval of the agreement, setting out its purposes and providing for general matters; and (2) amendments to bring federal legislation into conformity with international obligations (Steger 1997, 2010). The World Trade Organization Agreement Implementation Act was of a relatively minimalist nature, apparently because numerous necessary changes, such as those to investment, services, and intellectual property laws, had already been made (see Steger 1997, 246). The North American Free Trade Agreement Implementation Act (NAFTA Act), however, went further in postulating that all federal legislative acts related to implementation should be interpreted in a manner consistent with the agreement. Also, there is an assertion that nothing in that act limits the right of Parliament to enact legislation or to fulfil any of Canada's international obligations under NAFTA. Up to now it has been unclear, and not subject to jurisprudence, whether this language just constitutes a hortatory statement or in fact enshrines an expansive intention with respect to federal jurisdiction. Specifically, section 20 of the NAFTA Act provides the federal cabinet with the power to establish regulations giving effect to articles 312 and 313 of NAFTA, which deal with trade of wine and spirits, an area under provincial jurisdiction. However, this federal legislation has been neither used to address provincial non-compliance nor challenged by a province (despite an initial threat from Ontario) (VanDuzer and Mallet 2016, 118n164). Monahan (2001) believes that such a challenge would eventually have led to an upholding of this legislation.[6]

At the provincial level, NAFTA and GATT/WTO implementation was generally not regarded as a major issue, partly because the provinces had already fulfilled their respective obligations and partly because areas under provincial power had been carved out in Canada's schedules of commitments (VanDuzer and Mallet 2016, 97). For example, VanDuzer and Mallet (2016, 93) report that no provincial legislation was passed with respect to NAFTA obligations in investment and services. Some academic papers on implementation of the NAFTA and GATT agreements do not mention provincial involvement at all (e.g., Carmody 2014). In so far as provincial implementation was necessary at all, the federal government seemed to be successful in settling on voluntary or informal compliance agreements in advance (Skogstad 2002, 164). Overall, according to Paquin (2013, 549), NAFTA's main effect has been not to require new provincial legislation but to reduce the federal government's and the provincial governments' interventions in provincial economies in many areas.

Still, two special issues warrant attention with respect to the provincial implementation of NAFTA. First, Canada, the United States, and Mexico negotiated side agreements on labour rights and environmental protection, which in the case of Canada affect only willing provinces. Canada declared a list of provinces that would cooperate in the matters covered. For Canada, no obligations, but also no rights, arise vis-à-vis the United States and Mexico with respect to non-participating provinces. Quebec, Alberta, and Manitoba have ratified both side agreements (for details see VanDuzer and Mallet 2016, 98).

Second, NAFTA's controversial chapter 11 on investment protection and investor-state dispute settlement entitles investors to raise claims for compensation against the federal government for the full range of measures defined in the chapter even if the claims result from provincial-level decisions. This renders potentially problematic the lack of any right (or any obligation) of the provinces to participate in proceedings. At the same time, the federal government is legally solely responsible for paying any compensation that is determined by an arbitration tribunal set up under NAFTA's chapter 11, and, as of now, it has no legal recourse or authority to recoup the amounts paid from provincial governments (see, for example, Herman 2010).[7]

Several NAFTA chapter 11 proceedings against Canada have involved provincial-level measures. The most prominent case is probably that of AbitibiBowater Inc., a US pulp and paper manufacturer, against Canada, which referred to an alleged expropriation of Abitibi-Bowater's assets by the Government of Newfoundland. The Canadian government settled this claim in 2010 with a payment of CAD 130 million. Following the case, the prime minister directed the then Department of Foreign Affairs and International Trade to develop a mechanism for recouping such payments from the responsible provincial government, but no concrete mechanism has been proposed or implemented so far (VanDuzer and Mallet 2016, 101). Another example is the *Mobil Investments Inc. and Murphy Oil Corporation v. Government of Canada* case, in which claimant companies argued that the guidelines on research and development expenditures adopted by the Canada-Newfoundland and Labrador Offshore Petroleum Board (which reports to both the federal minister and the provincial ministers of natural resources but is not directly embedded in the administrative hierarchy) hurt their investments in the Hibernia and Terra Nova projects due to a de facto performance requirement (NAFTA, article 1106(1c)). The tribunal shared this view and in 2015 awarded the companies parts of their claims. No legislative consequences have been reported. A third important case was based on a 2012 claim filed by Windstream Energy, a US company that had signed a contract with the Ontario Power Authority in 2010 to build a hundred offshore wind turbines in Lake Ontario. In 2011 the Government of Ontario, following a policy review by the Ministry of the Environment, decided to defer offshore wind development. Windstream claimed CAD 425 million in compensation for loss of its investment, arguing that the decision was made in an "arbitrary and political manner." In 2016 a NAFTA arbitration tribunal dismissed a number of the claims but awarded Windstream a final amount of CAD 25.2 million in damages. In this case, perhaps surprisingly, the Government of Ontario paid the amount.[8]

GATT/WTO legal disputes in which the provincial implementation of commitments by Canada played a role are rare. One long-standing issue concerns the practices of Canadian liquor-control boards, which have historically administered a monopoly or near-monopoly position of provincial governments in the sale of alcoholic beverages. Suspected breaches of a 1979 statement of intent by Canadian provinces, which limited the capacity of liquor boards to regulate alcohol sales, led to a submission of the issue to a GATT dispute panel by the European Community (now the EU). The panel ruled in favour of the community in 1987 (and in favour of the United States in a similar case in 1992). A subsequent agreement between the European Community and Canada was reached with the knowledge and tacit consent of the majority of the provinces (Kukucha 2008). From the late 1990s the EU called for a further review of provincial liquor-distribution practices. Concerned provinces (Ontario, Quebec, and British Columbia) were directly involved in the ensuing governmental dialogue. Following a formal request for WTO consultations by the EU in 2006, a settlement was reached in 2009 that concerned tax- and tariff-related measures and therefore fell into federal jurisdiction.

A second WTO case concerned a local-content requirement in Ontario's Feed-In Tariff Program (FIT). In 2013 the WTO Appellate Body ruled this requirement to be inconsistent with WTO rules because it discriminated against foreign equipment providers, thereby infringing Canada's national treatment commitment under GATT. As a result, in 2014, Ontario abolished the requirement of domestically produced generation equipment for large projects and significantly lowered the local-content threshold for small- and micro-FIT projects.[9]

In sum, the separation between the Canadian federal government's competence to negotiate and conclude international trade agreements and the provinces' competence to implement commitments in their jurisdiction at their discretion enshrines a significant potential for ambiguity and conflict (see also Fafard and Leblond 2012). Up to now, such conflict has largely been avoided by a combination of adaptations of the commitments themselves and, more importantly, policy practices that reflect the predominantly collaborative style of Canadian federalism, at least as far as international trade policy is concerned (Skogstad 2012; Steger 2010). Moreover, provinces often have an economic self-interest in appropriate implementation, given the general benefits that they derive from international trade and investment. Nevertheless, the capacity of those arrangements to deal with implementation of a more complex and far-reaching agreement, such as CETA, is questionable.

The Canadian Free Trade Agreement

Canada's federal structure and its sharing of competences as enshrined in the Constitution historically implied significant barriers for interprovincial trade, which, following the conclusion of NAFTA in the early 1990s, led to what has been called the "paradox of Canadian trade policy": free trade abroad; restricted trade at home (Doern and MacDonald 1999, 30).[10] NAFTA instigated the negotiation and conclusion of the Agreement on Internal Trade (AIT) in 1994. This agreement was subsequently replaced by the Canadian Free Trade Agreement (CFTA) in 2017, in large part as a result of pressures related to Canada's agreeing to CETA, in which the provinces were closely involved (see the chapter by Paquin in this volume). As it turns out, the provincial implementation of international trade agreements and the regulation of trade and investment flows between provinces not only are obviously interrelated in substantive terms but also exhibit important institutional parallels.

Interprovincial trade is a field in which intergovernmental cooperation has slowly become denser as a consequence of international trade agreements, particularly after the conclusion of NAFTA. The AIT sought to institutionalize interprovincial cooperation by establishing a committee structure, an internal trade secretariat, and formal dispute-resolution mechanisms (government-to-government as well as person-to-government). However, the AIT's implementation was "unduly slow" according to a study by the Canadian Chamber of Commerce (2004), mostly because of "a lack of sustained political will by the signatories to the agreement, an unenforceable dispute resolution process, and the inadequate level of resources dedicated to implementing the agreement" (see also Hansen and Heavin 2010, 199).

The ineffective implementation of AIT and the continued existence of barriers to interprovincial trade motivated the establishment of the New West Partnership Trade Agreement" (NWPTA) between British Columbia, Alberta, and Saskatchewan in April 2010; Manitoba joined later. This agreement built on the Trade, Investment, and Labour Mobility Agreement signed by Alberta and British Columbia in 2006. The NWPTA's scope is much broader than the AIT's: NWPTA adopted a negative-list approach whereas AIT relied on a positive list (Hansen and Heavin 2010, 204).

The NWPTA and CETA negotiations created pressures for the provinces to revise and update the AIT. In 2017 they agreed to the more comprehensive CFTA. Similar to AIT, CFTA contains elaborate formal dispute-resolution mechanisms. With regard to the committee structure, CFTA takes over the Committee on Internal Trade from AIT as the leading forum for steering and implementation. The committee is composed of Cabinet-level representatives (or their designates). The committee chair rotates among provinces, with a one-year tenure. At the level of working groups, CFTA establishes a number of new, specialized formations (such as those on alcoholic beverages and fisheries). In addition, the agreement entitles parties to establish any additional committee and/or working group that they deem appropriate.

CFTA contains a new chapter on "regulatory notification, reconciliation, and cooperation," with the parts on reconciliation and cooperation in particular going further than AIT. It foresees the establishment and operation of a new Regulatory Reconciliation and Cooperation Table, whose representatives are appointed by first ministers. Parties are required to enter into negotiations to reconcile those regulatory measures (identified by a party) that act as a barrier to trade, investment, or labour mobility within Canada, with the aim of concluding a regulatory conciliation agreement, which may also contain tailored dispute-resolution processes. In preparing those agreements, the table is supposed to submit annual work plans to the Committee on Internal Trade and establish specialized working groups. Beyond reconciliation, parties may propose cooperation in the development of future measures in order to achieve positive economic effects, with the table being assigned a role as a discussion forum and assisting body.

CFTA contains a commitment to continued cooperation between the federal government and the provinces with respect to "achieving Canada's trade and economic goals in the international arena," and to a continued use of consultation mechanisms and participation by the provinces in international trade negotiations. It also says that "the Parties shall take appropriate steps to assess international obligations to ensure that the relationship between any international obligations and this Agreement is taken into account when new international obligations are negotiated or when international trade disputes arise."[11]

In sum, CFTA is an ambitious agreement in terms of both its institutional structure and the level of regulatory harmonization to which it aspires. It also establishes a direct link to the negotiation and conclusion of international trade agreements, albeit without specific reference to their implementation. There remains, however, scepticism as to the effectiveness of its implementation by the provinces, as was the case with AIT.[12]

Also, in April 2018, the Supreme Court of Canada confirmed, once again, that the provinces have the constitutional right to regulate economic activity in their territory, even if that might impede interprovincial trade. In what has become known as the Comeau case, the Supreme

Court ruled that it was legal for the province of New Brunswick, under its Liquor Control Act, to restrict the amount of beer that an individual could possess if the beer had not been purchased from a provincial liquor store. Mr Comeau had challenged this restriction by arguing that it was contrary to section 121 of the Constitution Act (1867), which states: "All Articles of the Growth, Produce, or Manufacture of any one of the Provinces shall, from and after the Union, be admitted free into each of the other Provinces." In its ruling the Supreme Court indicated that section 121 prohibits laws restricting interprovincial trade "but only when restricting trade is the laws' main purpose" (Roman 2018).

The Supreme Court's Comeau ruling clearly put the onus of achieving free trade within Canada on the provinces and on their cooperation to remove regulatory barriers to internal trade. Close cooperation is also crucial in order to implement Canada's next-generation international trade agreements.

Regulatory Cooperation and International Trade

Regulatory cooperation is a core feature of Canadian federalism and the effectiveness of twenty-first-century trade agreements. It therefore plays a key role in the implementation of CETA and other next-generation trade agreements. The Organisation for Economic Co-operation and Development (OECD) defines regulatory cooperation as "the range of institutional and procedural frameworks within which national governments, sub-national governments, and the wider public can work together to build more integrated systems for rule-making and implementation, subject to the constraints of democratic values, such as accountability, openness and sovereignty" (OECD 1994, 15). The scope of application and instruments of regulatory cooperation are correspondingly wide. For example, OECD (2013, 23) lists eleven different mechanisms of international regulatory cooperation, ranging from outright harmonization to a supranational or joint institution to international "soft law" and information exchange. International regulatory cooperation has been institutionalized among a considerable number of industrialized countries, such as between the United States and the European Union (United States-European Union High-Level Regulatory Cooperation Forum), the United States and Canada (United States-Canada Regulatory Cooperation Council), and Australia and New Zealand (in the context of the Australia-New Zealand Closer Economic Relations Trade Agreement [ANZCERTA]).

In the context of international trade, regulatory cooperation is commonly (though not uniformly) viewed as an instrument for reducing non-tariff trade barriers. The main tools for reducing these barriers in international trade agreements are regulatory harmonization and mutual recognition or equivalence of technical regulations, standards, and/or conformity assessment procedures. Important complementary instruments include obligations for information exchange and the increase of transparency (Steger 2012).

In addition to stating whether and how they can use those different instruments, international trade agreements can be distinguished by the degree to which they institutionalize regulatory cooperation (Krstic 2012; Steger 2012). For example, as Steger (2012) emphasizes, regulatory cooperation in NAFTA is characterized by an encouragement of voluntary initiatives but hampered by the lack of an institution with oversight of implementation.[13] ANZCERTA, in contrast, institutionalizes deep integration through joint accreditation and harmonization systems, establishment of joint regulatory agencies, and mutual recognition arrangements covering both occupational qualifications and product standards.

In the EU a soft mode of governance that is related to regulatory cooperation is the open method of coordination (OMC). While hard to define precisely, the OMC is conceptualized as a policy learning process, mainly consisting of periodic monitoring, evaluation, and peer review, supported by qualitative and quantitative indicators. This process helps member states to develop national policies in order to reach certain common EU goals and guidelines (for more details see Borrás and Jacobsson 2004, 188; Lisbon Council Conclusions 2000).[14] The OMC has become a relatively well-established mode of EU governance (Tholoniat 2010), which is partly due to its flexibility and adaptability to conditions in different policy areas. In contrast, its scope of application to Canada up to now has appeared to be limited (Townsend 2013).

In sum, the literature on and practice of regulatory cooperation and the OMC offer a set of governance instruments that are tailored to the achievement of a degree of regulatory convergence in an institutional environment that does not provide actors on the central level with any "hard" sanctioning devices. Effective regulatory cooperation, particularly if it is taking place on an expert level, requires a sufficient institutional density and frequency of interaction (Steger 2012). CETA attempts to satisfy these two requirements but falls short to some extent.

CETA's Implementation and the Canadian Provinces

CETA has been implemented at the Canadian level by the Canada-European Union Comprehensive Economic and Trade Agreement

Implementation Act, adopted on 16 May 2017.[15] Similar to the WTO and NAFTA acts, it contains a general part and a relatively elaborate list of federal-law amendments. It also uses the formulation from the NAFTA Act that any federal law that implements a provision of the agreement or fulfils an obligation of the Government of Canada under the agreement is to be interpreted in a manner consistent with the agreement.

In this section[16] we discuss two main CETA components that require significant provincial involvement in terms of implementation: government procurement and labour mobility. We also discuss CETA's framework for regulatory cooperation (given that the latter is a central feature of the agreement), including the recognition of professional qualifications as a necessary component for labour mobility. This provides the ground for the next section, which focuses on various options for improving intergovernmental cooperation.

Government Procurement

With its chapter 19, CETA aims to create a level playing field between Canada and the EU in the field of government procurement. When CETA negotiations began in 2009, EU firms did not have access to government procurement markets in Canada at the provincial and municipal levels. The plurilateral Agreement on Government Procurement, negotiated at the WTO, relieved European firms of the risk of nationality-based rejection only with respect to bids for federal government contracts. For this reason, the EU made access to provincial and municipal government procurement markets in Canada a key demand in the CETA negotiations.

As a result, EU firms now have (in principle) access to provincial and municipal government procurement markets in Canada. However, because Canadian provinces are not signatories to CETA, they can decide not to apply the provisions found in chapter 19. In such a case, affected EU firms would have to request the European Commission to launch a state-to-state dispute with the Canadian federal government under CETA's chapter 29. However, as discussed, the federal government has little, if any, effective legal means to force provinces (and municipalities) to mend their ways if they do not abide by the CETA provisions under which they are competent.

Therefore, it is important for provincial and territorial governments in Canada to pass implementation laws or adopt declarations that oblige government entities, whether municipal, regional, or provincial, to follow the provisions. For instance, the Government of Quebec has declared itself bound by the CETA provisions related to government procurement, thereby ensuring that chapter 19 applies in the province except where the Government of Quebec has negotiated specific exceptions (see the annexes to chapter 19, and Schram in this volume). For its part, the Government of Ontario has also declared itself bound by CETA and has directed municipalities to adapt their by-laws in accordance with CETA's public-procurement provisions (see Siles-Brügge and Strange in this volume on the municipal perspective). As for the Canadian federal government, although it cannot legally force provincial governments to do so, it can still encourage them to pass such laws and monitor their implementation.

Mobility of Natural Persons

CETA aims to make trade in services and investment between Canada and the EU easier by facilitating the mobility of people (professionals, investors, technicians, managers, etc.) between Canada and the EU. For example, in the case of professional services, a Canadian engineer or architect might have to spend a significant period of time in the EU to manage or supervise a project under a contract obtained by a Canadian engineering firm. In such a case the engineer or architect in question has to remain in the EU for more than the three-month limit currently in place for visitors. Moreover, in order to sign statutory documents that may be required by the authorities, this person would need to have his or her professional qualifications officially recognized in the EU.

CETA facilitates the movement of people for business purposes between Canada and the EU in two chapters, 10 and 11.[17] Chapter 10 establishes principles and rules for the temporary entry and stay of natural persons for business purposes. It provides measures that allow CETA business people to stay longer in Canada or the EU. For its part, chapter 11 calls for the mutual recognition of professional qualifications, which is necessary if business professionals, such as engineers, architects, and accountants, want to be able to offer their services in the other party's territory. It aims to get Canadian and European authorities to negotiate and sign mutual recognition agreements (MRAs) that allow qualified professionals (or technicians) to provide services, act according to their formal qualifications, and be legally recognized by the other party's authorities.

If chapter 10 on the temporary entry and stay of natural persons is the sole responsibility of the Canadian federal government, professional qualifications fall exclusively in the provincial domain. This means that the federal government has no authority or power to force provincial occupation regulatory bodies to negotiate MRAs with their European counterparts.[18] It can only encourage provincial bodies to propose and negotiate MRAs (see article 11.3.1).

CETA's Joint Committee on Mutual Recognition of Professional Qualifications (MRA Committee) provides the leadership (but not the legal authority) for occupation regulatory bodies in Canada and the EU to negotiate and conclude MRAs with each other so that Canadian and European recognized professionals and technicians can provide their services in the other party's territory. The MRA Committee is responsible, however, for the final approval of MRAs between Canadian and European authorities. Perhaps surprisingly, CETA's article 11.5 prohibits members of relevant authorities or professional bodies in Canada and the EU from chairing the MRA Committee; however, it is left open on whether delegates from these bodies or authorities can be committee members. Ideally they should be, given the responsibilities of the MRA Committee.

The MRA Committee faces a considerable challenge because there are more than four hundred and forty occupational and professional bodies in Canada, according to a joint study conducted by the European Commission and the Government of Canada (cited in Brender 2014, 15). To give a sense of the task at hand, Doutriaux (2015, 256) notes that seventy MRAs had been signed between French and Quebec bodies by the end of 2014, following the signature of the France-Quebec agreement on labour mobility seven years before, in the fall of 2008.

Ultimately, the professional and technical regulatory bodies at the provincial and member-state level decide if, when, and how they negotiate and conclude MRAs with each other. In Canada, provincial bodies first have to cooperate with each other in order to offer a common position to their European counterparts. In most cases the existence of national-level professional and technical associations will make this collaboration easier. Such national-level bodies may even act as the main interlocutors with similar EU-level associations, where they exist. For instance, in October 2018 the Canadian Architectural Licensing Authorities and the Architects' Council of Europe agreed to the Mutual Recognition Agreement for the Practice of Architecture among member states in the EU and Canada.[19]

CETA's Joint Committee on Mutual Recognition of Professional Qualifications should coordinate with (Canadian) provincial and (EU) member-state governments in the process of convincing such professional bodies to explore and undertake MRA negotiations. However, at the time of writing, the joint committee's first meeting had yet to be determined.[20]

Regulatory Cooperation

As mentioned, regulatory cooperation is a core feature of modern international trade agreements as well as of Canadian federalism. It is also at CETA's heart. While a detailed comparative assessment of regulatory cooperation in CETA is beyond the scope of this chapter, the agreement's degree of institutionalization in general appears to be relatively high.

In addition to establishing rules for specific fields, CETA devotes an entire chapter (21) to regulatory cooperation. The chapter "applies to the development, review and methodological aspects of regulatory measures of the Parties' regulatory authorities," that are covered by several chapters in CETA (see article 21.1). The main function of chapter 21 is to put in writing Canada and the EU's commitment[21] to further develop regulatory cooperation in light of their mutual interest in order to "(a) prevent and eliminate unnecessary barriers to trade and investment; (b) enhance the climate for competitiveness and innovation, including by pursuing regulatory compatibility, recognition of equivalence, and convergence; and (c) promote transparent, efficient and effective regulatory processes that support public policy objectives and fulfill the mandates of regulatory bodies, including through the promotion of information exchange and enhanced use of best practices" (CETA, article 21.2.4).

CETA's article 21.6 calls for the creation of a regulatory cooperation forum (RCF) to facilitate and promote regulatory cooperation between Canada and the EU. The RCF will be very high level because it "shall be co-chaired by a senior representative of the Government of Canada at the level of a Deputy Minister, equivalent or designate, and a senior representative of the European Commission at the level of a Director-General, equivalent or designate, and shall comprise relevant officials of each Party" (CETA, article 21.6.3). According to CETA's article 21.8, the forum will be responsible for consulting with private-sector stakeholders to inform its priorities, work plans, and assessments. In the spring of 2018 the Government of Canada and the European Commission conducted public consultations on the issues that the RCF should address;[22] however, at the time of writing, no date had been set for the forum's first meeting.

There is no mention of the RCF's relationship with the provinces, however. (CETA's chapter 21 is silent on the nature of federal-provincial regulatory cooperation.) CETA's article 21.9 specifies that, in addition to the RCF, there are contact points responsible for "communication between the Parties on matters arising under this Chapter." Article

21.9.2 states that "each contact point is responsible for consulting and coordinating with its respective regulatory departments and agencies, as appropriate, on matters arising under this Chapter." Chapter 21 is, however, silent on the relationship between these contact points and the RCF. Presumably, the contact points serve to support the forum's work on a more day-to-day basis.

In addition to the RCF and contact points mentioned in chapter 21, CETA's chapter 26 calls for the creation of an elaborate structure of committees. The most important committees are likely to be the following: Committee on Trade in Goods, Joint Management Committee on Sanitary and Phytosanitary Measures, Joint Customs Cooperation Committee, Joint Committee on Mutual Recognition of Professional Qualifications, Regulatory Cooperation Forum, and Committee on Government Procurement. These specialized committees are key to CETA's effective implementation, but they need to meet more often than the once-per-year minimum mandated by article 26.2.[23] Moreover, after more than a year of CETA's coming into force, several committees had yet to meet. The CETA Joint Committee, the key political discussion forum for CETA's governance, headed by Canada's trade minister and the European Commission's trade commissioner, had its first meeting on 26–7 September 2018, a year after CETA had entered into force. This lack of regular committee interaction raises concerns about the effectiveness of CETA's committee framework.

Improving Canada's Implementation of Next-Generation Trade Agreements

Although CETA sets out an extensive committee structure for implementing the agreement, it is silent on the role that the provinces are to play in the implementation process. At a minimum, where the provinces have competence, we expect that committees and contact points will closely involve the provinces and their relevant regulatory authorities as they go about implementing CETA, but this is not yet clear. Furthermore, it remains to be seen how effective the CETA committees will be. If CETA is to be effectively implemented in order for its expected benefits to be attained, then other options for improving provincial participation and coordination should be considered.

Formal Change at the Legal or the Executive Level

The precarious situation of implementing international trade agreements in Canada has not gone unnoticed by legal scholars. Some options for improvement have been discussed, all of which appear to be difficult to implement in the present political and legal environment.

One option would be to introduce expansive federal legislation based on the legislative powers of a general nature that are allocated to the federal level in the Constitution (sections 91 and 92). A potential basis is the "trade and commerce power" enshrined in section 91(2), which encompasses interprovincial and international trade (imports, exports, customs) as well as "general" trade and commerce-related fields (e.g., competition, trademarks).While the practical extent of this competence, and especially its relation to the provincial power to legislate in property and civil rights (section 92(13)) is not fully clear up to now, some see it as a valid constitutional defence of new federal legislation in order to implement international trade agreements (for detailed discussions, see Steger 1997, 268; and VanDuzer and Mallet 2016, 112). At a minimum, such legislation could at least act as a supportive device for selective intervention in areas that are related to federal competences.

A second potential basis for legislation is the federal power "to make laws for the Peace, Order, and Good Government of Canada" (section 91, introductory sentence) as a residual power for matters of national concern and emergencies. According to Steger (1997, 274), the doctrine has seen a certain resurgence in case law but would still likely provide only a supplementary argument for basing a federal competence on the trade and commerce power (see also VanDuzer and Mallet 2016, 114). In both cases, a change in constitutional jurisprudence would be needed, which does not appear likely for the time being. Courts have been generally hesitant to allow a modification of the long-established distribution of competences between the federal level and the provinces on the basis of general clauses; the resulting federal intrusion into provincial competences could amount to an arbitrary "constitutional reformulation by stealth" (VanDuzer and Mallet 2016, 117).

An alternative approach would be to establish an intergovernmental agreement that dealt explicitly with the provincial implementation of and compliance with Canada's international treaty obligations (Van-Duzer and Mallet 2016, 124). To be effective, such an intergovernmental agreement would have to contain formal commitments by the provinces to comply with treaty obligations that fall within their jurisdiction. It should also contain an internal dispute-settlement mechanism that would allow the federal and provincial governments to enforce these commitments.[24] To make such an arrangement work, the provinces would have to make significant concessions to the federal government. Given that the provinces are reluctant to grant more powers to the federal government in policy areas that fall under their competence, an intergovernmental agreement to implement Canada's international trade agreements appears unlikely for the time being. As a result, it may be more effective to consider softer modes of governance.

Soft Modes of Governance

As indicated, relying on CETA's committees and contact points to involve the provinces in ensuring that the agreement is effectively implemented may not be sufficient. More formal arrangements may be needed in order to coordinate and monitor CETA's implementation at both the general and very specific levels.

One option is to rely on the C-Trade Committee, a forum for regular formal consultation between the federal government and provincial governments in international trade negotiations (see Paquin in this volume for more detail), to coordinate implementation between the federal and provincial governments. The committee could then liaise with the CETA committees if and when it is necessary to do so. This would, however, require the C-Trade Committee to become a cooperative body rather than a consultative one. For this purpose, the committee would need to acquire significant financial and human resources, to which both the federal government and the provincial governments would contribute. As a result, the scope of the committee's remit would be expanded; it would deal not only with trade negotiations but also with the implementation of negotiated agreements. Expanding the C-Trade Committee's role in such a way would allow for more congruence between negotiations and implementation across the whole range of Canada's trade agreements.

The C-Trade Committee would set up intergovernmental working groups to deal with the technical nature of regulatory cooperation. These working groups would act as direct links to the various CETA committees in order to ensure coordination with their EU counterparts. As such, these working groups could follow the EU's OMC in terms of policy learning and regulatory convergence, as well as flexibility.

Finally, the provinces would have to coordinate themselves separately in order to provide effective input into the C-Trade Committee process. One option would be for the Council of the Federation to provide the institutional mantle for the province's coordination. However, as with the C-Trade Committee, this would involve a major upgrading of the council's scope and resources. Given its rather political nature and the technical nature of the coordinating work required, it is not at all clear that the council could perform effectively such regulatory cooperation duties.

An alternative option would be to rely on the committee structure provided by CFTA, which involves only the provinces. Given their technical nature, these committees may be better suited than the Council of the Federation to the task of feeding the C-Trade Committee's regulatory cooperation and trade-agreement implementation process. The Regulatory Reconciliation and Cooperation Table could then be used to discuss the implementation of international trade agreements as well. This would allow for greater congruence between those agreements and CFTA.

All these options would provide a richer framework for regular information exchange as well as policy learning not only within Canada but also possibly between the provinces and EU member states. Following a recommendation of Townsend (2013), they could also provide an opportunity to include a larger array of stakeholders, such as the professional associations relevant to labour mobility.

Conclusion

The issue of implementing international trade agreements in federal states is particularly important in Canada due to the far-reaching extent of relevant provincial competences, existing barriers to interprovincial trade, and the fact that the federal level does not dispose of a legal instrument to enforce provincial compliance with international commitments.

Next-generation trade agreements such as CETA exacerbate those issues because of their regulatory requirements with respect to a wide range of non-tariff trade barriers. Although Canada's experience with existing trade agreements – in particular, GATT/WTO and NAFTA – has shown that "collaborative" (and partly informal) federal arrangements have a certain capacity to ensure effective implementation, CETA requires a more elaborate institutional structure than presently exists if the federal and provincial governments are to work together effectively to put in place the regulatory rules, standards, and procedures necessary for proper implementation of the agreement's provisions.

The most straightforward way to achieve this would certainly be to institute reforms at the formal legal level – by either aiming for constitutional change or providing a formal executive-level framework in the form of a new intergovernmental agreement between the federal government and provincial governments. A more realistic approach, however, would be to extend and complement already existing arrangements. The C-Trade Committee could be the focal point for cooperation between the provinces and the federal government in implementing CETA. The committee's working groups could then coordinate with CETA's own committee infrastructure to ensure coordination with the EU. With respect to coordination between the provinces prior to their interaction with the federal government, the Council of the Federation could provide the institutional mantle for cooperation. Alternatively, the provinces could rely on the regulatory cooperation infrastructure created by the new Canadian Free Trade Agreement for interprovincial trade. In any case, the intergovernmental apparatus for the federal and provincial governments to cooperate in order to implement CETA could benefit from the EU's experience with the open method of coordination and other soft modes of governance.

NOTES

1 The agreement applies provisionally until all national (and regional, in some cases) parliaments of the European Union's member states have ratified CETA. Until then, some provisions are not applicable (for details see http://eur-lex.europa.eu.

2 For a discussion of the legal implementation of international trade agreements in Canada at the federal and provincial levels see the chapter by Paquin in this volume.

3 The role of the legislative branch in Canadian federal relations has traditionally been less important because of the weak position of the Senate – whose members are appointed without a formal role being attributed to provinces, and whose allocation of seats is based upon regional equality, not the size of provinces' populations – and the limited supportive role of political parties for federal cooperation and integration.

4 The distribution of legislative powers is set out in sections 91–3, as well as 94A and 95, of the Constitution Act, 1867 (British North America Act, 1867).

5 For a discussion of jurisprudence that is relevant to the implementation of international trade agreements, and a brief outline of constitutional doctrines used to delineate federal and provincial powers, see VanDuzer and Mallet (2016, 105).

6 In January 2018, Australia requested a consultation with the WTO regarding measures maintained by the Canadian government and the Canadian provinces of British Columbia, Ontario, Quebec, and Nova Scotia concerning the sale of wine. This request followed a complaint to the WTO by the United States about the restrictions imposed by the province of British Columbia on the sale of imported wines in grocery stores. In July 2018 the WTO's dispute-settlement body agreed to establish a panel to review the case. Under the agreed USMCA, Canada and the United States exchanged two side letters whereby the Government of

Canada "ensure[d]" that the province of British Columbia would modify, by 1 November 2019, its regulatory measures that allow only BC wines to be sold on supermarket shelves. At the time of writing (November 2018), it remained to be seen whether or how the Government of British Columbia would comply with the federal government's USMCA commitment.

7 Chapter 11 proceedings between the United States and Canada will be phased out should the USMCA enter into force, because this new agreement has removed provisions for investor-state dispute settlement for proceedings between the United States and Canada.

8 It is not clear why in this case the Government of Ontario chose to pay the award rather than leave it to the federal government. We can only speculate that the Government of Ontario wanted to preserve its reputation as an attractive investment location and had the means to pay the award, unlike the poorer Newfoundland government.

9 https://www.wto.org/english/tratop_e/dispu_e/cases_e/ds426_e.htm.

10 According to a study by the Canadian Chamber of Commerce (2004), the most common interprovincial barriers to trade were "overlapping of regulations between jurisdictions, multiple licensing requirements, and local preferences in awarding government contracts."

11 CFTA, article 1202(4), p. 193, https://www.cfta-alec.ca.

12 For example, when CFTA was agreed to, the provinces of British Columbia, Ontario, and Quebec announced that they would set up a common website for their residents to buy wine and spirits from all three provinces. At the time of writing, no such website had been created.

13 The lack of results on streamlining regulatory differences led subsequently to the establishment of the United States–Canada Regulatory Cooperation Council mentioned previously. Mexico and the United States have set up a similar high-level regulatory cooperation.

14 Available at http://www.europarl.europa.eu.

15 See http://www.parl.ca.

16 This section draws heavily from Leblond (2016).

17 "Temporary Entry and Stay of Natural Persons for Business Purposes," http://www.international.gc.ca; "Mutual Recognition of Professional Qualifications," http://www.international.gc.ca.

18 Professional and occupational regulatory bodies in the EU are national in nature; however, the European Commission has certain legal powers to enforce mutual recognition within the EU in order to promote the free movement of persons (e.g., Directive 2005/36/EC). For more information see http://ec.europa.eu/growth/single-market/services/free-movement -professionals/qualifications-recognition_en. However, the commission cannot oblige national regulatory or professional bodies to negotiate MRAs with their Canadian counterparts.

19 https://www.raic.org.
20 http://trade.ec.europa.eu/doclib/press/index.cfm?id=1811.
21 It is worth noting, however, that this commitment to regulatory
   cooperation is not an obligation; it is voluntary: "The Parties may
   undertake regulatory cooperation activities on a voluntary basis. For
   greater certainty, a Party is not required to enter into any particular
   regulatory cooperation activity, and may refuse to cooperate or may
   withdraw from cooperation" (CETA, article 21.2.6).
22 For Canada's consultation results see https://open.canada.ca. For the EU's
   consultation results see http://trade.ec.europa.eu.
23 Steger (2012, 124) underlines the importance of frequent meetings between
   the parties: "A ... Committee that meets only once a year will not be able
   to provide sufficient infrastructure and oversight to adequately ensure
   that the mutual recognition obligations are effectively carried out by the
   regulatory agencies concerned."
24 Beyond this, VanDuzer and Mallet (2016, 132) also suggest regulation
   of provincial financial responsibility for treaty-based dispute-settlement
   proceedings that are related to provincial measures, taking the EU
   regulation on financial responsibility in investor-state disputes as
   a model.

REFERENCES

Bickerton, James. 2010. "Deconstructing the New Federalism." *Canadian
   Political Science Review* 4 (2–3): 56–72.
Borrás, Susana, and Kerstin Jacobsson. 2004. "The Open Method of
   Co-ordination and New Governance Patterns in the EU." *Journal of
   European Public Policy* 11 (2): 185–208.
Brender, Natalie. 2014. *Across the Sea with CETA: What New Labour Mobility
   Might Mean for Canadian Business.* Ottawa, ON: Conference Board of
   Canada. https://www.conferenceboard.ca.
Canadian Chamber of Commerce. 2004. *Obstacles to Free Trade in Canada:
   A Study on Internal Trade Barriers.* Ottawa, ON: Canadian Chamber of
   Commerce. http://www.chamber.ca.
Carmody, Chios. 2014. "Canada's Implementation of the WTO Agreement." In
   Is Our House in Order? Canada's Implementation of International Law, edited
   by C. Carmody, 140–73. Kingston and Montreal: McGill-Queen's University
   Press.
Collins, Emmet. 2017. "Coming into Its Own? Canada's Council of the
   Federation, 2003–16." *IRPP Insight* 15: 1–21.
de Beer, Jeremy. 2012. "Implementing International Trade Agreements in
   Federal Systems: A Look at the Canada-EU CETA's Intellectual Property
   Issues." *Legal Issues of Economic Integration.* 39 (1): 51–71.

Doern, G. Bruce, and Mark MacDonald. 1999. *Free Trade Federalism: Negotiating the Canadian Agreement on Internal Trade*. Toronto: University of Toronto Press.

Doutriaux, Yves. 2015. "La reconnaissance des qualifications professionnelles: Entente France-Québec et AECG." In *Un nouveau pont sur l'Atlantique: L'Accord économique et commercial global entre l'Union européenne et le Canada*, edited by C. Deblock, J. Lebullenger, and S. Paquin, 265–80. Quebec, QC: Presses de l'Université du Québec.

Fafard, Patrick, and Patrick Leblond. 2012. *Twenty-First Century Trade Agreements: Challenges for Canadian Federalism*. Montreal: Federal Idea.

Hansen, Robin, and Heather Heavin. 2010. "What's 'New' in the New West Partnership Trade Agreement? The NWPTA and the Agreement on Internal Trade Compared." *Saskatchewan Law Review* 73 (2): 197–235.

Herman, Lawrence L. 2010. *Trend Spotting: NAFTA Disputes after Fifteen Years*. C.D. Howe Institute Backgrounder no. 133. https://papers.ssrn.com/sol3/papers.cfm?abstract_id=1706256.

Krstic, Stanko S. 2012. "Regulatory Cooperation to Remove Non-tariff Barriers to Trade in Products: Key Challenges and Opportunities for the Canada-EU Comprehensive Trade Agreement (CETA)." *Legal Issues of Economic Integration* 39 (1): 3–28.

Kukucha, Christopher J. 2008. *The Provinces and Canadian Foreign Trade Policy*, Vancouver: UBC Press.

Leblond, Patrick. 2016. *Making the Most of CETA: A Complete and Effective Implementation Is Key to Realizing the Agreement's Full Potential*. CIGI Papers no. 114. Waterloo, ON: Centre for International Governance Innovation. https://www.cigionline.org.

Minaeva, Yulia. 2012. "Canadian Federalism Uncovered: The Assumed, the Forgotten and the Unexamined in Collaborative Federalism." PhD diss., University of Ottawa. https://ruor.uottawa.ca.

Monahan, Patrick. 2001. "Canadian Federalism and Its Impact on Cross-Border Trade." *Canada–United States Law Journal* 27: 19–25.

OECD (Organisation for Economic Co-operation and Development). 1994. *Regulatory Co-operation for an Interdependent World*. Paris: OECD Publishing.

– 2013. *International Regulatory Co-operation: Addressing Global Challenges*. Paris: OECD Publishing.

Paquin, Stéphane. 2013. "Federalism and the Governance of International Trade Negotiations in Canada: Comparing CUSFTA with CETA." *International Journal* 68 (4): 545–52.

Poirier, Johanne. 2004. "Intergovernmental Agreements in Canada: At the Crossroads between Law and Politics." In *Canada, the State of the Federation 2002: Reconsidering the Institutions of Canadian Federalism*, edited by P.J. Meekison, H. Telford, and H. Lazar, 425–62. Kingston and Montreal: McGill-Queen's University.

Roman, Karina. 2018. Beer Not Freed: Supreme Court Upholds Law in Cross-Border Alcohol Case. *CBC News*. https://www.cbc.ca.

Skogstad, Grace. 2012. "International Trade Policy and Canadian Federalism: A Constructive Tension?" In *Canadian Federalism: Performance, Effectiveness, and Legitimacy*, edited by H. Bakvis and G. Skogstad, 203–22. New York: Oxford University Press.

Steger, Debra. 1997. "Canadian Implementation of the Agreement Establishing the World Trade Organization." In *Implementing the Uruguay Round*, edited by John H. Jackson and Alan Sykes, 243–84. Oxford: Clarendon Press.

– 2010. Implementation of Trade Agreements and Trade Policy Making in Canada. Presentation for TETE project. http://www.can-eu-tete.ca/.

– 2012. "Institutions for Regulatory Cooperation in 'New Generation' Economic and Trade Agreements." *Legal Issues of Economic Integration* 39 (1): 109–26.

Tholoniat, Luc. 2010. "The Career of the Open Method of Coordination: Lessons from a 'Soft' EU Instrument." *West European Politics* 33 (1): 93–117.

Townsend, Thomas. 2013. "Networked Learning in Complex Policy Spaces: A Practitioner's Reflection on the Open Method of Coordination." *Canadian Public Administration* 56 (2): 338–49.

VanDuzer, Anthony J., and Melanie J. Mallet. 2016. "Compliance with Canada's Trade and Investment Treaty Obligations: Addressing the Gap between Provincial Action and Federal Responsibility." *Alberta Law Review* 54 (1): 89–139.

3 Reconceptualizing Provincial Development: Evolving Public Procurement Practices in Quebec

SOPHIE SCHRAM

In late 2006, in Euro-Canadian diplomatic and business circles, the Canadian province of Quebec unexpectedly suggested subjecting the procurement contracts under provincial jurisdiction to a new bilateral trade and investment accord between Canada and the European Union (EU). By making this suggestion, Quebec paved the way for a new bilateral trade agreement between Canada and the EU, the Comprehensive Economic and Trade Agreement (CETA), which would put centre stage a deeper economic integration between the two economies by focusing on market access provisions and non-tariff barriers rather than on tariffs and quotas.

Quebec's suggestion to include sub-federal procurement represented a major and substantive policy change in provincial politics. In the past, Quebec and the other Canadian provinces had refused to subject provincial and municipal public procurement contracts – which were under their exclusive jurisdiction – to Canada's international trade agreements. Quebec's new policy stance would entail far-reaching consequences. First, giving European companies the right to participate in the bidding processes would considerably increase market competition for Quebec-based companies, which so far had enjoyed a privileged position in bidding for provincial contracts. In fact, public authorities could decide, in most circumstances, to consider only Quebec-based companies in the bidding processes, and even Canadian companies from other provinces could sometimes be disadvantaged. Second, and from the government's perspective, subjecting public procurement to a new trade agreement would prevent the provincial government from using public procurement contracts as a means to support certain companies or industrial sectors; in the past, governments had often granted public contracts in line with their respective political goals. Although all the provinces would face a similar situation, this process would be amplified in Quebec by its province-building project because public procurement was an important instrument of economic policymaking in which the federal order of government could not interfere.

Not only did Quebec change its substantive stance on public procurement and trade, but the provincial government also quite drastically changed the way it brokered this new position institutionally. Previously, the province had often used its available institutional resources to block Canada's advancements in public procurement and trade, but it now actively suggested including provincial public procurement in a new trade agreement with the EU. Given this track record of blocking Canada's efforts to open public procurement to foreign bidders, opposing further advances was part of Quebec's options from an institutional perspective. Yet, in an institutional setting in which the way the provinces participated in Canada's international trade negotiations was unclear, Quebec actively sought to alter its mode of participation to become a much more active partner before the implementation stage.

This is even more puzzling considering the scope of contemporary trade agreements. These new agreements focus on deep economic integration and involve an increasing number of issues that, in Canada, fall under provincial jurisdiction. This situation has considerably improved Quebec's position within the Canadian federal polity because the provinces must take steps to implement the provisions in Canada's international agreements that fall under their jurisdiction.[1] Quebec and the other provinces therefore have considerable latitude in blocking Canada's advancements in international trade provided those advancements fall under their jurisdiction. As an additional requirement in Quebec, the province can also require legislative ratification prior to implementation according to its domestic law (see Paquin in this volume).[2]

Hence, CETA's agenda-setting and early negotiation process represented a turning point at which Quebec significantly altered its position on the participation of foreign companies in provincial bidding processes, as well as its institutional strategy to pursue its policy position. The aim of the following account is to gain a better understanding of the motivations underlying Quebec's sudden policy change on public procurement, especially so early in the negotiation process, without pressure from Canada and as an offer to the EU.

To document the policy shift, I start by providing an account of both Quebec's past practices related to public procurement and its policy positions during previous trade negotiations. Second, I review existing accounts of the province's policy shift in the academic literature and in policymakers' accounts in order to highlight the extent to which the picture they draw remains incomplete. Third, I document how the provincial government changed the prevailing discourses underlying Quebec's procurement practices and thereby enabled the policy shift despite domestic resistance. The province advocated its new policy position on the international level during CETA's agenda-setting process (late 2006 to mid-2009) and early negotiation stage (mid-2009 to 2011).[3] My analysis is based on interviews with members of the provincial government, members of the National Assembly, provincial and federal diplomats, and provincial civil society organizations, as well as policy reports and plenary and committee sessions in Quebec's National Assembly.[4]

Changing Positions on Provincial Public Procurement (1979–2009)

Public procurement entered the agenda of international trade negotiations with the Tokyo Round of the General Agreement on Tariffs and Trade (GATT) in 1976. In order to foster the global trade agenda, the members of GATT promoted not only the participation of foreign companies in public procurement bidding processes but also internationally agreed procedures of notification, consultation, surveillance, and dispute settlement. Competition, transparency, and non-discrimination in public procurement practices were the leading principles shaping international negotiations on trade and public procurement. In 1979 the members of GATT reached an agreement and signed the Tokyo Round Code on Government Procurement, which set rules for the treatment of foreign bidders and the unfolding of tendering procedures (Graham 1983). This was the starting point of a process that fundamentally altered the ways in which governments procured goods and services.

With the evolution of international trade policy agendas in the late 1980s and early 1990s, Canadian sub-federal procurement contracts, which represented a major share of overall public procurement in Canada, became a substantive subject targeted in international trade negotiations. However, in many instances, the provinces refused to implement the provisions that had been negotiated by the federal government. During these negotiations the absence of a formal institutional procedure to develop Canada's trade policy position on topics involving provincial areas of jurisdiction had become apparent: the strict division of government spending authority between levels of government, including the exclusive jurisdiction by provinces over their procurement markets, allowed the provinces to pursue an exit strategy regarding their public procurement practices and to refrain from opening their procurement contracts to foreign bidders. Hence, the Canadian provinces were able to resist and insulate themselves from these international processes because of the rules and practices of Canadian federalism, and the federal government could not overcome this obstacle (Collins 2008). As a consequence of the provinces' exit strategy, provincial procurement was isolated from foreign market competition as well as the international tendering standards set out in multilateral and regional trade agreements. Hence, it was regulated solely by provincial legislation. At the same time, federal procurement practices were increasingly following the logics of competition, transparency, and non-discrimination.

During the negotiations of the Canada-United States Free Trade Agreement (CUSFTA, 1989) and the North American Free Trade Agreement (NAFTA, 1994) the provinces used their available institutional resources to refuse to extend privileged access to their procurement markets to US- and Mexico-based companies, leading to the exclusion of sub-federal public procurement from these agreements (Delagran 1992). In a similar way, during the negotiation of the plurilateral Agreement on Government Procurement (GPA, 1994) among fifteen members of the World Trade Organization (WTO),[5] the provinces' institutional resources with regard to their public procurement practices became apparent: although the federal government had signed the GPA and included the Canadian provinces in its market access· schedule,[6] the provinces, including Quebec, refused to implement these provisions, which therefore never came into effect. As a consequence, until CETA negotiations began, Canada's subsequent agreements on public procurement did not extend to the provinces (Collins 2008, 2011; McMurtry 2014).

The decision by Quebec not to subject its public procurement contracts to the GPA and NAFTA considerably deviated from its overall position on international trade. In fact, Quebec, together with Alberta, was among the most ardent supporters of free trade agreements in the late 1980s (Dufour 2006; P. Martin 1995a, 1995b; Rocher 2003a). According to Quebec policymakers from both the Liberal Party of Quebec and the Parti Québécois (PQ), free trade would enhance Quebec's provincial development. That being said, each political party supported free trade for partially different reasons (Campbell 1995; Robinson 1995). For the PQ, economic development, a certain degree of independence from the Canadian market, the promotion of francophone control and ownership in the economic realm, and the emergence of a corporate elite close to the provincial state underpinned the party's support for free trade. Free trade ultimately was a means to achieve a sufficient degree of economic independence in anticipation of political independence.

For the Quebec Liberals, to the contrary, free trade led to international economic interdependence, making political independence irrelevant (Brunelle, Bélanger, and Deblock 1999; Brunelle and Deblock 1997; Jockel and David 1997; Keating 1997; Paquin 2001, 2016).

In opposing international procurement provisions, Quebec departed from these discourses. Quebec's resistance to opening its procurement markets was to a large extent grounded in its wish to use provincial spending to foster provincial development by isolating public procurement from external (federal and international) interference. From the time of the Quiet Revolution[7] and until CETA, governments across party lines used public spending, among others through provincial Crown corporations (Bernier 1994), to meet their provincial socio-political, economic, and cultural objectives (McRoberts 1993, 360–1). Although the aim and extent of these practices varied, governments mostly acted according to a social and community logic, on the one hand, and an economic logic, on the other hand. For many years the link between community and economic development logics was strong, as I will show in the following.

First, the government used public contracts to develop less populated areas, including in Quebec's north. In the 1960s, during the Quiet Revolution, the government nationalized several electricity plants and invested massively in hydro-electricity. Subsequently, the government gave the Crown corporation Hydro-Québec the mandate to develop its sites through large-scale hydro-electricity projects, thereby generating electricity both for manufacturing plants, including those in the north, and for individual consumption, mainly in Quebec's cities situated towards the south of the province. These projects were part of a larger development project creating business opportunities for local companies. They contributed to local economic development as well as to social cohesion across the vastness of Quebec's territory (Bickerton and Gagnon 1984, 75).[8] Today Hydro-Québec's procurement contracts are worth almost CAD 3 billion per year (Hydro-Québec 2010, 43). In this sense, public procurement was used as a means of redistribution (especially from densely populated to less populated areas) by the state.

Second, Quebec's procurement activities also contributed to social cohesion and economic development by favouring bids from francophone businesses. By awarding public contracts to francophone Quebec-based companies, the province provided them with the opportunity to build expertise and subsequently expand internationally. Political leaders at the time were confident that these champions would contribute to a strong socio-economic provincial base. As McRoberts pointed out, this was the case especially for Bombardier and Lavalin, two provincial economic champions, which benefited considerably from extensive public contracts to build expertise and become international leaders in their respective fields (McRoberts 1993, 360–1).

Canadian federalism intensified this link between public procurement and economic and community development. When federal-provincial competition for economic and social authority and political loyalty increased in the 1970s and 1980s, the provinces, Quebec in particular, used provincial public procurement as a tool to steer their economic development without federal interference. As the federal government reduced its involvement in the economic realm – a process partially spurred by global and regional trade agendas – the provinces stepped into this gap to extend their activity in line with their respective province-building projects. In this context, provincial government spending played a major role in securing provincial community loyalty. By using public procurement contracts as a means of redistribution, Quebec government officials also fostered a sense of community and loyalty to the provincial government among the inhabitants of the province, thereby making public procurement an instrument for social cohesion (Jenson 1991, 62–5). In Quebec this process of federal-provincial competition was spurred further by Quebec's nation-building project (Jenson 1991, 1995).

The community and economic logics of provincial development associated with public procurement in Quebec extended well into the 2000s. In fact, shortly before they launched the CETA negotiations, Canada and the EU started to negotiate the Trade and Investment Agreement (TIEA), in 2004. In this negotiation the parties set out to achieve a far-reaching agreement on non-tariff issues including "investment facilitation, competition, mutual recognition of professional qualifications, financial services, e-commerce, temporary entry, small- and medium-sized enterprises, sustainable development, and science and technology" (Global Affairs Canada 2013). With regard to public procurement, they aimed "to undertake negotiations with a view to achieving the greatest possible extension of their commitments under the WTO Agreement on Government Procurement (GPA) and eliminating any remaining discriminatory measures and practices," thereby directly targeting provincial public procurement that was not subjected to the WTO's GPA (Global Affairs Canada 2013). This process failed, however, and negotiations were closed in 2006. A main cause of this failure was the provinces' refusal to comply with federal demands regarding their procurement markets. To a large extent, Canada's federal government was unsuccessful in convincing the EU of the benefit of the TIEA because the Canadian provinces were not committed to this process.[9]

Hence, in this instance, provincial public procurement represented an obstacle to the Canadian federal government in concluding a new trade and investment agreement. Its importance reached thus well beyond the issue itself and spilled over to Canada's overall trade relations.

From Exit to Voice: A Changing Institutional Strategy

Despite a long history of resistance to opening provincial procurement contracts to foreign bidders, underpinned by a discourse of provincial development, Quebec suddenly abandoned its opposition to opening its public procurement markets. In late 2006 the province actively suggested, first in diplomatic and business circles and later also during public events, including Canadian sub-federal procurement in a new economic agreement between Canada and the EU. By proposing to open public procurement bids to European competitors and by subjecting its public tendering procedures to the standards of an international trade agreement, Quebec not only significantly contributed to the launch of a new transatlantic trade and investment agreement, and hence deeper economic integration between Canada and the EU, but also suggested altering considerably its own public procurement practices.

At the core of academic explanations accounting for this puzzle are institutional arguments. These institutional perspectives document how the reconfiguration of intergovernmental relations in the Canadian federation accounted for substantive policy change in Canada's trade policy and argue that Quebec traded a new position on public procurement for access to the CETA negotiation table (Fafard and Leblond 2012, 2013; Kukucha 2011, 2013; Paquin 2010, 2013). Given the Canadian context of institutional ambiguity, Quebec was well equipped to pressure the federal government to accept provincial presence at the negotiation table in exchange for changing its position on provincial public procurement. In doing so, Quebec shifted from an exit towards a voice strategy.

This argument is compelling because the provinces did acquire access to the negotiation tables, which represented a major change in Canada's trade policymaking process. This was the first time that the provinces actively participated in Canada's international trade negotiations. Contrary to other trade negotiations, the provinces, represented by their official negotiators, were actively involved in the official negotiation process for chapters involving their areas of jurisdiction (see Paquin in this volume). Through its new institutional strategy Quebec sought to introduce its provincial priorities into the formulation and implementation of Canada's trade policy. In fact, Quebec's government and negotiation team highlighted the relationship between provincial activity in the negotiation process, and the coverage of provincial procurement markets. According to their accounts, CETA's far-reaching outcome on provincial procurement was related to active provincial participation in the formal negotiation rounds in Brussels and Ottawa (Johnson, Muzzi, and Bastien 2013).

This focus on inter-institutional configurations is also compelling because the European Commission (EC) exerted pressure on the federal government to include the provinces in the negotiation process. In an institutional context where the provinces could reject the outcome of Canada's international trade negotiations, the European commissioner for trade suggested that the EU would only launch a new negotiation process if Canada created institutional clarity. In turn, the provinces interpreted this requirement as an invitation to participate in the negotiation process. In fact, in an interview, a member of Quebec's negotiation team highlighted that the European commissioner for trade had told him at a meeting, with reference to a potential new trade agreement, "When you get your house in order, come and see me." According to the Quebec diplomat, the European commissioner thus insisted on including the provinces in the negotiation process.[10]

In this regard, Quebec's negotiation team also highlighted that the EC wished for a reconfiguration of Canada's intergovernmental relations during trade negotiations with the EU and, specifically, to include the Canadian provinces in the negotiation to ensure their commitment regarding their public procurement markets: "From the outset of the negotiations process, the EU, aware of the complexity of the jurisdictional landscape in Canada, requested that the provinces and territories be included, thereby ensuring EU access to their public procurement markets" (Johnson, Muzzi, and Bastien 2013, 561).

Yet, Quebec did not alter its policy stance only because the EC had pressured the Canadian federal government to increase the reliability of its negotiation commitments by including the provinces as partners. In fact, a comparison to other agreements casts doubt on these institutional explanations of Quebec's altered position.

During the CUSFTA, NAFTA, GPA, and recent TIEA negotiations the provinces were already being pressured to open their public procurement markets, yet they resisted in order to retain leverage over this important instrument of provincial development. In addition, the Canada-United States Agreement on Government Procurement (AGP, 2010) provides a case in point where the provinces agreed to implement an international public procurement agreement including provisions on sub-federal procurement despite their exclusion from the formal negotiation process. The AGP was brought to Canadian and US policy agendas well after CETA and as a consequence of the American Recovery and Reinvestment Act (2009), which included protectionist provisions on US public procurement. Contrary to the CETA negotiation process, the AGP's negotiation was led, on the Canadian side, by the federal government, and the provinces were not part of the official delegations (Clarke 2015). Even though the provinces were excluded from the official negotiation process, they implemented the provisions following from AGP. Hence, in this instance, institutional configurations were not the main reason that the provinces accepted to open their public procurement markets to US competitors.

The story of Quebec and CETA shows that the existence of multiple institutional resources alone cannot explain why Quebec changed its long-standing position and suggested including provisions on provincial and municipal public procurement in CETA. Even though being included as a negotiation partner was a positive side effect, Quebec did not merely open these markets to acquire a seat at the table or because it was pressured by the EC. Institutional ambiguity allowed Quebec to pursue its policy objectives more effectively by asking to be more actively involved in the negotiation process, yet it was not the main reason that Quebec suggested opening provincial public procurement to European competitors. Rather, Quebec fundamentally changed its position on the relation between public procurement and provincial development. Thus, rather than representing a mere tit for tat, Quebec had substantive reasons to broker this position, as I will show.

Shifting Logics of Provincial Development

Underpinning Quebec's substantive shift regarding procurement contracts and trade was a shift from an economic and social logic of provincial development guiding procurement practices to an emphasis on the economic logic and the addition of a political logic. In this process Quebec's Liberal government was the main driver of change. As it changed its discourse, it re-evaluated the role of public procurement for provincial development.

This process of normative change started well before CETA was launched. Under Quebec's Liberal government elected in 2003, the province started an internal process in which it reconfigured its procurement practices. In 2006 the National Assembly enacted a new law on the award of public procurement contracts (Loi sur les contrats des organismes publics, 2006, 2012), which replaced the existing legislation.

The law introduced transparent and factual selection criteria into the tendering procedures. According to the provincial government, the alteration of public procurement practices according to the rules of international trade would introduce and protect selection procedures based on objective and factual criteria. By subjecting provincial public procurement to the rules of international trade law, the government could foster this internal process.

During the negotiation of CETA, Quebec's Liberal government focused increasingly on the economic logic of provincial development and, specifically, on the benefits of international trade for the provincial economy. According to the provincial government's discourse, opening sub-federal procurement to European competitors would create new business opportunities for Quebec-based companies in the EU, whose public sector is highly integrated, extends from the European to the local level, and therefore offers promising business opportunities through procurement contracts. Unlike in past discourses, the government now focused on export opportunities for Quebec's companies and de-emphasised the importance of its own public procurement contracts for Quebec-based companies in favour of new opportunities created in the EU. Since Quebec's economy depended upon exports, gaining access to new markets was crucial to assure domestic economic development. By seeking new business opportunities abroad and by facing higher market competition domestically, Quebec-based companies would also be required to increase their production efficiency and innovation. In this way, opening public procurement contracts would strengthen the province's economic basis, a pillar of provincial development.

Quebec's government altered its discourse on provincial economic development also against the backdrop of reduced business opportunities for Quebec companies in the United States, Quebec's historical trade partner (Paquin 2016). In his speech opening the National Assembly's session on 10 March 2009, Premier Jean Charest pinpointed the US economic recession, the appreciation of the Canadian dollar vis-à-vis the US dollar, and mounting competition by emerging economies on global markets as the drivers of a reorientation of Quebec's trade policy. Accordingly, the government tried to render Quebec less dependent on the US economy by diversifying its trading partners, as Premier Charest explained in an article published by the Quebec daily *La Presse*:

Le marché américain devient de plus en plus difficile alors nous allons exporter davantage de produits Québécois vers l'Europe et les autres provinces canadiennes. Nous allons y arriver avec le lancement de négociations visant un accord transatlantique entre le Canada et l'Union européenne et avec la négociation d'un nouvel accord sur le commerce avec l'Ontario. (Charest 2008)

The objective of provincial development thus continued to underpin the policy position of Quebec, as it had during previous trade negotiations. Through references to provincial development Quebec's Liberal government established its substantive position and legitimized its suggestion to allow European companies to participate in provincial public-procurement-bidding processes.

This new discourse highlighting the economic benefits of opening public procurement for provincial development also allowed Quebec to bridge the domestic opposition to de-emphasizing the social dimension of provincial development (Trew 2013, 2014). As during the CUSFTA and NAFTA negotiations, many civil society organizations, including ATTAC-Québec, the Réseau québécois sur l'intégration continentale, the pan-Canadian Trade Justice Network, and the Council of Canadians, strongly opposed these new procurement provisions. Furthermore, public employees' trade unions in particular strongly opposed their government's new stance: both the Syndicat de la Fonction Publique et Parapublique du Québec and the Syndicat Canadien de la Fonction Publique (SCFP, Canadian Union of Public Employees) warned that opening procurement markets might engender massive job losses in the municipal sector. In fact, they feared that European providers might offer municipal services such as drinking water and waste management at lower costs, leading to lay-offs of municipal employees. Trade unions adapted their discourse to civil society groups and joined forces with them to oppose opening municipal service contracts to European companies. In this way they related their specific interests to general social motives and could appeal to a larger audience. According to the common discourse of trade unions and civil society organizations, Quebec's suggestion to allow foreign bidders on municipal procurement contracts would engender not only major cutbacks in municipal employment but also declining service quality. In fact, budgetary restraints might induce municipalities to contract out certain municipal services to less expensive foreign suppliers. In 2010, to prove this effect, the SCFP and the Council of Canadians published a joint study on the prospective dangers of opening drinking-water-management contracts to European companies (Coalition Eau Secours! 2012; Syndicat Canadien de la Fonction Publique and Conseil des Canadiens 2010).

The claims formulated by civil society and trade unions found some resonance in the political sphere. In fact, these groups aligned with some fractions within the PQ as well as the Québec Solidaire. For the PQ, the question of public procurement and trade was particularly complex. On the one hand, the party was historically rooted in trade union movements in Quebec, even though its historical links had recently been weakened (Tanguay 2003), inducing it to support trade unions' claims. Yet, on the other hand, the PQ had strongly supported free trade during the 1980s free trade debates, considering free trade an important instrument for the party's nation-building discourse. At the beginning of the CETA negotiation process, the PQ remained vague regarding the topic of public procurement. In 2012, however, when it formed the new government, the party had to make a decision about Quebec's position on public procurement and trade. The PQ fully endorsed the new trade negotiations and did not alter the chief negotiator's mandate. Its members mainly highlighted the positive effects of free trade for Quebec's provincial development. They could do so by referring to their party's historical support of free trade during the 1980s debates between Canada, the United States, and later Mexico (Martin 1995a, 1995b; Rocher 1994, 2003b). In evaluating its position, the PQ government highlighted that CETA's procurement provisions would not hamper the social logic of provincial development that had previously dominated the party's evaluation of public procurement and trade.

Embedding a shift in Quebec's position on public procurement in prevailing discourses on the benefits of free trade allowed the PQ to support opening procurement. Representing Quebec as a "trading nation," members of the PQ included the government's transformation of the quality and aim of public procurement in their national project favouring international trade. By doing so, the party extended its understanding that international trade fostered Quebec's autonomy and ultimately contributed to its independence project in the area of public procurement contracts.

In this regard, the minister for international relations and trade, Jean-François Lisée, referred to provincial procurement contracts in a speech given at the Conseil des relations internationales de Montréal on 11 February 2013. He underlined that opening these contracts to European and Canadian companies would create new business opportunities for Quebec-based companies in the EU, hence contributing to local economic development. Yet, Minister Lisée also continued to refer to a social logic of provincial development. According to his discourse, both logics were not at odds:

Notre objectif, dans les négociations commerciales, est certes de rendre nos entreprises plus actives dans le monde, et ainsi créer davantage d'emploi au Québec ... Rien n'entame notre capacité de favoriser des choix sociaux ou environnementaux. Il s'agit tout au plus de permettre à des entreprises européennes d'entrer en compétition avec des entreprises québécoises et canadiennes pour un plus grand nombre de contrats qu'auparavant, mais dans le cadre légal québécois d'aujourd'hui et de demain. (Lisée 2013)

Overall, Quebec's business community endorsed the government's support for opening public procurement contracts to European bids, as Quebec's chief negotiator Pierre-Marc Johnson reported in a public hearing in Quebec's National Assembly. Quebec's chambers of commerce were more explicitly supportive of a new trade agreement between Canada and the EU, including provisions on public procurement, than Ontario's, for instance, which warned its members about increased market competition from European companies during public-contract-bidding processes (Ontario Chamber of Commerce 2013).

Yet, in Quebec's business sector, support for opening provincial procurement was not unanimous. In particular, the provincial economic champion Bombardier, a mass-transit equipment company, made it difficult for Quebec's government to de-emphasize the social logic guiding provincial public-procurement practices. Bombardier had an ambivalent position and did not publicly endorse or refute CETA's procurement provisions. On the one hand, the company feared losing its privileged position for procuring to Europe and other Canadian provinces. Yet, on the other hand, it also hoped that CETA's rules of procedure might reduce the ability of provincial governments to impose performance requirements on its procurement activities, such as domestic production or content requirements, and thereby enhance the company's potential to benefit from global value chains, as van Assche pointed out (2016). Quebec's government partially catered to Bombardier's needs in areas that it considered of strategic importance to the future economic development of the province, including the subsistence of manufacturing plants.

The reconceptualization of the aim of public procurement contracts also introduced a political logic to provincial development, alongside the economic one. While the state had formerly been an instigator of social and economic development through the deployment of public contracts, strengthening the provincial state through procurement activities now became a goal in itself.

The introduction of transparent and facts-based selection procedures supported the restoration of the legitimacy of public spending practices after high-profile collusion scandals in which favouritism directed the award of public procurement contracts (Saint-Martin 2015). By subjecting the award of public contracts to international procedures and control, these risks might be minimized. Embedding the state's discourse on procurement in an argument about the legitimacy of public spending practices also had consequences for municipal support for the government's new position. By referring to price collusion, Quebec's government ensured the support of the municipal councils of large cities. In fact, an inquiry into the award and management of public contracts in the construction industry (the Charbonneau Commission) revealed in 2011 that both Montreal and Laval mayors were involved in unsound public procurement practices. By complying with CETA's provisions promoting transparency, integrity, and competition in the award of public contracts, Quebec's public authorities would be forced to adopt sound practices and re-establish their legitimacy. Unlike other major Canadian municipalities – Toronto's city council voted to exclude the city from the scope of CETA (Toronto City Council 2012) – Montreal's city council adopted a more cautious position. In a resolution on CETA, council members endorsed the agreement but also stressed the importance of preserving municipal regulatory capacity and service quality (Conseil Municipal de Montréal 2012) (on municipalities see Siles-Brügge and Strange in this volume).

In a public hearing in Quebec's National Assembly in 2011, Quebec's chief negotiator Pierre-Marc Johnson summarized this transition of public procurement from an instrument of social development to an instrument of economic and political development. He refuted the argument that procurement contributed to local development by favouring domestic companies and instead highlighted how increased competition could strengthen the provincial state:

> On voit souvent les marchés publics comme étant une occasion de créer des emplois ... Mais l'ouverture des marchés publics, au Québec comme ailleurs, qu'est-ce qu'elle vise? Elle vise à donner des meilleurs prix aux institutions qui achètent, premier objectif; deuxième objectif: de rendre visibles ces prix; troisième objectif: de réduire les occasions de collusion entre les pouvoirs publics puis les pouvoirs privés. (Assemblée Nationale 2011, 13–14)

Hence, opening procurement contracts to foreign bidders also aimed at reducing the cost of provincial procurement, thereby contributing to the consolidation of the provincial budget. Underlying this ambition was a discursive shift from the representation of public procurement contracts as a redistributive tool in line with a social logic to a political logic strengthening the government's hand.

Drawing on the argument that lower prices for public procurement contracts would contribute to a strengthening of the provincial state, the provincial government attempted to convince the Crown corporation Hydro-Québec of the benefits of opening procurement contracts to European competition. By highlighting the increasingly commercial role of Hydro-Québec (Bernier 2014) – and implicitly threatening that only profitable Crown corporations would survive in the long run – Quebec's negotiating team convinced Hydro-Québec to acquiesce to subjecting procurement bids to CETA provisions. At the same time – and this shows that political representatives were driven by an economic logic of provincial development – Quebec's government insisted on excluding certain knowledge-based areas of hydro-electric-energy production from the CETA provisions in order to maintain specific provincial expertise that was particularly beneficial to economic development.

When suggesting the inclusion of public procurement in a new agreement between Canada and the EU, the governing Liberal Party of Quebec also had the internal Canadian market in mind. In this regard, the two dominant logics of provincial development – economic and political – also interacted and reinforced each other. In fact, provincial public-procurement practices increasingly posed an impediment to Canadian internal market integration: the provinces closed their bidding processes not only to foreign companies but also to companies from other provinces, albeit to a lesser degree. Remaining interprovincial barriers restricted the full economic potential of the internal Canadian market in the eyes of Quebec Liberals, thereby representing an obstacle to economic development. Quebec's government aimed at creating new business opportunities for its companies in other provinces, similar to the economic logic applied to opening public procurement bids to European companies. At the same time, this economic logic also reinforced the Quebec Liberals' political conception of the relation among the Canadian provinces. While Quebec's Liberal party considered the Canadian internal market as a space for Quebec's provincial economic development and as a space to thrive politically, the PQ pursued a higher degree of independence from the Canadian internal market in order to prepare for political independence (Brunelle, Bélanger, and Deblock 1999; Brunelle and Deblock 1997; Campbell 1995; Jockel and David 1997; Robinson 1995, 2003). Through CETA the Quebec Liberals strengthened the economic logic of provincial development underpinning procurement practices among provinces and promoted their vision of Canadian federalism, characterized by cooperation among the provinces and the federal government, and of a high degree of internal market integration. I will comment on these two entangled processes in the following.

When procurement arrived at the forefront of the international trade agenda in the early 1990s, the procurement practices of the Canadian provinces were characterized by a tendency to closure among themselves. At that time, the federal government launched an initiative to integrate the highly heterogeneous Canadian internal market, which resulted in the Agreement on Internal Trade (AIT, 1995). Driven mainly by the federal executive, this agreement's provincial procurement chapter remained fairly limited, however, and even provided for a specific exception for regional and economic development projects (article 508). Each province wanted to preserve instruments to assure community loyalty through the award of public contracts, especially for the MASH sector and Crown corporations.

In an incremental process driven by provincial governments, however, the economic logic slowly grew in importance, while the social logic was de-emphasized with regard to interprovincial trade on procurement markets, from the mid-1990s on. Since then the boundaries of intra-Canadian procurement markets have shifted frequently because some provinces have engaged in closer economic cooperation through the formation of regional economic blocks, as I will show.

As early as 1994, Quebec and Ontario signed an agreement on reciprocal access, for their companies, to their procurement markets. In the preamble to this agreement they highlighted that closed procurement markets formed one of the most important internal trade barriers in Canada. However, the scope of their agreement remained limited to ministries and other governmental organizations, excluding the MASH sector. In 1999 the Canadian provincial and federal governments made considerable advancements on provincial procurement and included the MASH sector by way of the Third Protocol of Amendment in the AIT. Nevertheless, economic and social logics continued to coexist, as the relatively high thresholds (especially for the MASH sector) underscored. Since the late 1990s, some provinces have also engaged in processes of regional economic integration and competition. Dissatisfied with the advancements made in the framework of AIT, the governments of Alberta and British Columbia decided to engage in bilateral economic negotiations at their first Cabinet meeting in 2003 (Boutilier 2007). In April 2006 they signed the Trade, Investment, and Labour Mobility Agreement (TILMA, 2007), through which they reduced interprovincial trade barriers. This agreement was cast explicitly against the backdrop of economic competition from the central provinces of Ontario and Quebec (Boutilier 2007; Hansen 2007; Mar 2006). Thresholds for the applicability of TILMA to public procurement contracts were considerably lower than those of AIT, showing that the economic logic slowly replaced the social one. In 2010 the New West Partnership Trade Agreement between Alberta and British Columbia replaced TILMA. In this new agreement, provincial procurement played a major role: article 14 guaranteed an open and non-discriminatory bidding process above thresholds for all government entities, including for the MASH sector.

TILMA created pressure on the central provinces to keep a competitive business environment. Quebec and Ontario responded to this economic competition by engaging in a similar process of regional economic integration: in 2007 they signed a joint statement of intent, and in 2009 they signed the Ontario-Quebec Trade and Cooperation Agreement, which also included far-reaching provisions on provincial public procurement (Descôteaux 2009). The scope of the procurement provisions of the latter agreement extended to government entities, the MASH sector, and even Crown corporations. However, the thresholds remained somewhat higher than those of TILMA.

Hence, the transformation of the aim and quality of provincial public-procurement contracts described for Quebec was not an entirely new process; a shift from the mutually reinforcing social and economics logics towards a stronger focus on the economic logic had been under way since the mid-1990s among the Canadian provinces. In the mid-2000s, when Quebec suggested opening procurement contracts to European competitors, the Canadian provinces were already undergoing a process of intra-Canadian regional integration cast against the background of the competition of several groups of provinces with each other. Against the backdrop of a de-emphasis of the social logic in many provinces, convincing the other Canadian provinces to support the project was not a troublesome task. Quebec announced its support during a meeting of the Council of the Federation, an intergovernmental conference launched in 2003 that brings together provincial premiers twice a year. Most premiers quickly supported the project, as a member of Quebec's government reported: "Au Conseil de la Fédération, qui est le forum où nous retrouvons, l'adhésion a été assez spontanée. Ça n'a pas été problématique."[11]

On 20 February 2009 – three months before the official opening of negotiations between Canada and the EU – the Council of the Federation endorsed the project at its summit meeting in Quebec City (Council of the Federation 2009). In its statement the council announced full support for the negotiation of a new and comprehensive economic agreement with the EU. Premiers highlighted that the inclusion of the provinces in the negotiation process was key to assuring negotiation success. They drew attention to consultations between the federal and provincial governments on issues falling under provincial jurisdiction, thereby suggesting that prior involvement of the provinces would considerably ease the conclusion and implementation of the international agreement. Quebec's government interpreted this announcement as being a negotiation mandate given by the provinces to the federal government, similar to the mandate given to the EC by the member states.

As documented, Quebec re-evaluated and altered its position on public procurement and international and interprovincial trade against the backdrop of a slow and incremental reconfiguration of the role of public procurement in provincial development. Hence, the reconfiguration of its conception of the relation between public procurement and the logics underpinning provincial development triggered the development of a new policy position on public procurement and trade in Quebec. While maintaining a discourse referring to provincial development, the government of Quebec and its diplomatic team de-emphasized the social logic of provincial development, stressed the economic logic, and added a new political logic to provincial development. By doing so, they transformed the quality and aim of public procurement policies in Quebec's development project and considerably modified their interpretation of how best to achieve provincial development through public procurement practices.

Apart from pursuing provincial development through new means, Quebec achieved two additional, complementary aims that benefited its new position. First, it anchored an internal Quebec and interprovincial process in international trade law, thus adding another layer of legal certainty to provincial procurement practices. Second, it overcame regional competition among groups of provinces and furthered Canadian internal market integration.

Thus, discourse on provincial public procurement was a story of continuity and change. Still, discursively embedding procurement in Quebec's provincial development project while arguing that opening public procurement was an asset to provincial development was a thin line to walk. On the one hand, the government needed to emphasize the continuity of its new stance. Yet, on the other hand, it set out to fundamentally reconceptualize the function of public procurement as a tool for provincial development. In fact, the provincial government had to legitimize change in the province's procurement practices against the backdrop of far-reaching domestic opposition, which claimed that the government's plan would jeopardize provincial development.

Quebec's government and diplomats constructed a discourse accentuating the continuity of their policies in order to bridge domestic opposition. By embedding their policy shift in a discourse of provincial development and highlighting the benefits of free trade for Quebec's provincial development, they were able to quickly acquire domestic support for their new position on provincial procurement contracts and trade. As early as June 2008 the government had established a cross-party consensus in Quebec's National Assembly. In a joint motion adopted unanimously, Raymond Bachand (Liberal Party, minister for economic development, innovation, and export), Nicolas Marceau (Parti Québécois), and Gilles Taillon (Action démocratique du Québec) underscored Quebec's support for launching negotiations on a new economic agreement. Although the motion had no legal value, it exemplified the government's success in legitimizing its new stance on provincial procurement, which was a key issue in the province during the agenda-setting and early negotiation stage. Furthermore, the motion also documented a key goal of this negotiation in Quebec, namely the creation of new business opportunities in Europe:

> Que l'Assemblée nationale appuie les négociations en vue d'un partenariat économique plus étroit et de nouvelle génération avec l'Union européenne visant à favoriser le commerce des biens et services, ainsi que la circulation des capitaux et des travailleurs qualifiés, permettant au Québec d'atteindre de nouveaux marchés et de le confirmer comme principale porte d'entrée de l'Europe en Amérique du Nord. (Assemblée Nationale 2008, 4897)

In obtaining access to new procurement markets for its companies, Quebec no longer had an exit strategy that suited its policy position. Hence, Quebec needed to update its institutional strategy, moving from exit to voice.

Pursuing a New Position on Provincial Public Procurement

In order to pursue its new policy position, Quebec updated its institutional strategy and shifted from an exit strategy towards a voice strategy. It could do so because of the institutions of Canadian federalism and the context in which there was no formal process for provincial participation in formulating Canada's trade policy position – only the looming threat that the provinces might not implement the result of negotiations led by the federal government. Being aware that the successful conclusion of the CETA negotiation depended on provincial support, Quebec consciously exploited the ambiguous Canadian institutional context to create a situation in which provincial participation in the negotiation process became indispensable, thereby strengthening the province's international presence.

In deploying its new voice strategy, Quebec first addressed the European Commission. During the 2007 World Economic Forum in Davos, Quebec's premier, Jean Charest, sought to convince the initially reticent European commissioner for trade, Peter Mandelson, to launch negotiations of a new trade and investment agreement between Canada and the EU and to open provincial procurement markets in this context. Persuading Mandelson was not an easy task. In fact, the EC was reluctant to embark on new negotiations with Canada for three reasons. First, the recent failure of the Trade and Investment Enhancement Agreement had left the commission doubtful that a positive negotiation outcome between Canada and the EU could be achieved. Second, the EU had recently developed a new trade policy strategy, Global Europe (2006), which identified key bilateral partners, should the Doha Round fail. Canada was not among these potential partners. Third, the EU was also reluctant to start bilateral negotiations while the multilateral Doha Development Round of the WTO had not yet been concluded or discontinued, as a Canadian diplomat reported: "Around 2007 to 2008, when we started pushing this, the EU was not fully committed to the bilateral process. They were still very much hoping that the Doha Round would still produce results. So, they were not fully committed to the idea of bilaterals at that point."[12]

Provincial public procurement played a key role in convincing the EC that a new economic agreement with Canada was in the EU's interest. Quebec highlighted economic more than political benefits, to which Commissioner Peter Mandelson was more susceptible than his predecessor Pascal Lamy (Meunier 2007). From the EU's perspective, provincial public procurement was among the few sectors where European companies could substantially benefit from a new trade and investment agreement, given the relative size of the European and Canadian economies. Quebec's suggestion to include sub-federal public procurement in the new economic agreement considerably increased the value of the Canadian negotiation offer. In fact, it was a promising avenue for high-volume trade opportunities, with the total value of provincial procurement contracts exceeding that of federal ones: while the World Trade Organization estimated the value of provincial and territorial procurement at USD 20 billion per year, it estimated federal procurement at only USD 15 billion (World Trade Organization 2015). In addition, the share of federal spending in total Canadian public procurement had considerably decreased since the mid-2000s, as figure 3.1 demonstrates.

3.1 Evolution of Share of Total Public Procurement by Procuring Entity (1995–2012)

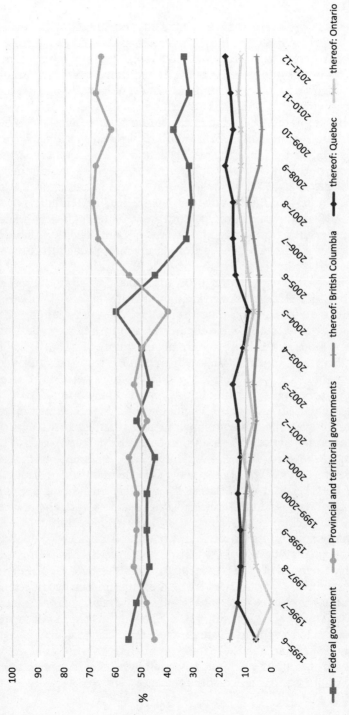

Source: Marketplace Canada (2017).

Note: The MARCAN (Marketplace Canada) reporting was developed under the AIT to help Canadian companies navigate the regulatory framework of Canadian federal and provincial public sector tender notice. It also provided statistics on government procurement contracts. The web page has been discontinued.

As the head of government of a politically influential province, Quebec's premier convinced the European commissioner that the Canadian provinces would agree to cooperate in opening their procurement markets to European companies. Once the EC was convinced of the benefits of a new bilateral trade agreement, and against the backdrop of its recent experience with TIEA, it insisted on including the provinces in the negotiation process in order to secure their future commitment and ensure a swift implementation of CETA's sub-federal procurement provisions. The EC's request to include the provinces as active negotiation partners provided Quebec with a new opportunity to extend its paradiplomatic activities (Balthazar 2003; Bélanger 1995; Kirkey, Paquin, and Roussel 2016; Paquin 2004, 2006), thereby feeding into provincial political development. Hence, the opportunity for Quebec to play a more active role in Canada's upcoming trade negotiation was a consequence and positive side effect of its substantive position on opening public procurement contracts and the benefits for provincial development.

As documented earlier, the other provinces supported Quebec's suggestion to include provincial public procurement in CETA. Subsequently, the EU and Canada officially launched negotiations at the European Union-Canada Summit in Prague in May 2009. Both delegations endorsed the Joint Report on the European Union-Canada Scoping Exercise (March 2009), in which public procurement played a key role and which underscored provincial commitment in the area of public procurement. According to this report, a new trade and investment agreement should aim "to achieve full coverage of central and sub-central government procurement in all sectors, to ensure inter alia treatment no less favourable than that accorded to locally-established suppliers" (Canada and European Union 2009, 6). Similar to the joint scoping report, the 2009 mandate of the Council of the European Union to the EC left no doubt about the European interest in gaining access for their companies to bid on public calls for tender at the Canadian provincial level, including procurement by the MASH sector and Crown corporations. According to the mandate, "the Agreement should aim for maximum ambition complementing the Government Procurement Agreement in terms of coverage (procuring entities, sectors, thresholds, services contracts). The Agreement will ensure mutual access to public procurement markets at all administrative levels (national, regional and local) in the traditional sector as well as in the field of public utilities, ensuring treatment no less favourable than that accorded to locally established suppliers. Market access provisions will extend to the relevant bodies governed by public law and to undertakings operating in the field of utilities" (Council of the European Union 2009).

Subsequently, Quebec's new institutional voice strategy materialized in participation by the provinces during the official negotiation tables in their areas of jurisdiction, represented by Quebec's official delegation (Fafard and Leblond 2013; Johnson, Muzzi, and Bastien 2013; Kukucha 2008, 2011, 2013, 2016; Paquin 2013; VanDuzer 2013). Its negotiation team also promoted provincial interests within the Canadian federal negotiation team. In this way, the incremental normative change underlying Quebec's altered position on public procurement triggered the reconfiguration of the institutional design of intergovernmental relations in Canada and during the CETA negotiation.

Conclusion

During the agenda-setting process of CETA the province of Quebec considerably deviated from the previous reluctance of Canadian provinces to open sub-federal public-procurement-bidding processes to foreign companies and actively proposed to subject public procurement under provincial jurisdiction to CETA. By doing so, Quebec deliberately relinquished an instrument of provincial development that had established community loyalty towards the government in the province – mainly through the creation of local employment – and the support especially of francophone companies, and thereby strengthened the tissue of Quebec as a political unit. In changing its position, Quebec enabled Canada and the EU to successfully pursue the CETA negotiation.

While many analyses have pointed to institutional dynamics to account for this empirical puzzle, I have highlighted the incremental normative change underpinning a reconceptualization of the role of public procurement in provincial development. Quebec's government engaged in a transformative process in which it reconceptualized provincial development, conferred a new meaning on its public procurement practices, and defended and explained this new discourse in the political arena. Gradually the economic dimension came centre stage in its discourse and replaced adjacent discourses on the social effects of public procurement practices, which used to accompany economic development. In this process the government de-emphasized the social and community dimensions of public procurement in favour of a focus on the creation of business opportunities abroad, on strengthening the provincial state, and on fostering Canadian internal market integration. Subsequently the cross-party consensus that free trade ultimately strengthened the province became the main discourse underscoring Quebec's procurement practices.

Hence, this policy change was by no means a story of Quebec being coerced by the Canadian federal government or the EU to change its stance on public procurement contracts. To the contrary, it was driven to a large extent by the province itself and supported by the other provinces, although Quebec had multiple institutional resources to avoid it, especially given its strengthened institutional position related to the numerous provisions in CETA that fell under provincial jurisdiction. When Quebec advocated the inclusion of provincial procurement contracts in CETA's procurement chapter in late 2006 and early 2007, institutions alone were thus not at the origin of this policy shift. Rather, the absence of a formal process establishing the relation between the federal and provincial orders in trade policymaking allowed Quebec to update its institutional strategy in order to strengthen its new policy position on public procurement. Although Quebec had previously and often used the significant institutional resources of Canadian federalism to refuse the implementation of international provisions on subfederal procurement, it now deliberately advocated their inclusion in CETA and changed its institutional strategy accordingly.

Furthermore, I have documented not only that the changing nature of international trade agreements had an impact on sub-national activity and domestic rules, norms, and practices, but also that domestic factors enabled international trade negotiations. By understanding Quebec's policy shift in light of altered domestic norms about the effects of public procurement contracts on provincial development, I highlighted that a reinterpretation of preferences at the sub-federal domestic level contributed to the changing nature of international trade policy. Hence, not only does the changing nature of trade policy influence sub-federal actors' mobilization but also the changing patterns of trade policy positions at the sub-federal level can shape the nature of international trade agreements.

NOTES

1 The provinces have sole jurisdiction over the procurement by provincial ministries and other government entities such as agencies, commissions, public funding authorities, the MASH sector (municipalities, municipal organizations, school boards, and publicly funded academic, health, and social service entities), and provincial Crown corporations. In Quebec, public procurement is currently regulated by the Loi sur les contrats des organismes publics (2006, amended 2012).
2 According to the Loi sur le ministère des affaires étrangères (1988, amended 2014), the minister for international affairs – jointly with the

minister for economic development in the case of trade agreements – usually ratifies international agreements (article 22.1). If the minister considers an international agreement to be important, he needs to refer it to the National Assembly of Quebec for scrutiny and approval (articles 22.2 and 22.4).

3 The official negotiation process was launched on 6 May 2009 in Prague and closed on 26 September 2014 in Ottawa.

4 This analysis is partially based on empirical material obtained for my doctoral thesis "Constructing Trade: The Negotiation of the Comprehensive Economic and Trade Agreement in Quebec (2006–2014)," Universität Trier and Université de Montréal.

5 Armenia, Canada, the European Union, Hong Kong/China, Iceland, Israel, Japan, Korea, Liechtenstein, Netherlands, Norway, Singapore, Switzerland, Chinese Taipei, and the United States. At present the agreement has nineteen parties comprising forty-seven WTO members.

6 Market access schedules are set out in annex 2 of the GPA (1994).

7 In the 1960s the province of Quebec entered a period of socio-economic and political change called the Quiet Revolution (Révolution tranquille), characterized by state expansion, retraction of the Catholic Church, the emergence of modern Quebec nationalism, the restructuring of the provincial economy, and a reconfiguration of the provincial party system (Dickinson and Young 2008, 305–44).

8 However, the contribution made to local development by these projects has become increasingly challenged with regard to environmental sustainability, the rights of local and especially First Nation communities, and economic development (Bernard, 2014; Martin, 2008; Prémont, 2014; Slowey, 2008).

9 Interview with Canadian diplomat (federal level), Brussels, 7 July 2014.

10 Interview with Quebec diplomat, Montreal, 9 October 2014.

11 Interview with member of Quebec Liberal government, Montreal, 24 October 2014.

12 Interview with Canadian diplomat, Brussels, 8 July 2014.

REFERENCES

Assemblée Nationale. 2008. *Journal des débats de l'Assemblée: Le vendredi 13 juin 2008* 40, no. 99. Quebec City. Accessed 11 November 2019. http://www .assnat.qc.ca.

– 2011. *Journal des débats de la Commission permanente des institutions: Le jeudi 8 decembre 2011* 42, no. 56. Quebec City. Accessed 11 November 2019. http:// www.assnat.qc.ca.

Balthazar, Louis. 2003. "Les relations internationales du Québec." In *Québec: Etat et Société*, edited by A.-G. Gagnon, 447–74. Montreal: Éditions Québec/ Amérique.

Bélanger, Louis. 1995. "L'espace international de l'État québécois dans l'après-guerre froide: Vers une compression?" In *L'espace québécois*, edited by A.-G. Gagnon and Alain Noël, 71–103. Montreal: Éditions Québec/Amérique.

Bernard, Jean-Thomas. 2014. "La rentabilité du développement hydro-électrique au Québec." In *Les défis Québécois: Conjonctures et transitions*, edited by R. Bernier, 313–24. Quebec City: Presse de l'Université du Québec.

Bernier, Luc. 1994. "L'évolution de sociétés d'État au Québec depuis 1960." In *Québec: État et société*, edited by A.-G. Gagnon, 199–220. Montreal: Les Éditions Québec/Amérique.

– 2014. "Hydro-Québec, la commercialisation d'une société d'État." In *Les défis Québécois: Conjonctures et transition*, edited by R. Bernier, 59–78. Quebec City: Les Presses de l'Université du Québec.

Bickerton, James, and Alain-G. Gagnon. 1984. "Regional Policy in Historical Perspective: The Federal Role in Regional Economic Development." *American Review of Canadian Studies* 14 (1): 72–92.

Boutilier, G. 2007. "How TILMA Will Affect Employers in Western Canada." Speech to the Western Canadian Forum on Employment Law, Calgary, 1 February.

Brunelle, Dorval, Yves Bélanger, and Christian Deblock. 1999. "L'intégration économique continentale et ses effets sur les gouvernements infra-étatiques: De l'ALE à l'ALENA et au-delà." *Cahiers de recherche sociologique* 32: 85–117.

Brunelle, Dorval, and Christian Deblock. 1997. "Free Trade and Trade-Related Issues in Quebec: The Challenges of Continental Integration." *American Review of Canadian Studies* 27 (1): 63–85.

Campbell, Robert Malcom. 1995. "Federalism and Economic Policy." In *New Trends in Canadian Federalism*, edited by F. Rocher and M. Smith. Peterborough, ON: Broadview Press.

Canada and the European Union. 2009. *Joint Report on the European Union–Canada Scoping Exercise*. http://www.esf.be. Ottawa: Government of Canada; Brussels: European Union.

Charest, Jean. 2008. "Un nouvel espace économique pour le Québec." *La Presse*, 26 March.

Clarke, S.F. 2015. Government Procurement Law and Policy: Canada. Washington, DC: Library of Congress. Accessed 11 November 2019. https://www.loc.gov.

Coalition Eau Secours! 2012. *Accord Canada–Union Européenne: Nos marchés publics de l'eau ouverts à la concurrence internationale?* 29 November. https://www.quebec.attac.org.

Collins, David. 2008. "Canada's Sub-central Coverage under the WTO Agreement on Government Procurement." *Public Procurement Law Review* 17 (1): 21–40.

– 2011. "Canada's Sub-central Government Entities and the Agreement on Government Procurement: Past and Present." In *The WTO Regime on Government Procurement: Challenge and Reform*, edited by S. Arrowsmith and R.D. Anderson. Cambridge: Cambridge University Press.

Conseil Municipal de Montréal. 2012. "Déclaration concernant l'accord économique et commercial global (AECG)." Montreal: Procès verbal de l'Assemblée ordinaire du Conseil municipal du 23 janvier 2012, 14 heures.

Council of the European Union. 2009. *Recommendation from the Commission to the Council in Order to Authorize the Commission to Open Negotiations for an Economic Integration Agreement with Canada*. Brussels: Coreper to Council.

Council of the Federation. 2009. *Support for the Negotiation of a New and Comprehensive Economic Agreement with the European Union*. Ottawa: Council of the Federation.

Delagran, Leslie. 1992. "Conflict in Trade Policy: The Role of the Congress and the Provinces in Negotiating and Implementing the Canada-U.S. Free Trade Agreement." *Publius: The Journal of Federalism* 22 (4): 15–29.

Descôteaux, David. 2009. *The Ontario-Quebec Trade and Cooperation Agreement: Economic Note on Trade Liberalization between Quebec and Ontario*. Montreal: Montreal Economic Institute.

Dickinson, John A., and Brian Young, eds. 2008. *A Short History of Quebec*. 4th ed. Montreal and Kingston: McGill-Queen's University Press.

Dufour, Pascale. 2006. "Projet national et espace de protestation mondiale: Des articulations distinctes au Québec et au Canada." *Canadian Journal of Political Science / Revue canadienne de science politique* 39 (2): 315–42.

Fafard, Patrick, and Patrick Leblond, eds. 2012. *Twenty-First Century Trade Agreements: Challenges for Canadian Federalism*. Montreal: Federal Idea.

– 2013. "Closing the Deal: What Role for the Provinces in the Final Stages of the CETA Negotiations?" *International Journal* 68 (4): 553–9.

Global Affairs Canada. 2013. *Canada–European Union Trade and Investment Enhancement Agreement*. Ottawa: Government of Canada.

Graham, W.C. 1983. "Government Procurement Policies: GATT, the EEC, and the United States." In *Federalism and the Canadian Economic Union*, edited by J.M. Trebilcock, J.R.S. Prichard, T. Courchene, and J. Whalley. Toronto: University of Toronto Press (for the Ontario Economic Council).

Hansen, Colin. 2007. *UBCM 2007: TILMA*. Speech at the Union of British Columbia Municipalities Convention 2007, 24 September. Accessed 9 November 2019.

Hydro-Québec. 2010. *Rapport annuel 2009: Façonner l'avenir*. Montreal: Hydro-Québec. http://www.hydroquebec.com.

Jenson, Jane. 1991. "All the World's a Stage: Ideas, Spaces and Times in
Canadian Political Economy." *Studies in Political Economy* 36: 43–72.
– 1995. "Mapping, Naming and Remembering: Globalization at the End
of the Twentieth Century." *Review of International Political Economy* 2 (1):
96–116.
Jockel, Joseph. T., and Charles-Philippe David. 1997. "Introduction: A
Sovereign Quebec and the United States." *American Review of Canadian
Studies* 27 (1): 9–10.
Johnson, Pierre-Marc, Patrick Muzzi, and Véronique Bastien. 2013. "The Voice
of Quebec in the CETA Negotiations." *International Journal: Canada's Journal
of Global Policy Analysis* 68 (4): 560–7.
Keating, Michael. 1997. "Stateless Nation-Building: Quebec, Catalonia and
Scotland in the Changing State System." *Nations and Nationalism* 3 (4): 689–717.
Kirkey, Christopher, Stéphane Paquin, and Stéphane Roussel. 2016. "Charting
Quebec's Engagement with the International Community." *American
Review of Canadian Studies* 46 (2): 135–48.
Kukucha, Christopher J., ed. 2008. *The Provinces and Canadian Foreign Trade
Policy*. Vancouver: University of British Columbia Press.
– 2011. "Provincial Pitfalls: Canadian Provinces and the Canada-EU Trade
Negotiations." In *Europe, Canada and the Comprehensive Economic and Trade
Agreement*, edited by K. Hübner. New York: Routledge.
– 2013. "Canadian Sub-federal Governments and CETA: Overarching
Themes and Future Trends." *International Journal: Canada's Journal of Global
Policy Analysis* 68 (4): 528–35.
– 2016. "Provincial/Territorial Governments and the Negotiation of
International Trade Agreements." Institute for Research on Public Policy,
Insight 10.
Lisée, Jean-François. 2013. "Québec: Des ambitions mondiales." Allocution
devant le Conseil des relations internationales de Montréal (CORIM) du
ministre des Relations internationales et de la Francophonie." 11 February.
https://www.mrif.gouv.qc.ca/fr/salle-de-presse/allocutions/2013/2013_02_11.
Mar, G. 2006. *Alberta International and Intergovernmental Relations*. Speech
to the Richmond Chamber of Commerce, 6 June 2006, Richmond, BC.
Accessed 9 November 2019. http://www.tilma.ca.
Marketplace Canada. 2017. Statistics on Procurement: Total by Party.
MARCAN reporting under the AIT, data last accessed on 19 October 2016.
Martin, Pierre. 1995a. "Le nationalisme québécois et le choix du libre-échange
continental." In *L'espace québécois*, edited by A.-G. Gagnon and A. Noel.
Montreal: Éditions Québec/Amérique.
– 1995b. "When Nationalism Meets Continentalism: The Politics of Free
Trade in Quebec." *Regional & Federal Studies* 5 (1): 1–27.
Martin, Thibault. 2008. "Hydro Development in Quebec and Manitoba:
Old Relationships or New Social Contract?" In *Power Struggles: Hydro*

Development and First Nations in Manitoba and Quebec, edited by T. Martin and S.M. Hoffman. Winnipeg: University of Manitoba Press, 2008.

McMurtry, John-Justin. 2014. "The Political Economy of Procurement." Supplement, *Canadian Public Policy / Analyse de Politiques* 40, no. S1: 26–8.

McRoberts, Kenneth H, ed. 1993. *Quebec: Social Change and Political Crisis*. 3rd ed. Toronto: McClelland and Stewart.

Meunier, Sophie. 2007. "Managing Globalization? The EU in International Trade Negotiations." *Journal of Common Market Studies* 45 (4): 905–26.

Ontario Chamber of Commerce. 2013. *5 Things You Need to Know about the Canada-EU Trade Deal*. Accessed 25 May 2017. https://occ.ca.

Paquin, Stéphane. 2001. *La revanche des petites nations: Le Québec, la Catalogne et l'Écosse face à la mondialisation*. Montreal: VLB.

– 2004. "La paradiplomatie identitaire: Le Québec, la Catalogne et la Flandre en relations internationales." *Politique et Sociétés* 23 (2–3): 203–37.

– ed. 2006. *Les relations internationales du Québec depuis la Doctrine Gérin-Lajoie (1965–2005)*. Quebec City: Presses de l'Université Laval.

– 2010. "Federalism and Compliance with International Agreements: Belgium and Canada Compared." *The Hague Journal of Diplomacy* 5 (1–2): 173–97.

– 2013. "Federalism and the Governance of International Trade Negotiations in Canada: Comparing CUSFTA with CETA." *International Journal: Canada's Journal of Global Policy Analysis* 68 (4): 545–52.

– 2016. "Quebec-US Relations: The Big Picture." *American Review of Canadian Studies* 46 (2): 149–61.

Prémont, Marie-Claude. 2014. "Hydro-Québec et le délestage des grandes régions productrices d'hydroélectricité." In *Les défis Québécois: Conjonctures et transitions*, edited by R. Bernier. Quebec City: Presses de l'Université du Québec.

Robinson, Ian. 1995. "Trade Policy, Globalization, and the Future of Canadian Federalism." In *New Trends in Canadian Federalism*, edited by F. Rocher and M. Smith. Peterborough, ON: Broadview Press.

– 2003. "Neo-Liberal Trade Policy and Canadian Federalism." In *New Trends in Canadian Federalism*, edited by F. Rocher and M. Smith. Peterborough, ON: Broadview Press.

Rocher, François. 1994. "Le Québec en Amérique du Nord: La stratégie continentale." In *Québec: État et société*, edited by Alain-G. Gagnon, 461–84. Montreal: Les Éditions Québec/Amérique.

– 2003a. "Le Québec en Amérique du Nord: La stratégie continentale." In *Québec: État et sociéte*, edited by A.-G. Gagnon. Montreal: Les Éditions Québec/Amérique.

– 2003b. "Le Québec dans les Amériques: De l'ale à la ZLE." In *Québec: État et sociéte*, edited by A.-G. Gagnon. Montreal: Les Éditions Québec/Amérique.

Saint-Martin, Denis. 2015. "Systemic Corruption in an Advanced Welfare State: Lessons from the Quebec Charbonneau Inquiry." *Osgoode Hall Law Journal* 53 (1): 66–106.

Slowey, Gabrielle A. 2008. "The State, the Marketplace, and First Nations: Theorizing First Nation Self-Determination in an Era of Globalization." In *Power Struggles: Hydro Development and First Nations in Manitoba and Quebec*, edited by T. Martin and S.M. Hoffman. Winnipeg: University of Manitoba Press.

Syndicat Canadien de la Fonction Publique and Conseil des Canadiens. 2010. *Eau publique à vendre: Comment le Canada va privatiser nos systèmes publics d'eau*. Rapport aux gouvernements provinciaux, territoriaux et municipaux concernant l'Accord économique et commercial global (AECG) entre le Canada et l'Union européenne. Ottawa: The Council of Canadians and CUPE.

Tanguay, Brian A. 2003. "Sclérose ou parfait état de santé? Examen du système de partis au Québec au xxie siècle." In *Québec: État et sociéte*, edited by A.-G. Gagnon. Montreal: Les Éditions Québec/Amérique.

Toronto City Council. 2012. *Request to Protect City of Toronto Interests and Existing Powers in Any Trade Agreement Signed between the Government of Canada and the European Union: Motion MM14.14 Referred by City Council on November 29, 2011*. City Council Decision. Toronto: Toronto City Council.

Trew, Stuart. 2013. "Correcting the Democratic Deficit in the CETA Negotiations: Civil Society Engagement in the Provinces, Municipalities, and Europe." *International Journal: Canada's Journal of Global Policy Analysis* 68 (4): 568–75.

– 2014. "Public Procurement." In *Making Sense of the CETA: An Analysis of the Final Text of the Canada–European Union Comprehensive Economic and Trade Agreement*, edited by S. Sinclair, S. Trew, and H. Mertins-Kirkwood. Ottawa, ON: Canadian Centre for Policy Alternatives.

Van Assche, Ari. 2016. "CETA: A New Type of Free Trade Agreement in Line with a New Global Trade Reality." In *The Comprehensive Econonic and Trade Agreement between Canada and the E.U.: An Overview*, edited by X. Van Overmerire and N. Nychay. Toronto: Lexis Nexis.

VanDuzer, Anthony J. 2013. "Could an Intergovernmental Agreement Increase the Credibility of Canadian Treaty Commitments in Areas within Provincial Jurisdiction?" *International Journal: Canada's Journal of Global Policy Analysis* 68 (4): 536–44.

Woolcock, Stephen B, ed. 2012. *European Union Economic Diplomacy: The Role of the EU in External Economic Relations*. Farnham, UK: Ashgate.

World Trade Organization. 2015. *Trade Policy Review: Canada*. Geneva: Trade Policy Review Body. Accessed 11 November 2019. https://www.wto.org.

4 Multilevel Trade in the United States: Federalism, Internal Markets, and Intergovernmental Relations

MICHELLE EGAN

While the Trump administration has generated global turmoil with its focus on restricting imports, the international consequences of its trade policy choices have reverberated at the domestic level as states have borne the brunt of the global retaliation against Washington's tariffs (US Chamber of Commerce 2018).[1] Though trade policy has generated intense political debates in the United States regarding job losses and depressed wages from foreign competition, charting a path forward is not easy given public views and expectations surrounding trade issues. Washington confronts a fraying consensus around trade policy where partisan divides about free trade agreements have been amplified by a new politics of trade in which the scope and comprehensiveness of many twenty-first-century trade negotiations reverberate within domestic politics at multiple levels. Yet research on trade negotiations has focused primarily on different producer interests and preferences without paying attention to the new political conflicts and patterns of policymaking that have emerged due to the expansion of the global trade agenda where divergent domestic rules have become an important target of trade negotiations.

While states are caught in the cross-fire of the escalating trade war, a more nuanced assessment of their specific role is required as they become entangled in international trade agreements. Although the international legal context normally allows only national governments to sign international binding agreements, state efforts to engage in foreign policy activities have often been contested in the courts when the "dormant" foreign power considers state laws impinging on foreign relations to be invalid. States have persisted through a wide range of mechanisms to engage in foreign economic relations, including regional economic investment activities, and seek to attract foreign investment through locational incentives as well as cooperative mechanisms that foster trans-border cooperation on a host of issues. Yet the United States has not adjusted its negotiating practices to integrate states in deliberations, even when these agreements cover regulatory aspects, because there is no risk of "veto" or "involuntary defection" by states in US trade policymaking.

As trade flows have expanded, more sectors have demanded market access in areas that have been regulated at the state level. It would, therefore, make sense that sub-federal economic interests seek to influence trade policy, especially as many of the new trade issues being pushed for greater liberalization infringe on the domestic regulatory competencies that are historically or constitutionally reserved to the states.[2] Today the role of states in American trade politics is very much shaped by the structure of the internal market. Despite the creation of national regulatory agencies and legislative initiatives limiting state power – particularly in key economic areas like banking, transportation, telecommunications, and security – states do have important legislative and regulatory powers. They also have constitutional protections, as well as specific "police powers" through which they exercise regulatory authority in procurement, agriculture, services, and professions, a product of American political and economic development in the nineteenth century (Egan 2015). As a result, the American internal market is fragmented and decentralized in many of those areas where trade partners want greater liberalization and non-discrimination to yield better market access. Hence, the new politics of trade puts pressure on sub-federal jurisdictions, drawing attention to the regulatory patchwork of rules and policies within the United States that are increasingly viewed as constraints in the promotion of market access and reciprocal liberalization.

The result is an institutional layering that complicates the existing trade framework but does not lead to institutional displacement with one level of governance being substituted by another (Broschek 2014, 53). The expansion of the trade agenda has inadvertently put the form and practice of federalism under scrutiny because the expansion of trade commitments has consequences for internal markets (Egan and Guimarães 2019). In the United States the regulatory differences and the discriminatory treatment of market actors from other sub-federal units are the product of past policy choices in which institutional authority over market integration led to specific state preferences and rules that still allow localities to maintain their rights to enact illiberal policies (Hoffmann, Parsons, and Springer 2017, 5). Yet trade scholars pay little attention to the protectionism of lower-level jurisdictions, although these rules are in fact some of the issues that have been deeply problematic for trade and investment negotiations. Even though the United States has de facto centralized trade policy authority, states are responsible for a number of trade-distorting measures that are the product of the historical allocation of competences between and among territorial jurisdictions.[3]

This chapter evaluates the impact of sub-federal jurisdictions in the United States on the new generation of "deeper" trade agreements. It looks at the form and practice of federalism in the negotiation and implementation of international trade agreements, the types of inter-governmental coordination in place to allow states to exercise voice in trade negotiations, and the degree to which the allocation of regulatory competences in the American internal market has an impact on the new generation of deep free trade agreements. The core argument advanced here is that the ability to reach agreement in the United States in key sectors such as agriculture, procurement, and services depends on the willingness to address persistent domestic trade barriers and to break up the protectionist practices of sub-national governments that continue to prevent deeper integration. The institutional design of federalism has led to "regulatory peaks" in a manner similar to that of the European internal market where there is a disconnection between internal trade liberalization and external obligations (Young 2004, 394). Although it is common for federations to pursue integrated markets to take advantage of reduced transaction costs and market efficiencies, there is greater attention now to the systemic influences and constraints of the global economy on domestic economic constituencies (Moravscik 1998, 18; Young 2016). By integrating the internal dynamics and external impact of the new politics of trade, the chapter sheds light on where the difficulties in reaching an agreement are likely to occur, as well as on the nature and workings of intergovernmental relations in federal systems.

Contemporary Trade Politics and American Federalism

Trade policymaking is a challenging proposition in the United States because it must navigate a wide range of agencies and interests in multiple and concurrent negotiations, over an ever-expanding set of issues that are outlined in various trade laws enacted by the US Congress. The myriad of local and state laws has led sub-federal jurisdictions to voluntarily opt out of specific trade commitments, to mobilize and lobby to gain exemptions, and to implement specific obligations that have carried substantial legal challenges to their domestic regulatory choices. This exposes sub-federal jurisdictions to international trade disputes, so that states have increasingly used federalism as a barrier to international trade liberalization. This has involved pressure to exclude issues from negotiations as well as refraining from participation in trade and investment commitments.

Most studies of trade policymaking focus on the horizontal division of powers between the executive and legislative institutions. While the US legislature has more power in the field of trade policy than have any of its federal counterparts in relations with the executive due to constitutional prerogatives over commerce, much of the scholarship has focused on the delegation of trade authority to the executive under fast-track authority. But even after an agreement has been reached, the respective responsibilities of the executive and legislature continue under a specific deadline for statutory approval. After the final text has been published, it is submitted to Congress for the adoption of the implementing legislation. Congress then considers the bill in committee, often working informally with the executive on the legislative text. This often generates legislative compromises, which are then negotiated through side agreements and other approaches into the implementing bill in order to generate broad-based support for ratification and approval. This support is critical because once the implementing bill has been formally introduced, no amendments are permitted; only a straight "yea" or "nay" vote for the agreement is allowed.

Although it appears that there is substantial partisan polarization on trade, the reality is more complex. The prevailing positions within each party have actually themselves been divided, with a sizable minority in one or both parties sharing the position of the other party's majority. In 2015, 15 per cent of House Democrats and 30 per cent of Senate Democrats joined 79 per cent of House Republicans and 90 per cent of Senate Republicans to grant the Trade Promotion Authority (TPA), which gave the executive broad negotiating power and facilitated congressional approval of trade agreements. However, many contemporary trade agreements also include a withdrawal clause; congressional approval is not required; therefore, if a president wishes to leave an existing commitment, there are few limits. Unless that power is restricted by statute, President Trump could seek to terminate designated trade agreements. In the case of the North American Free Trade Agreement (NAFTA), chapter 22, article 2205 provides the option to withdraw from the agreement six months after written notification has been given (this is also the case for agreements with Australia, Chile, Colombia, Korea, Panama, Peru, and Singapore), although it may remain in force for the remaining parties. Though neither Congress nor federal courts will deter Trump from carrying out trade threats, his policies can generate disputes or retaliation by aggrieved trade parties, with the prospect of unilateral trade mechanisms and remedies being put to greater use (Lighthizer 2017).

Unlike earlier, first-generation agreements that included numerous exemptions, low utilization of trade preferences, and problems surrounding rules of origin, recent free trade negotiations incorporate more far-reaching commitments to address non-tariff trade barriers, as well as new issues concerning state-owned enterprises and data-localization requirements. While some governments have resorted to structural adjustment programs to mitigate the effects of increased competition by linking these programs to trade agreements, such compensation has been decoupled from liberalization in the United States. The notion of trade adjustment has not been fully supported, due to conservative concerns that the adjustment might become a long-term federal subsidy, and to liberal concerns that it might provide compensation without significant job growth. However, trade adjustment has been made more complicated as the shift towards transnational production and global supply chains has also led companies to decentralize production, which makes import protection a more difficult proposition for governments due to the pressures of regional and global integration. Trade adjustment assistance has been frequently used as a means to promote political support in Congress for trade liberalization in the face of growing public dissatisfaction with free trade agreements.

Although this direct form of compensation to deal with market adjustments is indicative of what Ruggie (1982) termed "embedded liberalism," it has not stemmed the rising protectionist pressures and the fraying domestic consensus for further liberalization in the United States. Immediately upon Trump taking office, his administration triggered renegotiations of NAFTA and the Free Trade Agreement between the United States of America and the Republic of Korea, withdrawal from the Trans-Pacific Partnership (TPP), and reconsideration of all existing free trade agreements. The Transatlantic Trade and Investment Partnership (TTIP) negotiations have also been placed on hiatus but may resume at some point. The US debate over the advisability of including investor-state-dispute-settlement mechanisms emerged again in NAFTA renegotiations, with three hundred state legislators urging US trade representative Robert Lighthizer to eliminate the mechanisms (Inside U.S. Trade, 14 September 2018). Federal executive action by the Trump administration to "Buy American and Hire American" has also enhanced restrictive domestic-preference laws. Whatever the consequences of possible ruptures in traditional American trade policy, Trump is not the first president to complain about trade deals. Barack Obama also campaigned against NAFTA but embarked on major trade negotiations once he was in office. The Trump administration focuses on reducing the trade deficit, using trade remedies aggressively, and tackling perceived unfair trade practices, as a means to divert investment domestically and promote job growth through a fiscal stimulus.

Attention among states turned towards the consequences of renegotiations for specific sectors, notably agriculture, automotives, textiles, and medical devices that are tightly woven into North American supply chains (*New York Times*, 27 April 2017). NAFTA has helped the Midwest states by allowing the automotive sector to compete with China. By contributing to the development of cross-border supply chains, NAFTA lowered costs, increased productivity, and improved US competitiveness (Autor, David, and Hanson 2016). While NAFTA offers substantial benefits to a variety of US agricultural exporters across different states, exports are much higher to Mexico than to Canada. Mexico imports hundreds of billions of dollars of varied agricultural products from the United States, but the supply-management system for dairy and poultry products in Canada has been a source of grievance in NAFTA renegotiations despite a trade surplus of US exports (Noll and Litan 2018). Moreover, NAFTA rules have encouraged agricultural product testing at the state or provincial level whenever possible, rather than requiring national approvals. US trade agreements regarding textiles have included product-specific rules of origin. Cheaper imports have displaced domestic production in the United States. However, NAFTA accelerated the redistribution of labour-intensive manufacturing away from the United States to Mexico, with two-thirds of Mexican finished goods being made from American yarn or fabric as cotton growers, yarn spinners, and fabric makers have found a strong export market for their goods. Despite the changing rhetoric, any subsequent trade negotiation will also face some political challenges that are the result of the institutional design of federalism.

The impact of trade agreements thus varies by state and sector. With NAFTA, thirty-three states export more goods to Canada than to any other country, and seven states count Mexico as their biggest export partner (Chamber of Commerce 2018). Thus, the scope of liberalization pursued by the US Trade Representative in conjunction with other federal agencies is directly relevant to states that have different, sometimes conflicting, economic interests. The federal government has full constitutional powers to bind states to any trade agreement, but many of the issues that are increasingly subject to international trade negotiations will affect domestic state laws. State governments have primary or shared competencies with the federal government in a number of areas and have asked trade negotiators to address concerns related to internet gambling, licensing of professionals, insurance, and education, which reflects the language in the TPA to remove barriers that "unreasonably restrict the establishment and operation of service suppliers." For states, the recent effort under the TPA to promote "unreasonable barriers to investment," as well as the efforts to promote regulatory compatibility and mutual recognition in labour and services, raises concerns about the degree to which an agreement locks in specific goals and objectives that may not address state-specific concerns (Kukucha 2015). Although there is language to allow states to exclude certain provisions and to provide exceptions, some of which became salient in the TTIP negotiations in Europe as well, such as public health and social services, specific exclusions (e.g., gambling, minority set-asides) are tempered with broad commitments that were often included to secure access in other trade negotiations. These may open up state regulatory regimes to challenge on specific issues. Areas such as insurance and utilities that involve effectively state-owned enterprises or highly regulated monopolies may be subject to increased market competition (Kukucha 2013).

States have no involvement in ratification as this is the prerogative of the federal level, and the implementing acts of the WTO, NAFTA, and other trade agreements allow the federal executive to prevail over states and bring suit against states in case of non-compliance with the agreement. However, there have been growing tensions at the state level about the respective commitments undertaken, with various actions being carried out by state governors, legislatures, and attorneys general to seek carve-outs in the General Agreement on Trade in Services, rescind prior state commitments, and create trade commissions in order to advance state interests on trade policy. Yet unlike the federal level, which can impose tariffs and remedies (protectionist or retaliatory), states are constrained from taking protectionist actions. While the federal government can undertake trade liberalization without the consent of states, it would require federal courts to invalidate these state laws, state legislative repeal, or non-implementation by state agencies in order to foster greater liberalization within the US internal market.

Deliberative Intergovernmentalism and Advocacy Coalitions

Although international trade negotiations have had an increasing impact on subnational jurisdictions, the degree of intergovernmental coordination varies across federal systems. This has meant that the institutional preferences expressed by sub-federal units depend on the degree to which territorial interests have a role in the negotiation and implementation stage (Fabbrini 2017; Jachtenfuchs and Kasack 2017). In the United States few studies have focused on the role of states in negotiations of trade agreements as distinct from their traditional role in trade and investment promotion and economic development initiatives, in which states are primarily focused on expanding access to international markets and protection of sensitive sectors or industries (Kukucha 2013, 2015; Weiler 1994). Nevertheless, sub-federal jurisdictions in the United States, whether they be legislative or executive agencies, have increasingly engaged in policy deliberations in order that this cross-jurisdictional coordination effort does not displace the horizontal coordination between the federal executive and legislative branch in trade negotiations. Instead, what has emerged is a two-fold strategy regarding trade agreements: deliberative intergovernmentalism where states have been accorded a formal advisory role, and more traditional lobbying activities through advocacy networks (Puetter 2012; Sabatier and Jenkins-Smith 1993).

An important role for states in international trade negotiations emerged in the aftermath of the Trade Act in 1974. The act led to the creation of an advisory trade committee known as the Intergovernmental Policy Advisory Committee on Trade (IGPAC) to express state and local concerns (Weiler 1994). This statutory consultation meant that states and localities could advise on issues pertaining to their jurisdictions. However, it is one of twenty-eight such advisory committees that reflect a range of different constituencies and interests interacting with the US Trade Representative as well as other federal agencies. Although the committee is composed of a number of state and local representatives, not all states are included in the advisory committee, which is required to report on any substantive trade agreements. The body provided input into the Uruguay Round of negotiations in the General Agreement on Tariffs and Trade in 1994, giving recommendations on services, procurement, and trade-related investment measures; supporting provisions on intellectual property and subsidies and countervailing duties; and urging the federal government to assist sub-federal jurisdictions in complying with many requirements such as technical barriers to trade and government procurement. Pushing for trade and adjustment assistance in several areas affected by GATT, the states have frequently advocated for more resources to assist in the implementation of trade agreements given their experience with WTO obligations (IGPAC 1994). Their argument that the federal government was no longer the sole source of trade policymaking and implementation was meant to highlight the way in which many of the issues would require adjustment in existing state and local rules to bring them into compliance with treaty commitments on subsidies, product standards, and food and agricultural regulations, as well as a myriad of services that were now brought under international trading rules (IGPAC 1994, 3).

IGPAC has continued to provide reviews of various trade agreements under the Trade Act of 2002, but its formal role comes at the end of negotiations. After a continually changing roster of state officials, depending on individual state resources and commitment, the succession of reports on bilateral trade deals with partners ceased with the demise of trade promotion authority in 2007. The consultative framework languished until the adoption of trade promotion authority under the Obama administration again provided an avenue for states to address their views, this time on the TPP agreement; they have more limited input in the stalled TTIP negotiations. Recognizing that these new, ambitious, deep trade agreements have an impact on state regulatory practices, federal agencies have provided informal briefings on a wide range of issues, especially during the recent negotiations on TTIP and TPP.[4] Although members of the advisory committee were invited to all the TPP and TTIP negotiation sessions, there were no funds to support their active participation. The result was a patchwork of engagement and involvement by states, covering a range of state, local, and municipal bodies and institutions (IGPAC 2004).[5] With the need to generate state support for trade liberalization efforts, federal trade officials have opted for a *deliberative* intergovernmental method. They aim for greater policy coherence through intensified intergovernmental coordination to promote policy consensus. This has led them to seek state input through regular consultations, meeting with the National Conference of State Legislators (NCSL), the National Governors' Association (NGA), regional governors' associations, and local chambers of commerce (Congressional Hearing before a Subcommittee of the Committee on Appropriations 2010). Increasingly, a number of states, including Maine, Utah, Michigan, and Texas, have sought to exercise their own voice, mobilizing trade commissions or legislative committees to provide a forum for reviewing trade policy and advising state and federal officials on trade issues that affect their local economies.

Another very important option has been the more traditional advocacy and lobbying efforts by state associations in an effort to shape policy outcomes. As the federal government has sought specific exemptions in trade agreements, states have mobilized through particular trade and professional associations to defend their interests (Cammissa 1995; Schaeffer 2001). These advocacy coalitions involving multiple actors across different levels of government serve as policy brokers to promote collective action to influence policymaking. The seven main associations, including the NGA, the NCSL, the National Association of State Attorneys General, the Council of State Governments, and the US Conference of Mayors, coordinate intergovernmental relations for more than eighteen thousand government entities. These associations represent different sub-federal jurisdictions across a range of policy issues; therefore, their interests can and do vary, making collective action difficult.[6]

The success of the associations in translating their concerns into policy is hard to gauge. Sub-federal jurisdictions have been wary of federal pre-emption regarding state and local regulatory practices and have sought to ensure that they are not liable for federal trade commitments. Many state legislatures have passed resolutions to provide consent before they are bound by any trade obligations, because governors had decided on their commitment to successive procurement agreements with limited legislative intervention. The Uruguay Round's initial thirty-seven states that committed to opening up state procurement has declined in subsequent agreements. Only nineteen states chose to commit to the Dominican Republic-Central America Free Trade Agreement in 2004, and subsequently nine states committed to the free trade agreement with Peru in 2006 – a significant diminishing of support from that of the WTO procurement agreement a decade earlier. The NCSL urged the Obama administration to safeguard the rights of sub-federal jurisdictions in international trade agreements by affirming the president's executive order on pre-empting state laws and extending it to international as well as domestic decisions (NCSL 2013; Public Citizen 2009). The NCSL lobbied for explicit congressional action if state laws were pre-empted, as well as for indemnity for states from any claims brought against the United States for state regulatory actions. Similar concerns were raised by attorneys general and by other state and local organizations such as the NGA and the National Association of Counties about how compliance with international obligations could undermine state and local regulatory initiatives.

While the administration has identified certain trade-related dispute-resolution mechanisms that it wants to change or even eliminate, investor-state dispute has become a flashpoint in trade negotiations at the state level. State-specific concerns were evident in the final TPP agreement in terms of the right to "regulate in the public interest," albeit this did not go far enough in addressing state concerns about investment agreements. These issues were equally salient in TTIP discussions, as states have raised ongoing concerns about their liabilities under prior trade commitments that undermined their public welfare objectives at the state level in areas such as health, safety, and environmental regulations (Kukucha 2016, 15; Public Citizen 2009). The NCSL pushed a resolution rejecting the TPP on the grounds that the provisions in the agreement infringed further on their sovereign legal and regulatory rights. Furthermore, NCSL indicated that it would not support any bilateral investment treaties or free trade agreements containing investor-state-dispute-settlement provisions (NCSL 2013). More than thirty states were actively engaged in deliberations on the TPP and TTIP negotiations, bringing together more than three hundred state representatives at various annual conventions and forums hosted by the major national associations.[7] However, the NGA has not taken a stance on either TTIP or TPP, preserving its brokerage function in a more partisan political climate.[8] Although some individual governors have taken positions on specific trade negotiations, they are also conscious of the politicization and contention surrounding trade deals; therefore, they tend to focus on related issues such as investment incentives, logistics, competiveness, and partnerships. Specific state-level caucuses have more forcibly expressed their views. The state environmental caucus has focused its opposition on environmental and energy issues as a result of the provisions sought by trading partners on the export of gas and oil from the United States, and the labour and development caucus wants sovereignty impact assessments for any international trade and investment agreements under negotiation (NCSL 2013).

American Internal Market and International Trade

The institutional design of the American internal market is now under increased scrutiny, as domestic regulations are proving problematic for international trade agreements. The management of that interstate regulatory diversity has been addressed differently in federal systems because the allocation of regulatory competences has been significantly shaped by the institutional alignments that occurred early in the formative stages of federations. Although barriers to the free movement of goods, services, labour, and capital exist in a number of federations (Anderson 2012; Egan 2015), generating a variety of efforts in Australia, Europe, and Canada to promote internal trade liberalization, the issue has been markedly absent in the US literature. While, in principle, US markets are more integrated in terms of free flow of goods, services, and factors of production as a result of constitutional adjudication to promote interstate commerce, the durability of states in the economic sphere is a product of constitutionally sanctioned police powers. The effect is to allow regulatory diversity across jurisdictions. Although these regulatory powers may be legitimate exercises of state autonomy if they are in the public interest, they may not be discriminatory against out-of-state producers if they apply equally to all producers (Hinarejos 2012, 4). Where states opt for specific requirements to address local concerns or protect local producers, this can pose an additional burden on out-of-state producers, leading to direct discrimination. Regardless of regulatory intent, the activity of sub-federal jurisdictions through the so-called police powers is being reshaped by the shift from tariff liberalization to regulatory liberalization (Young 2016). Trade partners are advocating for the removal of discriminatory local and state provisions in the new generation of trade agreements. States are now being drawn into trade negotiations across a breadth of issues. As economic integration is a long-term driver of the new trade agenda, it puts pressure on divergent local standards and practices. In some areas US rules are less centralized and liberalized than in other federal systems. As the United States continues to promote market opening, seeking to incorporate new obligations on government procurement, investment, intellectual property, and services, it faces domestic constraints stemming from the resilience of its internal barriers to trade, which have been criticized by trade partners seeking reciprocal liberalization.

Nevertheless, a closer look at the US internal market shows that it is much less integrated than the European Union (EU) one, which may seem surprising as the United States is a federal state (Egan 2012, 2015; Hoffman, Parsons, and Springer 2017). US state regulations cover services, energy, procurement, licensing, and a number of agricultural and product standards where the possible negative effects of trade discrimination have led trade partners to push for sub-federal liberalization. Not surprisingly, states exhibit a defensive zeal to protect their policies from liberalization commitments. Yet domestically state actions have generally been reviewed in terms of interstate commerce, which is an exclusive federal power. Many of the state measures restricting interstate trade have remained in place if they burden internal trade indirectly (Schütze 2017). States can point to a legitimate policy objective to maintain trade-restricting measures with the result that certain regulatory powers remain at the sub-federal level in the absence of congressional action. Given that some of the issues under negotiation fall under exclusive or shared competencies in the United States, the more recent trade agreements cover fields as diverse as services, energy, procurement, licensing, and technical barriers to trade where the regulatory activity of states is significant. Assessing the trade effects of such domestic policies is difficult because regulatory choices can vary by state; in some states, for example, licensing rules cover specific trades, and in other cases there are no licensing, certification, or legal requirements to practice. For instance, California regulates 385 occupations, whereas Washington regulates only 32; overall licensing covers around 30 per cent of the workforce, and in some cases occupational licensing laws forbid the offering of services if state requirements have not been met. Absent federal leadership, states can generate a patchwork of policies that can create uncomfortable trade-offs between jurisdictional sovereignty and trade liberalization, as they seek economic investment while placing some sectors off limits through the continuation of subsidies and exemptions.

To illustrate, several areas of contention in recent trade agreements highlight how sub-federal jurisdictions have complicated TTIP and TPP and further complicated the renegotiation of NAFTA. In trade talks with the United States, the EU has pushed for disciplines on subsidies, which have exploded at the sub-federal level. The United States has not included subsidies disciplines in past trade agreements. While the EU includes restrictive provisions on state aids and subsidies, US local governments and states continue to offer a myriad of tax incentives to business. The sheer scale of US subsidies considerably dwarfs that of Europe's. Between 2010 and 2014 the United States had seventy-four subsidy packages over USD 100 million each, the EU just six (Thomas 2012, n.d.). The deal that Donald Trump brokered with Carrier Corporation offered another manifestation of this strategy. Although constitutional limits have not been placed on such widespread subsidies and investment practices under the commerce clause, the EU has lobbied to counteract such trade-distortive subsidies at the subnational level (Inside U.S. Trade, 26 April 2013). Even though research has shown that tax breaks to encourage economic relocation are economically inefficient and wasteful, the United States has not included subsidies disciplines in past bilateral or regional trade agreements. The United States does not have anything similar to the European state-aid code, and the federal government has the legal authority only to control state subsidies that are exempt from WTO rules. Although the EU pushed for more transparency on subsidies in the United States, more than half of local and state subsidies went to large corporations, amounting to around USD 80 billion per year (*New York Times*, 1 December 2012).

A second area affecting sub-federal jurisdictions is the massive public-procurement market, with a significant portion of contracts being at the state and local level. It is estimated that the market is USD 1 trillion at the state and local levels, making this around 80 per cent of the total market, with procurement amounting to 10 per cent of US gross domestic product (Hufbauer and Moran 2015). The United States discriminates by allowing domestic producers to have a price advantage over foreign firms; specific state preferences for local residents and firms; and minority set-asides. Consequently, federal, state, and local government procurement rules often discriminate against out-of-state bids. For example, motor oils and fuels in Alabama for the Department of Transportation must be bought in the county where they will be consumed. In Colorado, state agencies must give preference to Colorado firms for the purchase of professional services, and in Idaho, all those awarded municipal, state, and local contracts for school construction and maintenance must employ 95 per cent local residents.

Although the potential gains from liberalizing government procurement are substantial, it is predominantly US federal entities that are included in specific trade agreements. Sub-federal jurisdictions were added to the WTO's Agreement on Government Procurement in 1994, but commitments differed between states, with specific exemptions being requested by individual states. NAFTA allowed for sub-federal jurisdictions to join on a voluntary basis. The United States has faced increased pressure from trade partners, but this is unlikely to change the impact on states.

The United States indicated that the TPP would not cover any new state or local government procurement commitments, declaring that sub-federal coverage was off the table according to past practice. The voluntary approach to procurement has received widespread criticism from trade partners, notably Canada and the EU, especially as the bulk of procurement contracts are at the state and local level. When states are participants – as distinct from regulators in the marketplace – they can discriminate with specific provisions favouring in-state firms or products, preferential bids from local suppliers, or outright bans on goods and services from outside of the home state (Hoffman, Parsons, and Springer 2017). The EU pushed the United States, with limited success, to open up procurement in states and cities to allow European firms to bid on public contracts, but it was able to push Canadian provinces and territories to make broad commitments in CETA negotiations (see Schram in this volume for an alternative view). The EU has argued that federal procurement open to European companies is much lower than US figures suggest. The openness of the market is reduced by the set-aside for American companies under various provisions of US law for small and medium-sized enterprises, "Buy American" requirements, and restrictions put in place by the Berry Amendment for military contracts.

While the multiplicity of regulatory practices can hinder imports and raise market-entry barriers, states can also be sources of policy diffusion and emulation across sub-federal markets. For example, the making of environmental or consumer regulations is not the exclusive realm of federal politics. State laws could in fact serve as a catalyst to promote regulatory cooperation in international trade. While TTIP sought to promote sectoral coordination in cosmetics, it was stymied by differences in animal testing between the United States and the EU. Yet three states – New Jersey, California, and New York – have banned animal testing, bringing them into alignment with European norms. Similarly, differences between the United States and the EU on genetically modified foods have been divisive in the trade arena. Yet legislation on genetically modified food labelling has been introduced in thirty states and successfully passed in several states, including Vermont, Maine, and Connecticut, though implementation is contingent on neighbouring states adopting similar requirements. Concerns about the consequences of such a regulatory patchwork of standards have led to unsuccessful legislative efforts to pre-empt state laws by establishing federal rules for genetically modified food labelling. Although states have opted to expand regulatory protections in some instances, aligning their policies with prospective trade partners, they have also continued to support trade-distorting measures that undermine the internal market. While Canada, Australia, and Europe have focused on dismantling the barriers that continue to inhibit internal trade, with varying degrees of success, the United States has not focused on the relationship between internal and international trade. There is no conscious policy to address internal trade barriers that compares to the legislative efforts in Europe and Canada. The United States has not consciously employed different modes of integration to tackle different regulatory barriers to trade across the entire market. Yet the United States has a number of tools to foster intergovernmental cooperation and promote multistate cooperation across a number of policy areas. Although interstate administrative agreements, mutual reciprocity, and state-administered compacts coordinate state activities, they are voluntary tools and are often only partial in coverage. Instead there are regulatory "peaks" where barriers remain as state rules continue to diverge; firms have to comply with multiple requirements, with limited pressures for coordination or approximation (Young 2004, 393). Although American trade policy is centralized, trade partners have criticized internal market fragmentation and the persistence of US state barriers that foster illiberal practices (Weiler 1994).

Conclusion

International trade agreements have encroached upon domestic areas of jurisdiction as trade agendas have expanded to include many behind-the-border issues. This has created pressure on federal governments to ensure the compliance of sub-federal jurisdictions. Most scholars in this volume note that deep integration agreements create institutional constraints that make agreement more problematic. Yet the United States has not adjusted its negotiating practice to integrate sub-federal jurisdictions. In the United States, states are not directly included in trade policy negotiations, though there are established consultative mechanisms at the federal level to provide formal review of any negotiated trade agreement. States are one of the many interests engaged in advocacy and lobbying for their institutional self-interest, but they are dwarfed by the influence and access of trade associations, business groups, and individual corporations. States have also been on the receiving end of both intense lobbying efforts by third countries, including Canada, Mexico, and the EU, to mitigate the effects of punitive tariffs, and trade discussions regarding NAFTA renegotiation and TTIP.

For US states, the core issue in trade politics is more about the federally adopted trade commitments and the politics of intergovernmental management involved in the implementation of any international trade agreement. Many observers argue that states lack the resources to follow ongoing trade negotiations; their interest is more in terms of promotional programs and activities to attract foreign trade and investment. The result is a patchwork of activities, with some states being more engaged at the sub-federal level in following trade negotiations through legislative or bureaucratic advocacy and deliberation. What has become a lightning rod of criticism for most states is the investor-state provisions that challenge state authority, generating long-standing lobbying efforts to exclude them from the free trade agreement.

US states are concerned about their ability to maintain jurisdiction over certain economic, agricultural, and labour issues because the US internal market is not uniform. As such, the United States is characterized by asymmetrical trade liberalization, in contrast to the EU where the common commercial policy and its obligations apply to all member states, creating a credible commitment that arises from treaty obligations. As the Trump administration seeks changes in trade agreements, the re-emergence of trade as a high-profile political issue in the United States should not ignore the opportunities for sub-federal jurisdictions to seek specific outcomes. As states continue to see manufacturing sectors suffer from the effects of cheap imports and economic decline, they may push for trade remedies rather than trade liberalization. Alternatively, states may seek to preserve trade commitments if they perceive specific benefits for local industries or if they have become integrated into supply chains and are more exposed to any changes in trade agreements.

Although trade politics may focus primarily on the horizontal relations between the legislature and the executive in the United States, sub-federal jurisdictions complicate the negotiation and implementation of international trade agreements. Trade agreements tend to expose regulatory inconsistencies throughout federal systems, clarifying the barriers *between* different sub-federal jurisdictions that could impede commerce. While Canada, Australia, and the EU have sought to address such internal constraints through political and legislative initiatives, the United States does not view internal barriers arising from divergent state rules as necessitating further reform, even though they have complicated recent trade negotiations and are likely to be salient issues in any future trade negotiations.

NOTES

1 An earlier version of this chapter was presented at the EUSA Biennial Conference in Miami on 5 May 2017. I am grateful to Laurie Buonomo and Maria Helena Guimareas for comments on an earlier draft. This research was funded by a DSRA grant from the School of International Service and a Council of Foreign Relations fellowship.
2 Under the tenth amendment to the United States Constitution, the powers not delegated to the federal government are reserved to the states or to the people. Police power is exercised by the legislative and executive branches of the various states through the enactment and enforcement of laws.
3 There is not an optimal distribution of federal versus state power. The United States is premised on a "dual federalism" model in which state and federal institutions govern largely separate spheres defined by regulatory subject matters. State powers are often referred to as "police powers."
4 Personal interview, July 2016.
5 Personal interview, July 2016.
6 Personal interview, 2017.
7 Personal interview, 2017.
8 Personal interview, 2017.

REFERENCES

Anderson, George. 2012. *Internal Markets and Multi-Level Governance*. Oxford: Oxford University Press.

Autor, David, D. Dorn, and G. Hanson. 2016. "The China Shock: Learning from Labor Market Adjustment to Large Changes in Trade." National Bureau of Economic Research Working Paper, January.

Broschek, Jörg. 2014. "Pathways of Federal Reform: Australia, Canada, Germany, and Switzerland." *Publius* 45 (1): 51–76.

Broschek, Jörg, and Patricia Goff. 2016. Introductory paper presented at the Multilevel Politics of Trade conference, Waterloo, Ontario, 14–15 October 2016.

Cammissa, Anne Marie. 1995. *Governments as Interest Groups: Intergovernmental Lobbying and the Federal System*. Santa Barbara, CA: Prager.

Congressional Hearing before a Subcommittee of the Committee on Appropriations. 2010. House of Representatives, One Hundred Eleventh Congress, first session, part 4.

Egan, Michelle P. 2012. "Single Market." In *Oxford Handbook of the European Union*, edited by E. Jones, A. Menon, and S. Weatherill, 407–21. Oxford: Oxford University Press.

– ed. 2015. *Single Markets: Economic Integration in Europe and the United States*. Oxford: Oxford University Press.

Egan, Michelle, and Helena Guimarães. 2019. "The Dynamics of Federalism, Subnational Markets and Trade Policy-Making in Canada and the US." *Regional & Federal Studies* 29 (4): 459–78.

Fabbrini, Sergio. 2017. "Intergovernmentalism in the European Union: A Comparative Federalism Perspective." *Journal of European Public Policy* 4: 580–97.

Hinarejos Alicia. 2012. "Free Movement, Federalism, and Institutional Choice: A Canada-EU Comparison." *Cambridge Law Journal* 71: 537–66.

Hoffmann, Leif, C. Parsons, and B. Springer. 2017. "Hayek, Polanyi, and Single Markets: Or How Europe's Single Market Surpassed America's." European Union Studies Association biennial conference, 4–7 May 2017, Miami.

Hufbauer, Gary, and Tyler Moran. 2015. "Government Procurement in US Trade Agreements." Working paper. Florence, Italy: European University Institute.

IGPAC (Intergovernmental Policy Advisory Committee on Trade). 1994. "The Uruguay Round of Multilateral Trade Negotiations." Unpublished. January

– 2004. Recommendations for Improving Federal-State Policy Coordination Memo. Unpublished. August.

Jachtenfuchs, Markus, and Christiane Kasack. 2017. "Balancing Sub-unit Autonomy and Collective Problem-Solving by Varying Exit and Voice: An Analytical Framework." *Journal of European Public Policy* 24 (4): 598–614.

Kukucha, Christopher J. 2013. "Canadian Sub-federal Governments and CETA: Overarching Themes and Future Trends." *International Journal* 68: 528–36.

- 2015. "Federalism Matters: Evaluating the Impact of Sub-Federal Governments in Canadian and American Foreign Trade." *Canadian Foreign Policy Journal* 21 (3): 224–37.

Lighthizer, Robert. 2017. Congressional Testimony as Nominee for USTR. https://www.congress.gov.

Moravscik, A. 1998. *The Choice for Europe*. Ithaca, NY: Cornell University Press.

NCSL (National Conference of State Legislatures). 2013. *Free Trade and Federalism*. http://www.ncsl.org.

Noll, Roger, and Robert E. Litan. 2018. "Extra Milk Exports to Canada under Trump's Rebranded NAFTA Will Be a Drop in the Bucket." Brookings Institution, 8 October 2018. https://www.brookings.edu.

Public Citizen. 2009. *State Rights and International Trade*. Washington, DC: Public Citizen.

Puetter, Uwe. 2012. "Europe's Deliberative Intergovernmentalism: The Role of the European Council." *Journal of European Public Policy* 19 (2): 161–78.

Ruggie, John G. 1982. "International Regimes, Transactions and Change: Embedded Liberalism in the Postwar Economic Order." *International Organization* 36 (2): 379–415.

Sabatier, Paul A., and Hank C. Jenkins-Smith. 1993. *Policy Change and Learning: An Advocacy Coalition Approach*. Boulder, CO: Westview Press.

Schaeffer, Matthew P. 2001. "Conscientious State Legislators and the Cultures of Compliance and Liberalization Relating to International Trade Agreements." *Proceedings of the Annual Meeting (American Society of International Law)* 95: 52–7.

Schütze, Robert, ed. 2017. *From International to Federal Market*. Oxford: Oxford University Press.

Thomas, Kenneth. 2010. *Investment Incentives and the Global Competition for Capital*. London: Palgrave Macmillan.

- n.d. *How Corporate Giveaways Hurt American Communities*. Scholars Strategy Network. https://scholars.org.

US Chamber of Commerce. 2018. Trade Works, Tariffs Don't. 2 July 2018. https://www.uschamber.com/tariffs

Weiler, Conrad. 1994. "Foreign-Trade Agreements: A New Federal Partner?" *Publius* 24 (3): 113–33.

Young, Alasdair R. 2004. "The Incidental Fortress: The Single European Market and World Trade." *Journal of Common Market Studies*, 42, 393–414.

- 2016. "'Not Your Parents' Trade Politics': The Transatlantic Trade and Investment Partnership Negotiations." *Review of International Political Economy* 23 (3): 345–78.

5 Mexican Sub-federal Actors and the Negotiation and Implementation of Free Trade Agreements

JORGE A. SCHIAVON AND MARCELA LÓPEZ-VALLEJO

The participation of sub-federal actors – sub-federal governments, business, and civil society – in the drawing up of free trade agreements (FTAs) points to a new type of multilevel trade governance, either because they demand to participate in negotiation and implementation or because the counterparts of the treaty invite them to do so. Such is the case of two recent European Union (EU) FTAs – one with Canada and the other with the United States. However, this participation is not a common practice and cannot be generalized to all federal states and to all FTAs. Sub-federal participation in Mexico, the EU's other North American partner, shows a different story. Mexico is one of the countries with the most international treaties and FTAs signed worldwide, yet Mexican sub-federal actors have not fully participated in their negotiation and decision-making processes. This is the case of the FTA signed with the EU in 1999 and renegotiated in 2017: civil society was consulted only in the first stage, and sub-federal governments had no say. In the 1994 North American Free Trade Agreement (NAFTA), also renegotiated during 2017–18, sub-federal governments were not consulted, and, although some non-governmental organizations (NGOs) were present in the debates in Congress, only one part of civil society was considered in the actual negotiations: business. This situation can also be seen when analysing bilateral FTAs signed by Mexico.

We contend that, as in most federations worldwide where democracy and accountability are not substantive practices, sub-federal actors participate only in the ratification and implementation phases. For sub-federal actors to participate in other stages of the FTAs, a more inclusive legal framework and more institutional capacities are necessary.

The current legal framework in Mexico allows sub-federal governments (states and municipalities) and civil society to participate in public debates led by Senate commissions, a power granted by the 2004

Law on the Approval of Economic International Treaties (LAEIT) (Diario Oficial de la Federación 2004). Since the 1990s, sub-federal actors have increasingly requested to participate in all stages of FTAs, and especially in the twenty-first century when the transition to democracy was forged and civil society found political space to fight for concrete topics. In the case of states and municipalities, this desire can be explained by a legal power that they have had since 1992, which allows them to sign inter-institutional agreements (IIAs). This means that they have the capacity to sign international agreements without requiring the Senate's approval. State and municipal governments have increasingly used this capability granted by the Law on Celebration of Treaties (LCT) of 1992 (Diario Oficial de la Federación 1992) for many purposes, mainly economic cooperation.

The central argument of this chapter is that even though Mexican civil society has become more involved in the negotiation process of FTAs during the last two decades, the role of sub-federal governments has remained limited. This limitation comes from the restrictive legal framework in which vertical federalism operates and from a lack of institutional capacities to support these negotiation activities. In Mexican federalism the decentralization of competences (e.g., promoting the signing of IIAs by sub-federal governments) competes with the centralization of resources at the federal government. Centralization of fiscal revenue and the lack of capacities of sub-federal units to collect taxes (other than by municipalities from real estate and for public lighting, and by states from vehicles, tourism, and entertainment) create dependency on the federal government, promote "clientelism" (party favouritism and political favours), and prevent sub-federal units from developing capabilities for negotiation and implementation of FTAs.

Institutional design also limits civil society's participation to public debates in Congress, where opinions generally legitimize the decisions that have already been made. This shows that the inconsistency of democratic practices and the lack of substantive democracy prevent civil society from promoting FTA agendas and participating in the decision-making process. Therefore, civil society generally contests FTAs; these agreements are perceived as favouring political elites, rather than benefiting the broader population. This claim was at the core of the renegotiation of NAFTA, where the equalizing of salaries for automotive workers in all three countries conditions the signing of the treaty and especially its implementation. Similarly, in the renegotiation of the EU-Mexico Free Trade Agreement it was reiterated that civil society participation in all stages of the negotiation was crucial. Nonetheless, in this agreement it fell short of what was expected.

Although participation by NGOs and the role of business and municipalities are fundamental for legitimizing and implementing FTAs, this chapter focuses primarily on the legal instruments and institutional capacities that Mexican states have in order to participate in FTA negotiations and implementation, and assesses how much they actually participate in these activities. The chapter is divided into four sections. The first analyses the constitutional and legal provisions regarding the powers of Mexican states to conduct international relations. We underscore a dual approach to free trade: through federal FTAs to be implemented in a vertical federal scheme, and through IIAs signed directly by states to attract investment, promote their exports, and seek international decentralized cooperation. The second section explains the participation of Mexican sub-federal governments in the process of economic liberalization in Mexico. We argue that even though states have not participated in the negotiation of major bilateral and multilateral FTAs, they have dealt with their implementation. As the general argument notes, legal restrictions and institutional capacities determine the level of involvement by Mexican states in trade. The third section conducts an in-depth study of the capacities of Mexican sub-federal governments to participate actively in the negotiation and implementation of FTAs. The fourth and last section analyses the state of Jalisco's participation in the EU-Mexico Free Trade Agreement. Finally, the conclusions summarize the most important findings of the chapter.

The Legal Framework for Sub-federal Participation in Free Trade Agreements

In Mexico the Constitution establishes the legal framework for conducting foreign policy, and the powers of the three branches of government are clearly defined. Although there is no provision giving the states the power to participate directly in international affairs, there is no explicit prohibition either. Article 124 of the Constitution establishes that "the powers that are not explicitly defined in the Constitution ... are reserved for the states." In the specific case of treaties it is more precise, establishing that "states cannot, in any case, enter alliances, treaties or coalitions with other states or foreign powers" (article 117.I). The Constitution also states that the Supreme Court of Justice has the power to solve the conflicts of competencies between the three levels of government (federal, state, and municipal) (article 105) in all topics, including foreign policy and international agreements.

The specific attributions on foreign policy are defined in the Organic Law of Federal Public Administration, in which article 28.I establishes that the Secretariat of Foreign Affairs (Secretaría de Relaciones Exteriores, SRE) has the power to coordinate the external actions of all the ministries and agencies of the federal executive and sub-federal governments without affecting their powers. As such, the SRE's main responsibility is to conduct and coordinate foreign policy. To do so, the secretariat has the power to participate in all types of treaties, agreements, and conventions in which the country takes part.

The regulation for the negotiation of treaties can be found in the Constitution and the LCT of 1992. There are two types of international instruments: first, the treaty, which is the agreement typified in the Constitution that must be approved by the Senate to be valid; and second, the IIA, which is defined as "the agreement ruled by public international law, concluded ... between any ministry or decentralized agency of the public federal, state or municipal administrations, and one or many foreign government agencies or international organizations" (article 2.II).

Article 76 of the Constitution, alongside the LCT and the LAEIT, mandates that all treaties are to be ratified by the Senate. The Senate must ratify treaties as a whole with no possibility to change or exclude parts of them. States have no say in the negotiations of these treaties, although the fate of treaties lies indirectly in their hands, as most of the provisions are implemented at the local level. The LAEIT also establishes that in the FTA negotiation process, Senate commissions should be appointed to oversee the debate on the advantages and disadvantages of the agreement, with other federal public agencies being involved. During this stage, articles 11 and 12 of LAEIT note that all ideas coming from citizens, business, unions, civil associations, and state and municipal governments should be addressed in public hearings. The commissions are the filters for these opinions. After the debates take place, the commissions must give an opinion about the FTA to the executive agency or secretary that is representing Mexico in the negotiations, almost always the secretary of economy and the SRE. In this sense, sub-federal governments have the legal prerogative to participate in the deliberations about the FTA within the Mexican federal scheme. At the time of implementation, states and municipalities are usually implicated in dispute-resolution mechanisms or in building institutional capacity to operate FTAs.

One of the most important contributions of the LCT is that it incorporates the figure of IIAs, thereby establishing the legal basis for sub-federal governments to participate in the international arena. At the same time, this law states explicitly that "the areas covered by inter-institutional agreements must be strictly circumscribed within the powers of the ministries or decentralized agencies of the different levels of government" (article 2.II). The law also states that the bureaucratic agencies that enter into these types of agreements must keep the SRE informed and that the SRE has the power to revise the IIAs and determine if they are legal. If they are, the secretariat registers them and keeps an official record (article 7) through the Registry of IIAs, which had 894 IIAs on record by July 2018.

Most international counterparts to Mexican states are governmental, accounting for more than two-thirds of all IIAs. Some IIAs have been signed with international organizations (12 per cent), especially from the United Nations system; NGOs (3 per cent); and private partners (17 per cent), mostly universities and research centres. Only the state of Chiapas concentrates most of its international cooperation on partners other than governments, such as international organizations, NGOs, and private actors, including the United Nations, the EU, and foreign universities. More than one-third of the states (twelve out of thirty-two) have IIAs only with governmental counterparts (Schiavon 2015).

The international activities of Mexican states are restricted to those areas in which they have powers; therefore, it is not surprising that the areas covered by the IIAs concentrate on the strengthening of human capital through education, culture, science, technology, and human-resource training; the generation of welfare through the promotion of trade, investment, and tourism; and, to a lesser extent, the improvement of the environment, urban development, and security (Schiavon 2015).

A huge variation in the number of IIAs signed by Mexican states can be observed, ranging from nil (Baja California Sur) to 139 (Jalisco). More than two-thirds of the IIAs (468 of 668, representing 70 per cent of the total) have been signed by only ten states (less than one-third of the Mexican federal units). Almost one-third (32 per cent) of the IIAs are concentrated in two states only: Jalisco and Chiapas. Taking into consideration the level of government that signs the IIAs, there is a balance between state and municipal actors; 366 (55 per cent) were signed by state authorities, and 302 (45 per cent) by municipal governments. The preferred type of IIA concluded by Mexican states is a sisterhood agreement, which accounts for 42 per cent of all the IIAs signed. The Sisterhood agreement was the first form to link cities prior to the LCT of 1992. This cooperation strategy started in the 1950s with the organization Sister Cities International and was used by Mexican municipalities. Originally, they promoted exchanges of administrative personnel, decision makers, students, and society. These agreements evolved, and today they are regulated by SRE and represent an intention for cooperation

5.1 Inter-institutional Agreements by Federal Unit, Level of Government, and Type of Agreement

Federal unit	IIAs	% total	Level of government						Type of agreement				
			State	% total	Municipal	% total	Sisterhood	% total	Other	% total
Aguascalientes	7	1.05	3	42.86	4	57.14	4	57.14	3	42.86
Baja California	14	2.10	6	42.86	8	57.14	4	28.57	10	71.43
Baja California Sur	0	0.00	0	0.00	0	0.00	0	0.00	0	0.00
Campeche	9	1.35	3	33.33	6	66.67	5	55.56	4	44.44
Chihuahua	28	4.19	22	78.57	6	21.43	4	14.29	24	85.71
Chiapas	74	11.08	62	83.78	12	16.22	7	9.46	67	90.54
Coahuila	9	1.35	2	22.22	7	77.78	7	77.78	2	22.22
Colima	1	0.15	1	100.00	0	0.00	1	100.00	0	0.00
Mexico City	38	5.69	38	100.00	0	0.00	15	39.47	23	60.53
Durango	15	2.25	13	86.67	2	13.33	2	13.33	13	86.67
Guanajuato	20	2.99	8	40.00	12	60.00	11	55.00	9	45.00
Guerrero	6	0.90	2	33.33	4	66.67	2	33.33	4	66.67
Hidalgo	17	2.54	10	58.82	7	41.18	7	41.18	10	58.82
Jalisco	139	20.81	90	64.75	49	35.25	43	30.94	96	69.06
State of México	49	7.34	17	34.69	32	65.31	33	67.35	16	32.65
Michoacán	37	5.54	11	29.73	26	70.27	25	67.57	12	32.43
Morelos	7	1.05	1	14.29	6	85.71	6	85.71	1	14.29
Nayarit	6	0.90	4	66.67	2	33.33	1	16.67	5	83.33

(Continued)

5.1 Continued

Federal unit	IIAs	% total	Level of government				Type of agreement			
			State	% total	Municipal	% total	Sisterhood	% total	Other	% total
Nuevo León	39	5.84	7	17.95	32	82.05	28	71.79	11	28.21
Oaxaca	16	2.40	14	87.50	2	12.50	1	6.25	15	93.75
Puebla	21	3.14	8	38.10	13	61.90	12	57.14	9	42.86
Querétaro	15	2.25	6	40.00	9	60.00	5	33.33	10	66.67
Quintana Roo	23	3.44	6	26.09	17	73.91	16	69.57	7	30.43
San Luis Potosí	14	2.10	1	7.14	13	92.86	12	85.71	2	14.29
Sinaloa	2	0.30	1	50.00	1	50.00	0	0.00	2	100.00
Sonora	14	2.10	13	92.86	1	7.14	1	7.14	13	92.86
Tabasco	6	0.90	5	83.33	1	16.67	0	0.00	6	100.00
Tamaulipas	6	0.90	0	0.00	6	100.00	6	100.00	0	0.00
Tlaxcala	2	0.30	2	100.00	0	0.00	0	0.00	2	100.00
Veracruz	15	2.25	1	6.67	14	93.33	13	86.67	2	13.33
Yucatán	11	1.65	7	63.64	4	36.36	2	18.18	9	81.82
Zacatecas	8	1.20	2	25.00	6	75.00	4	50.00	4	50.00
TOTAL	668	100.00	366	54.79	302	45.21	277	41.47	391	58.53

Source: Schiavon, 2015.

(like a memorandum of understanding), technical transfers, or a specific program.

Mexican federal units, especially those with higher degrees of external activities, use IIAs as legally binding mechanisms to regulate and sustain their international relations with foreign counterparts. Most of the IIAs (97 per cent) were signed after the initiation of NAFTA, on 1 January 1994, and the opening of the Mexican economy. NAFTA opened two areas of opportunity for local development by Mexican states: a huge market with reduced barriers for their exports, and an important source of foreign direct investment. These two opportunities generated the incentives for Mexican states to promote themselves actively internationally, thus leading to decentralization in external economic promotion.

The activity of Mexican states has increased over time. Before NAFTA, only twenty-one IIAs had been signed (3 per cent of the current total); the number of IIAs increased during the following administrations. Under the Enrique Peña administration (2012–18), in only two years (2012–14), seventy-one (11 per cent) IIAs were signed and registered by the SRE.

Mexico's Free Trade Agreements and the Role of States

In the 1980s Mexico started a liberalization process, dismantling the protectionist scheme that had been in place since the 1940s, in which the import-substitution model had relied on national industries, especially on Petróleos Mexicanos (PEMEX, the state oil monopoly). In 1986 the country entered the General Agreement on Tariffs and Trade (GATT), opening its economy to free trade. One of the main drivers of this decision was the collapse of oil prices, which resulted in the reduction of more than 50 per cent of Mexican oil exports during the period from 1985 to 1986 (Cárdenas 2015, 680–5).

The trend towards free trade intensified in the 1990s, with the country seeking to insert itself in a neoliberal free-trade world, which would grant Mexico a position as an emerging and competing economy. The main goal of liberalization was to strengthen international ties and normalize trade relations with strategic partners, especially with the United States. The United States had already signed an FTA with Canada in 1989, and Mexico set its sights on such an agreement. Canada was reluctant at first to participate in the negotiation of a trilateral agreement, due to fears about job relocation to a more flexible Mexican market in terms of labour and environmental regulation. The government of Brian Mulroney eventually joined the trilateral negotiations, presenting this new negotiation process as an opportunity to redeem the mistakes of the Canada-United States Free Trade Agreement, such as protecting cultural and indigenous industries (Ketterer, Bernhofen, and Milner 2014; Morales 2008; Vega Cánovas 2010; Wise 2011).

The negotiation of NAFTA took place in the three countries without the presence of sub-federal governments. During the negotiations Mexico's government approved the LCT, including the instrument of IIAs. This move may have been a palliative to the fact that no sub-federal government had been invited to the NAFTA negotiations. Other actors had much more influence in the process. NAFTA's chapter XI on investment protection opened the space for some multinational companies to participate at several negotiation tables, such as the three main US automakers (Gutiérrez-Haces 2008; Studer 2006). Twenty-three years later, NAFTA was renegotiated; the participation of business eclipsed that of both civil society and sub-federal governments once again. Nonetheless, certain Mexican and transnational civil-society organizations condemn FTAs by arguing that they are a political failure when they do not deliver promises of prosperity and well-being for workers (urban and rural) (RQIC 2017). Local governments in Mexico did not design strategies to participate actively in either the original NAFTA or its renegotiation.

In addition to entering GATT (which would be transformed in 1995 into the World Trade Organization, and Mexico immediately becoming a member) and signing NAFTA, Mexico entered the Organisation for Economic Co-operation and Development, in 1994, a few months after NAFTA came into force. The strategy of visibility and participation in key multilateral organizations led Mexico to become a member of the Asia-Pacific Economic Cooperation mechanism in the same year (Derbez 2002). This vigorous trade liberalization set the path for Mexico to sign several bilateral FTAs and other types of economic agreements with partners worldwide. The first FTAs enacted by Mexico were with Costa Rica (1994), Nicaragua (1999), and Chile (1999). Some other trade agreements were signed to achieve "economic complementarity," a formula established by the Treaty of Montevideo in 1980, with specific goals and a sectoral approach (Secretaría de Economía 2016b).

The 1990s trade liberalization had several effects in Mexico: (1) a new relationship with private companies and corporations under the negotiated rules (especially for investment and for labour and environmental standards); (2) the division of the economy into sectors with different rates of success or failure in achieving liberalization goals; (3) a lack of technical and financial capacity to reach competitive standards for some industries; (4) migration of workers out of sectors with little or no competitiveness; (5) a separation of the relationship between growth and development; (6) a new legal and normative relation with national and international partners to solve controversies (by international panels); (7) the need to create and redesign institutions to manage the new reality (for example, the need to reform article 27 of the Constitution, regarding land ownership); (8) the privatization of more than 90 per cent of state-owned companies to compete in a free market; and (9) an increasing divide in society and public opinion, and contestation over the costs and benefits of free trade (for example, in the transportation and corn sectors) and of non-tariff barriers (Cárdenas 2015; García-Zamora 2011; Morales 2008; Vega Cánovas 2010).

The road to free trade was far from smooth. Strong protests against NAFTA and free trade took place all over the country, alongside the Zapatista indigenous rebellion that started on the same day as NAFTA's entry into force, 1 January 1994. In addition, the euphoria of free trade and the Mexican opening to the world was blurred by one of the worst financial crises faced by the country, the "Tequila Crisis" in December 1994 (Cárdenas 2015).

At the end of the 1990s Mexico signed its second most important FTA, the Global Agreement with the European Union, which included an EU-Mexico Free Trade Agreement. The "democratic clause" in this agreement established that respect for human rights, and democratic processes, were essential conditions for the signing of the treaty.[1] Although the treaty had no direct relationship with sub-federal governments, Mexican society expected free and open participation at local levels (politically and economically). However, the voice of states was heard only through some Senate discussions during the negotiation.

During 2017 and 2018 this agreement was renegotiated and included new topics such as transparency, anti-corruption, sustainable development, competitiveness of small and medium-sized enterprises, digital trade, and telecommunications. Albeit in a very limited way, the agreement promoted states' participation in public consultations in the first stages of the negotiation (European Commission 2016, 2018), as will be discussed in section four of this chapter. A complementary FTA was also signed with the European Free Trade Association (Iceland, Liechtenstein, Norway, and Switzerland) in 2000; its review mechanism agreed in 2016 included consultation for stakeholders, among them state governments. Relations with the EU are driving Mexican states to look for a new generation of agreements in which a multi-stakeholder approach during the entire process of negotiation guarantees better implementation, closing the gap between the traditional exclusivity of foreign policy (for trade) and the day-to-day reality of localities and territories.

Although sub-federal governments have participated little at bilateral and multilateral FTA negotiation tables, they experience the direct effects of free trade. On the one hand, new opportunities are created to attract foreign direct investment. On the other hand, some sub-federal governments realize that their economies and population are not prepared for competition at a global level, experiencing massive migration flows to Mexico City or the United States (Durand 2016). In some cases, social protests spark another type of relations between the European Parliament and some of these communities. In 2014 two members of the Parliament visited some wind farms in Oaxaca that had been developed with European investment, to check the legitimacy of local social claims.

Under the strong belief that a spillover effect would generate development in Mexican states and localities, the country has continued to foster more trade liberalization through FTAs in the twenty-first century. New FTAs were signed with Israel (2000), El Salvador, Guatemala, and Honduras (2000), Uruguay (2003), Japan (2004), Central America (Costa Rica, El Salvador, Guatemala, Honduras, and Nicaragua, 2012), and Panama (2015). Some bilateral FTAs are still under negotiation (with Turkey and Jordan). Sub-federal governments have not participated directly in any of these negotiations to date (OAS 2016).

In addition to these treaties the Mexican federal government found mechanisms to refine negotiation schemes to facilitate liberalization. Agreements for economic complementarity were negotiated and enacted with Bolivia in 2010 and with Mercosur partners in 2003 (reinforcing existing ones, such as the one with Brazil). Sectoral agreements were established with Paraguay (2000) and Ecuador (2007). Mexico has also negotiated more than thirty agreements for investment protection since 2000 and participated in several comprehensive regional forums (which seek trade liberalization, among their objectives), such as the Pacific Alliance (2012) (Secretaría de Economía 2016).[2]

The most emblematic treaty was the Trans-Pacific Partnership (TPP).[3] Mexican sub-federal governments were not included in the negotiations, despite annex I-A of chapter 1's recognition of the regional level of government, which in the case of Mexico meant states (municipalities and other jurisdictions were not included). Article 2.3(2) established that "the treatment to be accorded by a Party means [in agreement with article III of GATT 1994], with respect to a regional level of government, treatment no less favorable than the most favorable treatment that the regional level of government accords to any like, directly competitive or substitutable goods, as the case may be, of the Party of which it forms a part" (OAS 2016). Although no further mention is made of states, by including this clause the TPP was the first FTA to recognize that a key component of trade is local participation, especially when national treatment rules are being defined and addressed.

Institutional Capacities of Sub-federal Governments for Agreement Implementation

The participation of Mexican sub-federal governments in FTAs takes place only at the implementation phase. We argue that even though they are willing to have a more active role in this phase (and in negotiations), limited institutional capacities prevent most of them (especially municipalities) from participating effectively in the process. To understand better the institutional structure, activities, personnel profile, and financial and legal capacities – as well as the central objectives, concerns, needs, and successes of the agencies or offices in charge of the international relations of sub-federal governments in Mexico – a comprehensive survey tackling all these points was conducted during the second semester of 2014.[4]

The central findings of the survey are contrasted with the information on the international relations of states and the IIAs previously discussed, to provide a comprehensive analysis. The first variable to be analysed is the type of organizations and agencies in charge of international affairs in the Mexican federal states. Of the twenty-six cases, seventeen (65 per cent) have a specific area, office, or agency in charge of coordinating the international relations of the state government. It is important to mention that most of the international relations areas were created recently. Only two states (Jalisco and Sonora) had established an international affairs agency before 2000. The institutional and administrative adscription of these agencies or areas also varies, although most (fifteen) are under the office of the governor.

Of all the state international agencies, only ten have institutionalized and regular budgets for their activities, and the rest depend on the budgets of the areas to which they are linked. Only two states have considerable budgets of more than USD 1 million per year (Puebla, with a yearly budget of MXN 50 million, and the State of Mexico, with MXN 27 million).[5] The rest of the agencies have substantially smaller budgets, ranging from MXN 0.5 million to 11.5 million. It should not be surprising that the states with institutionalized budgets also have the most full-time personnel.

In terms of their legal and statutory capacities, there is a huge variation in the legal documents that support not only the activities of the international agencies but also their strategic planning and organization. Most of the areas (fifteen of twenty-six) derive their responsibilities and activities from the State Development Plan (Plan Estatal de Desarrollo), a document that the state executives develop during their first year in office to establish the central objectives and priorities of their administrations. This document is more political than legal in nature and is therefore not legally binding, not only for the administration that proposes it but also, most important, for the next administration. Sixteen of the international areas have legally binding rules of action, twelve of them in the form of internal rules of procedure, two (Chiapas and the State of Mexico) in an organizational manual, one (Puebla) in an executive decree of creation, and one (Oaxaca) in the organic law of the state. The relevance of these legally binding documents is that they generate a bureaucratic structure that can become institutionalized, facilitating their permanence between administrations. Finally, fifteen of the international areas have strategic planning, and twelve of them develop yearly working plans that establish the specific activities that will be enacted during the year.

One of the strategies that states use to promote themselves internationally is the opening of representation offices abroad. Currently, only ten Mexican federal states have such offices: Baja California in San Diego (California); Chiapas in Salt Lake City (Utah); Colima in Lynwood (California); Mexico City and Durango, both in Los Angeles (California) and Chicago (Illinois); the State of Mexico in Houston (Texas), Chicago (Illinois), and Los Angeles (California); Guerrero in Santa Ana (California) and Chicago (Illinois); Jalisco in Chicago (Illinois); Oaxaca in Los Angeles (California); and Puebla in New York City (New York), Passaic (New Jersey), and Los Angeles (California).

What are the most important international and coordination activities conducted by the agencies in charge of the international relations of states in Mexico? As has been widely discussed, state governments conduct international activities to promote local development and welfare, especially through external promotion (to attract foreign direct investment and tourism; for international cooperation in education, culture, science, and technology; and for exports, among others).

To coordinate with other states in their process of internationalization, fifteen states said they were official members of the Asociación Mexicana de Oficinas de Asuntos Internacionales de los Estados, and one more state, Morelos, was in the process of becoming a member.[6] Twenty of them participate directly or indirectly in the international affairs commission of the Conferencia Nacional de Gobernadores, where political coordination between state governors takes place. The most important institutional relation of the international areas at the federal level is, not surprisingly, with the SRE, where all of them except Tlaxcala have direct and constant relations. Finally, most have contact and relations with Mexican representations abroad, twenty-one of them with Mexican embassies, and eighteen with Mexican consulates, especially with the network of fifty Mexican consulates in the United States, where 98.5 per cent of Mexican migrants reside.

To conduct their activities in terms of local coordination and external projection, the international affairs areas face considerable challenges (see table 5.2). Only half of them (fourteen) consider that their current legal and operative status facilitates the fulfilment of their responsibilities, and the most important challenges that they face in their everyday activities are insufficient budgets and staff members, as well as a lack of highly professional staff in international affairs at the local level.

How do these international affairs areas face and, to some extent, try to solve these challenges? Unfortunately they have limited intergovernmental mechanisms to coordinate with the activities of other state ministries, to communicate their actions locally and externally, and to evaluate their performance. Only twelve of them have permanent coordination mechanisms with other state agencies and ministries, nine have developed a communications strategy to share their activities at the local and external level, nine have institutional mechanisms to evaluate the fulfilment of their objectives, and nine have published books, newsletters, and reports of their accomplishments. What is surprising in the age of the internet and social networks is that only six states have an official web page for the international affairs office (Colima, Durango, State of Mexico, Guerrero, Puebla, and Sonora).

When the states are asked to qualify their international activities vis-à-vis Mexico's foreign policy, it is extremely interesting that twenty-one out of twenty-five states (84 per cent) consider their international affairs to be complementary to Mexico's foreign policy. Only two states (Querétaro and Guanajuato) think these activities are competitive, and Hidalgo perceives them as autonomous.

Finally, three open questions were included in the survey, asking the states to share up to three of the most important challenges they face, three of their current training needs, and three of the most relevant actions they have carried out to institutionalize and consolidate their internationalization into the future. The most cited challenges were being able to transition after a change of state governor; to strengthen interministerial coordination mechanisms; to solve the insufficiency of

State	Legal rules of procedure	Budget	Human resources	Knowledge and training	Inter-institutional coordination	Federal coordination	Strategic planning	Political support	Total challenges
Aguascalientes	No	No	No	No	No	No	No	No	0
Baja California	No	Yes	Yes	No	Yes	Yes	No	Yes	5
Baja California Sur	Yes	Yes	Yes	Yes	Yes	Yes	Yes	No	7
Chiapas	No	No	No	Yes	Yes	No	Yes	Yes	4
Chihuahua	N/A	N/A	N/A	N/A	N/A	N/A	N/A	N/A	N/A
Colima	No	Yes	Yes	Yes	No	No	No	No	3
Federal District	Yes	No	No	No	No	No	No	No	1
Durango	Yes	Yes	No	Yes	Yes	Yes	Yes	Yes	7
State of Mexico	Yes	Yes	Yes	Yes	No	Yes	No	No	5
Guanajuato	No	Yes	Yes	Yes	No	No	No	No	3
Guerrero	No	Yes	Yes	No	Yes	No	Yes	Yes	5
Hidalgo	Yes	No	Yes	Yes	Yes	Yes	Yes	Yes	7
Jalisco	Yes	Yes	No	Yes	Yes	Yes	No	No	5
Michoacán	Yes	Yes	No	Yes	Yes	Yes	Yes	Yes	7
Morelos	No	No	Yes	No	No	No	Yes	No	4
Nuevo León	Yes	No	No	No	No	No	Yes	No	2
Oaxaca	No	Yes	No	No	No	No	No	No	1
Puebla	No	No	No	No	No	No	No	No	0

State									
Querétaro	No	Yes	No	Yes	No	Yes	No	No	3
Quintana Roo	No	No	No	Yes	Yes	No	No	No	2
San Luis Potosí	No	No	No	No	No	No	No	No	0
Sonora	No	Yes	Yes	Yes	No	No	No	No	3
Tabasco	No	No	No	Yes	No	Yes	No	No	2
Tamaulipas	No	No	No	No	No	No	No	No	0
Tlaxcala	Yes	Yes	Yes	Yes	No	Yes	Yes	No	6
Yucatán	Yes	Yes	Yes	Yes	No	No	No	No	4

Source: Schiavon 2016.

budget and staff; to provide a legal framework and rules of procedure to the area; and to coordinate at the state level the international activities of the municipal governments.

The Participation of Mexican Sub-federal Governments in Free Trade Agreements

Although more than 85 per cent of its exports go to North America (mainly to the United States), Mexico receives 30 per cent of its investment from the EU, and trade with the EU was four times larger in 2017 than in 2000, when the agreement was enacted (Centro de Estudios Internacionales Gilberto Bosques 2018). This section underscores two instances of Mexican states' involvement in the EU-Mexico Trade Agreement. The first one accounts for the "democratic clause" included in the agreement, whereby states (business and civil society) had to participate in the negotiation process. The second exemplifies how some Mexican states, such as Jalisco, profit from the implementation of FTAs, especially from the agreement with the EU.

The EU-Mexico Free Trade Agreement and States' Limited Participation

Mexico signed the Global Agreement with the EU in 1997. As stated in the report of the twentieth Joint Parliamentary Commission in 2016,

> the European Union established itself as Mexico's third-largest global trading partner in the last 15 years, and its second-largest export market. The 251% increase in trade between the two parties between 1999 and 2014 and the European Union's 8.1% share of Mexico's worldwide trade are proof of this. (EU-Mexico Joint Parliamentary Committee 2016)

This relationship had trade-offs. As noted before, the agreement included a democratic clause, which in the 1990s the Mexican government interpreted only as procedural democracy in which new parties could compete in elections. This limited interpretation prevented compliance with the clause (Icaza 2016). Indeed, the joint mechanism for dialogue and information exchange during and after negotiations was the European Union-Mexico Joint Parliamentary Council, which pressed the Mexican federal government to comply with the democratic clause. The Mexican government considers this council lacking in enforcement powers because it does not involve the Senate. As a result, the council has been very inefficient and offers only non-enforceable recommendations (Aguirre Reveles and Pérez Rocha 2007; Icaza 2016).

Only through some activities involving the Senate were states indirectly involved in the negotiation process. For example, at the end of the 1990s the Partido de la Revolución Democrática hosted public seminars in the Senate to inform society about the EU-Mexico Free Trade Agreement. It was the only mechanism to listen to society's opinions during the negotiation process, yet it informed senators' votes (Lombaerde and Schulz 2009). Most of the contestation and analysis of this agreement was directed by networks of civil-society organizations, which linked either directly to the European Union or through some federal secretariats in Mexico; for example, the SRE was more open to this dialogue than was the secretary of economy (Icaza 2016). In 2001 the European Foreign Service, in coordination with the Mexican government and with the collaboration of the European Economic and Social Committee, established the European Union-Mexico Civil Society Forum to promote societies' involvement in cooperation and dialogue on trade. By 2014 six meetings of this forum had taken place. A transverse topic during all forums was human rights. For example, in the first forum an advisory council in Mexico and a commission to supervise commitments in this area were created. With the aim of including more stakeholders in trade and human rights discussions, a Social Observatory and a joint advisory committee made up of business, trade unions, farmers, academia, and civil organizations were inaugurated at the fourth forum (Delegation of the European Union to Mexico 2016; Secretaría de Relaciones Exteriores 2016).

Regarding trade, participants in these forums analysed the achievements of the Mexico-European Union agreement, the Doha Development Agenda, workers' rights, and the performance of small and medium-sized enterprises in the bilateral market. At the last two forums (2012 and 2014) a general evaluation of the Global Agreement between Mexico and the EU was presented. However, sub-federal governments were not involved in these forums, with the exception of the third one, in which the EU expressed concern about states' and municipalities' weak institutional capacities and transparency (CANAINTEX 2017; Centro de Estudios Internacionales Gilberto Bosques 2016b; Secretaría del Relaciones Exteriores 2016).

The EU-Mexico Free Trade Agreement was renegotiated in 2017–18. After ten rounds of negotiations, a preliminary agreement was reached on 23 April 2018 and included, for the first time in a Mexican FTA, a commitment by the EU to sign agreements with Mexican states and municipalities in order to offer European companies access to trade procurement; this gave them direct institutional guarantees to operate locally (European Commission 2018). As the original EU-Mexico Free

5.3 Origin of EU Investment in Mexico (2000–2017)

	2000	2005	2010	2015	2017
Origin of investment	%	%	%	%	%
Spain	54	41	29	43	42
Netherlands	16	28	42	3	0
United Kingdom	15	8	4	6	5
Germany	4	8	18	16	17
Belgium	1	0	1	10	13
Italy	1	2	1	8	16
France	0	12	4	11	6
Other	9	1	1	3	1

Source: Compiled by the authors with information from Secretaría de Economía, 2018.

Trade Agreement stated, democracy was very important to the European partners. The 2018 agreement includes other political-institutional elements, such as transparency, labour, and sustainability. Civil society, in this sense, is fundamental to revise, provide information on, and even denounce violations of the three topics in all stages of the process (European Commission 2018).

As the involvement of civil society is crucial to EU partners, the participation of states in the new version of the EU-Mexico Free Trade Agreement is justified when analysing the investment that has arrived to the states, outside Mexico City. From 2000 to 2017 most of the EU investment in Mexico was concentrated in a few states and came mainly from seven EU members, as tables 5.3 and 5.4 show.

Parallel to the presence and active participation of civil society, there is direct support of Mexican business with the aid of the European Commission and the Mexican federal government through the program PROCEI-ProMéxico. Under this joint program, fifteen projects in seventeen Mexican states have been developed with a sector- or product-based approach (in coffee, honey, avocado, mezcal, textiles, shoes, plastics, aeronautical industry, and information technologies, among others). Some of the benefiting states are Baja California, Chiapas, Chihuahua, Jalisco, Mexico City, Morelos, Nuevo León, Oaxaca, Puebla, Querétaro, San Luis Potosí, and Mexico (ProMéxico 2015). This program also includes a certification fund for specific products. For example, it granted the certification of sustainable management in 2015 to some agribusiness companies in the state of Morelos. Despite

5.4 Foreign Direct Investment Flows from the EU* to Mexican Top Ten States, 2000–2017 (in USD million)

2000		2005		2010		2015		2017	
Mexico City	2,219	Mexico City	2,334	Nuevo León	3,510	Mexico City	1,550	Mexico City	1,353
Nuevo León	1,188	State of Mexico	956	Mexico City	1,699	San Luis Potosí	1,028	State of Mexico	766
Querétaro	294	Nuevo León	394	State of Mexico	1,071	Guanajuato	582	Coahuila	625
Jalisco	230	Tamaulipas	315	Veracruz	1,055	Jalisco	563	Puebla	595
San Luis Potosí	221	Quintana Roo	257	Jalisco	831	State of Mexico	526	Jalisco	404
Tamaulipas	213	Baja California	249	Puebla	786	Puebla	455	Guanajuato	384
State of Mexico	104	Veracruz	249	Querétaro	562	Chihuahua	428	San Luis Potosí	379
Baja California Sur	89	Jalisco	208	Guanajuato	542	Querétaro	315	Tamaulipas	360
Quintana Roo	84	San Luis Potosí	192	San Luis Potosí	466	Morelos	244	Quintana Roo	298
Baja California	80	Querétaro	156	Baja California	464	Tamaulipas	225	Oaxaca	298

*No investment is registered from other EU members: Bulgaria, Croatia, Cyprus, Estonia, Greece, Hungary, Latvia, Lithuania, Malta, Romania, Slovakia, Slovenia, and Sweden.

Source: Compiled by the authors with information from Secretaría de Economía, 2018.

these efforts, the bilateral support for implementing the FTA has not been enough, as the EU-Mexico Joint Parliamentary Committee (2016) acknowledges. It noted that until 2013 the EU was Mexico's second-largest trading partner, before it was displaced by other markets. This situation was central at the discussions for the FTA renegotiation.

Although some state governments, such as Jalisco, were most involved and benefited most from the EU-Mexico Free Trade Agreement, they did not take part directly in the decision-making process of the agreement or in the renegotiation process; they only participated in its implementation, mainly through the federal government.

Jalisco and the Implementation of the EU-Mexico Free Trade Agreement

As previously discussed, Jalisco is one of the most active states in international relations, with 43 sisterhood agreements and 139 IIAs.[7] Since 1996 it has worked on developing international relations through the state's Office of International Affairs, one of the first such offices to be created in the country. Internationalization has diversified, and currently several other state government agencies have their own areas through which to conduct international activities or regional relations (Gobierno de Jalisco 2016). During the current administration the Office of International Affairs has been working under the direct supervision of the Governor's Office. There are also other offices related to internationalization, such as the Office for International Affairs of the Secretaries of Education and Health. To provide services to Jalisco's migrants, there is a specific office under the Secretary of Development and Social Integration. Finally, for trade promotion, the Secretary of Economy has an office for promoting trade and investment together with the Jaltrade Institute for Trade Promotion. In support of internationalization, Jaltrade opened an office in Chicago (called Casa Jalisco) in 2012 to help promote industrial, commercial, and touristic activities; several Jalisco secretaries are represented there. This office also works to create networks with the business community, workers, migrants, and students living in the United States (Gobierno de Jalisco 2012). To balance the relationship with the United States and to support the relationship with the EU, the Government of Jalisco created two offices in 2002: the Información y Difusión de la Unión European Jalisco (CIDUE, Centre for Information and Diffusion of the European Union in Jalisco) and the Commercial Office SEPROE-Jalisco in Madrid (Moreno Pérez 2008).

Because of this dispersion of activities, the state government recognizes that there is still not an integral international affairs strategy.

Coordination issues and overlap have been the main obstacles. Another problem has been that most of the signed agreements are not functional (Gobierno de Jalisco 2016; Villarruel 2013). In other words, the state seems to reproduce the federal government's pattern of signing international instruments (especially FTAs) and having the capacity to implement only a few of them.

In terms of trade relations, Jalisco's 2030 State Development Plan (Plan Estatal de Desarrollo 2030) establishes the goal of profiting from Mexico's FTAs, especially to promote trade, investment, and employment (Gobierno de Jalisco 2016; Moreno 2008). Jalisco is one of the top five recipients of foreign direct investment (FDI) and imports. This locates it at ninth place in general competitiveness, which is low considering that the state has the third-largest economy in the country. This might be explained by low levels in other internationalization indicators such as economic innovation, labour, environment, and political stability (Instituto Mexicano para la Competitividad 2014). In addition, FDI in Jalisco is concentrated mainly in a few external partners (Germany, Japan, Luxembourg, Spain, and the United States) (Gobierno de Jalisco 2016).

The Government of Jalisco also acknowledges that most exports and imports take place with NAFTA countries, accounting for 75 per cent and 50 per cent of total exports and imports, respectively (Gobierno de Jalisco 2016); the fact that Jaltrade has an office in Chicago supports this assessment. To find unexplored markets, the state has focused recently on other partners such as the EU. Jalisco is the state that has benefited the most from this transatlantic relation (Villarruel 2013). According to data from the EU, total trade between the Union and Jalisco increased by 472 per cent from 2003 to 2013, while accumulated investment represented 53 per cent of the state's FDI.

The sectors that benefited most from EU investment were pharmaceuticals, commercial transportation, electronics, and beer (Delegación de la Unión Europea en México 2015). This strong trade relation has been boosted recently. In 2015, economic and trade advisers from the embassies of EU members in Mexico and from the representation of the EU in Mexico visited Jalisco to analyse business opportunities (Delegation of the European Union in Mexico 2016). New sectors were promoted, including agriculture. According to the agriculture adviser from the EU, some products could be easily exported to the EU market: tequila, meat products, berries, avocado, and organic foods (Secretaría de Desarrollo Rural–Jalisco 2016). Some other products and sectors have also been supported, and PROCEI-ProMéxico has facilitated the entry of Jalisco industries into the EU market, especially in manufacturing, shoes, textiles, aeronautics, information technologies, steel, and plastics (ProMéxico 2016; Gobierno de Jalisco 2014).

Another example of the partnership between the Jalisco government, EU PROCEI (Programa de Competitividad e Innovación), and ProMéxico is found in the fashion industry. From 2011 to 2013 this joint program trained eighty Jalisco companies from the fashion and innovation industries. The training experience was framed under a larger project called MIND (México Innovación y Diseño), on which the EU spent over one million euros. The results have been very successful: participating companies are now entering markets in Germany, Italy, and Spain (ProMéxico 2015). The European Secretariat for Cluster Analysis awarded this project its bronze seal. Another example of the way in which Jalisco is expanding its trade network towards the EU is the Program for Jalisco's Competitiveness (Jalisco Competitivo). In the budget approved for 2016, some companies received support for the international promotion of their products in the European market (Secretaría de Economía–Jalisco 2015a, 2015b).

In sum, Jalisco is trying to expand its market to the EU, taking advantage of the EU-Mexico Free Trade Agreement and of the inertia of the renegotiation process, but the lack of a grand strategy is still preventing the state from finding the necessary governmental coordination to profit more from Mexico's FTAs.

Conclusion

This chapter presented an overview of the role of Mexican sub-federal governments in the FTA process. We have shown that these governments have not participated in the negotiation of FTAs. Although participation through Senate commissions is limited, it is a first step towards a new generation of FTAs, in which the involvement of states could be more profound and not limited to consultation. We also argued that Mexican sub-federal governments participate directly in economic and trade relations in the implementation of FTAs. The federal government considered the regional spillover effect of FTAs to be the inevitable consequence of economic liberalization, but the performance of FTAs in governance schemes that have an impact on local regulation and economic networks are already in place. Most Mexican states have faced problems in keeping up with and implementing the federal government's aggressive liberalization scheme, which has included the signature of a wide array of FTAs (and other forms of agreements) in the last three decades.

We presented the case for indirect participation of sub-federal governments in FTAs via IIAs for economic promotion and attraction of investment. Although the federal government, through the SRE, is making a great effort to update the registry of all these agreements, there are many still not reported, some of them dealing with economic cooperation.

One of the most important reasons that sub-federal governments do not participate in FTA negotiations alongside the federal government is their limited institutional capacities. First, the lack of information exchange between both the SRE and the secretary of economy (in charge of negotiating FTAs) and the states and municipalities excludes the states and municipalities from participation in negotiations. One interesting finding is that sometimes sub-federal governments are not even aware of what is being negotiated, and the secretary of economy generally does not know what states and municipalities are negotiating about economic exchanges.

Second, sub-federal governments rarely participate in the Senate commission in charge of negotiating and ratifying FTAs. The LAEIT grants this ability, yet local authorities have rarely used it. A third institutional weakness is the lack of a proper office (and professional officials) to conduct international and economic relations abroad. This situation makes it difficult for states and municipalities to negotiate actively with the federal government and other international actors; it also makes it more difficult to monitor and evaluate the implementation of agreements. In addition, the lack of continuity of local political and economic projects due to electoral processes is a barrier that reduces the confidence of foreign counterparts.

Limited capacities, a lack of links between sub-federal governments and the secretary of economy, the lack of an updated database of states' and municipalities' foreign activities, and a great diversity of interests and goals among them seem to be the main problems preventing a more active participation of states in international trade networks and in FTA negotiations. Some sub-federal governments are starting to build and strengthen their capacities to become more active players in FTA negotiation and implementation processes. FTA partners have encouraged this change; the EU included civil society, businesses, and sub-federal governments in the renegotiation process for updating the EU-Mexico Global Agreement.

Not all states and municipalities have been proactive in this process. For example, even though the state of Jalisco is very active internationally, having signed many IIAs, it has few that are operational. In addition,

Jalisco has tried to expand its market to the EU, yet the federal government has led this project through PROCEI-ProMéxico, leaving the state as a passive and reactive actor. In this case, as in the rest of the country, centralization of trade and the lack of institutional capacities play a fundamental role in limiting states' proactiveness in FTA negotiations.

In sum, Mexican sub-federal governments have been historically absent from the negotiation processes of FTAs, but they have had important relations with partners abroad through IIAs and sisterhood agreements. Ironically, this international experience seems to contrast with their passivity in dealing directly with FTAs. For Mexican states to participate more actively in FTA negotiation and implementation, more inclusive legal provisions at the federal level, and more institutional capacity at the state and local levels, are necessary.

NOTES

1 See title I, article I, of the Economic Partnership, Political Coordination and Cooperation Agreement (the Global Agreement) between Mexico and the European Union.
2 Of all these FTAs the only one denounced (by Venezuela in 2004) was the trilateral agreement signed with Colombia and Venezuela (the G3), but in 2006 Mexico and Colombia renegotiated the FTA bilaterally.
3 Members of the partnership are Australia, Brunei, Canada, Chile, Japan, Malaysia, Mexico, New Zealand, Peru, Singapore, the United States, and Vietnam.
4 Jorge A. Schiavon developed the survey in July 2014. With support from the General Direction for Political Coordination of the SRE (the SRE area in charge of relations with sub-federal goverments in international affairs) and the Asociación Mexicana de Oficinas de Asuntos Internacionales de los Estados (the only organization in the country that brings together and coordinates the actions of state agencies in charge of the international relations of twenty-one states), the survey was sent to all thirty-two states in August 2014. The level of response was very high: twenty-seven (84 per cent) of the thirty-two federal states answered the request, with twenty-six answering almost every question. See Schiavon (2016).
5 Exchange rate (2016), USD 1 = MXN 18.
6 By September 2018, twenty-one out of thirty-two states were members of the Asociación Mexicana de Oficinas de Asuntos Internacionales de los Estados.
7 We thank Dr Daniel Villarruel Reynoso, professor of the Universidad de Guadalajara, for his insights on the Jalisco case study.

REFERENCES

Aguirre Reveles, Rodolfo, and Manuel Pérez Rocha. 2007. *The EU-Mexico Free Trade Agreement Seven Years On: A Warning to the Global South*. Mexico City: Transnational Institute, Mexican Action Network on Free Trade, ICCO.
CANAINTEX. 2017. Avances 3ª Ronda de Modernización del TLCUE. Brussels, 3–7 April. http://www.canaintex.org.mx.
Cárdenas, Enrique. 2015. *El largo curso de la economía Mexicana: De 1780 a nuestros días*. Mexico City: El Colegio de México and Fondo de Cultura Económica.
Centro de Estudios Internacionales Gilberto Bosques. 2016a. *Principales aspectos del nuevo Tratado de Libre Comercio entre México y la Unión Europea (TLCUEM): Oportunidades, logros y desafíos*. Mexico City: Centro de Estudios Internacionales Gilberto Bosques and Senado de la República.
– 2016b. *XXI Reunión de la Comisión Parlamentaria Mixta México–Unión Europea*. Brussels: Centro de Estudios Internacionales Gilberto Bosques and Senado de la República.
Delegación de la Unión Europea en México. 2015. *Consejeros de la Unión Europea analizan oportunidades de negocio en Jalisco: Comunicado de prensa*. Mexico City: Delegación de la Unión Europea en México. http://eeas.europa.eu.
Delegation of the European Union to Mexico. 2016. *The European Union–Mexico Political Relations, 2016*. http://eeas.europa.eu.
Derbez, Luis Ernesto. 2002. México y el mecanismo de Cooperación Económica Asia Pacífico. *Comercio Exterior* 52 (10): 866–73.
Diario Oficial de la Federación. 1992. *Ley de Celebración de Tratados*. Mexico City: Diario Oficial de la Federación.
– 2004. *Ley sobre la Aprobación de Tratados Internacionales en Materia Económica*. Mexico City: Diario Oficial de la Federación.
Durand, Jorge. 2016. *Historia mínima de la migración México–Estados Unidos*. Mexico City: El Colegio de México.
EU-Mexico Joint Parliamentary Committee. 2016. *Joint Declaration: 20th Meeting*. Mexico City. https://polcms.secure.europarl.europa.eu.
European Commission. 2016. *Consultation Strategy Linked to Impact Assessment of the Proposal to Modernize the Trade Pillar of the EU-Mexico Global Agreement*. http://trade.ec.europa.eu.
– 2018. *New EU-Mexico Agreement: The Agreement in Principle and Its Texts*. Brussels: European Commission. http://trade.ec.europa.eu.
García-Zamora, Rodolfo. 2011. "Migración bajo el TLCAN: Exportación de bienes y gente." In *El Futuro de la Política de Comercio en América del Norte: Lecciones del TLCAN*, edited by K.P. Gallagher, E. Dussel Peters, and T.A. Wise, 93–7. Mexico: Editorial Miguel Ángel Porrúa.

Gobierno de Jalisco. 2012. *Casa Jalisco en los Estados Unidos–Matriz Chicago, Illinois.* http://transparencia.info.jalisco.gob.mx.

– 2014. *Convenio de colaboración con ProMéxico (Subprograma Jalisco Competitivo).* Gobierno de Jalisco. http://info.jalisco.gob.mx.

– 2016. *Plan Estatal de Desarrollo, 2013–2030 del Gobierno de Jalisco.* http://sepaf.jalisco.gob.mx.

Gutiérrez-Haces, Teresa. 2008. Impacto del capítulo XI del TLCAN sobre la estrategia de la Inversión extranjera directa en México desde la óptica del Pacto Federal. In *Agenda del Desarrollo, 2006–2020,* vol. 1, edited by J.L. Calva, 169–99. Mexico City: UNAM, Universidad de Guadalajara.

Icaza, Rosalba. 2016. "NAFTA Parity in Real Time: The 'Making' of the EU-Mexico Partnership." In *The EU and World Regionalism: The Makability of Regions in the 21st Century,* edited by P. de Lombaerde and M. Shulz, 115–30. London: Ashgate Publishing.

Instituto Mexicano para la Competitividad. 2014. *Índice de Competitividad 2014.* IMCO. http://imco.org.mx.

Ketterer, Tobia D., Daniel Bernhofen, and Chris Milner. 2014. "Preferences, Rent Destruction and Multilateral Liberalization: The Building Block Effect of CUSFTA." *Journal of International Economics* 92 (1): 63–77.

Lombaerde, Philippe de, and Michael Schulz. 2009. *The EU and World Regionalism: The Makability of Regions in the 21st Century.* London: Ashgate Publishing.

Morales, Isidro. 2008. *Post-NAFTA North America: Reshaping the Economic and Political Governance of a Changing Region.* Farnham, UK: Ashgate Publishing.

Moreno Pérez, Raquel. 2008. "La vinculación internacional del gobierno de Jalisco." In *Diplomacia local: Las relaciones internacionales de las entidades federativas mexicanas,* edited by C. Dávila, J.A. Schiavon, and R. Velázquez Flores, 205–46. Mexico City: UNAM.

OAS (Organization of American States). 2016. *Trans-Pacific Partnership Agreement.* http://www.sice.oas.org.

ProMéxico. 2015. *Resultados PROCEI: México–Unión Europea; Boletín de prensa 39/15.* http://www.gob.mx.

– 2016. *Programa de Competitividad e Innovación México–Unión Europea: El cierre de cinco años de promover relaciones exitosas.* http://www.promexico.gob.mx.

RQIC (Réseau Québécois sur L'intégration Continental). 2017. *Political Declaration of the Encounter of Social Organizations of Canada, United States, and Mexico.* Quebec City: Réseau Québécois sur L'intégration Continental. http://rqic.alternatives.ca.

Schiavon, Jorge A. 2015. "Una década de acción internacional de los gobiernos locales mexicanos (2005–2015)." *Revista Mexicana de Política Exterior* 104: 103–27.

– 2016. "The International Relations of Sub-state Governments in Mexico: A Comparative Analysis with Ten Federal Systems." PhD diss., University of California, San Diego.

Secretaría de Desarrollo Rural–Jalisco. 2016. Inicia Jalisco y la Unión Europea nueva etapa de intercambio comercial.

Secretaría de Economía. 2016. *Comercio Exterior / Países con Tratados y Acuerdos firmados por México.* http://www.gob.mx.

– 2018. *Información estadística de flujos de IED hacia México por país de origen desde 1999.* https://datos.gob.mx.

Secretaría de Economía–Jalisco. 2015a. *Jalisco competitive.* http://sedeco.jalisco .gob.mx.

– 2015b. *Proyectos aprobados en convocatorias.* http://sedeco.jalisco.gob.mx.

Secretaría de Relaciones Exteriores. 2016. *México–Unión Europea.* http:// www.gob.mx.

Studer, Isabel. 2006. "El TLCAN y la industria automotriz en México: Hacia la armonización de los estándares ambientales en América del Norte." In *Tercer Simposio de América del Norte sobre Evaluación de los Montreal: Efectos Ambientales del Comercio,* 3–59. Montreal: Commission for Environmental Cooperation.

Vega Cánovas, Gustavo. 2010. *El Tratado de Libre Comercio en América del Norte, Visión retrospectiva y retos a futuro.* Mexico City: El Colegio de México.

Villarruel Reynoso, Daniel. 2013. "Salir al mundo ¿Para qué? El Interés Local Internacional (ILI) como estrategia de posicionamiento global. El caso de Jalisco: una paradoja." *Trabajos y Ensayos* 16. Universidad del País Vasco, Spain.

Wise, Carol. 2011. "Sitting in Limbo: North American Free Trade Agreement." In *National Solutions to Trans-border Problems? The Governance of Security and Risk in a Post-NAFTA North America,* edited by I. Morales, 5–25. Farnham, UK: Ashgate Publishing.

6 Civil Society, Multilevel Governance, and International Trade in North America

CHRISTOPHER KUKUCHA

For several decades the scope of international trade agreements has expanded to include issues of sub-federal jurisdiction, such as services, technical standards, procurement, health care, labour, and the environment. This chapter argues that the "behind the border" nature of these developments and the institutional realities of federalism in Canada, the United States, and Mexico have directly influenced the mobilization, organization, and impact of civil-society groups, often limiting democratic participation. As such, all three factors outlined in the introduction – evolving international trade policy and agreements, federal institutional configuration, and social movement activity – are at play. Specifically, the marginalization of US states, due to an institutional and fiscal process whereby Congress typically dictates sub-federal engagement, has opened up policy space for social mobilization around trade issues and matters of states rights, albeit often tied to financial support from specific sources. These dynamics do not exist in Canada, however, due to different federal structures, resulting in a relatively cooperative system of intergovernmental relations with fewer civil-society groups related to international trade, and with arguably less impact on government policy, despite the quality of input. In Mexico, national labour groups have increased activity in this policy area, but mobilization is ad hoc, reflecting Mexico's history of one-party dominance and its highly centralized system of federalism. Perhaps more importantly, however, this chapter also seeks to transcend institutional understandings of multilevel trade politics in North America. Specifically, the emergence of transnational societal linkages suggests the need for a more fluid consideration of actors not easily categorized into various organizations and levels of analysis. Civil-society groups mobilizing in the area of international trade also include counter publics and counter discourses that challenge neo-liberal economic foundations and the dominance of rationalist and material understandings of the global political economy. These discursive narratives are not well understood by other institutions and actors but are arguably crucial to securing the legitimacy and acceptance of contemporary international trade agreements.

Societal Groups and Foreign Trade Policy in North America

The literature focusing on societal groups and policymaking varies in Canada, the United States, and Mexico. One area of the Canadian literature, for example, clarifies the differences between interest groups and social movements. On the one hand, interest groups vary in organization and focus but are generally accepted to have formal structures and the ability to articulate positions with the goal of altering policy preferences, albeit without assuming elected office (Pross 1975). As an extension, studies examining "policy communities" and "networks" focus on the formal and informal interaction of interest groups and the state (Coleman and Skogstad 1990). On the other hand, social movements lack formal organization, with membership consisting of a wide range of societal actors (Brodie 1995). Contributions have also argued that neo-liberalism has altered the nature of political institutions and democracy in Canada (Smith 2005). This study will include aspects of civil society falling under each of the categories.

There are also numerous, though increasingly dated, studies focusing on societal considerations and Canada's foreign trade policy, especially in relation to the failed Multilateral Agreement on Investment (MAI), the Seattle meetings of the World Trade Organization (WTO), and the Organization of American States (OAS) summit in Quebec City regarding the Free Trade Area of the Americas (FTAA) (Kirton 2001–2). One empirical study from the early 2000s also focused on public attitudes related to international trade, identifying a "permissive consensus" in Canada based on the perception that foreign trade agreements increase prosperity without undermining the welfare state (Wolfe and Mendelsohn 2005). Those opposing this view, however, critiqued the apparent exclusion of non-corporate interests and suggested that the cooptation of these actors created serious social and democratic implications (Macdonald 2002). Specific attention to these conclusions is most apparent in studies examining the "anti-globalization movement" in Canada (Ayres 1998, 2004).

The US literature tends to focus on the role and impact of interest groups and other non-governmental actors in the American policy process. One subfield concentrates on the role of these interests in American election campaigns and financing (Boatright 2011; Rozell, Wilcox, and Franz 2011). Others, however, look more closely at the impact of specific women's, religious, ethnic, and consumer groups on US policy (Goldberg 1990; Slavin 1995; Weber and Jones 1994). Finally, there are studies emphasizing the relevance of civil-society organizations (CSOs) on specific policy areas, such as immigration, health care, and education (Facchini, Mayda, and Mishra 2011). As with Canada, there are also several contributions that concentrate specifically on nongovernmental interests and trade policy. Some emphasize the role of civil society within the institutional process of the US federal government (Deardorff and Stern 1998; Grossman and Helpman 2002; Pastor 1980). Others probe the relevance of domestic actors in the context of larger multilateral trade regimes, with a specific emphasis, much like Canada, on protests associated with the MAI and the WTO Seattle meetings (Dam 2004; Thomas 2000; Wall 2001). It should also be noted that the expansive literature focusing on the role of sub-federal governments in US foreign policy typically excludes any discussion of civil society (Fry 1998, 2004; Kincaid 2003; Sager 2002).

The academic literature in Mexico follows similar trends, concentrating on the role of non-governmental actors in the policy process (Barnes 2011; Bayes and Gonzalez 2011). Many of these contributions highlight the lack of strong societal groups in Mexico due to the country's long history of statism and clientelism, albeit with reference to some emerging binational coalitions with US groups on labour, environmental, and human rights issues (Fox 2001; Sabet 2008; Shefner 2007). Similar linkages were identified in matters of international trade, especially in the context of the North American Free Trade Agreement (NAFTA) and the MAI (Von Bülow 2009). Some, however, highlighted a decline in cross-border labour cooperation between the United States and Mexico post-2000 (Nolan Garcia 2011) due in part to a shift in focus by Mexican unions towards domestic bargaining issues and protectionism, although some ties continued between smaller groups and Canadian unions (Clarkson 2008). Others, however, presented a more favourable analysis of Mexican CSOs, arguing that transnational networks provided opportunities to frame resistance to neo-liberal frameworks (Johnston and Laxer 2003).

Therefore, with the exception of some focus on Mexico, the literature on civil society and international trade in North America typically reflects Western, developed, and democratic experiences in state-societal relations, even with several Mexican studies written by Canadian and American scholars. It also has a tendency to portray state and society as "monolithic entities" in direct competition with one another, typically underplaying alliances that exist between state elites and social groups as they seek to advance their own agendas (Engle-hart 2011, 340–1). A graver weakness is the absence, again with some Mexican exceptions, of state-societal relations representing developing and non-democratic experiences (Hann and Dunn 1996). Further, and perhaps most importantly for this chapter, many of these contributions emphasize civil-society activity at separate international, national, and local levels, thereby missing relevant modes of inquiry that are able to integrate the actual interconnectedness of civil society within and between states (Macdonald and Ayres 2016, 329–30).

As such, it is constructive to place the activity of North American civil society within broader theoretical debates in the global political economy literature, which are dominated by material and rationalist assumptions of international economic relations (Anderson and Kuku-cha 2016, 3–10). Communitarian and state-centric perspectives, for example, whether mercantilist or liberal in interpretation, often treat societal forces as secondary variables or exclude them entirely (Gilpin 1987; Grieco 1990). Even Marxists emphasize the exploitive material nature of capitalism and the importance of class-based forces as a means of change (Lenin 1939; Marx 1962). By the 1980s, however, a number of scholars, including Canadian Robert Cox (1981), began challenging these traditions, albeit still from a material perspective, by highlight-ing the socially constructed and politicized nature of knowledge. Oth-ers were more critical of transnational market forces and endorsed the principle of cosmopolitan democracy, or "globalization from below," which called for the democratization of international institutions and the development of a form of citizenship that extended beyond the nation state (Falk 1997; Held 1995). Social-movement approaches also focused on identity and culture as mobilizing influences, especially in terms of Latin America and Mexico (Alvarez, Dagnimo, and Escobar 1998; Brysk 2000).

As Laura Macdonald and Jeffrey Ayres have noted, these contribu-tions only provide partial insight into the importance of civil society in international trade relations. Specifically, Macdonald and Ayres argue that the "global political economy cannot be understood without refer-ence to the discursive, symbolic, and cognitive power of civil society, and civil society is also central to any potential norms-driven transfor-mation of the international system" (2016, 329). As such, civil society is central to understanding and challenging the role of language, cat-egories, concepts, and identities in existing economic narratives. This study, with its focus on federalism and multilevel governance, obvi-ously contributes to the existing material and rationalist dominance of the literature. It will also focus on transnational linkages between CSOs in North America and the normative dialogue that has emerged as a result of this process, which also includes the concerns of counter publics seeking to challenge the neo-liberal order. In doing so, it will highlight possible causes of, and solutions to, the current crisis of legitimacy surrounding issues of international trade.

Federalism, International Trade, and Societal Engagement in North America

One comparative framework for understanding federalism in Canada and the United States is the distinction between *interstate* and *intrastate* federal systems (Kukucha 2015a; Loewenstein 1965; Smiley 1971).[1] *Interstate* models, such as Canada, typically have legislative arrangements where the upper and lower houses operate in "complete separation from one another" (Hueglin and Fenna 2006, 222). The Canadian Senate, for example, has limited regional representation, with appointments traditionally made on the basis of party and not province. Canada's Senate also has limited parliamentary power, namely an inability to introduce money bills and an unwillingness to defeat legislation passed in the House of Commons. Central and sub-federal governments are also separate, limiting legislative coordination between Ottawa and provincial or territorial governments. This places an emphasis on intergovernmental relations, or executive federalism, which can be competitive but also provides flexibility for negotiated solutions in institutionalized or less formal settings, albeit with limited access for societal interests (Smiley and Watts 1985).

The United States is an example of *intrastate* federalism, with an emphasis on the horizontal distribution of powers between Congress and the executive branch. American presidents, for example, are much more engaged with Congress than with US states. Although pragmatic and cooperative intergovernmental relations have evolved over time, few formal institutional mechanisms exist to include sub-federal governments in federal decision making. The US system also has a tradition of weak party linkages between both levels of government and an absence of party discipline, creating an environment conducive to lobbying by individuals, firms, and other societal interests (Hueglin and Fenna 2006, 64–7). This mix of institutional and societal actors, however, ultimately creates competition and challenges for governments to control the policy process.

In contrast, the form and practice of Mexican federalism does not facilitate intergovernmental relations or societal engagement, especially in terms of international trade. Historically, Mexico has a centralized system of government, with extensive executive control. The president is the head of both state and government and from 1929 to 2000 was selected from one party, the Partido Revolucionario Institucional (PRI). During that period the president, as leader of the PRI, held extensive powers of appointment within government and also had the authority to remove state governors, usually by negotiated resignations. Historically, Mexican states were also fiscally constrained, with the federal government controlling most public revenue. Rules limiting consecutive sub-federal re-election also prevented a consistent means of advocating for state rights (Ward, Rodríguez, and Mendoza 1999, 66–7; Weldon 1997). Significant changes, however, have occurred during the last two decades, including an end to PRI dominance and the emergence of the Partido Acción Nacional (PAN) and the Partido de la Revolución Democrática (PRD) (Remes 2006, 185). Mexico has also established forums for sub-federal consultation. The first, in 1999, was the Asociación Nacional de Gobernadores, followed by the Conferencia Nacional de Gobernadores in 2002. It is important to note that, nevertheless, foreign policy remains the exclusive domain of the federal government, and only two Mexican states currently have bureaucratic departments exclusively committed to international affairs (Jalisco and Chiapas) (see Schiavon and López-Vallejo in this volume). The Mexican constitution also has no provisions allowing for intergovernmental consultation on matters of foreign policy. Any discussions with state or municipal officials are ad hoc and limited to specific issue areas.

Civil Society in Canada

Historically, Canadian non-governmental actors, especially related to international trade, represented Canada's corporate and business sector, usually in the form of sectoral organizations, such as the Canadian Cattlemen's Association, or as "umbrella groups" representing numerous sectors, such as the Business Council of Canada. In 1995, however, Don Abelson noted the increasing importance of "advocacy think tanks" in Canada and the United States, prioritizing free markets, limited regulation, and other pro-business issues, currently best represented by the Fraser Institute and the C.D. Howe Institute (Abelson 1995a, 1995b). Today deep linkages and networks exist between all sectoral, umbrella, and think-tank organizations. As William Carroll and Murray Shaw have pointed out, this enables ongoing and organized conversations that reinforce narratives and basic principles of neo-liberal, capital priorities (Carroll and Shaw 2001). The role of diaspora communities in Canada has also influenced the country's foreign trade relations, especially in the pursuit of specific trade agreements such as the Canada-Ukraine Free Trade Agreement (Carment and Landry 2015).

In contrast, "critical" societal groups in the policy area of foreign trade relations are fewer and less organized, albeit with a long history of activity in Canada. In 1931, for example, the League for Social Reconstruction was founded, consisting largely of early labour activists and intellectuals, to challenge the perceived shortcomings of capitalism after the Great Depression. The league would eventually serve as a cornerstone of the Co-operative Commonwealth Federation, with several members helping to write the Regina Manifesto in 1933. In most cases, however, these early alternative groups lacked the budget, personnel, and infrastructure to have a long-lasting impact, although some did publish pamphlets and other documents (Carroll and Huxtable 2014). Many also disappeared in the 1940s and 1950s as the country turned its attention to the cold war and alleged threat of communism in Canada and the United States.

The first organized group to counter this trend was the Institute for Policy Studies, founded in 1963. Although it helped establish the Transnational Institute in Amsterdam in the 1970s, hoping to build linkages between alternative CSOs in a range of countries, it had limited impact in Canada. By the 1980s, however, a small collection of union activists and academics had begun to question the increasing popularity of neo-liberal policies in Western developed economies, eventually forming the Canadian Centre for Policy Alternatives (CCPA). From the outset, the centre was focused not on the destruction of capitalism but on the re-establishment of previous understandings between labour and capital in the form of a Keynesian welfare state (Carroll and Huxtable 2014). The CCPA quickly became part of a larger international wave of mobilization around the Canada-United States Free Trade Agreement (CUSFTA) and NAFTA. The Council of Canadians (COC), founded in 1985, had a similar agenda, as did other Canadian groups, including the Canadian Labour Congress. The Pro-Canada Network, a coalition of these and other CSOs, also emerged during this period, affecting the Canadian political discourse and platforms of the New Democratic and Liberal parties (Macdonald and Ayres 2016, 338). From the outset, though, many of these interests suffered from a lack of financial resources, which limited the hiring of staff and the publication of research, but this began to change as fund-raising and institution-building efforts improved in the 1990s.

NAFTA was also significant because it contributed to the building of transnational networks between groups throughout North America.

In fact, the Pro-Canada Network was instrumental in this process, providing some inspiration for new coalition groups such as the Citizens Trade Campaign (CTC) and the Alliance for Responsible Trade. The Mexican Action Network on Free Trade (Red Mexicana de Acción Frente al Libre Comercio) was also created to serve as an umbrella organization for over a hundred grassroots environmental, indigenous, labour, women's rights, and neighborhood groups. The result was a series of joint conferences and lobbying efforts targeting NAFTA, which some observers credit for leading to President Bill Clinton's pursuit of the environment and labour side deals in NAFTA. These groups also continued to mobilize in the post-NAFTA era, and CTC and the Alliance for Responsible Trade successfully campaigned against the renewal of US presidential fast-track authority in 1997–8 and protested at the WTO's Seattle meetings in 1999 and the 2001 FTAA discussions in Quebec City (Gabriel and Macdonald 2011; Macdonald and Ayres 2016, 338; Nolan Garcia 2011).

Today Canadian groups, especially the COC and CCPA, remain actively engaged in promoting an alternative agenda, especially on matters of foreign trade policy. These groups have also expanded existing pan-Canadian and transnational linkages with other like-minded groups. For example, the CCPA has ties with the Canadian Environmental Law Association, the Canadian Teachers Federation, and Winnipeg-based CHOICES, often drafting alternative federal budgets, opening provincial offices, and producing research studies and surveys. The COC and CCPA also played a crucial role in establishing the Trade Justice Network (TJN) in 2010, when several environmental, social justice, and Indigenous groups met in Ottawa to discuss a lack of dialogue and transparency related to ongoing Canada-European Union Comprehensive Economic and Trade Agreement (CETA) negotiations. The TJN later expanded to include several Canadian municipalities and a range of similar like-minded societal groups in Europe, starting with a combined meeting in Brussels in the summer of 2010 after the fourth round of CETA negotiations (Trew 2013). More recent efforts shifted to the renegotiation of NAFTA, including participation in three days of meetings with other societal groups in Mexico City in May 2017. Recent student protests across Canada, and the emergence of the Occupy movement, have further focused attention on neo-liberal inequalities, not all related to international trade.

A number of public sector unions in Canada also forged alliances with US and Mexican labour groups in the post-NAFTA period. These included the Canadian Union of Postal Workers, the Public Service Alliance of Canada, and the Canadian Union of Public Employees. For the most part, these ties were limited to information sharing and research, especially related to the impact of liberalized trade on public services. One example was the Coalition to Defend Public Education, a group of over five hundred thousand teachers in the United States, Canada, and Mexico, which was concerned about the potential commercialization of public education. Telecommunications was another area of cooperation with evolving ties between the Communications, Energy, and Paperworkers of Canada, the Communication Workers of America, and the Sindicato de Telefonistas de la República Mexicana (Telephone Workers' Union of the Mexican Republic). Other examples include Mexican labour representatives participating in a protest at a Sprint call centre in San Francisco, and the United Steelworkers of America and the Canadian Autoworkers jointly participating in proceedings related to NAFTA's North American Agreement on Labour Cooperation (Clarkson 2008, 107–8).

Civil-society activity in Canada also permeates the provincial and territorial level, although the significance of these initiatives typically varies from region to region (Kukucha 2015b). In Ontario most societal engagement focuses on contentious issue areas, such as services or trade and the environment. Pressure, however, is not usually directed at the Ministry of Economic Development and Growth – formerly the Ministry of Economic Development, Employment, and Infrastructure and, prior to that, the Ministry of Economic Development and Trade (MEDT) – which is responsible for foreign trade policy, but at other line departments such as the Ministry of Environment and Climate Change (water) and Ministry of Education (services). In some cases, however, the former MEDT engaged with some groups, such as the CCPA, but, in the words of one senior policy adviser, it did "not define the province's final negotiating position on these issues."[2]

Quebec, by contrast, has a corporatist tradition that does not exist in other provinces, with a high degree of labour involvement and non-governmental engagement. The province's largest trade unions provide an organizational base for labour interests. Unlike other provinces, Quebec has a civil society that benefits from "peak associations," such as the Fédération des Femmes du Québec, which draws together groups with similar interests (Montpetit 2003). In matters of foreign trade policy, however, contact is again typically made directly with line departments, and information is then passed to other relevant officials within the provincial bureaucracy. In response to pressure from civil society before and after the OAS Summit of the Americas in Quebec City, the Parti Québécois (PQ) created a formal panel, the Quebec Observatory on Globalization, in the fall of 2001, although it failed to produce any meaningful engagement. Jean Charest's Liberal government ended these efforts, relying instead on specialized think-tanks and university groups for its non-governmental input.[3]

As in Quebec, British Columbia has a long legacy of societal engagement with labour movements, environmental groups, and First Nations interests. Environmental issues first gained prominence in the province during New Democratic Party (NDP) governments in the 1990s, as did consultation with First Nations due to judicial land claims and the Nisga'a Treaty, although neither the NDP nor the First Nations has a significant interest in foreign trade policy (Hoberg 2001, 24–7). Labour does have an interest in this policy area, influencing British Columbia's decision to adopt its observer-only status position during NAFTA negotiations and influencing its position on WTO negotiations related to labour standards and services. As one senior representative suggested, however, labour "did not drive government policy, especially on matters of international trade."[4] Not surprisingly, the relevance of societal groups further declined during the Liberal governments of Gordon Campbell and Christy Clark, with the exception of several proposed pipeline projects.[5] This will potentially change under the recently elected NDP government of John Horgan.

For the most part, societal activity in other provinces mirrors the realities in Ontario and British Columbia. Manitoba, for example, has a long tradition of activist interest groups, but access to government often depends on the party in power, with Conservatives favouring agriculture, business, and Métis groups, and the NDP focusing on organized labour and Indigenous interests (Brock 1996, 110–11).[6] In other provinces, such as Saskatchewan, provincial interaction with societal groups, especially in the area of international trade, is dominated by industry associations and often limited to a small range of line departments, although Alberta also previously organized information sessions on services with a wide range of interests, including teachers, health-care professionals, and representatives from labour.[7] In Atlantic Canada, consultation with industry occurs within a small range of departments, and any contact with civil society is minimal and typically takes place within larger federal consultations.[8] Not surprisingly, many of these industry groups are tied to the region's resource-based economy, especially fisheries, offshore oil, and hydroelectricity. Historically, there are close ties between merchants and political elites, especially in Newfoundland and Labrador, but these ties have declined as competing sectoral and labour associations have emerged (Kukucha 2015b).[9]

Despite these regional differences, national CSOs did target and interact with provinces and territories during CETA negotiations. As early as 2008, societal groups such as the COC became aware of provincial efforts, notably in Quebec, Ontario, and Manitoba, to promote trade talks with European Union officials. The COC responded by approaching provinces that were potentially receptive to input from the group. Manitoba and Nova Scotia were targeted due to their NDP governments with strong ties to labour, as were Ontario and Quebec due to predictable provincial concerns related to procurement, supply management, and liquor distribution boards (see Schram in this volume). Over a span of three years the COC met with officials from Nova Scotia and Manitoba on several occasions. In Quebec another group, the Réseau Québecois sur l'Intégration Continentale, also met with provincial officials, as did the CCPA and the Trade and Investment Research Project in Ontario. The Canadian Union of Public Employees commissioned a legal opinion on potential provincial vulnerabilities related to CETA and services (Trew 2013).

Typically, meetings between government officials and civil society consisted of a briefing from a senior trade representative, followed by a question-and-answer session. Ultimately, however, civil-society groups had mixed opinions of the effectiveness of CETA consultations. Although some provinces were open to meeting and receiving unsolicited reports, others were less receptive. Quebec groups were initially optimistic about the potential openness of the newly elected PQ government that followed the Charest Liberals, but were ultimately disappointed. Frustrated by a lack of progress with provincial officials, these groups soon refocused efforts on consultations at the municipal level and the TJN. The goal also shifted from influencing federal and provincial negotiating positions to having a formal public review of CETA prior to it being signed by the Canadian government, which did not occur (Kukucha 2015b; Trew 2013). As noted, however, the TJN remained actively engaged regarding the renegotiation of NAFTA, with Canadian representation from the COC, CCPA, the Canadian Labour Congress, the Canadian Union of Public and General Employees, the National Farmers Union, and the Public Service Alliance of Canada. Sub-federal representation included the British Columbia Teachers Federation, Quebec's Fonds de solidarité, and the Réseau Québecois sur l'Intègration Continentale.

Civil Society in the United States

Historically, US trade policy was dominated by the economic priorities of producers who wielded considerable influence in Congress. Civil society was, for the most part, silent on international trade. Business leaders, academics, and unions engaged in debates on the issue, but most groups supported liberalized trade. In fact, during the post-war period, up until the 1960s, the American Federation of Labor and Congress of Industrial Organizations (AFL-CIO) supported the pursuit of free trade agreements under the assumption that American competitiveness would ensure employment and high wages for US workers (Von Bülow 2009, 6).

By the 1980s, however, trade negotiations had begun focusing on issues with a broader societal context. Attempts to reduce subsidies had the potential to affect domestic agricultural production, which has been viewed as part of an "American" way of life, and intellectual property issues had implications for the pharmaceutical industry and the health and welfare of American citizens. Ultimately, it was NAFTA that highlighted divisions between labour, trade, and environmental groups. As noted, the NAFTA side deals were enough to defuse criticism from environmental interests but, interestingly, not from organized labour. In fact, the AFL-CIO continued to oppose NAFTA as Bill Clinton fought to get the agreement through Congress (Destler 2005, 253–5).

At the sub-federal level, state and local interests have only mobilized on international trade issues for slightly more than a decade. In the first decade of the 2000s this activity focused primarily on legislative initiatives, which in some states were packaged together in one bill, consistently titled the Jobs, Trade, and Democracy Act (Public Citizen 2012b). In Oregon, House bill 3340 called for the creation of an office of trade enforcement and a citizens' commission on globalization, at the request of the Oregon Fair Trade Coalition in March 2007. In the same year, Iowa also attempted, and failed, to pass bills in two consecutive sittings of the legislature (SF 171, the Jobs, Trade, and Democracy Act; and SF 168, proposing an advisory council on international trade and globalization). In Hawaii, Senate bill SB1030, and its companion legislation House bill HB30, both calling for state legislative approval of procurement rules, was passed in May 2007. In addition, House resolutions calling for an end to presidential Trade Promotion Authority (TPA) were passed in Alabama (HR 121), Pennsylvania (HR 276), and Hawaii (HR 63) in 2007. Other states pursuing similar legislative agendas, with varying degrees of success, include Minnesota, Wisconsin, Montana, California, New York, Maine, Vermont, New Hampshire, Utah, and Washington State (Kukucha 2015b).

Many of these state legislative initiatives were part of a larger campaign driven by Public Citizen, a national group founded by Ralph Nader in 1971 that relies on private donations and funding. During this period, it was the Global Trade Watch division of Public Citizen that actively opposed trade initiatives at federal and state levels of government with an eclectic range of programs focusing on "alternatives to corporate globalization," democracy, sovereignty, federalism, deregulation, services, the environment, health care, and employment. State legislative initiatives were part of this campaign, with Public Citizen often providing financial support and, in many cases, draft language for tabled legislation related to TPA and other pertinent international trade issues (Public Citizen 2012a). These efforts dwindled later in the decade, however, as financial support for Global Trade Watch began to decline and/or shift to other priorities.

At the same time, the AFL-CIO focused on a wide range of concerns, including health care, retirement, education, immigration, and workers' rights, but it did not actively engage sub-federal governments on these issues. Comparatively, the Forum on Democracy and Trade covered a wide range of foreign trade issues with direct implications for US states, including services, procurement, and investment. In recent years, however, the forum has not engaged new international trade issues, such as the Trans-Pacific Partnership (Forum on Democracy and Trade 2012).

A unique dynamic in the United States is the existence of civil-society groups with an emphasis on international trade at the state level. Many of these groups are coalitions consisting of members from organized labour, churches, environmental groups, and other social justice and democratic rights organizations. Several are also closely affiliated with, or members of, the CTC, a nationally based coalition founded in 1992 with close ties to Public Citizen and Global Trade Watch (Citizens Trade Campaign 2012). One of the oldest state-level groups, established in 2004, was the Maine Fair Trade Campaign, which was created when the state government was passing its Jobs, Trade, and Democracy Act (Maine Fair Trade Campaign 2012). The Oregon Fair Trade Campaign was also founded in 2004, by the Oregon branch of the AFL-CIO and the Sierra Club (Oregon Fair Trade Campaign 2012). In Washington state, the Washington Fair Trade Coalition served a similar function (Washington Fair Trade Coalition 2012). Other CTC-affiliated state coalitions emerged in Wisconsin, Florida, California, New York, Minnesota, Ohio, Pennsylvania and Texas. In many cases, however, these state organizations had nothing more than a name and contact information. Those sub-federal groups with a web presence posted similar information and agendas, often with direct links to the main Public Citizen website. Today many of these initiatives have stalled or no longer exist. The New Hampshire Citizens Trade Policy Commission, for example, was eliminated in 2011, and Vermont's commission last took action in 2010 (Vermont Legislature 2012).

Reasons for diminished activity appear to be directly related to decreased funding from groups such as the Ford Foundation, the Rockefeller Brothers Fund, and the Charles Stewart Mott Foundation. Others have cited the increasingly polarized nature of American politics, driven by ideological and financial considerations. Gone are former defenders of states' rights and key moderate Republicans in state legislatures and Congress, ending a previous spirit of bipartisan cooperation. Added to this is what one observer has called a "tsunami of money" from specific partisan interests, such as Charles and David Koch. As such, the representation of American sub-federal interests on matters of trade policy now hinges on the ability and willingness of the Office of the United States Trade Representative to prioritize state concerns in international negotiations.[10] The focus on international trade in the Donald Trump administration, including the renegotiation of NAFTA, however, could renew interest and financial support in this policy area in the future.

Civil Society in Mexico

As already noted, Mexican federalism, and generations of PRI rule, did not foster an environment conducive to societal engagement in any policy areas. Representation did exist, but it was a corporatist model, in which the PRI created groups to represent various social sectors. Starting in the 1930s, for example, PRI efforts focused on the military but also on peasants, labour, and other agrarian groups that served as the foundation of Mexico's revolutionary past. The PRI then provided benefits in exchange for the political support of these groups. All other forms of societal organization were openly discouraged by government. When opposition groups did mobilize, they were typically repressed, often with the use of force and, in some cases, intervention by the military (Mackinlay and Otero 2004).

The PRI's focus on working- and middle-class Mexicans continued in the post-war period with the government's protectionist trade policies and state investment in specific sectors of the economy. These economic priorities rewarded citizens responsible for producing manufactured goods. State subsidies for food, gas, transportation, and housing also benefited these segments of Mexican society. The result was a labour and middle class that enjoyed comparatively high wages, a favourable standard of living, better education, and increased life expectancy.

The Mexican debt crisis of the 1980s, however, offered new opportunities for social protest. In exchange for financial assistance from the United States and the International Monetary Fund, the Mexican government implemented a number of austerity programs, including the elimination of subsidies and social programs designed to provide assistance to the corporatist groups on which the PRI had long relied for political support. Citizen unrest also increased as government resources were diverted to debt servicing, the dismantling of previous protectionist policies, and privatization. Ultimately, the PRI was no longer able to provide state-based patronage and support to its traditional political base. Wages also dropped, resulting in greater inequality in Mexican incomes.

It is important to remember that social mobilization outside the old corporatist model had started to emerge prior to the debt crisis. One catalyst was the Tlatelolco massacre, during which the military killed large numbers of student protesters in 1968. Other acts of oppression further facilitated linkages between a wide range of groups, including independent unions, community organizations, Indigenous movements, and farming and middle-class interests that had previously supported the PRI (Foweraker 1993; La Botz and Boyer 1988). Initially these groups called for improved services, increased wages, and social programs. Quickly, however, the agenda expanded to include fair elections and human rights. A number of non-governmental interests also ran candidates in elections and offered support to unions, Indigenous groups, debtors, and peasants, including the Zapatista rebels. The result was a mix of organizations linking middle-class interests with lower-class (working and peasant) groups (Macdonald and Ayres 2016, 337).

Despite this coalescence, different strategies were adopted by varying factions. Middle-class efforts were focused primarily within CSOs focusing on electoral reform and human rights. These actors typically avoided mass mobilization and instead focused on strategies designed to create legislative and electoral pressure. Lower-class interests tended to prioritize demonstrations, hunger strikes, barricades, and other forms of public protest. The linkages between middle- and lower-class groups, however, created larger and more representative coalitions, which represented a significant shift in Mexico's democratization process.

The institutionalization of this dissent occurred with the formation of the PRD, which had considerable early success in state and local elections during this period. Middle-class CSOs also continued to work with Mexico's most poor and vulnerable citizens, especially on issues related to fair elections and electoral reform. Despite this success, the PRD was limited in its impact. The rise of other legitimate opposition parties undercut its electoral support, numerous militants in the party hierarchy were jailed at various times, and the divergent interests of members often resulted in significant internal party divisions. Ultimately, it would be the PAN, under Vicente Fox, that would sweep to power in the 2000 federal elections (Shefner 2007).

As noted earlier, Mexican societal groups began to mobilize during the negotiation of NAFTA, though not always from a unified position. For example, the Mexican Confederation of Labour (CTM) – in contrast to other domestic groups, such as the Mexican Action Network on Free Trade – supported NAFTA. Initially, the Mexican government adopted previous corporatist strategies by allowing the CTM and other select groups access to various forums, such as the Advisory Council for International Trade Negotiations, initially formed in 1993 as a consultative mechanism for the Department of Commerce and Industry Support, which later became the Department of Economy. In its early stages, the advisory council consisted of representatives from labour, agriculture, business, and academia, with regional councils selected directly by the secretary of commerce. Ultimately, however, its input on NAFTA was secondary to that of the Coordination of Business Organizations in Foreign Trade, which was formed in 1990 with representatives from fourteen sectoral associations and various chambers of commerce. Similar trends followed under the Fox and subsequent Felipe Calderon (2006–12) PAN governments. As such, the 2000s to date have represented the ongoing prioritization of large manufacturing interests, through selective protectionism, and the liberalization of services and agriculture (Vieira 2016; Von Bülow 2009).

Like Canada, the United States began to develop transnational linkages with Mexican societal groups. In 1998 John Sweeney, the president of the AFL-CIO, became the first prominent labour leader to visit Mexico in seventy-four years. During his visit Sweeney met with a wide range of groups including the CTM, but also new organizations such as the National Union of Workers. This broadening of engagement subsequently strengthened the Inter-American Regional Workers Organization, an organization coordinating labour groups throughout the Americas (Saguier 2011). The relatively negative NAFTA experience for many CSOs resulted in a call for greater cooperation between civil-society groups in order to avoid labour's perceived marginalization in future negotiations. These efforts were not limited to the United States and Mexico but also included the involvement of groups in Brazil and Chile, such as the Unified Workers' Central. This cooperation resulted in the creation of the Hemispheric Social Alliance, a broad coalition of labour, non-governmental organizations, and other civil-society groups that actively opposed FTAA negotiations between 2000 and 2004.

It is important, however, not to overstate these transnational linkages. Almost immediately, tensions began to emerge between groups advocating an end to capitalism and international trade, and "moderate" organizations such as the Inter-American Regional Workers Organization and the AFL-CIO. Some groups, such as the CTM, refused to participate in the Hemispheric Social Alliance. The broadening of the coalition of CSOs also resulted in an agenda that transcended trade and included a wide range of environmental and social issues (Von Bülow 2009, 8–15). As is the case today, cooperation between American and Mexican labour groups was also difficult. Put simply, foreign workers are viewed as a threat to US jobs, which often provides motivation for American protectionism.

International Trade and Multilevel Societal Activity in North America

My analysis highlights all three factors under consideration in this volume, namely the increasingly intrusive nature of international trade policy and agreements into domestic policy space, the form and practice of federalism in all three countries, and the evolving, and often limited, nature of civil-society activity related to trade policy in North America. Sub-federal governments in North America have varying levels of legitimacy in the negotiation and implementation of international trade agreements. Canadian provinces, for example, have the longest history of involvement due to a level of constitutional ambiguity on matters of foreign trade policy (see Paquin, and Hederer and Leblond in this volume). In the United States and Mexico, however, international trade is clearly a federal responsibility, outside of a small number of sectors such as procurement (see Egan and Schram in this volume). At the current time, with the exception of Canada, there is limited access for sub-federal institutional actors in the foreign trade policy of all three North American states.

Not surprisingly, these institutional realities have a direct impact on the activity of civil society. In Canada there is a long history of corporate representation on economic issues, but "alternative" voices on trade policy failed to gain prominence until the CUSFTA and NAFTA periods, albeit with limitations based on funding and resources. There are also distinct sectoral and regional differences influencing the activity of non-governmental actors in Canada. In Ontario, linkages tend to be driven by business, although First Nations groups have established a role in the forestry sector. Quebec has attempted to initiate formal consultative frameworks in the past, but the Liberals and the PQ have returned to a more elite-driven process of interaction. Alberta faces negligible demands from societal considerations and continues to focus on concerns raised by industry. Although the NDP in British Columbia improved access during the 1990s, the role of labour and the environment diminished considerably during the past decade. The recent CETA negotiations also suggest a limited impact for societal actors at the sub-federal level.

The United States also has a pattern of sub-federal activity by nongovernmental actors related to foreign trade policy. Well-funded national groups such as Public Citizen, with some involvement from organized labour, led by the AFL-CIO, have targeted numerous state legislatures in an attempt to introduce legislation focusing on state involvement in the negotiation and implementation of international trade agreements and presidential TPA. These legislative initiatives also helped create a number of state citizen commissions that include elected and bureaucratic members of government, as well as representatives from civil society. Another unique feature of US states is the existence of societal groups with an emphasis on international trade. In most cases, these organizations consist of members from organized labour, churches, environmental groups, and other social justice and democratic rights organizations. The majority of these groups are also closely affiliated with, or are members of, the Citizens Trade Campaign or Public Citizen.

Despite this proliferation of activity, it is clear that US sub-federal initiatives have only a minor impact on either state or federal foreign trade policy. Interest in sub-federal international trade peaked during a small window of activity between 2004 and 2009. During the first wave of activity these societal groups targeted the expiration of TPA in 2007, which was ultimately not extended. Building support for the Democratic challenge to the Republicans in the 2008 presidential election was also part of the strategy. Today, however, Public Citizen and labour have shifted attention and resources away from sub-federal international trade to other campaigns, such as governor recall efforts and new challenges related to the Donald Trump administration (Yakabuski 2012).

This raises a question as to why national groups, such as Public Citizen, would adopt a strategy of targeting US states in an attempt to influence Congress. Again, one possible explanation is the nature of American federalism. Specifically, the United States has a tradition of weak party linkages between federal and state governments. There is also an absence of robust party discipline, which, combined with an executive branch that is typically less powerful than the legislature, creates an environment conducive to lobbying by individuals, firms, and state governments. Although Canadian parties also have difficulty transcending federal and provincial politics, durable traditions of party discipline, and a strong executive government, tend to promote a less confrontational form of "executive" federalism (Smiley 1987). Although Canada has nationally based groups with a focus on international trade, these organizations have typically engaged provinces by providing studies critical of specific trade issues or by having informal conversations and lobbying.

Finally, Mexico has a different pattern of civil-society involvement, once again driven by the realities of Mexican federalism. Historically, societal activity was tied to corporatist relations between the ruling PRI and select labour and non-governmental groups until the economic crisis of the 1980s. The emergence of new groups representing the interests of Mexico's middle and lower classes, however, challenged the status quo, focusing on human rights and fair elections as opposed to international trade. Many of these groups also adopted very different strategies to influence government, with some coalitions highlighting legislative electoral pressure and others pursuing other forms of mass mobilization, such as demonstrations, hunger strikes, and other protests. These groups captured the attention of new political parties, such as the PRD and PAN, which both attempted to tap into the potential electoral support.

These observations allow for a better understanding of the impact of civil society on foreign trade policy in North America. Where activity does occur, it is often limited to "process" issues and not typically tied to policy outcomes at the federal or the international level. It is important to note, however, that challenges for societal groups are not solely tied to federalism. Organized labour, for example, has suffered from a decline in manufacturing jobs, most of which were well paid, secure, and unionized. The rise of the service sector, with minimal union representation, as well as a new generation of workers with a general antipathy for unions, further contributes to a decline in influence. Even public sector unions remain particularly vulnerable in the aftermath of the 2008 global economic crisis as opinion turns against the perception of high wages, overly generous benefit packages, and rich pensions. Traditional political influence within the NDP in Canada and the Democrats in the United States is also in decline as these parties begin to distance themselves from electorally unpopulated allegiances.

On another level, broader societal engagement is limited by a series of other problems, such as consultation fatigue. Just as governments face limited resources, so do non-governmental interests, and most groups do not have the capacity to engage in dialogue with different ministries at both levels of government. There is also the reality that "civil society" is not a monolith, and different groups have varying interests. In Canada, for example, organized labour, the environment, and Indigenous groups have all actively engaged government on softwood lumber and have enjoyed some success at various times, despite very different agendas. Another reality is that foreign trade is an extremely complicated and technical issue that often goes beyond the basic understanding of observers who are not directly involved in the actual policy process. It is also clear that the events of 11 September 2001 shifted the North American policy agenda from the completion of the FTAA and Doha Round negotiations to broader security concerns.

Despite these limitations, it is crucial to include civil society in any analysis of the multilevel governance of foreign trade policy. Doing so provides an understanding of the actions and impact of civil society in matters of international trade. As this study suggests, civil society includes a wide range of institutionalized groups that actively engage the policymaking process at the domestic, international, and transnational levels. For the most part, their activity consists of outreach to mainstream and material institutions and actors, such as governments, the media, universities, and other similarly engaged groups. What also exists, albeit more on the margins, is the participation of alternative activist ideas and communities. As Nancy Fraser has suggested, these counter publics consist of "parallel discursive arenas where members of subordinated social groups invent and circulate counter discourses, which in turn permit them to formulate oppositional interpretations of their identities, interests, and needs" (1990, 67). These typically include ideas that transcend international trade, encompassing a wide range of social justice and environmental issues.

According to Carroll and Huxtable (2014), this situation creates a dual level of engagement within civil society between institutionalized actors and counter publics, allowing for alternative and discursive narratives that challenge the neo-liberal order. Based on the discussion of civil society in North America herein, it is clear that these voices exist regarding international trade, albeit to a lesser degree than those of the more organized, arguably "elite" CSOs. It is also clear that more work is needed to understand the concerns and motivations of the marginalized narratives. From an academic perspective, this is interesting as it challenges the dominance of material, rationalist knowledge in the global political economy. On a more practical level, however, greater awareness and inclusion is needed to address normative concerns

178   Christopher Kukucha

related to international trade, which will only expand the legitimacy of
future international trade initiatives.

NOTES

1 The distinction between interstate and intrastate federalism is similar but
   less differentiated than the distinction between self-rule and shared rule.
   Generally, interstate federalism promotes self-rule capacities and reflects
   the principle of *séparation des pouvoirs*. By contrast, intrastate federalism
   promotes shared rule and the principle of *distribution des pouvoirs*. For a
   detailed discussion see Broschek (forthcoming).
2 Personal interview, 31 August 2005.
3 Personal interview, 4 June 2003.
4 Personal interview, 14 July 2004.
5 Personal interview, 28 August 2002.
6 Personal interview, 2 June 2004.
7 Personal interview, 31 May 2004, and personal interview, 19 July 2004.
8 Personal interview, 28 May 2003, and personal interview, 29 May 2003.
9 Personal interview, 2 September 2005.
10 Personal interview, 18 March 2015, and personal interview, 20 March 2015.

REFERENCES

Abelson, Donald. 1995a. "Environmental Lobbying and Political Posturing:
   The Role of Environmental Groups in Ontario's Debate over NAFTA."
   Canadian Public Administration 38 (3): 352–81.
– 1995b. "From Policy Research to Political Advocacy: The Changing Role of
   Think Tanks in American Politics." *Canadian Review of American Studies* 25
   (1): 93–126.
Alvarez, Sonia E., E. Dagnimo, and A. Escobar, eds. 1998. *Culture of Politics,
   Politics of Culture: Re-visioning Latin American Social Movements*. Boulder,
   CO, and Oxford: Westview Press.
Anderson, Greg, and Christopher J. Kukucha. 2016. "Back to the Future: IPE
   and the Evolution of Global Politics." In *International Political Economy*,
   edited by G. Anderson and C.J. Kukucha, 2–23. Don Mills, ON: Oxford
   University Press.
Ayres, Jeffrey M., ed. 1998. *Challenging Conventional Wisdom: Political
   Movements and Popular Contention against North American Free Trade*.
   Toronto: University of Toronto Press.
– 2004. "Political Economy, Civil Society, and the Deep Integration Debate in
   Canada." *American Review of Canadian Studies* 34 (4): 621–47.
Barnes, Nielan. 2011. "North American Integration? Civil Society and
   Immigrant Health Policy Convergence." *Politics and Policy* 39 (1): 69–90.

Bayes, Jane, and Laura Gonzalez. 2011. "Globalization, Transnationalism, and Intersecting Geographies of Power: The Case of the Consejo Consultivo del Instituto de los Mexicanos en le Exterior (CC-IME): A Study in Progress." *Politics and Policy* 39 (1): 11–44.

Boatright, Robert G. 2011. *Interest Groups and Campaign Finance Reform in the United States*. Ann Arbor: University of Michigan Press.

Brock, Kathy. 1996. "Lifting Impressions: Interest Groups, the Provinces, and the Constitution." In *Provinces: Canadian Provincial Politics*, edited by C. Dunn, 95–122. Peterborough, ON: Broadview Press.

Brodie, Janine. 1995. *Politics on the Margin: Restructuring and the Canadian Women's Movement*. Halifax, NS: Fernwood.

Broschek, Jörg. Forthcoming. "Bicameralism and the Consequences of Political Structuring in Canada: Lost Alternatives, Future Options." In *Canadian Federalism and Its Future: Actors and Institutions*, edited by J. Poirier and A.-G. Gagnon. Montreal and Kingston: McGill-Queen's University Press.

Brysk, Alison, ed. 2000. *From Tribal Village to Global Village: Indian Rights and International Relations in Latin America*. Stanford, CA: Stanford University Press.

Carment, David, and Joe Landry. 2015. "Civil Society and Canadian Foreign Policy." In *Readings in Canadian Foreign Policy*, 3rd. ed., edited by D. Bratt and C.J. Kukucha, 277–89. Don Mills, ON: Oxford University Press.

Carroll, William K., and David Huxtable. 2014. "Building Capacity for Alternative Knowledge: The Canadian Centre for Policy Alternatives." *Canadian Review of Social Policy* 70: 93–111.

Carroll, William K., and Murray Shaw. 2001. "Consolidating a Neoliberal Policy Bloc in Canada, 1976–1996." *Canadian Public Policy* 27 (2): 1–23.

Citizens Trade Campaign. 2012. What Is Citizens Trade Campaign? http://www.citizenstrade.org/ctc/about-ctc/what-is-citizens-trade-campaign/

Clarkson, Stephen. 2008. *Does North America Exist? Governing the Continent after NAFTA and 9/11*. Toronto: University of Toronto Press.

Coleman, William D., and Grace Skogstad. 1990. "Policy Communities and Policy Networks: A Structural Approach." In *Policy Communities and Public Policy in Canada*, edited by W.D. Coleman and G. Skogstad, 14–33. Toronto: Copp Clark Pitman.

Cox, Robert. 1981. "Social Forces, States, and World Orders: Beyond International Relations Theory." *Millenium: Journal of International Studies* 10 (2): 126–55.

Dam, Kenneth W. 2004. *The Rules of the Global Game: A New Look at US International Economic Policymaking*. Chicago, IL: University of Chicago Press.

Deardorff, Alan V., and Robert M. Stern. 1998. *Constituent Interests and US Trade Policies*. Ann Arbor: University of Michigan Press.

Destler, I. Mac. 2005. *American Trade Politics*. 4th ed. Washington, DC: Institute for International Economics.

Englehart, Neil A. 2011. "What Makes Civil Society Civil? The State and Social Groups." *Polity* 43 (3): 337–57.

Facchini, Giovanni, A.M. Mayda, and P. Mishra. 2011. "Do Interest Groups Affect US Immigration Policy?" *Journal of International Economics* 85 (1): 114–28.

Falk, Richard. 1997. "Resisting 'Globalization-From-Above' through 'Globalization-From-Below.'" *New Political Economy* 2, 17–24.

Forum on Democracy and Trade. 2012. *Trade and Federalism*. http://www.forumdemocracy.net/section.php?id=121

Foweraker, Joe. 1993. *Popular Mobilization in Mexico: The Teachers' Movement, 1977–87*. Cambridge: Cambridge University Press.

Fox, Jonathan A. 2001. "Evaluacion de las coaliciones binacionales de la sociedad civil a partir de la experiencia Mexico–EstadosUnidos." *Revista Mexicana de Sociologica* 63 (3): 211–68.

Fraser, Nancy. 1990. "Rethinking the Public Sphere: A Contribution to the Critique of Actually Existing Democracy." *Social Text* 25 (26): 56–80.

Fry, Earl H. 1998. *The Expanding Role of State and Local Governments in US Foreign Affairs*. New York: Council of Foreign Relations Press.

– 2004. "The Role of Sub-national Governments in North American Integration." In *The Art of the State, II: Thinking North America*, edited by T.J. Courchene, D.J. Savoie, and D. Schwanen, 3–31. Montreal, QC: Institute for Research on Public Policy.

Gabriel, Christina, and Laura Macdonald. 2011. "Citizenship at the Margins: The Canadian Seasonal Agricultural Worker Program and Civil Society Advocacy." *Politics and Policy* 39 (1): 45–68.

Gilpin, Robert. 1987. *The Political Economy of International Relations*. Princeton, NJ: Princeton University Press.

Goldberg, David H. 1990. *Foreign Policy and Ethnic Interest Groups: American and Canadian Jews Lobby for Israel*. Westport, CT: Greenwood Press.

Grieco, Joseph M. 1990. *Cooperation among Nations: Europe, America and Non-tariff Barriers*. Ithaca, NY: Cornell University Press.

Grossman, Gene M., and Elhanan Helpman. 2002. *Interest Groups and Trade Policy*. Princeton, NJ: Princeton University Press.

Hann, Chris, and Elizabeth Dunn. 1996. *Civil Society: Challenging Western Models*. New York: Routledge.

Held, David. 1995. *Democracy and the Global Order: From the Modern State to Cosmopolitan Governance*. Stanford, CA: Stanford University Press.

Hoberg, George. 2001. "Policy Cycles and Policy Regimes: A Framework for Studying Policy Change." In *In Search of Sustainability: British Columbia Forest Policy in the 1990s*, edited by Benjamin Cashore, Michael Howlett,

Jeremy Wilson, George Hoberg, and Jeremy Rayner, 3–30. Vancouver: UBC Press.

Hueglin, T.O., and A. Fenna. 2006. *Comparative Federalism: A Systemic Inquiry*. Peterborough, ON: Broadview Press.

Johnston, Josée, and Gordon Laxer. 2003. "Solidarity in the Age of Globalization: Lessons from the Anti-MAI and Zapatista Struggles." *Theory and Society* 23 (1): 39–91.

Kincaid, John. 2003. "Globalization and Federalism in the United States: Continuity in Adaptation." In *The Impact of Global and Regional Integration on Federal Systems: A Comparative Analysis*, edited by H. Lazar, H. Telford, and R.L. Watts, 37–86. Montreal and Kingston: McGill-Queen's University Press.

Kirton, John. 2001–2. "Guess Who Is Coming to Kananaskis?" *International Journal* 56 (1): 101–27.

Kukucha, Christopher J. 2015a. "Federalism Matters: Evaluating the Impact of Sub-federal Governments in Canadian and American Foreign Trade Policy." *Canadian Foreign Policy Journal* 21 (3): 224–37.

– 2015b. "Lacking Linkages: Labour, Civil Society, and Sub-federal Trade Policy in North America." In *Regional Governance in Post-NAFTA North America: Building without Architecture*, edited by G. Anderson and B. Bow, 110–29. New York: Routledge.

La Botz, D., and Richard Boyer. 1988. *The Crisis of Mexican Labor*. New York: Praege.

Lenin, Vladimir I. 1939. *Imperialism: The Highest Stage of Capitalism*. New York: International Publishers.

Loewenstein, Leiman M. 1965. *Political Power and the Governmental Process*. Chicago, IL: University of Chicago Press.

Macdonald, Laura C. 2002. "Governance and State-Society Relations: The Challenges." In *Capacity for Choice: Canada in a New North America*, edited by G. Hoberg, 187–223. Toronto: University of Toronto Press.

Macdonald, Laura C., and Jeffrey Ayres. 2016. "Civil Society and International Political Economy." In *International Political Economy*, edited by G. Anderson and C.J. Kukucha, 329–42. Don Mills, ON: Oxford University Press.

Mackinlay, Horacio, and Gerado Otero. 2004. "State Corporatism and Peasant Organizations: Towards New Institutional Arrangements." In *Neoliberal Globalism, the State and Civil Society*, edited by G. Otero, 72–88. New York: Zed Books.

Maine Fair Trade Campaign. 2012. Home. http://www.mainefairtrade.org/.

Marx, Karl. 1962. *Capital*. 4th ed. Translated by Eden Paul and Cedar Paul. London: Dent.

Montpetit, Éric. 2003. *Misplaced Distrust: Policy Networks and the Environment in France, the United States, and Canada*. Vancouver: UBC Press.

Nolan Garcia, Kimberley A. 2011. "The Evolution of United States–Mexico
    Labor Cooperation (1994–2009): Achievements and Challenges." *Politics and
    Policy* 39 (1): 91–118.
Oregon Fair Trade Campaign. 2012. Home. http://www.citizenstrade.org
    /ctc/oregon/.
Pastor, Robert A. 1980. *Congress and the Politics of US Foreign Economic Policy,
    1929–1976.* Berkeley: University of California Press.
Pross, Paul A. 1975. "Pressure Groups: Adaptive Instruments of Political
    Communication." In *Pressure Groups Behaviour in Canadian Politics*, edited
    by A.P. Pross, 1–27. Toronto: McGraw-Hill Ryerson.
Public Citizen. 2012a. Globalization and Trade. http://www.citizen.org.
– 2012b. Spotlight on Your State. http://www.citizen.org/Page.aspx
    ?pid=1195.
Remes, Alain de. 2006. "Democratization and Dispersion of Power: New
    Scenarios in Mexican Federalism." *Mexican Studies / EstudiosMexicanos* 22
    (1): 175–204.
Rozell, Mark J., C. Wilcox, and M.M. Franz. 2011. *Interest Groups in American
    Campaigns: The New Face of Electioneering.* 3rd. ed. New York: Oxford
    University Press.
Sabet, Daniel. 2008. "Thickening Civil Society: Explaining the Development
    of Associational Life in Mexico." *Democratization* 15 (2): 410–32.
Sager, Michelle. 2002. *One Voice or Many? Federalism and International Trade.*
    New York: LFB Scholarly Publishing.
Saguier, Marcelo. 2011. "Transnational Labour Mobilisation in the Americas."
    In *Civil Society and International Governance: The Role of Non-state Actors in
    Global and Regional Regulatory Frameworks*, edited by D. Armstrong, V. Bello,
    J. Gilson, and D. Spini, 181–97. New York: Routledge.
Shefner, Jon. 2007. "Rethinking Civil Society in the Age of NAFTA: The Case
    of Mexico." *Annals of the American Academy of Political and Social Science*, 610,
    188–93.
Slavin, Sarah. 1995. *US Women's Interest Groups: Institutional Profiles.* Westport,
    CT: Greenwood Press.
Smiley, Donald V. 1971. "The Structural Problem of Canadian Federalism."
    Canadian Public Administration 14 (3): 326–43.
– 1987. *The Federal Condition in Canada.* Toronto: McGraw-Hill Ryerson.
Smiley, Donald V., and Ronald L. Watts. 1985. *Intrastate Federalism.* Vol. 39,
    Research Studies Prepared for the Royal Commission on the Economic
    Union and Development Prospects for Canada. Toronto: University of
    Toronto Press.
Smith, Miriam. 2005. *A Civil Society: Collective Actors in Canadian Political Life.*
    Peterborough, ON: Broadview Press.

Thomas, Janet. 2000. *The Battle in Seattle: The Story behind and beyond the WTO Demonstrations*. Golden, CO: Fulcrum Publishers.

Trew, Stuart. 2013. "Correcting the Democratic Deficit in the CETA Negotiations: Civil Society Engagement in the Provinces, Municipalities, and Europe." *International Journal* 68 (4): 568–75.

Vermont Legislature. 2012. *Commission on International Trade and Sovereignty: 2011–2012 Legislative Session*. http://www.leg.state.vt.us.

Vieira, Vinícius R. 2016. When Procedural Legitimacy Equals Nothing: Civil Society and Foreign Trade Policy in Brazil and Mexico. *Contexto Internacional* 38 (1): 349–84.

Von Bülow, Marisa. 2009. "Networks of Trade Protest in the Americas: Toward a New Labour Internationalism?" *Latin American Politics and Society* 51 (2): 1–28.

Wall, M. 2001. *The Battle in Seattle: How NGOs Used the Internet to Challenge the WTO*. Seattle: University of Washington Press.

Ward, Peter M., Victoria Rodríguez, and Enrique C. Mendoza. 1999. *New Federalism and State Government in Mexico: Bringing the States Back In*. Austin: University of Texas at Austin.

Washington Fair Trade Coalition. 2012. Home. http://washingtonfairtrade.org/.

Weber, Paul J., and Landis Jones. 1994. *US Religious Interest Groups*. Westport, CT: Greenwood Press.

Weldon, Jeffrey. A. 1997. "The Political Sources of Presidentialism in Mexico." In *Presidentialism and Democracy in Latin America*, edited by S. Mainwaring and M.S. Shugart, 225–58. Cambridge: Cambridge University Press.

Wolfe, Robert, and Matthew Mendelsohn. 2005. "Values and Interests in Attitudes toward Trade and Globalization: The Continuing Compromise of Embedded Liberalism." *Canadian Journal of Political Science* 38 (1): 45–68.

Yakabuski, Konrad. 2012. "Democrats in a Fretful State over Wisconsin." *Globe and Mail*, 26 May.

SECTION TWO

Europe and Australia – Multilevel Trade Politics in Comparative Perspective

7 Federalism in Times of Increased Integration: The Participation of the Cantons in Swiss Trade Policy

ANDREAS R. ZIEGLER

Switzerland's federalism is generally known as being a prime example of power-sharing between a federal government and states. It is still based on the ideas enshrined in the first constitution of the consolidated nation state of 1848. What is less known is how cantonal involvement in trade policymaking has changed over the last twenty-five years. As elsewhere, due to increased globalization and economic integration – in particular, at the European level – the mechanisms to involve the cantons have evolved considerably, leading to the creation of new institutions and procedures. While some of them are formalized, others are more informal and still in the making. At the same time, the capacity of the relatively small sub-federal entities in Switzerland heavily limits their possibilities to influence directly the international relations of Switzerland in a systematic and comprehensive way. The federal government still enjoys exclusive competence in this field (like in all its foreign policy), yet it must now take into account the particular interests of the cantons and consult them in those areas. The final ratification of trade agreements does not normally involve the cantons directly but only through their representation in Parliament.

Using the especially important agreements between Switzerland and the European Union as an example, this chapter demonstrates the changing role of the cantons in trade policy that has taken place since the early 1990s. Overall, it concludes that increased sub-federal involvement has resulted in better acceptance of the negotiation results by the cantons (and thereby the population in general), but at the price of slower and more complicated communication procedures, which affects the flexibility of the federal government. One can probably say that in Switzerland the strong engagement of the cantons is primarily a consequence of two factors: strong institutional resources and the changing nature of trade policy. Societal mobilization also plays a certain role, but the role of societal actors and political parties in trade policy is mostly visible at the federal level because the country is relatively small, and many of the cantons are very small. For parties, nongovernmental organizations (NGOs), and lobbies it is more efficient to work at the federal level, mostly through their offices in the capital.

Situating the Swiss Case

Like many federal states, Switzerland was created as a modern state in the nineteenth century from a group of formerly independent territories. Some of these territories, traditionally known as cantons, had concluded military alliances as early as the thirteenth century;[1] others were created as a result of wars and territorial agreements between European powers only in the nineteenth century. During the Napoleonic occupation in the early nineteenth century they had for a short period been joined in a centrally organized state (the so-called Helvetic Republic) following the French tradition, but they only became a modern unified federal state in 1848 when (after a short civil war) the Constitution of the Swiss Confederation was adopted (Federal Constitution 1848). This constitution underwent a major reform in 1874 (Federal Constitution 1874) and was updated (though not fundamentally altered) in 1999 (Federal Constitution 1999).[2] The constitution of 18 April 1999 contains the basic rules on the participation of the Swiss cantons in foreign policy, including trade policy.

Before becoming part of the new federal state, the cantons had, in principle, their own foreign policy, including trade policy. In order to strengthen the international position of the cantons, the agreements between them most often involved questions regarding their political and military relations with foreign powers. Important treaties were concluded from the fifteenth century onwards between most or all of the cantons and France, the Habsburg Empire, Spain, Milan, Venice, Savoy, the Holy See, the Netherlands, and England (see Behr 2014).[3] The Swiss cantons heavily depended on the income from trade with these powers (in particular, exports of livestock and milk products) and from the sale of mercenaries, an ancient type of modern human trafficking or trade in services. Many treaties were concluded to obtain trade preferences and a guaranteed market access. The import of salt was of fundamental importance and often an important element of these treaties. In the eighteenth century, exports of textiles became important. Already in 1815, the power to conclude military alliances and trade agreements was, in principle, transferred to the central organ of the cantons for joint decision making, but the remaining powers of the cantons to conclude economic agreements were still relatively important (see Kreis 2012).

The constitution of the newly created federal state of 1848 contained the basic model of the cantons' participation in foreign affairs (including trade policy), which is still in force today. In principle, the constitution introduced the full competence of the federal state to declare war and conclude treaties, even in those areas where the cantons were competent domestically. The text mentioned explicitly that the federal competence included the conclusion of customs and trade agreements with foreign states (Federal Constitution 1848, article 8). At the same time, the cantons kept the right to conclude their own treaties with foreign states in the areas of the state economy, cross-border transport, and police cooperation, as long as these treaties did not infringe the rights of the federal level or other cantons (article 9). In these areas, direct negotiations and contacts between the cantons and foreign entities were allowed; in all other questions, they had to be arranged through the federal government (article 10). The constitution of 1874 contained exactly the same provisions.

Although Switzerland is often studied, and sometimes admired, as a well-functioning federal state, one should not forget the specific geopolitical and geographic conditions under which it has evolved. Today the whole country has approximately 8.4 million inhabitants. Of these, approximately two million are foreigners who have no voting rights at the federal level (and normally neither at the sub-federal level nor at the local level). The country is made up of twenty-six cantons. These differ enormously in actual size and even more so in the size of their population and economic structure. Zurich alone has approximately 1.4 million inhabitants and thus is home to one-sixth of the total population, but there are at least eight cantons with less than 100,000 inhabitants (and are therefore smaller than an average town in most countries). Another five cantons have less than 200,000 inhabitants. Among the bigger cantons (after Zurich), it takes only four more cantons – Berne (980,000 inhabitants), Vaud (718,000 inhabitants), Aargau (613,000 inhabitants), and St Gallen (479,000 inhabitants) – to reach more than half of the population of the country. An additional issue is the fact that the country has four official languages, and therefore the balance between the Germanic part of the country (approximately two-thirds of the population) and the Latin part (one-third of the population, comprising the French, Italian, and Romansch languages) is an important factor in daily politics (see Wouters, Van Kerckhoven, and Vidal 2016).[4]

Institutional Foundations of Cantonal Participation

The constitution of 1999 did not totally change the principles governing the involvement of the cantons in foreign policy matters but essentially led to a more detailed description of the rights and duties of the federal level and the cantons (for an account under the old constitution see Schmitt 1994, 362).[5] The foreign relations power is now described at the very beginning of the second chapter of the constitution (1999) relating to the powers of the federal level (articles 54–6, sec. 1; articles 57–61, sec. 2).[6] In addition, chapter 3 of the constitution speaks about how the federal government and Parliament share their powers when dealing with foreign relations (articles 184, 186).[7] As we will see, the cantons normally deal directly with the federal government, but they can also use certain mechanisms to influence the federal parliament.

Competencies

The most important cantonal powers currently lie in the areas of education, health care, police, construction, and local infrastructure, including public transport and energy and water supply.[8] In addition, the cantons often have the task of implementing federal policies – that is, in the area of labour conditions, immigration, or some aspects of environmental policy (for an example related to environmental policy see Casado-Asensio and Steurer 2016). As a consequence, these are the areas in which more examples of friction between Switzerland's foreign affairs and their activities and interests exist.

An important addendum to the constitution of 1999 is a provision that states explicitly for the first time that the federal level in its relations with foreign states "shall respect the powers of the cantons and protect their interests" (article 54, paragraph 3). Furthermore, the cantons are given specific procedural rights to participate in the making of foreign-policy decisions by the federal level (article 55).

Besides these new elements in the constitution of 1999 and some added details regarding existing principles, in the very same year a new federal law was adopted to fill these provisions with meaning, the Federal Law on the Participation of the Cantons in the Foreign Policy of the Swiss Confederation, on 22 December (BGMK 1999).[9] This law is mostly concerned with increased participation in the negotiations of international agreements, and the ratification of these agreements is governed by the ratification provisions in the constitution (which shall be treated in the next section).

Intergovernmental Relations

The BGMK was Switzerland's first attempt to find solutions to the increased importance of international developments and, in particular, binding international agreements at the local level. This process is often associated with the phenomenon of globalization, though one can show that developments of a similar nature had already taken place in the late nineteenth century. Nevertheless, as in many other countries, the developments since the Second World War (especially in the 1980s and 1990s) have led to a widespread and intense perception that local autonomy and existing powers are more and more affected by increased cooperation at the global and European level. The resulting rules and principles do limit the scope for national and sub-federal decision making (see Füglister and Wasserfallen 2014). As international negotiations are traditionally the responsibility of the federal government, the federal parliament, citizens (direct democracy), and the cantons were looking for ways to influence this process, be it before, during, or after the negotiation of binding international rules or even of legally non-binding rules that could still de facto limit their impact (see Cina 2016).[10] Consider the following:

- Article 1 of the BGMK takes up the general principle that the cantons must be allowed to participate in all processes (i.e., decision making) led by the federal government internationally whenever the processes affect areas in which the cantons are competent at the domestic level or, generally, where their essential interests are concerned. According to the text of the constitution, the essential interests of the cantons are always concerned when such international decisions lead to important implementation tasks at the cantonal level (paragraph 2). Although the law states that this participation in the decision making should not hamper the effectiveness of Swiss foreign policy (paragraph 3), there are no clear indications on how this should be prevented or when this would be the case.
- Article 2 states the objectives of cantonal participation in the negotiations. The cantons will have an opportunity to defend their interests regarding the outcome of the negotiations as such and the necessary implementation that they will have to ensure. Where possible, they should be given the chance to prevent an erosion of their own powers. In addition, it is hoped that this participation gives domestic legitimacy to the outcome of the negotiations by the federal government.

- In general, cantons and the federal government are to exchange as much information as possible. In particular, the federal government will inform the cantons early and comprehensively on the issues at stake in upcoming negotiations whenever they ask for it (article 3). Before negotiations are undertaken, the federal government must give the cantons an opportunity to express their views in a consultation process. This special consultation process comes in addition to the existing consultation of various stakeholders that is traditionally undertaken for major negotiations (just as for special legislative projects). Whenever the position of the cantons is not respected, though their domestic powers are affected, the federal government needs to provide justification (article 4).
- The federal government can include representatives of the cantons in the preparation of a specific negotiation mandate as well as in the negotiating teams themselves. Whenever their powers are affected, they normally have a right to such representation. The cantons must decide among themselves how they want to nominate the respective representative(s), although the official appointment is the prerogative of the federal government (article 5).
- All information exchanged between the cantons and the federal government is to be treated as confidential (article 6).
- In the final operative provision of the law (article 7), the generally accepted (but so far unwritten) principle of Swiss constitutional law is codified for the first time, that the cantons have a legal obligation to implement international commitments entered into by the federal government.

The existence of the specific BGMK does not mean that other policy instruments that had already existed before the coming into force of this new law cannot be used by the cantons to defend their strategic trade interests. One such instrument is the so-called Cantonal Initiative (Standesinitiative) (Federal Constitution 1999, article 160, paragraph 1).[11] Under this rule a policy proposal must be treated by the federal parliament and can potentially lead to a binding decision for the federal government (for a description of the role of the federal parliament, see Granat 2017).[12] Although this was traditionally not often the case, these requests can concern the foreign trade policy of the country. It seems that the use of such initiatives has increased in recent years. A good example is a recent cantonal initiative by the canton of Vaud. In April 2016 this canton's parliament adopted a cantonal initiative to request that, in the ongoing negotiations between Switzerland and Malaysia, market access liberalization for palm oil not be included. Although several NGOs and lobbies had already submitted similar proposals, mostly for ecological reasons that see the production methods of palm oil in Malaysia as unsustainable, the request by this canton was mostly motivated by economic, that is, protectionist reasons. Vaud has a relatively important agricultural sector and produces a fair amount of colza (rapeseed) oil (BauernZeitung 2016). In July 2016 a parallel initiative was discussed by the big chamber of the canton of Thurgau, another canton with an important agricultural sector. The federal government had always rejected a total ban or exclusion from the negotiations because this is an important sector for Malaysia, and the federal government would prefer to find rules regarding the production methods (to ascertain sustainability) and/or quotas to limit the negative effects (*Neue Zürcher Zeitung* 2016). This is not the first time that the importation of palm oil has been discussed in the federal parliament following a cantonal initiative. In 2012 a general ban, which was not limited to a specific negotiation of a free trade agreement with a known partner, for the import of palm oil was requested by the canton of Fribourg. Ultimately, however, this initiative was rejected by Parliament in 2013.[13]

Another example of a cantonal initiative that concerns directly international trade negotiations is the one submitted by the canton of Geneva, which hosts the WTO among other international organizations, in early 2015. It requested the federal government to disclose immediately the available information on the negotiations for a trade-in-services agreement and to promise not to make any commitments leading to privatizations or a reduction of public services. In addition, this cantonal initiative wanted the federal parliament to endorse a request to subject the result of the negotiations to a referendum in which both the majority of the voting citizens and a majority of all cantons would have to vote positively. Equally, this initiative was rejected by Parliament in 2016. In this case, it became apparent that the parliament of the canton of Geneva was very concerned about the legitimacy of services negotiations in general and questioned not only the way this agreement was being negotiated but also the potential outcome. The idea that public services should be of a high level and that there be less room for the private sector in the areas of health care or education is heavily influenced by neighbouring France and, thus, is an important political issue in this region of the country.

So far, the cantonal initiatives in the area of foreign trade have seldom been accepted by the federal parliament, but an increase in their use seems apparent. Generally, the federal parliament defends a position that allows the federal government to participate actively in international and bilateral trade negotiations. This does not mean that protectionist policies do not influence the Swiss position in negotiations, but the federal parliament has so far been confident that the federal government itself knows the politically acceptable limits when it comes to liberalization of access to the Swiss market, particularly in the areas of agriculture, public services, and migration. Yet, the possibility that certain cantons will try to limit the negotiating freedom of the federal government in advance or during negotiations, through cantonal initiatives submitted to the federal parliament, should not be neglected in the future.

As in other federal states (for example, Belgium), the ratification process of certain international agreements is subject to approval by cantons in addition to the more common approval by the two chambers of the federal parliament. This procedure was codified in more detail even before the entry of the new constitution of 1999 and before the rules on participation in ongoing negotiations just outlined. Although the constitutions of 1848 and 1874 foresaw the approval of certain treaties by the federal parliament, an amendment in 1921 was voted to subject certain important treaties to additional approval by the citizens in a referendum (direct democracy) (Popular Initiative 1921, article 89, paragraph 4).[14]

Much later, in 1977, this provision was extended to include the approval by a majority of the cantons in certain rare cases. Interestingly, when the first constitution was discussed in 1848, at least one canton requested that all treaties should be approved by a majority of the cantons – a proposal that was rejected.[15] Similar proposals by Members of Parliament in the nineteenth century did not receive much support. For the first time, in 1972, when Switzerland concluded its first bilateral trade agreement with the European Union (at that time the European Economic Community), the federal government decided to submit the agreement to a referendum, which, for the agreement to be accepted, required a majority of the voting citizens and a majority of the population of each canton to vote in favour of it. This was controversial because it was not explicitly foreseen in the constitution. The federal government argued that the ratification of such an important agreement should be treated like a change of the constitution, which requires the application of this procedure. The idea that agreements of the same importance to the country as a change in the constitution should be accepted by a majority of the cantons was formally introduced by an amendment to the constitution in 1977. Since then, all treaties leading to membership in an international organization in the area of collective defence or of a supranational character have been subjected to approval by both the majority of all voting citizens and a majority of the cantons (Federal Constitution 1874, amend. 1977, article 89, paragraph 5).

Additionally, for a wider group of treaties eight cantons can request that the approval of the treaty be subject to a referendum in which a majority of those who vote have to support it. It is extremely rare that eight cantons decide together to use this prerogative, and it has so far never happened with regard to foreign policy issues (for news coverage see *Neue Zürcher Zeitung* 2013).[16] This solution in the constitution of 1999 is still in force today (article 140, paragraph 1b).

Interestingly, as had been done in 1972 with regard to the first free trade agreement concluded with the European Union, the ratification of the comprehensive trade agreement creating a European Economic Area, between the European Union and members of the European Free Trade Association (EFTA), in 1992 was subjected to approval by both a majority of the voting citizens and a majority of the cantons. This was done despite the fact that legally the agreement did not require such a double majority under the constitution, because it neither led to membership in an international organization in the area of collective defence nor was it of a supranational character. In this case, the federal government felt that the economic and political consequences of the agreement were so important that they justified such a procedure. The debate on whether this constituted a violation of the constitution was intense but ultimately without consequence. As a matter of fact, this agreement was very comprehensive and basically would have led to an integration into the internal market of the European Union without proper membership.[17]

In 2012 a proposal for another amendment of the constitution was voted that would have extended the number of cases in which a majority of the cantons would have to vote in favour of the ratification of an international agreement. More than 75 per cent of the voting citizens and all the cantons rejected this proposal. Nevertheless, discussions continue regarding which international treaties should be subject to joint approval by the majority of the voting citizens and the majority of the cantons.[18]

While it is thus rare that a majority of voters in a majority of cantons have to approve a specific treaty by way of a referendum, the cantons can always try to influence the federal parliament before it has to ratify the treaties. The situation in which Parliament has to approve international treaties is much more common, in particular when it comes to trade agreements that are normally not subject to a referendum (though it is more common today for NGOs to request it). It is not always easy to isolate, from other interest groups, the influence of specific cantons on the federal parliament when it approves international treaties, but there are rare instances in which it was generally agreed that the view of one or several cantons influenced the outcome of a vote (which was negative, an unusual result).

The most striking example in recent years was probably the negative vote by the federal parliament regarding an agreement with Germany on air traffic originating at Zurich airport. This airport (like all Swiss airports) is relatively close to the border and thus leads to regular complaints by the German border regions that are most affected by the noise. It is by far Switzerland's biggest airport and since the 1990s has increasingly been used as a hub, with many passengers in transit. One can thus consider this a case of trade in services because Swiss and foreign airlines create jobs and tax income in the Zurich area by servicing international (transiting) passengers who could otherwise use another airport in Europe. In 2001 a new agreement was negotiated between the German and Swiss governments that was considered relatively restrictive by the German Land of Baden-Württemberg on behalf of its local population. Consequently, discussion in the Swiss federal parliament was very heated. The bigger chamber of Parliament rejected the treaty on 19 June 2002, and the smaller chamber did so on 18 March 2003.[19] It was generally held that the negative comments of the canton of Zurich had had a decisive influence on the Members of Parliament. Ten years later a new agreement was negotiated by the Swiss and German governments. A member of the Zurich cantonal administration (from the unit responsible for foreign affairs and, in particular, European affairs) had been included in the Swiss delegation during these negotiations. The outcome was even less favourable from a Swiss perspective, but this time the canton of Zurich supported the ratification of the treaty,[20] which led to a positive vote in the Swiss parliament; the German side never submitted the treaty to Parliament.

As elsewhere in Europe, the debate on the effects of globalization on society intensified in the 1980s and early 1990s; some would even say that it started in the 1970s. For the cantons this discussion mostly focused on the need to safeguard their interests in the negotiations, in the conclusion of international treaties, and in the formulation of common policies in international organizations, mostly at the regional European level but also at the global level. This need was particularly important due to the relative openness of the Swiss economy and the strong need to have access to international markets in view of the small size of the economy and the absence of natural resources. Two important milestones in this debate were the negotiation of a European Economic Area with the European Union (1989–92) (see Schweizer 1992, 59) and the conclusion of the Uruguay Round leading to the creation of the World Trade Organization (WTO) in 1995 (see Wasescha 1996).

These discussions and developments triggered the creation of a body in which the cantons discuss and coordinate their interests regarding Switzerland's foreign policy: the so-called Conference of the Cantonal Governments (Konferenz der Kantonsregierungen, KdK).

It became apparent, and is still vividly discussed today, that the request for better inclusion in foreign policymaking also required the cantons to increase both their ability to participate actively and their expertise in the area. This was particularly felt with regard to European integration because Switzerland over time was increasingly surrounded by members of the European Union to and from which most products, migration, and capital flow. The KdK was seen as the first institutional improvement that could help the cantons to strengthen their position. It was established on 8 October 1993 as a permanent body under a specific treaty between all twenty-six cantonal governments.[21] The KdK has a secretariat based in Berne, Switzerland's capital. Regular meetings of a plenary assembly are foreseen, but in practice many specific working groups do most of the substantive work. These groups deal with areas of cooperation between Switzerland and the European Union that are particularly important for the cantons because they touch upon their domestic powers (such as migration, security, and recognition of diplomas).[22]

Many of the working groups deal with topics that today are included in modern comprehensive trade agreements, like the free movement of workers and professionals who provide services, or of specific services sectors (education, air transport), but no working group is devoted to trade in general that is not related to the European Union. Owing to the paramount importance of Europe for Swiss foreign trade policy, all working groups focus on the European Union. The KdK acknowledges, however, that at the global level Switzerland's foreign economic policy (in particular when it involves the liberalization of certain services, migration, and investment flows, for example) affects also the cantons and their interests. As an example, the granting of market access to foreign service suppliers can lead to specific quotas for workers that need to be controlled at the cantonal level, as the federal authorities have no staff and administrative bodies to do this. The same is true when it comes to the recognition of diplomas or the issuance of work permits. The representation of the KdK's interests at the federal level is undertaken by the secretariat of the KdK. The members of the secretariat can represent the KdK in working groups or other bodies established by the federal government, as well as in delegations that participate in international negotiations, as foreseen in the Law on the Participation of the Cantons in the Foreign Policy of the Swiss Confederation. In addition to European integration, the KdK is particularly interested in the negotiations of the WTO and bilateral free trade agreements.[23] This is due to the fact that, so far, the access to domestic services markets for foreign companies and their detached workers has been discussed mostly in these settings.

One additional area of foreign trade that interests the cantons particularly is public procurement. It is also increasingly common to subject the purchase of goods and services by sub-federal entities to the disciplines negotiated in the framework of the Government Procurement Agreement of the WTO and respective chapters in free trade agreements. Public procurement issues are dealt with by a separate body created by the governments of the cantons through a convention in 2009, the Conference of Directors for Planning, Construction, and the Environment (Bau-, Planungs- und Umweltdirektoren-Konferenz, BPUK).[24] Like the KdK, it is a public body, composed of the members of each cantonal government responsible for planning, construction, and the environment. In addition, this body has a member from the Principality of Liechtenstein and the Association of Towns and the Association of Communes. It is not legally related to the KdK, as are several other such bodies created by the cantons for coordination in specific areas. Nonetheless, all these bodies use the infrastructure of the KdK and meet regularly in its offices in Berne. The BPUK, which deals not only with international negotiations, is in charge of public procurement because construction projects are particularly important when it comes to public procurement at the local level.

The secretariat of the KdK is managed by an independent institution, the Ch Foundation for Confederal Cooperation, which the cantons created in 1967.[25] Within this body one staff member (of a total of three working at the headquarters) is in charge of foreign affairs. Currently this is Roland Mayer, who has held the position for many years and thereby has become part of the foreign policy landscape in this small country. He is in charge of an additional three persons who have their workplace directly within federal government offices. Two members of staff are delegated to the federal Ministry of Foreign Affairs unit in charge of negotiations with the European Union, the Directorate for European Affairs. A third person is delegated to the federal Ministry of Foreign Affairs, not in Berne but in the Swiss Mission to the European Union in Brussels.[26]

At the local level, it must be remembered that obviously the bigger cantons simply have more resources than the others to deal with foreign affairs. The smallest canton of Appenzell Innerhoden with its sixteen thousand inhabitants acts differently than the biggest, the canton of Zurich, with its 1.4 million inhabitants. The latter, like many other large cantons, has created within its administration a special unit to deal with external matters, although this often includes not only relations with other states or international organizations but also issues pertaining to other cantons or neighbouring regions.[27] Some of these bodies are quite active when it comes to, for instance, the promotion of their economic interests abroad. As a recent example, we can mention the organization of a networking meeting between Chinese investors and the local authorities in Zurich.[28] Even the biggest of these sub-national actors are too small, however, and their administrative capacities are too limited to shape the foreign relations of the country as a whole in a systematic and direct matter. Their influence is sometimes even further reduced by the absence of a common standpoint among the cantons (or absence of even totally opposite views). As the number of cantons is relatively high, the likelihood of finding a common denominator is small, and their economic situations are so diverse that they hardly ever fight together for a specific point. In this sense, sectoral lobbies (such as farmers, financial services providers, and the pharmaceutical industry) are more likely to succeed. They may be supported by those cantons to which their specific economic activity is particularly important.

A good recent example in this respect is the response by Switzerland to pressure within the Organisation for Economic Co-operation and Development (OECD) and from the European Union to revise its domestic corporate tax system. The issue had led to tensions between Switzerland and its neighbours since the early 2000s, escalating after the financial crisis in 2008. As corporate tax is, to a large extent, within the competence of the cantons, any revision of the corporate tax system would immediately affect their regulatory authority and have a direct impact on the income available to them. The negotiations in the OECD and with the European Union led to the threat of blacklisting Switzerland if some favourable tax treatments available to multinational companies (e.g., tax breaks on overseas earnings) were not ended. This required a total overhaul of the corporate tax system for all companies, leading to a discussion of the extent to which this would affect the attractiveness of certain cantons to multinational companies. Not all cantons were affected by this question in the same way, as some regions of the country are more attractive to multinational companies than others. The federal government involved the cantons heavily in a reform proposal that ultimately had to be submitted to a popular vote in a referendum. In this case, all cantons were directly affected by the international pressure and thus had an interest in finding a solution. They issued a common statement on 13

January 2017, inviting voters to adopt the proposal (in order to avoid being blacklisted at the international level).[29]

The Second Chamber

Since 1848 the Swiss constitutional system has been characterized by a two-chamber system, which some say was due to the liberal elite's admiration of the system introduced in the United States. One chamber, the Nationalrat (National Council), is made up of representatives of the people (with larger cantons having more representatives than smaller ones), and the other chamber, the Ständerat (Council of States), represents the cantons; that is, each canton has two representatives (the Council of States).[30] The cantonal representatives in the Council of States do not have to take instructions from their respective cantonal governments, but they are usually considered to be taking into account the interests of their local voters and thereby, to a large extent, the interests of their canton. In some cantons liaison with the cantonal representatives in the federal parliament (both chambers) is officially undertaken by the special units, with the administration dealing with foreign affairs. One would think that the members of the Council of States would see their role as mostly defending the interests of their cantons. This, however, is usually not the case. In both chambers one can observe that the votes of the representatives are normally more related to the party affiliation of the cantonal delegates than to the cantons they represent. Some observers even think that this may be an additional reason to create the KdK as another, informal "state organ" (not foreseen in the constitution) (see Vatter 2016, 342). This seems also true in the area of trade, where delegates in both chambers may defend or take up specific, important issues that affect their canton, but here again the ideological view of a particular delegate normally prevails.

Functioning of the Current System

Despite the fact that the participation of the Swiss cantons was codified in more detail in 1999 than it had been previously, and the cantons have since created institutions to effectively use their rights, the system is still considered insufficient by many observers. The cantons have repeatedly stated that they are not happy with the current system; they see the need for a more in-depth reform of Swiss federalism and of the cooperation between themselves and the federal government when it comes to foreign trade policy. Again, this is mostly triggered by the very complex and comprehensive relations with the European Union. More recently, they made public statements on 24 June 2011 and 13 December 2013 that they would only support the federal government in its future negotiations with the European Union if domestic reforms regarding the federal structure and democratic participation were launched.[31] The cantons want to achieve an even more far-reaching participation in the foreign policy of Switzerland, and they have made several concrete proposals for reform:

1. The cantons want to be informed early – not only when their powers are concerned but also, generally, when their interests (even potentially in the future) are concerned.
2. The cantons want to have at least three months before presenting their own position. Only this would allow them to consult stakeholders meaningfully. A shorter period seems to them to be unrealistic and threatens their right to participate actively in the decision-making process.
3. When it comes to questions regarding European integration, often on the subject of trade, the cantons want to enhance the weight of their own position. The government should only be allowed to defend another position if preponderant foreign-policy interests can be invoked.
4. The existing informal dialogue between the federal government and the cantons is considered to be insufficient. The cantons would like to see the creation of a standing body for the sole purpose of discussing foreign affairs with the federal government and the cantons. This body should be used for all areas of foreign policy-making, though the complexity and abundance of decisions related to the European Union are again at the origin of this proposal.
5. So far, there is a foreign-policy dialogue between the federal government and the cantons. The cantons, however, see that the federal government is also influenced by Parliament, and thus they would like to participate in the meetings and discussions of the specialized parliamentary committees, through either written submission or active participation in the meetings. Already at this stage it is not uncommon for the parliamentary committees to invite representatives of the cantons to hearings.

On several occasions the representatives of the cantons have voiced their concern regarding the current system and the importance of adopting the suggested reforms. Most recently, the president of the KdK has even threatened to sue the federal government before the Supreme Federal Court, exercising a type of constitutional jurisdiction in this context. The KdK is of the opinion that the federal system as a whole is in need of reform to take into account the increasing complexity of decision making at the federal level, which often affects, directly or indirectly, the cantons. Foreign affairs and trade play an important role in this, but the phenomenon is more widespread.

Conclusions

The discussion on how the relationship (and the institutional balance) between the cantons and the federal level in Switzerland is affected by increasingly intense and far-reaching foreign affairs has been significant in the country over the last thirty years. The most important part of Swiss foreign policy has always been trade and economic integration. This has been exacerbated by the creation of the European Union, where purely economic and other aspects of cooperation and integration often converge. Switzerland is one of the few remaining European states that is not a member of the Union, and as a rather small, export-oriented state, it depends on its European markets. As a result, its foreign policy is heavily dominated by its bilateral relations with the European Union. The perceived change in the federal structure in Switzerland is, therefore, often discussed because of European integration.

But this does not mean that other areas of trade with partner countries that are farther afield or within global organizations like the WTO or the OECD could not affect the powers and autonomy of the cantons. One example that has been shown is the liberalization of market access for agricultural goods, where rural cantons naturally have strong interests in protecting the local agricultural sector from foreign market competition. Another example is the liberalization of trade in services, where existing monopolies and prerogatives in areas such as health, education, and public utilities lead to important challenges for the existing structures and traditions of the cantons. This is also true in the area of public procurement, where changes introduced at the global level (in the Government Procurement Agreement of the WTO) and at the European level have totally altered the procurement practices of the cantons in the last twenty years. Finally, the increasing demand to allow migration as a part of trade negotiations (supply of services through seasonal workers, access to the labour market, etc.) leads to additional concerns that influence the traditional fields of cantonal politics.

Amendments to the constitution and the adoption of the Federal Law on the Participation of the Swiss Cantons in the Foreign Policy of the Federal State in 1999 tried to accommodate the increased need to involve the cantons in foreign policy and the conclusion of international treaties. The cantons have also discovered the use of cantonal initiatives to influence the federal parliament in areas where they fear that the federal government is not sufficiently taking their problems into account.

The cantons have had to adapt their institutions in order to use these instruments. At the internal level, many of them have increased the resources dedicated to foreign affairs, in particular European integration). At least the bigger cantons now normally have specialized agencies in the administration that not only promote the canton to foreign investors but also follow developments in foreign policy, in particular economic aspects that might be of relevance to the canton and its direct interaction with other cantons and the federal government and parliament. Together the cantons have created bodies (in particular the KdK) and arrived at a common position towards the federal government – or simply coordinated their policies and views. The fact that the federal government even accepts permanent representatives of this body in its own ministries and missions abroad (in addition to the ad hoc nomination of members of international delegations) is remarkable. At the same time, one should not overestimate the potential of the cantons in the area of foreign policy and, particularly, trade. Even the bigger cantons that can employ trade specialists may face the problem that it is not easy to convince local politicians and members of cantonal parliaments and governments with regard to the sometimes rather dry questions of international trade. Expertise in the area of trade is not evenly spread among all the Swiss cantons and their representatives at both cantonal and federal levels.

In addition, important differences between the cantons can make it difficult to come up with common positions. In recent years the divide between urbanized regions and rural areas has seemed apparent, albeit mitigated by the continuous urbanization of most of the country. Here, as in other areas of Swiss federalism, it has been voiced that the urban centres should have their own role to play in the political system, but concrete measures have not been taken so far. In these cases, the bigger (and richer) cantons may find it easier to defend their own positions directly at the federal level, something that is difficult for the smaller cantons to do.

Overall, it can be said that increased sub-federal involvement has resulted in better acceptance of the negotiation results by the cantons and therefore by the population in general, but at the price of slower and more complicated communication procedures that affect the flexibility of the federal government. The cantons have already asked for increased participation and even threatened to sue the government if a total reform of the federal system is not achieved soon (not only with regard to trade or foreign affairs in general). The increased use of cantonal initiatives, as well as the more common idea of using cantonal referendums against federal government decisions, in the area of trade and foreign affairs underlines this trend.

NOTES

1 Most famously, such an agreement between Uri, Schwyz, and Unterwalden of early August 1291 – the Rütlischwur, one of many military alliances, i.e., Bundesbriefe (in German) or Pactes fédéraux (in French) – is traditionally used as a historic origin for the country and justifies the celebration of a national holiday on 1 August. The decision to refer to this particular document as a historic starting point is, however, rather controversial and mostly the result of the nation-building process in the second part of the nineteenth century.
2 The Federal Constitution of 18 April 1999 was entered into force on 1 January 2000.
3 For a historic case study in English see Behr (2014).
4 For an interesting study of why tensions between the language regions are less of a problem in Switzerland than in Belgium, see Wouters, Van Kerckhoven, and Vidal (2016).
5 For an account under the old constitution and before the entry into force of the Federal Law on the Participation of the Cantons in the Foreign Policy of the Swiss Confederation of 1999, see Schmitt (1994).
6 Section 1, articles 54–6, of the constitution of 1999; security, national defence, and civil defence are treated in section 2 of the same chapter (articles 57–61).
7 Articles 184 and 186 of the constitution of 1999.
8 Those relating to trade (including trade in services and public procurement) and trade-related migration are addressed in this chapter, and for other areas the following studies may be interesting: health, Trein (2017); education, Behrens (2016).
9 Bundesgesetzüber die Mitwirkung der Kantone an der Aussenpolitik des Bundes (BGMK) of 22 December 1999, AS 2000 1477, https://www.admin.ch.
10 See for an example a recent interview given by the president of the Conference of Cantons (Konferenz der Kantonsregierungen, KdK) in which he complains about the erosion of cantonal powers and political autonomy due (inter alia) to international agreements, in Cina (2016).
11 Article 160, paragraph 1, of the constitution.
12 For a description of the role of the federal parliament in the federal system see Granat (2017).

13 See the official record, https://www.parlament.ch/de/ratsbetrieb
/suche-curia-vista/geschaeft?AffairId=20120313.

14 Article 89, paragraph 4, of the Swiss constitution of 1974, introduced by
referendum (Popular Initiative) in 1921.

15 See the detailed description of the historic development by the
government in the official journal (Botschaft des Bundesrates
an die Bundesversammlung über die Neuordnung des
Staatsvertragsreferendums vom 23. November 1974, BBl 1974 II 1133–6).

16 In a recent debate about the ratification of an agreement between
Switzerland and Germany and regarding the use of German airspace in
connection with flights from and to Zurich airport, the employment of this
instrument was discussed but rejected by the responsible parliamentary
committee of the canton of Zurich. See the coverage in *Neue Zürcher
Zeitung*, 29 August 2013, https://www.nzz.ch.

17 As a consequence, Switzerland did not join the European Economic
Area, and the other EFTA members all became parties to the EEA. Today
Norway, Iceland, and Liechtenstein are the remaining EFTA members in
the EEA, and the others have since joined the European Union.

18 For a discussion of this proposal by the Conference of Cantons (KdK)
see http://www.kdk.ch/de/themen/allgemeine-aussenpolitik
/staatsvertragsreferendum/.

19 For an official summary of the negotiations see the government statement
of 10 September 2003 at https://www.parlament.ch.

20 See the interview with the responsible member of the government of the
canton of Zurich, Ernst Stocker, in *Tagesanzeiger*, 6 July 2012, http://www
.tagesanzeiger.ch; and the official press release of the canton, https://vd.zh
.ch. Some parties were not so happy and suggested that the canton reject
the proposed text and even launch a procedure to request a referendum at
the national level.

21 The text of the Convention on the Conference of Cantonal Governments is
available in English at http://www.kdk.ch.

22 The list of working groups is available online at http://www.kdk.ch.

23 See the respective statement on the home page of the KdK: http://www
.kdk.ch.

24 For detailed information on this body see its home page, http://www
.bpuk.ch. The current statute dates from 20 September 2012 and has
replaced the original of 18 September 2009. It is available online on the site
of the organization.

25 For details on this body, a foundation under Swiss private law, with its
seat in Solothurn see http://www.chstiftung.ch.

26 For details see http://www.kdk.ch/de/die-kdk/sekretariat/.

206   Andreas R. Ziegler

27 See, for the canton of Zurich, https://aussenbeziehungen.zh.ch; and for
    the canton of St Gallen, http://www.aussenbeziehungen.sg.ch.
28 See the press release "Volkswirtschaftsdirektion vernetzt chinesische
    Unternehmer im Kanton Zürich," at https://aussenbeziehungen.zh.ch.
29 See KdK press release of 13 January 2017, "Les Cantons disent OUI à la
    réforme de l'imposition des entreprises" (The Cantons say "yes" to the
    corporate tax reform), https://kdk.ch.
30 The Ständerat (Council of States) is the second chamber, representing the
    twenty-six cantons (similar to the US Senate). It comprises forty-six elected
    Ständeräte (councillors): two represent each of the twenty "full" cantons,
    and one represents each of the six so-called half cantons.
31 See the two press releases at https://kdk.ch/de/aktuell
    /medienmitteilungen/.

REFERENCES

BauernZeitung. 2016. Waadt fordert Ausschluss von Palmöl Freihandel. 21
    April. https://www.bauernzeitung.ch.
Behr, Andreas. 2014. "The Representation of the Swiss Cantons at the
    Spanish Court at the End of the Seventeenth Century: A First Approach."
    Dimensioni e problemi della ricerca storica 27 (1): 165–92.
Behrens, Matthis. 2016. "Switzerland: Between the Federal Structure and
    Global Challenges." In *Education in Non-EU Countries in Western and
    Southern Europe*, edited by T. Sprague, 75–98. London: Bloomsbury
    Publishing.
Casado-Asensio, Juan, and Reinhard Steurer. 2016. "Mitigating Climate
    Change in a Federal Country Committed to the Kyoto Protocol: How Swiss
    Federalism Further Complicated an Already Complex Challenge." *Policy
    Sciences* 49 (3): 257–79.
Cina, Jean-Michel. 2016. Wir prüfe eine Klage gegen den Bund. *Neue Zürcher
    Zeitung*, 3 December. https://www.nzz.ch.
Federal Constitution of the Swiss Confederation of 12 September 1848. 1848.
    http://www.verfassungen.de.
Federal Constitution of the Swiss Confederation of 29 May 1874. 1874. http://
    www.verfassungen.de.
Federal Constitution of the Swiss Confederation of 18 April 1999. 1999.
    https://www.admin.ch.
Füglister, Katharina, and Fabio Wasserfallen. 2014. "Swiss Federalism in a
    Changing Environment." *Comparative European Politics* 12 (4–5): 404–21.
Granat, Katarzyna. 2017. "National Parliaments as Political Safeguards
    of Federalism: Interparliamentary Cooperation in the EU, the US, and
    Switzerland." In *National Parliaments after the Lisbon Treaty and the Euro*

Crisis: Resilience or Resignation?, edited by D. Jančič, 263–80. Oxford: Oxford University Press.

KdK (Konferenz def Kantonsregierungen). 2017. Les cantons disent OUI à la réforme de l'imposition des entreprises. 13 January. https://kdk.ch/fr/

Koordination Aussenbeziehungen. 2017. Volkswirtschaftsdirektion vernetzt chinesische Unternehmer im Kanton Zürich. 12 May. https://aussenbeziehungen.zh.ch.

Kreis, Georg. 2012. Aussenpolitik. *Historisches Lexikon der Schweiz*. http://www.hls-dhs-dss.ch.

Neue Zürcher Zeitung. 2016. Kommission lehnt Kantonsreferendum ab. 29 August. https://www.nzz.ch.

Schmitt, Nicolas. 1994. "The Foreign Policy of Spanish Autonomous Communities Compared to That of Swiss Cantons." In *Evaluating Federal Systems*, edited by B. de Villiers, 362–93. Dordrecht, Netherlands: Martinus Njihoff.

Schweizer, Rainer J. 1992. "Die Schweizer Kantone vor der Europäischen Herausforderung." *Jahrbuch des öffentlichen Rechts der Gegenwart* 40: 59.

Trein, Philipp. 2017. "Europeanisation beyond the European Union: Tobacco Advertisement Restrictions in Swiss Cantons." *Journal of Public Policy* 37 (2): 113–42.

Vatter, Adrian. 2016. *Das Politische System der Schweiz*. 2nd ed. Baden-Baden, Germany: Nomos.

Wasescha, Luzius. 1996. "Die Auswirkungen der Uruguay-Runde (GATT/WTO) auf Kantone und Länder." In *GATT 94 und die Welthandelsorganisation: Herausforderung für die Schweiz und Europa*, edited by S. Kux and D. Thürer, 117–27. Zurich: Schulthess.

Wouters, Jan, Sven Van Kerckhoven, and Maarten Vidal. 2016. "The Dynamics of Federalism: Belgium and Switzerland Compared." In *Weak States, Strong Societies: Power and Authority in the New World Order*, edited by A. Saikal, 38–58. London: I.B. Tauris.

8 Parallel Pathways? The Emergence of Multilevel Trade Politics in Austria and Germany

JÖRG BROSCHEK, PETER BUßJÄGER, AND
CHRISTOPH SCHRAMEK

The European Union (EU) has considerably expanded its authority over internal and external trade policy. Historically, this has been, for the most part, a unidirectional development. Institutional authority over the formulation and conduct of trade policy has migrated from the member states to the supranational level. This process of institutional change displayed patterns of encompassing reforms through the creation and modification of quasi-constitutional treaties, from the treaties of Paris and Rome in the 1950s to the Maastricht Treaty in the 1990s to the Treaty of Lisbon in 2009. Such major institutional innovations were followed by episodes of gradual and adaptive changes (see also Maria Garcia's chapter in this volume). Notably, the European Court of Justice further stretched supranational jurisdiction in trade policy, rather than constraining it, as a means of facilitating "negative integration" (Scharpf 1999; Woolcock 2015).

In the wake of new, deep, and encompassing trade agreements, however, the legitimacy and scope of supranational trade-policy authority has been put into question. Although most member states have either endorsed or at least tacitly accepted the evolution of a supranational trade order, more recently sub-federal entities in Belgium, Austria, and Germany have emerged as powerful actors with considerable potential to slow down or even block the ratification of trade agreements. Trade policy has become truly multilevel rather than merely bi-level in character, as the Belgian regions and communities, along with the Austrian and German Länder, are in the process of asserting a new role in this policy space. If the Transatlantic Trade and Investment Partnership (TTIP) was a "game changer," as Ferdi De Ville and Gabriel Siles-Brügge (2016) suggest, then this occurred not only because of an unforeseen level of social mobilization but also because of the looming anticipated threat of sub-federal entities frustrating the ratification of new trade agreements.

In this chapter we reconstruct how trade policy has mobilized the Austrian and German Länder since about 2013. Although this activism is a rather new development, it is, at the same time, part and parcel of the more encompassing and ongoing process of Europeanization. Accordingly, the Länders' attempt to engage more actively in trade policy reflects a general concern about political marginalization within the European political order in which member states and supranational institutions have increasingly decided on the institutional and policy changes. In this respect, the desire to become more involved in trade politics reflects contestation over political authority, and bureaucratic self-interest has driven the Länders' new activism. This is evident, for example, in their vehement opposition to the establishment of investor-state-dispute-settlement mechanisms or potential constraints on the right to regulate.

Bureaucratic self-interest, however, is only one part of the explanation. The changing nature of trade politics in both cases can only be fully understood in light of the increasing social mobilization and politicization of an inherently technocratic policy domain. Sub-federal concern about supranational transgressions through trade policy is, therefore, reinforced through party politics, highlighting the importance of interaction effects between trade policy, institutions, and the state-society dimension. Civil-society organizations and political parties increasingly perceive the Land level as an institutional access point to shape trade politics. Notably, sub-federal activities and outcomes such as resolutions, bills, and hearings address a wide range of issues that indicate political conflict about trade policy in general. However, the interference of party politics and federalism in trade politics has different consequences. On the one hand, Austria and Germany have highly institutionalized systems of intergovernmental relations. In both countries, sub-federal actors have utilized these structures to form a joint position on pending trade agreements, most notably the TTIP and the Canada-European Union Comprehensive Economic and Trade Agreement (CETA). On the other hand, differences in the composition and power of the second chambers explain why the German Länder have the potential to emerge as pivotal actors in trade politics, while the Austrian Länder lack the power to veto the ratification of trade agreements.

This chapter demonstrates how the interaction of institutional and socio-political factors has shaped the emergence of multilevel trade politics in Austria and Germany. It argues that small yet significant differences between both federations matter for the conduct and, possibly, the medium-term consequences of trade policy. In Germany the powerful Bundesrat has the potential to effectively veto the ratification of at least certain elements of trade agreements. This creates a typical dilemma of "joint decision making" (Scharpf 1988; Scharpf, Reissert, and Schnabel 1976) especially for Land governments where either the Social Democratic Party (Sozialdemokratische Partei Deutschlands, SPD) or the Greens is a coalition partner. By contrast, Austrian Land governors cannot directly veto trade agreements through the Bundesrat, and the federal level can unilaterally impose trade-agreement ratification on them. However, the Länders' ongoing uniform opposition has the potential to undermine the legitimacy of unilateral decisions by the federal government.

Entering the Trade Policy Arena: Länder Engagement since 2013

Trade policy has gained remarkable prominence within the federal arena in Austria and Germany since about 2013. Issue salience has increased considerably within this period. Trade policy has entered the agenda of different Land legislatures, intergovernmental institutions, and the federal level itself, a trend that has been reflected in the passing of several resolutions, in parliamentary hearings and bills. Moreover, the heightened level of activity in the federal arena has been accompanied by growing social mobilization. Both countries witnessed a series of rallies unfolding in 2015 and 2016, backed by a large alliance of important civil-society groups ranging from environmental groups to churches to unions. The streets of major German and Austrian cities were filled with more than 10,000 people participating in demonstrations against the TTIP and CETA, with one event in Berlin attracting at least 150,000 in October 2015.

These developments indicate similarities between the two federal systems. A closer examination, however, also reveals important differences. In both federations the Länder are in the process of finding a new role in trade politics, a policy field that used to be a domain shared exclusively between the federal and the European level. Trade politics, therefore, has become truly "multilevel" as sub-federal entities, which also include municipalities,[1] participate in various ways in the formulation and ratification of trade agreements (see Siles-Brügge and Strange in this volume). The nine Austrian and sixteen German Länder share a concern about the effects of new trade agreements like TTIP and CETA, which are expected to have the potential to negatively affect their competencies and right to regulate. These concerns about the detrimental effects for the institutional integrity of the Länder are complemented and, increasingly, reinforced through party politics and more political preferences of individual Land governments. In Austria this has led to a broad consensus among party leaders and governments from both tiers to stop TTIP and CETA in their current form. In Germany, however, several Land governments have become more cautious. Although Länder have not revoked their claim to have a formal say in the ratification of mixed agreements like CETA, there was no outcry when the federal government announced in February 2017 that it was still ascertaining whether or not the CETA-ratification bill would be introduced as a consent bill (*Zustimmungsgesetz*) or an objection bill (*Einspruchsgesetz*), with only the former affording the Bundesrat the power to veto the bill (Deutscher Bundestag 2017). This is remarkable in so far as the federal government now appears to call into question the promise of former economic affairs minister Sigmar Gabriel to give the Länder effective participation rights in the ratification process via the Bundesrat (Bundesregierung 2016). The absence of vocal Länder protest against this potential reversal indicates a paradoxical situation: while the German Länder, in principle, insist on their right to participate in trade policy, several Land governments appear to be increasingly concerned that this may threaten the ratification of free trade agreements such as CETA. The governments of politically and economically powerful Länder like Bayern, Hesse, and Baden-Württemberg are especially confronted by this paradox.

Before we analyse how trade policy has sparked sub-federal activity in Austria and Germany, it is necessary to clarify briefly the institutional configuration of both federations. Austria and Germany represent the Continental European tradition of federalism (Hueglin and Fenna 2015; Thorlakson 2003). As such, they differ in several respects from the Anglo-Saxon federations like the United States, Canada, and Australia, but also from Belgium, which became a federal state in 1993. Generally, and as outlined in the introductory chapter of this book, Austria and Germany (along with Switzerland; see Ziegler's chapter in this volume) lean more towards the shared-rule pole of federalism.

First, Anglo-Saxon federations are organized around a dual allocation of competencies. Accordingly, each governmental tier – the federal level and the sub-federal level – has exclusive responsibility for legislative, executive, and administrative functions within its sphere of authority. By contrast, Continental European federations feature an integrated division of competencies, which means that the sub-federal level often implements federal legislation. As a consequence, both governmental tiers are highly intertwined in most policy areas. The high degree of interdependence creates a strong incentive for sub-federal entities to participate directly in areas of federal legislation through the system of intergovernmental relations or the second chamber.

Second, this division of labour requires close coordination between both levels on an ongoing basis, which is an additional reason that federations in this tradition exhibit a dense, highly institutionalized system of intergovernmental relations. Third, neither Austria nor Germany has adopted the senate model to ensure that regional interest is represented through the second chamber. The German Bundesrat exemplifies the council model, which allows for the direct representation of sub-federal governments in the second chamber instead through elected or appointed senators. Bundesrat members are not elected but are delegated by Land governments. The Bundesrat delegation of each Land usually consists of the head of government (the Ministerpräsident), Cabinet members, and sometimes top-level bureaucrats (Staatssekretäre). Each Land must cast its vote *en bloc*, with votes ranging from three to a maximum of six for Länder with a population of more than seven million. The Austrian Bundesrat, however, is unique and difficult to classify. The sixty-one Bundesrat members are elected through the Landtage (the sub-federal parliaments), and the seats allocated to each of the nine Länder are roughly proportional to population size, ranging from three to twelve. Moreover, although the German Bundesrat has evolved as a powerful institution with an absolute veto right in most important legislative areas such as taxation, social insurance, and economic affairs, the Austrian Bundesrat is a rather weak second chamber that, apart from a few exceptions, can only exercise a suspensive veto.

Similarities in the institutional architectures of the two federations are important to understand why and how the Austrian and German Länder initially responded to the changing nature of trade policy. From the Länders' viewpoint, the emergence of a new generation of trade agreements negotiated by the EU has represented a recent instance of Europeanization, a dynamic that is generally seen as having the potential to further constrain the Länders' already limited capacity for autonomous action.[2] The transfer of authority since the creation of the single market and the harmonization of national law has narrowed Länder autonomy significantly as the EU has become involved in almost every policy area. This has directly impinged on the Länders' few legislative (e.g., education, cultural, and media policy; environmental policy) and broad administrative competencies. Moreover, considering that the German Länder enjoy powerful participation rights in important fields of federal legislation through the Bundesrat, Europeanization also indirectly reduced their role in the federal arena as authority migrated from the federal to the supranational level.

Scholarship on regional mobilization has identified two main institutional channels available to sub-level actors to protect their interests within EU politics (Hooghe and Marks 2016; Swenden and Bolleyer 2014; Tatham 2016).[3] Regions can either focus on domestic institutional arrangements ("intra-state channels") or directly act on the supranational level, for example through the European Committee of the Regions or the creation of offices in Brussels ("extra-state channels"). Although the Austrian and German Länder have deployed both strategies, intra-state channels provide them with more leverage to shape political processes and outcomes. Accordingly, they carry more weight and represent the Länders' preferred route to shape multilevel trade governance.[4] This pattern is consistent with a deeper historical pattern of institutional adaptation in both federations. The German Basic Law (Grundgesetz) formally designates most matters as concurrent legislation. The federal level pre-empted most of these jurisdictions during the 1950s and 1960s, but the Länder were compensated simultaneously with a strengthening of participation rights through the Bundesrat. In short, Länder gave up autonomy in exchange for constitutional privileges in the legislative process at the federal level (Lehmbruch 2000; Scharpf 2009). This pattern was replicated when the dynamics of Europeanization intensified in the mid-1980s. The Länder made the ratification of the Single European Act (SEA) and the Maastricht Treaty contingent on the formal entrenchment of new participation rights in certain matters of Europeanization. Negotiations on the SEA led to rather focused and comparatively weak provisions requiring that the federal government consider the opinion submitted by the Bundesrat whenever exclusive Land jurisdictions are affected. During the negotiations on the Maastricht Treaty, however, the Länder were able to wrest major concessions from the federal government. The compromise included a new constitutional provision (article 23 GG) that entrenched encompassing but staged co-decision rights in matters of Europeanization. The Austrian Länder emulated this process during the negotiations over Austria's accession to the EU in the early 1990s, which led to the creation of article 23d ff of the federal constitution (Bundes-Verfassungsgesetz, B-VG). This provision looks similar to its German counterpart; however, considering the weakness of the Austrian Bundesrat in terms of its composition and authority, it has not afforded the Austrian Länder the same political veto power as the German Länders'.

The Austrian and German Länder responded to trade-policy innovation on the European level in a path-dependent manner. Consistent with their adaptive reaction to Europeanization dynamics since the 1990s, Land governments were put on the alert by bureaucratic self-interest in anticipation of the potential implications of looming trade agreements like TTIP, CETA, and the Trade in Services Agreement, and existing intra-state channels served as the main route to become involved in the political process. As we show in the following sections, however, the institutional self-interest of Länder governments alone cannot adequately account for the unfolding dynamic. Rather, it is its interaction with policy preferences and party politics that has produced important differences between the two federations.

Austria

The Austrian Länder enjoy participation rights in European affairs as well as in external matters generally, which allow them to submit binding uniform statements to the federal government if their competencies are affected by supranational legislative proposals or international treaties. The Austrian federal constitution (B-VG) differentiates between treaties concluded within the framework of the EU and treaties concluded between the federal government and other states. In practice, the Länder have made use of their participation rights more often in European affairs than with respect to international treaties concluded beyond the EU framework. This is hardly surprising as Austria's accession to the EU in 1995 had a deep impact on Länder competencies. Although the Länder established representation offices at the supranational level and are also represented within the Austrian delegation to the Committee of the Regions, the main institutional focus for protecting their interests within the emerging multilevel architecture has remained the domestic federal framework, most notably the Bundesrat and the system of intergovernmental relations, especially through the horizontal Landeshauptleutekonferenz (LHK), the Conference of State Governors.[5]

The Austrian federal constitution contains a section with provisions concerning the EU (articles 23a ff). These provisions were implemented with a federal constitutional law (EU-BegleitBVG)[6] prior to the Austrian accession to the EU. For the Länder, article 23d of the B-VG is of particular importance in so far as it entails rules concerning the participation of the Länder and municipalities in the EU decision-making-process

(Egger 2017). Section 1 of this provision states that the federal government must inform the Länder without delay regarding all projects within the framework of the EU that affect the autonomous sphere of Länder competencies or could otherwise be of interest to them. Furthermore, the federal level must give the Länder the opportunity to present their views within a reasonable interval to be fixed by the federal government.[7] The same holds for the municipalities in so far as their own sphere of competence or other important interests are affected. Following this, section 2 provides the possibility for the Länder to give a uniform opinion on a project concerning matters in which legislation is their business.

As a result, article 23d of the B-VG provides different possibilities for the Länder to give an opinion. A general opinion can be given by one Land, or more or all Länder (section 1) (Öhlinger and Konrath 2013). This type of opinion is basically not binding for the federal level. The other possibility is a uniform opinion according to article 23d, section 2, of the B-VG. The federal government may depart from a uniform opinion only for compelling integration and foreign-policy reasons. It must advise the Länder of these reasons without delay. In this sense, a uniform opinion has a limited binding effect (Öhlinger and Konrath 2013). Article 23d of the B-VG does not determine the requirements for the establishment of such a uniform opinion. These requirements can be found in a separate agreement among the Länder according to article 15a of the B-VG. In any case, one can assume that uniformity exists when the majority of the Länder agree without any dissent (Bußjäger 2015, 363–4).

For international treaties that are concluded between the EU and non-member states, article 23d of the B-VG can be applied when the aforementioned requirements of this provision are met (Egger 2017). This means that the Länder have certain rights to participate in the procedure, including general or uniform opinions, if their autonomous sphere of competence is affected by the international treaty.

In addition, the Bundesrat can take part in the internal coordinating procedure in EU matters. According to article 23e, section 1, of the B-VG, the federal government must inform the Bundesrat without delay about all projects within the framework of the EU and afford it the opportunity to express its opinion. Article 23e, section 4, of the B-VG also allows the Bundesrat to give a limited binding opinion if a project within the framework of the EU aims to pass a binding legal act that either requires the passing of constitutional amendments limiting the competencies of the Länder in legislation and executive powers pursuant to article 44, section 2, of the B-VG, or contains regulations that can only be passed by such regulations (Gamper 2006). However, this provision is of limited importance. In practice there has been no known case of its application.

Regarding international treaties without EU participation, for a long time the Austrian Länder had only the right to give a non-binding opinion if the respective treaty included necessary implementation measures affecting the sphere of Länder competencies or if the autonomous sphere of Länder competencies was affected in another way. In the course of an amendment of the B-VG in 2008,[8] new provisions on the participation of the Länder were entered into the constitution. Based on the model of the aforementioned article 23d, the former article 10, section 3, of the B-VG was expanded to the extent that the provision now contains the possibility of the Länder giving a uniform opinion (Bußjäger 2013, 111; Wiederin 2011).[9] Therefore, it states that the federal government, if it is in possession of a uniform opinion from the Länder, is bound thereby when concluding the state treaty. The federal government may deviate therefrom only for compelling foreign-policy reasons.

At first glance, the distinction between article 10, section 3, and article 23d of the B-VG is clear. Certainly, one has to consider that international treaties regarding trade policy – like TTIP and CETA – are classified as so-called mixed agreements (see Mögele 2012, 39), which not only concern the framework of the EU but also fall within the competencies of the member states. Therefore, one has to scrutinize the two articles to see which one should be applied. The solution – to apply article 23d for the EU parts of the agreement and article 10, paragraph 3, for those parts that lie within the scope of the member states – may be appropriate but in practice difficult to manage (Egger 2017). It would be more practicable to permit the application of both articles.

Within this institutional framework the Austrian Länder sought to find a common position in light of new trade agreements negotiated at the EU level. Although the Länder considered primarily TTIP and CETA in their deliberations, it is clear that these trade agreements represent a general trend that put them on alert. For example, the sub-federal parliaments like the legislature of Niederösterreich – geographically the largest Land, second in terms of its population, and economically highly dependent on exports – adopted a resolution entitled "Stop TTIP, CETA and TiSA – Now!" in October 2015 (Landtag von Niederösterreich 2015). As well, the Japan-EU Free Trade Agreement has recently emerged on the agenda of Land legislatures. The salience of trade policy at the Land level is reflected, first of all, in a growing number of parliamentary debates, motions, and resolutions. The Land

Salzburg was among the first, passing a unanimous resolution, which was carried by all political parties represented in the legislature, in June 2014 (Land Salzburg 2014). The Länder Vorarlberg (2016), Tirol (2016), Niederösterreich (2016), and Steiermark (2016), among others, followed. These activities reveal an unusual degree of agreement among all political parties across the political spectrum from the left (the Greens) to the far right (Freiheitliche Partei Österreichs, FPÖ). Although political parties have variously supported different motions or, as was the case with the Land Salzburg's second resolution on the ratification of CETA in April 2016 (Land Salzburg 2016), supported specific demands included in one motion, there exists broad-based scepticism or even outright opposition towards core elements of European trade policy.

Second, a similar all-encompassing political consensus emerged among the Land governors. The Austrian Länder and the Bundesrat released several statements on TTIP and CETA. In May 2014 the Länder gave a uniform opinion according to article 23d, section 2, of the B-VG regarding TTIP (Stadt Wien 2014a). In this opinion the Länder stated that they acknowledged the reduction and gradual elimination of trade barriers. Nevertheless, economic growth should not be the exclusive criterion for the conclusion of such an agreement. Instead, they called for environmental and social aspects to be considered more seriously in the course of the negotiations. Furthermore, the Länder criticized the lack of information from the federal government and pointed out that it had violated the constitutional obligation to inform the Länder without delay according to article 23d, section 1, of the B-VG. In general, the Länder faulted the insufficient transparency in the wake of the negotiations concerning TTIP. Additionally, the Länder requested a cost-benefit analysis from the federal government that would contain the effects of the agreement not only from an economic point of view but also regarding different sectors, like the social, health care, or environment sector. Although the Länder had little information about the contents of TTIP in 2014, they gave their opinion on several content-related questions concerning public services, investment protection, and public procurement. In conclusion, the Länder invited the federal government to consider these common positions of the Länder within negotiations regarding TTIP.

At this point the LHK has to be mentioned. Although it is not provided in the federal constitution, this horizontal intergovernmental body plays an important role and, as an institution representing the Länder, is a significant element of cooperative federalism in Austria (Bußjäger 2003, 2013). The conference meets usually twice a year and is informal, voluntary, and consensus based. The resolutions that are passed in the wake of the particular conferences have no legal force. Nevertheless, they can, under certain circumstances, unfold a political signal effect (Bußjäger 2003, 84).

After the aforementioned uniform opinion of the Länder in May 2014, the LHK passed a resolution in November 2014 regarding TTIP (Stadt Wien 2014b). With reference to the uniform opinion in May, the conference asked the federal government to ensure that the negotiations proceeded in a transparent way, that the Länder received sufficient information about the negotiations, and that it maintained existing high environmental and social standards. In addition, the Land governors stated that the possibility of initiating an arbitral procedure should be provided and that free trade agreements like CETA and TTIP must be concluded in the form of a mixed agreement.

Two years later, in May 2016, the Land governors passed another resolution (Stadt Wien 2016), in which they confirmed the resolution from May 2014 and stated that the claims from then, as far as they concerned TTIP, also applied to CETA. Again, the Land governors demanded comprehensive information about the progress of negotiations. Furthermore, they encouraged the federal government to oppose a provisional application of CETA and TTIP and to ensure that enacted regulations would not be restricted or amended. The resolution also demanded that the federal government withhold the conclusion of CETA and TTIP if the claims of the resolution were not fulfilled. In addition, the Land governors declared the resolution to be a binding uniform opinion of the Länder according to article 23d, section 2, of the B-VG.

Subsequently, the Bundesrat gave an opinion according to article 23e of the B-VG (Republik Österreich 2016). In this opinion the federal government was invited to consider the concerns of the Länder on the EU level regarding CETA that they had expressed in their previous resolutions from 2014 and 2016. Finally, the Länder issued another opinion, on 1 October 2017, in which they reinstated their concerns for all pending and future trade agreements (Stadt Wien 2017).

Surprisingly, however, the federal government gave its consent to the provisional application of CETA in September 2016 (*Die Presse* 2016), and the federal parliament (both chambers) eventually ratified the agreement in June 2018. These developments obviously are barely compatible with the uniform opinions of the Länder, in which they called upon the federal government to oppose the provisional application of CETA and TTIP and the ratification of CETA in its original form. What is more, the federal government's unilateral approval of

CETA deviates in at least two ways from the general pattern of federal politics in Austria. First, it is unusual that the federal government deliberately ignores uniform opinions by the Länder. Second, Austria's vertically highly integrated political parties make it difficult for Land governors to deviate from policy commitments made by the federal organizational unit. Accordingly, even if territorial divisions occur within a political party, political party loyalties often mitigate these conflicts and result in programmatic uniformity among the federal and sub-federal units (on the role of political parties in Austria's federal system see for example Fallend 2013). In the case of CETA, the federal government decided to support the ratification despite widespread opposition.[10] Considering the political costs of this approach, it may become increasingly difficult for the incoming federal government to support the ratification of future trade agreements in a similar way.

Germany

Similar to Austria, the growing prominence of trade policy in Germany's federal arena needs to be seen in the larger context of Europeanization. Europeanization has had a profound impact on the German Länder. The gradual expansion of authority at the EU level has affected not only the few exclusive Land competencies but, perhaps even more importantly, the core function of the Länder within Germany's federal architecture: their broad responsibility for implementing federal law. Since the 1950s the Länder had adopted different strategies to defend their institutional integrity within a continuously changing multilevel environment, but from the 1990s these efforts became much more visible as a consequence of unification and the creation of the single market (Laufer and Münch 2010, 206).

The Länders' strategies revealed both patterns of "exit" and patterns of "voice." Exit strategies are aimed at protecting the sub-federal capacity to act autonomously. Charlie Jeffrey, for example, has argued that the integration of the five new Länder in 1990 contributed to a differentiation of Länder interests and desolidarization among them, which in turn spurred the economically strong Land governments to demand more policy and fiscal autonomy in order to reposition themselves within the European market (Jeffrey 1999). Indeed, considering indicators like gross domestic product and population, Nordrhein-Westfalen, Baden-Württemberg, and Bayern compare to other medium-sized EU member states, with Nordrhein-Westfalen ranking higher than the Netherlands, and Bayern and Baden-Württemberg being still larger and more prosperous than Belgium, Sweden, or Austria (Scharpf 2009, 67). Voice strategies, in contrast, seek to strengthen the Länders' participation rights in Europeanized decision-making processes. Two types of voice strategies can be distinguished. First, Länder have sought to assume a more active role at the European level through extra-state channels. As early as 1956 they had established an official observer (Länderbeobachter) who, as a formal member of the German delegation, represented the Länder in meetings of the Council of the European Union. Since the mid-1980s the Länder have also installed representative offices in Brussels, replicating the creation of the quasi-diplomatic representative offices in Berlin. Second, the Länder have been eager to strengthen domestic or intra-state voice channels, especially by furnishing the Bundesrat with more power in federal legislation.

Overall, intra-state channels have remained the most important and, presumably, most effective strategy to defend Länder interests. The Länder have pushed for the institutionalization of intra-state channels that would allow them to participate in international and European affairs since the 1950s. The Agreement of Lindau (Lindauer Abkommen) of 1957 was the first major step in this process, detailing procedural requirements of Länder participation in different types of international treaties. The agreement obliges the federal government to inform and consult Länder early on whenever their competencies may be affected directly or indirectly by an international treaty. In addition, the agreement provides that the federal government and the Länder reach a consensus if an agreement directly affects exclusive Länder competencies (Deutscher Bundestag 2016b). When Europeanization dynamics intensified during the 1980s after a period of stalemate, the Länder successfully pressed the federal government to include explicit provisions that more firmly entrenched their participation rights in the ratification bill of the SEA in 1986, and to draw up a new framework agreement. The ratification of the Maastricht Treaty in 1992 eventually required a number of constitutional changes. The Länder threatened to refuse their approval unless the federal government was willing to make further concessions concerning their involvement in EU politics. As a result, the new article 23 of the Basic Law introduced encompassing provisions that guaranteed the Länder constitutionalized participation rights (Kropp 2010, 160; Laufer and Münch 2010, 208; Sturm and Pehle 2001, 80). Most notably, article 23(4) stipulates that the "Bundesrat shall participate in the decision-making process of the Federation insofar as it would have been competent to do so in a comparable domestic matter, or insofar as the subject falls within the domestic competence of the Länder" (Deutscher Bundestag 2016a, 29).[11]

Consistent with this historical pattern, Land governments activated intra-state channels to situate themselves in the field of trade policy. Interestingly, even before trade policy came into the limelight of public debate in Germany through TTIP and CETA, the Bundesrat had to decide on the free trade agreement between the EU and Colombia and Peru (European Union-Colombia/Peru Trade Agreement). The federal government introduced the ratification bill as a consent bill in accordance with article 84(1) of the Basic Law because it was considered to affect implementation competencies of the Länder. The bill also indicated the agreement's mixed character (Deutscher Bundesrat 2013b). Interaction effects emanating from the state-society dimension, which reinforced bureaucratic interests in the mobilization of Land governments, became apparent at this point as well. A broad alliance of forty-five religious, human rights, developmental, and environmental associations identified the Bundesrat as an institutional veto point that could be activated to jeopardize the free trade agreement's ratification. In an open letter published on 5 April 2013 the alliance called upon the members of the Bundesrat to reject the ratification bill in its second reading on 3 May.[12] This letter echoed concerns of the SPD, the Greens, and the Left (Die Linke), who opposed the bill in the Bundestag. The bill barely passed, but the SPD-Green government of Nordrhein-Westfalen succeeded in pressing the Bundesrat to pass an accompanying resolution (Deutscher Bundesrat 2013b). Through this resolution the Länder indicated their preference for multilateral trade agreements through the World Trade Organization and expressed concerns about the proliferation of bilateral and mixed agreements. In particular, the Bundesrat criticized the asymmetry between binding and stringent obligations that guarantee market access in industry and agriculture, the liberalization of public services and procurement on the one hand, and the lack of corresponding binding and stringent obligations that provide complementary labour, social, environmental, and consumer rights on the other hand (Deutscher Bundesrat 2013b).

Only a few weeks later, in June 2013, the Bundesrat passed a second resolution on the TTIP negotiations between the EU and the United States. Although in the case of the first resolution the Bundesrat's position had reflected primarily different party positions over trade policy, the TTIP resolution also raised concerns about the institutional integrity of the Länder generally. Party politics aligned with territorial interests of different Land governments, regardless of their partisan position. Through the resolution the Bundesrat endorsed negotiations between the EU and the United States on TTIP and emphasized the potential economic benefits of the agreement (Deutscher Bundesrat 2013a). At the same time, however, the resolution called upon the federal government to ensure that the agreement would not undermine high European regulatory standards in social policy, environmental policy, food security, and data protection. The resolution also placed emphasis on the need to include specific provisions in the area of agriculture to ban genetically modified products and meat from animals treated with hormones from entering the EU. Considering the broad mandate to negotiate a deep trade agreement, the resolution pointed proactively to the constitutional competencies of the Bundesrat and to the requirement to consult the Länder in accordance with the Agreement of Lindau and urged the federal government to insist on transparent negotiations.

The tone and tenor of a third resolution that was passed one year later, in July 2014, was even more critical. The resolution was concerned with the modalities of investment protection and addressed directly to the European Commission (Deutscher Bundesrat 2014). It reaffirmed the Bundesrat's earlier explicit acknowledgment of the potential benefits of TTIP but reiterated and specified the Länders' main concerns. In particular, the Länder demanded that the precautionary principle not be weakened and that existing higher regulatory standards in areas such as health, environment, food, social welfare, and data protection prevail. The Bundesrat also insisted that the right to regulate as a principle is non-negotiable and may not be violated, directly or indirectly, through any form of investment protection. In addition, the Länder rejected any form of investor-state-dispute-settlement mechanisms as dispensable and fraught with risk. Instead, disputes should be resolved by national courts. The rather vague language concerning the Bundesrat's involvement entailed in the first resolution of 2013 was replaced with an explicit statement designating TTIP as a mixed agreement. Finally, in an opinion submitted to the European Commission in December 2015, the Bundesrat reaffirmed these concerns in detail and stated explicitly that it rejected a provisional implementation of CETA due to concerns over investment-protection mechanisms and their potential constraints for exercising the right to regulate (Deutscher Bundesrat 2015).

These concerns and corresponding demands were echoed within Germany's dense and highly institutionalized system of intergovernmental relations. The Länder devoted significant attention to trade policy and sought to consolidate a common position through horizontal cooperation. The Conference of Ministers for European Affairs, for example, discussed TTIP and other planned trade agreements in detail in 2015. In addition to the issues raised by the Bundesrat, the Land ministers emphasized the potential negative effects on cities and municipalities and explicitly insisted on the formal requirement to make the ratification of such agreements subject to approval by the Bundesrat, a requirement that was seen to flow from their mixed character (Europaministerkonferenz 2015, 11). Similar concerns were expressed by the Conference of Ministers for the Environment (Umweltministerkonferenz 2014), the Conference of Ministers for Economic Affairs (Wirtschaftsministerkonferenz 2014) and the Conference of Ministers for Consumer Protection (Verbraucherschutzministerkonferenz 2014).

The emerging trade-policy-governance structure, therefore, was consistent with Germany's dominant mode of interaction, joint decision making. Fritz W. Scharpf identified this mode of intergovernmental bargaining in the 1970s and defined it as an institutionally generated actor configuration in which decisions of the federal (or supranational) level are dependent on the agreement of sub-level governments (Scharpf 1988; Scharpf, Reissert, and Schnabel 1976). Joint decision making represents the strongest form of collaboration between intergovernmental actors because it is a compulsory form of negotiation. While cooperation implies that intergovernmental actors seek to forge a compromise on a voluntary basis, in the case of joint decision making a change of the status quo requires that most actors agree. The predominance of joint decision making in German federalism has been criticized by political scientists and, increasingly since the 1990s, by the broader public, for it encourages lowest-common-denominator decisions or even stalemate. Several efforts to disentangle both governmental tiers since the 1990s, however, have largely failed (Benz 2016; Broschek 2015; Scharpf 2009). The inability to effectively overcome an institutional decision-making structure that is widely seen as problematic is consistent with Scharpf's concept of the joint-decision trap. The anticipated short-term advantages of this institutional configuration make it almost impossible to reach an overall agreement on unlocking it.

In order to prevent stalemate, political actors often seek to minimize the conflict intensity of issues, for example by removing certain items from the agenda, by redefining a given problem, or by attempting to facilitate agreement through a sequential negotiation of agenda items (Benz, Detemple, and Heinz 2016). Such strategies, however, are problematic when party politics are superimposed on negotiations in the federal arena (see Lehmbruch 2000). Accordingly, political parties in opposition to the federal government may utilize the Bundesrat to jeopardize federal legislation. This pattern has re-emerged especially when a coalition government on the federal level does not have a clear majority in the Bundesrat, and when a bill is potentially polarized.

These conditions have been present, at least to some extent, in the case of trade policy. The increasing polarization of trade policy has confronted with a serious problem the governing elites in Berlin as well as many Land governments. Overall, the grand coalition consisting of the SPD and the CDU/CSU (Christlich Demokratische Union Deutschlands and the Christlich Soziale Union in Bayern),[13] at the federal level, has been supportive of the EU's trade-policy agenda.[14] Land governments, however, have become increasingly divided over trade policy (table 8.1). Bayern, Hamburg, Mecklenburg-Vorpommern, Niedersachsen, Saarland, and Sachsen indicated support for CETA (though not necessarily TTIP). The governing coalitions of Berlin (SPD-Linke-Grüne) and Thüringen (Linke-SPD-Grüne) explicitly oppose trade agreements like TTIP and CETA, and the seven remaining Land governments have indicated that they were either in the process of ascertaining their position or that they would abstain in case of a Bundesrat vote, with the latter option being the common practice for coalition governments when they are divided on an issue in the Bundesrat. Although the ratification of the European Union-Colombia/Peru Trade Agreement found support in 2013 and the first resolution on TTIP still indicated support in principle, the Bundesrat has emerged as a potential veto point for any future trade agreements, as indicated in its detailed, still nuanced, but also clear, 2015 opinion to the European Commission. Indeed, as the focus of debate shifted away from TTIP and towards CETA, the federal government could only rely on a limited number of Land governments who endorsed CETA. At the time of writing, these Länder currently have twenty-five votes in the Bundesrat, but for a consent bill to pass, at least thirty-five votes are required. With the newly elected conservative-liberal coalition government of Nordrhein-Westfalen (since May 2017), one more large Land now supports CETA, but any bill would still miss an absolute majority.

8.1 Coalition Governments, Trade-Policy Preferences, and Bundesrat Votes of the German Länder (as of December 2018)

Land	Governing party or coalition	Parties in Landtag (strongest party first)	Trade-policy preference in ratification of CETA	Expected Bundesrat vote in case of ratification of CETA	Votes in Bundesrat
Baden-Württemberg	Grüne/CDU	Grüne, CDU, AfD, SPD, FDP	Tentatively supportive of CETA	Support or abstain	6
Bayern	CSU-FW	CSU, SPD, FW, Grüne, AfD	Supportive of CETA and TTIP	Support	6
Berlin	SPD-Linke-Grüne	SPD, CDU, Linke, Grüne, AfD, FDP	Opposed	Oppose	4
Brandenburg	SPD-Linke	SPD, CDU, Linke, AfD, Grüne	Linke is clearly opposed	Abstain	4
Bremen	SPD-Grüne	SPD, CDU, Grüne, Linke, FDP, AfD, BiW	Conditionally supportive, but Grüne was opposed to CETA in May 2016 form	Abstain	3
Hamburg	SPD	SPD, CDU, Grüne, Linke, AfD, FDP	Supportive of CETA	Support	3
Hessen	CDU-Grüne	CDU, SPD, Grüne, Linke, FDP, AfD	Conditionally supportive, but still assessing the implications of CETA (2016)	Support or abstain	5
Mecklenburg-Vorpommern	SPD-CDU	SPD, AfD, CDU, Linke	Supportive	Support	3
Niedersachsen	SPD-CDU	CDU, SPD, Grüne, FDP, AfD	Supportive	Support	6

(*Continued*)

8.1 Continued

Land	Governing party or coalition	Parties in Landtag (strongest party first)	Trade-policy preference in ratification of CETA	Expected Bundesrat vote in case of ratification of CETA	Votes in Bundesrat
Nordrhein-Westfalen	CDU-FDP	CDU, SPD, FDP, AfD, Grüne	Supportive	Support	6
Rheinland-Pfalz	SPD-Grüne-FDP	SPD, CDU, AfD, FDP, Grüne	Grüne is opposed	Abstain	4
Saarland	CDU-SPD	CDU, SPD, Linke, AfD	Supportive	Support	3
Sachsen	CDU-SPD	CDU, Linke, SPD, AfD, Grüne	Supportive	Support	4
Sachsen-Anhalt	CDU-SPD-Grüne	CDU, AfD, Linke, SPD, Grüne	Grüne is opposed	Abstain	4
Schleswig-Holstein	CDU-Grüne-FDP	CDU, SPD, Grüne, FDP, AfD	Grüne is opposed	Abstain	4
Thüringen	Linke-SPD-Grüne	CDU, Linke, SPD, AfD, Grüne	Opposed	Oppose	4

Note: AfD (Alternative für Deutschland); BiW (Bürger in Wut); CDU (Christlich Demokratische Union Deutschlands); CSU (Christlich Soziale Union in Bayern); FDP (Freie Demokratische Partei); FW (Freie Wähler); Grüne (Bündnis 90/Die Grünen); Linke (Die Linke); SPD (Sozialdemokratische Partei Deutschlands).

Source: Authors' compilation based on an examination of legislative proceedings, government communiqués, and coalition agreements.

Conclusion

After the federal elections held in Austria and Germany in the fall of 2017, the new federal governments in both countries faced different challenges in their efforts to ensure the ratification of looming free trade agreements negotiated by the EU. In the case of Austria, the ÖVP was able to commit the new junior coalition partner FPÖ to a pro-EU agenda. In a statement issued during the final stage of the coalition negotiations, FPÖ chairman Heinz-Christian Strache explained that the political legacy of the previous grand coalition could not be easily reversed, including the ratification of CETA. Indeed, the new coalition government succeeded in the ratification of CETA in June 2018. However, it is not clear if the unanimous opposition of Land governors, backed by most political parties at the Land level, can be ignored and unilaterally by-passed again in the future. In Germany uncertainty prevails. It is far from clear when the renewed grand coalition government will introduce a CETA ratification bill. A first ratification bill introduced by the liberal Freie Demokratische Partei in February 2018 (Deutscher Bundestag 2018b) was defeated in April 2018 because the CDU/CSU and SPD did not see any compelling reason to ratify the agreement at that point. The CDU also justified its decision not to support this motion because a final clarifying ruling of the constitutional court on CETA was still pending (Deutscher Bundestag 2018a).

As we have shown, the institutional architecture of both federations shares similarities that are evident if they are compared with the Anglo-Saxon federations. In addition, Europeanization and the high degree of social and political mobilization of trade policy are contextual factors that are similar in both countries and help in the understanding of the emergence of multilevel trade politics in Austria and Germany since 2013. At the same time, however, the patterns of sub-federal engagement reveal important differences, which can be explained by institutional variation.

In Germany the dominant mode of interaction between the federal level and the Länder is joint decision making, which requires broad consensus among actors representing different tiers of government. Joint decision making is notoriously prone to generating stalemate, especially if issues are salient and contested between political parties (Lehmbruch 2000). The composition and political power of the Bundesrat affords Land executives the opportunity to veto the ratification of encompassing trade agreements. As has been shown, this is not an entirely unrealistic scenario, especially since abstention – the default option if coalition governments are divided upon an issue – ultimately counts as a "no" vote. The ongoing fragmentation of party systems on the federal and sub-federal levels, the corresponding diversity of coalition governments on the Land level, and the polarization of trade policy make it increasingly difficult for governments to deploy negotiation strategies facilitating agreement in Germany's highly entangled system of joint decision making. In fact, this combination of institutional and political factors has the potential to become a "joint-decision trap," particularly for those Social Democratic or Green Party Land governments that support trade agreements like CETA in principle; while they have a strong interest in exercising the right to participate in the ratification process, they also want to avoid ratification failure.

In Austria the higher degree of hierarchy between the federal and Land levels mitigates these effects. Although the system of intergovernmental relations is highly institutionalized, like in Germany, the strong position of the federal level simultaneously allows for unilateral action to avoid deadlock. More than in the German case, collaboration between the Länder and the federal government takes place under the shadow of hierarchy. Hence, the former federal grand coalition (until 2017) and the ÖVP-FPÖ coalition government (2017–19) supported the EU's recent free trade agreements, despite being confronted with opposition stemming from a broad alliance of all the Land governments and all the other major political parties at the federal level.[15] Even more remarkable, the territorial division between the federal level and the Land level has pitted the Sozialdemokratische Partei Österreichs (SPÖ)-ÖVP federal coalition (2013–17) against SPÖ- or ÖVP-led coalition governments in the nine Länder, a rare phenomenon in light of Austria's highly integrated political parties. Unlike in Germany, sub-federal actors in Austria – political parties and Land governors – have been unanimous in their criticism of the new direction of supranational trade policy in terms of conduct and substance. In particular, the high degree of harmony among Land governors and their coordinated action through the LHK compensate somewhat for their lack of institutional power. Although the Austrian Länder were unable to prevent the ratification of CETA, future federal governments will find it difficult to ignore their concerns in upcoming ratification processes such as the Japan-EU Free Trade Agreement.

NOTES

1 German and Austrian sub-federal units include so-called city states, which are a Land and a municipality at the same time. In Germany these are the Länder Berlin, Bremen, and Hamburg, three out of sixteen Länder. In Austria the Land Vienna is a city state.
2 Interview, Bayerische Staatskanzlei, Munich, 28 July 2017.
3 The distinction between "intra-state" and "extra-state" channels builds on Tatham (2016).
4 This sets the Länder apart from most other regions, which seem to put greater emphasis on extra-institutional channels.
5 For an assessment of Länder activities on the European level see Rossbach (2016). The annually published federalism report of the Institute of

Federalism consistently records uniform opinions according to article 23d of the B-VG. In contrast, a uniform opinion according to article 10, section 3, of the B-VG, which established the legal framework for Länder participation in external matters outside the EU, has not been located since the establishment of this provision in the year 2008.

6 *Federal Law Gazette*, no. 1013/1994.

7 More detailed provisions with respect to article 23d, paragraphs 1 to 3, of the B-VG are established in an agreement between the federation and the Länder according to article 15a of the B-VG (*Federal Law Gazette*, no. 775/1992 as amended by *Federal Law Gazette* I, no. 2/2008). Concerning deadlines, see article 4 of this agreement.

8 *Federal Law Gazette* I, no. 2/2008.

9 The term *uniform opinion* has to be understood in the same sense as in article 23d, section 2, of the B-VG. Therefore, it is again down to the Länder to enact corresponding regulations, which lay down the rules for the establishment of a uniform opinion. See Bußjäger (2013).

10 Besides, since April 2017, a popular initiative against CETA and TTIP, which has reached more than five hundred thousand signatures, has sat in the Nationalrat (the lower house of Parliament) for further processing. However, the popular initiative has no legally binding effect. According to article 41, section 2, of the B-VG, an initiative that is supported by at least a hundred thousand voters has to be considered by the Nationalrat. Therefore, the federal constitution does not oblige it to decide upon the initiative.

11 In addition, the general constitutional provisions of article 23 of the Basic Law were further specified in an accompanying law, the Gesetz über die Zusammenarbeit von Bund und Ländern in Angelegenheiten der Europäischen Union in 1993.

12 Offener Brief an die Mitglieder des Deutschen Bundesrates, Berlin, 5 April 2013, accessed 22 December 2017, https://www.kolko.net.

13 The CSU, the CDU's sister party, only operates in Bayern.

14 While certain reservations existed towards TTIP, within the SPD more so than within the CDU, the debate began to focus on CETA, and TTIP faded into the background from 2016. After negotiations with CETA opponents within the SPD, Economic Affairs Minister Sigmar Gabriel was able to secure a majority vote in favour of CETA during the party convention in Wolfsburg on 19 September 2016.

15 Except for the rather small Das Neue Österreich und Liberales Forum. Moreover, the SPÖ is divided internally upon this issue. Although Germany's former minister of economic affairs Social Democrat Sigmar Gabriel was able to secure his delegates' support for CETA in

a party convention held exclusively to address CETA in Wolfsburg in September 2016, Austrian SPÖ members broadly rejected the provisional implementation of CETA in an internal vote. Spiegel Online, "Österreichs SPÖ stellt sich gegen Freihandelsabkommen," 20 September 2016.

REFERENCES

Benz, Arthur. 2016. *Constitutional Policy in Multilevel Government: The Art of Keeping the Balance*. Oxford: Oxford University Press.

Benz, Arthur, Jessica Detemple, and Dominic Heinz. 2016. *Varianten und Dynamiken der Politikverflechtung im deutschen Bundesstaat*. Baden-Baden, Germany: Nomos.

Broschek, Jörg. 2015. "Pathways of Federal Reform: Australia, Canada, Germany, and Switzerland." *Publius* 45 (1): 51–76.

Bundesregierung. 2016. Regierungspressekonferenz vom 1. Juli. https://www.bundesregierung.de/Content/DE/Mitschrift /Pressekonferenzen/2016/07/2016-07-01-regpk.html.

Bußjäger, Peter. 2003. "Föderalismus durch Macht im Schatten? Österreich und die Landeshauptmännerkonferenz." In *Jahrbuch des Föderalismus 2003*, edited by Europäisches Zentrum für Föderalismus-Forschung Tübingen, 79–99. Baden-Baden, Germany: Nomos Verlagsgesellschaft.

– 2013. "Die Mitwirkung der Länder beim Abschluss von Staatsverträgen." *Zeitschrift für öffentliches Recht* 68 (1): 111–24.

– 2015. "Mitwirkung der Länder an der Rechtsetzung in der Europäischen Union." In *20 Jahre EU-Mitgliedschaft Österreichs*, edited by S. Griller, A. Kahl, B. Kneihs, and W. Obwexer, 359–81. Vienna: Verlag Österreich.

Deutscher Bundesrat. 2013a. "Entschließung des Bundesrates zur Aufnahme von Verhandlungen zwischen der EU und den USA über ein transatlantisches Handels- und Investitionsabkommen (TTIP)." *Drucksache 464/13*. Bonn.

– 2013b. "Gesetz zu dem Handelsübereinkommen vom 26. Juni 2012 zwischen der Europäischen Union und ihren Mitgliedstaaten einerseits sowie Kolumbien und Peru andererseits." *Drucksache 2013, 259/13*. Bonn.

– 2014. "Entschließung des Bundesrates anlässlich des öffentlichen Konsultationsverfahrens der Europäischen Kommission über die Modalitäten eines Investitionsschutzabkommens mit Investor-Staat-Schiedsgerichtsverfahren im Rahmen der Verhandlungen über eine Transatlantische Handels- und Investitionspartnerschaft zwischen der EU und den USA." *Drucksache 2014, 295/14*. Bonn.

– 2015. "Mitteilung der Kommission an das Europäische Parlament, den Rat, den Europäischen Wirtschafts- und Sozialausschuss und den Ausschuss der Regionen: Handel für alle – Hin zu einer verantwortungsbewussteren Handels- und Investitionspolitik." *Drucksachen Ausschussempfehlung 2015, 500/1/15.* Bonn.

Deutscher Bundestag. 2016a. *Basic Law for the Federal Republic of Germany.* English translation. Berlin: Deutscher Bundestag.

– 2016b. *Fragen zum sog. Lindauer Abkommen und der Ständigen Vertragskommission der Länder. Wissenschaftliche Dienste.* WD 3–3000–240/16. Berlin: Deutscher Bundestag.

– 2017. "Antwort der Bundesregierung auf Kleine Anfrage 'Offene Fragen zum Freihandelsabkommen CETA.'" *Drucksache 18/11068.* Berlin.

– 2018a. 'Beschlussempfehlung und Bericht des Ausschusses für Wirtschaft und Energie.' *Drucksache 19/1767.* Berlin.

– 2018b. "Gesetzentwurf." *Drucksache 19/958.* Berlin.

De Ville, Ferdi, and Gabriel Siles-Brügge. 2016. *TTIP: The Truth about the Transatlantic Trade and Investment Partnership.* Cambridge: Polity Press.

Die Presse. 2016. "EU-Staaten stimmten Ceta zu." 29 October.

Egger, Alexander. 2017. "Art 23d B-VG." In *Rill-Schäffer-Kommentar Bundesverfassungsrecht,* edited by B. Kneihs and G. Lienbacher. Vienna: Verlag Österreich.

Europaministerkonferenz. 2015. Bericht der 68. Europaministerkonferenz. 21 May.

Fallend, Franz. 2013. "Austria: A Federal, a Decentralized Unitary, or a 'Hybrid' State? Relations between the Welfare State and the Federal State after 1945." In *Routledge Handbook on Regionalism and Federalism,* edited by J. Loughlin, J. Kincaid, and W. Swenden, 235–47. Abingdon, UK: Routledge.

Gamper, Anna. 2006. "The Austrian Bundesrat." In *A World of Second Chambers,* edited by J. Luther, P. Passaglia, and R. Tarchi, 781–828. Milan, Italy: Giuffrè Editore.

Hooghe, Liesbeth, and Gary Marks. 2016. *Community, Scale, and Regional Governance: A Postfunctionalist Theory of Governance, Volume II.* Oxford: Oxford University Press.

Hueglin, Thomas, and Alan Fenna. 2015. *Comparative Federalism: A Systematic Inquiry.* 2nd ed. Toronto: University of Toronto Press.

Jeffrey, Charlie. 1999. "From Cooperative Federalism to a 'Sinatra Doctrine' of the Länder?" In *Recasting German Federalism: The Legacies of Unification,* edited by C. Jeffrey, 329–42. London: Pinter.

Kropp, Sabine. 2010. *Kooperativer Föderalismus und Politikverflechtung.* Wiesbaden, Germany: Springer VS.

Land Niederösterreich. 2016. Resolutionsantrag des Abgeordneten Mag. Riedl betreffend TTIP, CETA und TiSA. Ltg.-987/V-4/8–2016 15 June.

Land Salzburg. 2014. Nr. 614 der Beilagen zum stenographischen Protokoll des Salzburger Landtages. *2. Session der 15. Gesetzgebungsperiode.* 4 June.

232   Jörg Broschek, Peter Bußjäger, and Christoph Schramek

- 2016. Nr. 337 der Beilagen zum stenographischen Protokoll des Salzburger Landtages. *4. Session der 15. Gesetzgebungsperiode*. 27 April.
Land Steiermark. 2016. Landtagsbeschluss Nr. 217, 13. Landtagssitzung, XVII. Gesetzgebungsperiode. *EZ/OZ 857/4*. 10 May.
Landtag von Niederösterreich. 2015. *Ltg.-724–1/A-3/74–2015*. 22 October.
Land Tirol. 2016. Entschließung betreffend Ratifizierung des CETA-Freihandelsabkommens. *GZ 250/16*. 30 June.
Land Vorarlberg. 2016. CETA: Keine vorläufige Anwendung! Beilagennummer 50/2016. 6 June.
Laufer, Heinz and Ursula Münch. 2010. *Das föderale System der Bundesrepublik Deutschland*. Munich: Bayerische Landeszentrale für politische Bildungsarbeit.
Lehmbruch, Gerhard. 2000. *Parteienwettbewerb im Bundestaat: Regelsysteme und Spanungslagen im politischen System der Bundesrepublik Deutschland*. 3rd ed. Wiesbaden, Germany: Springer VS.
Mögele, Rudolf. 2012. *AEUV Art. 216*. Edited by R. Streinz. Munich: Verlag C.H. Beck.
Öhlinger, Theo, and Christoph Konrath. 2013. Art 23d. In *Österreichisches Bundesverfassungsrecht*, edited by K. Korinek, M. Holoubek, and A. Martin. Vienna: Verlag Österreich.
Republik Österreich. Bundesrat. 2016. Stellungnahme gemäß Art. 23e B-VG des EU-Ausschusses des Bundesrates vom 31. Mai 2016. 4/S-BR2016. Vienna Republik Österreich Bundesrat.
Rossbach, David. 2016. "Domestic Institutions and Regional Representation in the European Union: The Case of Austria." *Regional and Federal Studies* 26 (1): 25–43.
Scharpf, Fritz W. 1988. "The Joint-Decision Trap: Lessons from German Federalism and European Integration." *Public Administration* 66 (2): 239–78.
- 1999. *Governing in Europe: Effective and Democratic?* Oxford: Oxford University Press.
- 2009. *Föderalismusreform: Kein Ausweg aus der Politikverflechtungsfalle?* Frankfurt and New York: Campus.
Scharpf, Fritz W., Bernd Reissert, and Fritz Schnabel. 1976. *Politikverflechtung: Theorie und Empirie des kooperativen Föderalismus in der Bundesrepublik*. Königstein, Germany: Athenaum.
Stadt Wien. 2014a. Beilage zu VSt-7437/20 vom 5. Mai 2014. Vienna: Stadt Wien.
- 2014b. VSt-7437/82. 19 November. Vienna: Stadt Wien.
- 2016. VSt-7437/229, 11 May. Vienna: Stadt Wien.
- 2017. Vst-7437/259, 31 October. Vienna: Stadt Wien.
Sturm, Roland, and Heinrich Pehle. 2001. *Das neue deutsche Regierungssystem*. Opladen, Germany: Leske und Budrich.

Swenden, Wilfried, and Nicole Bolleyer. 2014. "Regional Mobilization in the 'New Europe': A Research Agenda." *Regional and Federal Studies* 24 (3): 249–62.

Tatham, Michaël. 2016. *With, Without, or Against the State? How European Regions Play the Brussels Game.* Oxford: Oxford University Press.

Thorlakson, Lori. 2003. "Comparing Federalism Institutions: Power and Representation in Six Federations." *West European Politics* 26 (2): 1–22.

Umweltministerkonferenz. 2014. *82. Ergebnisprotokoll.* 9 May. Konstanz, Germany: Umweltministerkonferenz.

Wiederin, Ewald. 2011. Art 10/3. In *Österreichisches Bundesverfassungsrecht*, edited by K. Korinek, M. Holoubek, and A. Martin. Vienna: Verlag Österreich.

Verbraucherschutzministerkonferenz. 2014. *Ergebnisprotokoll der 10. Verbraucherschutzministerkonferenz am 16. Mai 2014 in Rostock-Warnemünde.* Schwerin, Germany: Verbraucherschutzministerkonferenz.

Wirtschaftsministerkonferenz. 2014. *Beschlusssammlung der Wirtschaftsministerkonferenz am 4./5. Juni 2014 in Berlin.* Berlin: Wirtschaftsministerkonferenz.

Woolcock, Stephen. 2015. "Trade Policy: Policy-Making after the Lisbon Treaty." In *Policy-Making in the European Union.* 7th ed., edited by H. Wallace, M. Pollack, and A. Young, 388–406. Oxford: Oxford University Press.

9 Trade Politics and the Australian States and Territories

ANNMARIE ELIJAH

The proliferation of ambitious bilateral and mega-regional free trade agreements across the globe has altered the trade-policy agenda. Many of the new deals seek to liberalize the "behind-the-border" barriers embedded in domestic policy instead of tariffs or quotas. These agreements have special complexity for federal states, and Australia is no exception.

This chapter suggests that the intergovernmental politics of trade policymaking in Australia has changed over time and in relation to the various agreements, with their differing complexity and reach. It investigates the proposition that the governance burden on the federation has grown as Australia's international trade obligations have stretched further behind borders. It suggests that the Australian states and territories are integral to the adequate implementation of new-generation trade agreements and to any prospect of comprehensively reviewing them.

The existing literature that specifically addresses questions around the role of Australia's sub-national actors in trade policy is small. Australian research reflects the international division between internal and external trade policy, with scholars focusing on either federalism or international political economy. This chapter draws on the small directly relevant, secondary literature and the separate literatures on Australian federalism and Australian trade policy. It relies heavily on the publicly available documentary evidence in each of the Australian jurisdictions, and two extensive parliamentary reviews into the Australian treaty-making process (Australia 1995, 2015). Research on the Australian federation is limited by some transparency issues and access to materials, a problem acknowledged in the literature and elaborated in this chapter.

The chapter proceeds in three sections. First, it seeks to establish the institutional mechanisms used for intergovernmental cooperation and consultation in trade politics. Which actors are involved in multilateral trade policymaking? What are the dominant modes of decision making? What is the timing of sub-federal actors' involvement in the politics of trade, and where in the policy cycle do they participate? The chapter evaluates the options for Australian states and territories where their interests do not align with central government priorities. It traces how this process has changed over time, with reference to the changing international trade-policy landscape and the specific demands of the agreements in question. Second, the chapter briefly sets out the cases of three agreements to illustrate these changes since the early 1980s: the "deep" trade agreement between Australia and New Zealand (1983), the Australia-United States Free Trade Agreement (2005), and the Korean-Australian Free Trade Agreement (2014). It is clear that each agreement followed a different path through Australia's intergovernmental institutions; together they provide a snapshot of the changing multilevel landscape. The second section also canvasses likely challenges for the Australian federation relating to the prospective Australia-European Union agreement launched in 2017. At this early stage it is clear that the states and territories will need to be involved. Third, the chapter reviews these findings in relation to Hirschman's framework of *exit*, *voice*, and *loyalty* (Hirschman 1970). What are the options for Australian states and territories as they engage in multilevel trade politics? Which strategies are being employed, and to what effect? Does this framework enhance our understanding of the Australian case?

The chapter demonstrates that the nature and effectiveness of intergovernmental cooperation varies significantly over time. In part these changes can be attributed to the demands made on the sub-federal governments in terms of commitment and implementation and to the prevailing political and societal influences on trade policy at a given time. However, the institutional landscape of Australian intergovernmental relations in trade has also changed in untidy ways. This draws our attention to some peculiarities of the Australian case.

The Institutional Landscape: Trade Policy and Australian Intergovernmental Relations

Viewed comparatively, Australia is one of the more centralized examples of contemporary federal systems (Broschek 2015; Phillimore 2013). In the first decade of this century Saunders noted the "long

history of cooperation" in the federation and the increasing centralization that had resulted (2002, 69). Similarly, Hollander and Patapan
wrote that in Australia's case "the pull of the centre has tended to
overcome the tug of the periphery" (2007, 280). The history of Australian intergovernmental relations reflects the complex – and at times
colourful – politics around these centripetal forces. Wiltshire wrote in
the early 1990s that the media had come to regard federal-state relations "as a bloodsport" (1992, 171). In the mid-1970s Reid argued that
Australian politics was "a complex web of political strategy and counter strategy between governments. There are threats, counter-threats,
reprisals, bluffs, non-cooperative moves, retreats and advances" (Reid
1974, cited in Parker 1977).

The main institutions of Australian intergovernmental relations
have also altered significantly since federation in 1901. These are best
described as ad hoc, responding on a case-by-case basis to the perceived
need for consultation and cooperation. Hollander and Patapan describe
the Australian federation as "problem defined and problem driven."
They argue that the system has considerable strengths, such as being
"non-doctrinal," but that there are certain dangers in this approach, for
example unintended consequences (Hollander and Patapan 2007, 291).

Australian trade policy is no exception to these federal dynamics. All
evidence suggests that it is dominated by the Commonwealth, is institutionally ad hoc and pragmatic, and is at times the subject of political
manoeuvring. The main players in the institutional landscape are the
Council of Australian Governments (COAG) and its ministerial councils; the Treaties Council; Parliament, particularly the Joint Standing
Committee on Treaties (JSCOT); and the bureaucratic structures and
officials' groups that serve the relevant portfolio ministers and these
councils and committees. The chapter finds that the officials' groups are
particularly important.

Australian sub-national governments (of six states and two territories) do not have international legal personality and do not enter into
treaty-level agreements. As in many other federal systems, trade-policy
authority lies with the central government. The government of the Commonwealth of Australia retains the power to enter into treaties and to
implement them, as set out in sections 61 and 51(xxix) of the Australian
constitution, respectively. Despite its federal system, Australia speaks
"with one voice" internationally. The Department of Foreign Affairs
and Trade (DFAT) is the lead agency in relation to trade agreements.

The allocation of these powers relating to treaties, and trade agreements in particular, is not formally contested internally (see, for example, Australian Senate 1995, 2015). This is not to suggest that the politics

of trade inside the federation is straightforward. Historically, the key point of contention among Australian jurisdictions has centred on meaningful and timely consultations.

The Council of Australian Governments

The dynamics of Australian federalism altered significantly in the early 1990s with the establishment of the COAG. The changes extended and formalized existing intergovernmental relations in the federation and, importantly, linked these institutions to the prevailing consensus around economic reform. The COAG generally meets at least annually and consists of the prime minister, the premiers, the chief ministers, and the president of the Australian Local Government Association. Its work is supplemented by ministerial councils across portfolio areas. The establishment of the COAG and its links to the reform agenda have been covered in the literature on Australian federalism (see, for example, Painter 1998; Wiltshire 1992).

The COAG process and its ministerial-council structures have at times provided the institutional architecture for the meetings of Australian trade-policy ministers. Like many of the ministerial councils, however, the trade ministers' council has undergone multiple restructures throughout its history. It has changed in name and form several times and been rolled into and then removed from the formal auspices of the COAG. In its latest iteration, and further to central agency reviews of the ministerial-council system in 2011, the council continues to meet but not formally as a COAG council. It is therefore removed from the centralized set of conventions relating to ministerial councils (Australia 2016a).

Given the prevailing tendency for consensus-style decision making and the clear dominance of the Commonwealth in this policy area, the removal of the council from the auspices of the COAG may make no practical difference to the adequacy of consultations on trade. Nevertheless, full involvement as a COAG council and the oversight of the COAG secretariat in the Department of the Prime Minister and Cabinet oblige a council and its officials to observe certain governance norms (including voting procedures) that might be useful where there is disagreement. Further, formal involvement in the COAG gives ministers across all jurisdictions clear recourse to high-level consideration by heads of government as required.

A review of the scant publicly available material relating to the trade ministers' council since the early 1990s reveals that ministers have focused on a range of issues: collective attempts to identify export opportunities, discussion of prospective trade agreements, closer coordination of overseas representation, forthcoming international events, and World Trade Organization issues. Topical issues also surfaced at these meetings: drought, for example, and possible collective work on the millennium bug. Releases from 2014 and 2015 show a renewed focus on investment issues.

In accordance with COAG principles, detailed accounts of the meetings are not available, and the information publicly released often reflects the views of one jurisdiction, often the Commonwealth and occasionally the hosting jurisdiction. The lack of transparency relates not so much to the highly sensitive nature of discussions but to the long-standing COAG convention that material is not released without permission from all jurisdictions. Where cross-jurisdictional clearance does not occur, documents are not released, and the proceedings are not discussed publicly (Australia 2016a; Saunders 2002, 73).[1] As Walsh and others have noted, the tendency towards secrecy in intergovernmental decision making has implications for Australian federalism and democracy, particularly in relation to the role of state and territory parliaments (Walsh 2012, 45). Saunders also concluded that decision making through Australian "executive federalism" reduces accountability (2002, 73).

The lack of detailed accounts or documentary evidence of intergovernmental relations limits this and other research into multilevel policymaking. In trade policy this difficulty is compounded by the Australian bureaucracy's risk-averse consultation procedures. A review into treaty-making, conducted through the Senate's Foreign Affairs, Defence and Trade Committee in 2015, set out the issue in detail. It noted the "common practice" of negotiating trade agreements confidentially. The vast majority of submissions to the committee called for greater transparency, with the exception of evidence from DFAT, which suggested that it was difficult to reform the current procedures: "if you start releasing your bottom line, your negotiating strategy, and everyone can see it, then you are not going to get the best outcome" (Holmes, cited in Australian Senate 2015, 43). DFAT's position was criticized in the final report of the opposition-led committee.[2]

Direct concerns relating to the Australian states and territories did not feature heavily in the 2015 committee report. In fact, the committee received just two submissions from states and territories, despite terms of reference specifically concerning the intergovernmental institutions and consultation processes (Australia 2015, 1). The Queensland submission attested to the usefulness of the current practices. The Australian Capital Territory submission was critical, noting difficulties with insufficient time frames and an inability to understand where in DFAT the states and territories should direct their inquiries (Australia 2015, 55). Other jurisdictions did not lodge submissions, leading the committee to wonder if state and territory involvement in the treaty-making process was no longer "the burning issue that it once was in the mid-1990s" (Australia 2015, 10).

The 1996 Reforms and the Treaties Council

The current intergovernmental framework on trade policy owes much of its form and function to a landmark review of Australian treaty-making in 1995, after which the treaty-making architecture was reformed. In *Trick or Treaty? Commonwealth Power to Make and Implement Treaties* the Senate Committee put forward a number of revisions to the treaty-making process. In relation to states and territories it suggested the establishment of a high-level treaties council that would comprise parliamentary representatives from each jurisdiction, including opposition members. The COAG duly established the Treaties Council, and it met in November 1997, consisting of the prime minister, premiers, and chief ministers (Australia 1997). The committee report envisaged that the council would meet regularly and provide a political forum for resolving outstanding matters relating to Australian treaty negotiations and obligations (Wiltshire 1992, 175); ultimately it would be "more than a clearing house for information" (Australia 1995, ch. 13). In principle the existence of the Treaties Council could have changed dramatically the institutional landscape for trade policy. In practice the council's first meeting was also its last.

The lack of meetings for the Treaties Council can, on the one hand, be interpreted as evidence that intergovernmental cooperation on treaties is working adequately, with no need for governments to resort to high-level scrutiny. On the other hand, given the evidence of state and territory interest in the council, it is far more likely that the Commonwealth Government does not see the process as convenient or advantageous and has exercised its agenda-setting powers by simply not convening the council. Following recent changes to the COAG's public information on intergovernmental processes, the Treaties Council appears to have disappeared altogether from the institutional landscape.

Other recommendations from the 1995 review fared better. The five "pillars" of the reforms are summarized in the 2015 Senate Committee report. In brief, the measures included the establishment of the Treaties Council, parliamentary scrutiny of treaties prior to binding treaty action by the government, preparation of a national interest analysis for each treaty, the establishment of the parliamentary JSCOT to review and report on treaties, and the establishment of an online treaties library. The reforms complemented the existing set of rules (agreed in 1982, revised in 1983 and 1992) known as the *Principles and Procedures for Commonwealth-State Consultation on Treaties*. State and territory interest in treaty-making remained at high levels through the late 1990s, with various practical measures proposed to enhance existing processes. The 2015 parliamentary review found "no evidence" that these proposals "gained any traction" or were revisited by state or territory parliaments (Australia 2015, 9). With the exception of the Treaties Council, the 1996 reforms remain in place, with varying degrees of effectiveness.

Bureaucratic Arrangements

Australian trade-policy consultation with state and territory bureaucracies does not take place via a single institutional platform. It is split primarily between the Commonwealth-States Standing Committee on Treaties (SCOT) – which preceded the ill-fated Treaties Council but would have served as its bureaucratic arm – and the senior officials' standing committee serving the ministerial council on trade in all of its different iterations. The standing committee is variously referred to as the Senior Trade Officials Group and the Standing Committee of Officials in government documentation.

The SCOT meets twice yearly and is convened by the Department of the Prime Minister and Cabinet. It has the following responsibilities: deciding on the forum for intergovernmental consideration of a treaty; monitoring and reporting on treaty implementation where it is relevant for states and territories; ensuring states and territories are adequately informed; and coordinating state and territory representation on delegations, where appropriate (New South Wales Government 1997). Note that the standing committee provides the institutional framework for *all* treaties, not simply trade treaties. It deals with a significant volume of information, channelled through central agencies. In the context of the 1995 treaty-making review, the standing committee was roundly criticized by the states and territories, which argued in a joint submission that it was not politically accountable, that the process was used by the Commonwealth as a clearing house, that information was provided too late, and that consultation was "patchy" and varied "immensely from treaty to treaty." The Senate report recommended that the standing committee be abolished (Australia 1995, esp. 9–12 and 22). This contrasts with the 2015 report, in which the committee was not criticized at all and in fact was commended by one jurisdiction as "highly valuable" (Australia 2015, 55).

The SCOT may well be the most important venue for intergovernmental cooperation on trade policy. The officials meet regularly, with the agenda being dictated by the issues at hand. References to the committee's work can be found in DFAT and Austrade annual reports and in accounts of treaty-making by senior trade officials (see, for example, Mugliston 2009). Given the COAG conventions and the sensitive nature of trade policymaking, there is little on the public record that might enable analysis and an assessment of whether cooperation or discord generally prevails. This leaves a series of research questions unanswered. Which Australian jurisdictions are the most engaged in trade policymaking? Do consultations focus primarily on forthcoming negotiations, implementation of existing agreements, or both? Do states and territories work together to formulate policy positions? Is practical experience of implementation fed back to the Commonwealth in a process of policy learning so that future trade agreements might be improved?

The history of Australian intergovernmental relations on trade suggests that there is absolutely no appetite – at least in the Commonwealth Government – to elevate trade-policy consultations to the political (ministerial) level or to debate the issues transparently through state and territory parliaments and legislatures. Importantly, states and territories are also ambivalent on whether such processes are necessary (Australia 2015).

The key actors in the governance of Australian trade policy are theoretically embedded in the intergovernmental decision-making process at high levels. In reality the bulk of the work is handled in officials' groups. The dominant mode of decision making in this context is consensus. Where there is dissent, it is not always clear how issues are resolved, but they are rarely elevated to the ministerial level. There is some evidence that consultations are useful, particularly for those jurisdictions that are sufficiently well resourced to pursue their interests. There is some evidence that trade-policy consultation with the states and territories has improved in the twenty-year period between the two parliamentary reviews of Australian treaty-making.

Multilevel Trade Politics in Australia: A Snapshot

This section provides a brief description of the intergovernmental processes related to the negotiation of three different Australian trade agreements, summarized in table 9.1. The different institutional path

9.1 Examples of Australian Intergovernmental Relations on Trade, 1980–Present

Agreement and year of entry into force	Intergovernmental measures
Australia-New Zealand Closer Economic Relations Trade Agreement, 1983	• Discussed briefly at Premiers' Conference* • Ad hoc meeting of officials ahead of Commonwealth consultations, with promise of full and meaningful consultation through the Premiers' Conference, with additional officials' meetings as required • Expansion of intergovernmental coordination as economic integration progressed, including cross-jurisdictional intergovernmental agreements with New Zealand
Australia-United States Free Trade Agreement, 2005	• Ministerial consultations across jurisdictions • State and territory submissions to Joint Standing Committee on Treaties (JSCOT) (8 submissions) • Consultations with states and territories before and after each negotiating round • State and territory representatives joined as observers in rounds • Standing Committee on Treaties process
Korea-Australia Free Trade Agreement, 2014	• Invitation to join public submissions to Department of Foreign Affairs and Trade (2 submissions) • Senior Trade Officials Group meetings • Standing Committee on Treaties process • Consultations on specifics: services, investment • No JSCOT submission by any state or territory

* The Premiers' Conferences were the institutional precursor to the Council of Australian Governments.

taken in each case reflects, first, the nature of the bilateral relationship in question; second, the timing of the negotiations in terms of the development of Australian trade policy; and, third, the content of the proposed agreement and the extent to which it impinges on state and territory competences. This brief snapshot confirms the importance of investigating each trade agreement as a separate intergovernmental proposition. The previous section explained the changing intergovernmental landscape – for example, the different iterations of the ministerial councils and officials' groups, and the enhanced role of Parliament after the 1996 reforms. This section shows that different intergovernmental mechanisms are used for different trade agreements, even where institutional continuity can be found.

Australia-New Zealand Closer Economic Relations

Australia and New Zealand have a long-shared history of economic relations and a history of formal trade agreements dating from 1922. Negotiations for the present treaty, known as the Comprehensive Economic Relations Trade Agreement (CER), began in the late 1970s. Its existence and form are widely attributed to a combination of global and domestic challenges faced by the governments of both countries. The CER quickly progressed from a comprehensive but straightforward agreement on trade in goods (1983) to an ambitious agenda of economic integration. Briefly summarized, the measures following from the CER encompass agreement on trade in services, including the use of a negative-list approach (1988); technical barriers to trade (1988); business law (1988); customs (1988, 1992, and 1996); standards and accreditation (1990); securities (1994); food standards (1995); government procurement (1997); mutual recognition of goods and occupations (1998); and investment (2013). This list is by no means exhaustive, and the Australian Government estimates that the bilateral relationship is underpinned by "more than 80" bilateral treaties, protocols, and arrangements (Australia 2016b).[3] CER has proved to be a model "living agreement," with frequent built-in reviews, and the two countries have worked towards the stated objective of a single economic market since 2004. The depth and extent of trans-Tasman economic integration has been established elsewhere (Leslie and Elijah 2012). Relevant here is the extent to which the CER program – with many of the characteristics of a "deep" trade agreement – has ventured behind borders and had an impact on the Australian states and territories.

The Australian government alerted the states and territories to the prospect of the CER early in the negotiations, undertaking to keep them informed and fully consulted. Details of Commonwealth Government thinking on the process have been made available as part of a set of historical documents published by the DFAT. It demonstrates that the intergovernmental framework on trade policy was scant but that all parties could see the significance of the potential agreement for sub-national governments. In response to state and territory questions, officials were assured that "Commonwealth officials were under very strict marching orders that the consultations *must* be meaningful. This was reflected in the Communique and the PM's statement to the Parliament and in the fact that *no decisions* had been taken up on what form any closer Australia New Zealand economic relationship might take. *Full* account would be taken of the views and comments of the States, industry and other interested parties. It would be many months before any matters were ready for decision and in the interim, there would be full discussions" (Andre, Payton, and Mills 2003, 297; italics in the original).

The Premiers' Conference was to serve as the institutional basis for this consultation, supplemented by officials' talks as required. Later documentation suggests that in fact CER was discussed for only a few minutes at the relevant meeting due to the heavy agenda (Andre, Payton, and Mills 2003, 504).

As the trans-Tasman agenda of economic integration progressed – arguably well beyond the parameters of standard trade agreements at the time – consultation with the states and territories became increasingly important. State and territory involvement in the measures appears to have been dealt with on a case-by-case basis. In two instances where measures directly involved sub-national governments (standards and accreditation, and mutual recognition of goods and occupations), states and territories were not merely consulted but were actually signatories to intergovernmental agreements governing the trans-Tasman arrangements (see New Zealand Ministry of Foreign Affairs and Trade 2003, 267, 365). In the case of mutual recognition of goods and occupations, agreement with New Zealand was preceded by an internal arrangement with the same objectives. The Australian Mutual Recognition Agreement (1992), and the Trans-Tasman Mutual Recognition Arrangement (1998) that followed, are perhaps the clearest examples of Australian attempts to embed domestic reform objectives relating to the federation in an international trade agreement.

The intergovernmental process inside the federation around trans-Tasman economic integration was extensive. The parties were able to use existing institutions (COAG and its ministerial councils) as the institutional framework to enable negotiation, agreement, signature, and review of these measures, and this was possible because the Commonwealth had long allowed New Zealand to participate in what were otherwise "domestic" intergovernmental institutions. Despite the assorted institutional reforms to the COAG and the ministerial councils that had taken place since their inception, New Zealand participation remains codified and observed in this system (Australia 2016b). New Zealand's close involvement in the governance structures of the Australian federation has greatly influenced the institutional method for dealing with sub-national involvement in CER. Faced with the prospect of a comprehensive trade agreement and the sub-national issues that arose from it, the parties acted pragmatically and utilized existing institutions to manage cooperation. In terms of the multilevel politics of trade, the innovative institutional arrangements governing the CER and trans-Tasman economic integration are an exception internationally and, as the next two examples show, for Australia as well.

The Australia-United States Free Trade Agreement

Australian states and territories were active participants in the negotiation process that preceded the signing of the Australia-United States Free Trade Agreement (AUSFTA). AUSFTA has attracted considerable academic attention in Australia (see, for example, Thurbon 2015), but in large part this work has not focused on state and territory involvement and implications. Rather, the agreement has been criticized for its social-policy implications, the political imperatives that dictated its signing, and the lack of positive economic outcomes for Australia (Capling and Ravenhill 2015; Weiss, Thurbon, and Mathews 2005).

The intergovernmental process that preceded the signing of AUSFTA can be summarized as follows: the agreement was discussed at the trade ministers' council; officials' meetings were held before and after each negotiating round; state and territory representatives joined the Australian delegation as observers; and the agreement went through the SCOT process. State and territory governments also fully used the Commonwealth parliamentary process in this instance, making a total of eight submissions to the JSCOT.

The politics around the participation of states and territories in the six negotiating rounds is particularly interesting. In July 2003 the Victorian premier made his displeasure publicly known when the United States allegedly declined to allow a nominated state-and-territory delegate to attend the negotiations, on the basis that US state representatives might request the same. The incident provoked the premier to call immediately for the Treaties Council to be convened (Nicholson 2003). In the event, the states and territories did attend the bulk of the negotiating rounds. The JSCOT report on state and territory consultations outlines the process as follows: one state-and-territory representative attended the third round of negotiations, three attended the fourth round, two attended the fifth round, and one attended the final round (Australia 2004a). The Treaties Council was not convened.

The Australian Capital Territory submission to the JSCOT was highly critical of the AUSFTA, and the state and territory consultation relating to it. The chief minister described the text as "disappointing" and listed a series of concerns (consistent with civil-society concerns) including health and environmental implications, together with uncertain economic gains. On consultation specifically, the Australian Capital

Territory argued that there were "significant deficiencies" in the process. States and territories were not given access to the full working texts but rather to four relevant chapters. The submission argued that consultation worsened in the final stages of negotiations and did not adequately involve the states and territories at the political (ministerial) level. Further, the submission alleged that procurement gains through AUSFTA were limited by the Australian Government's inability to engage with the US states (ACT Chief Minister 2004). Notwithstanding some clear differences of opinion, the final text of AUSFTA shows that at least some state and territory interests were compiled and reflected in the outcomes; see, for example, chapter 15 on government procurement, especially the exceptions listed by jurisdiction in the annex.

The Korea-Australia Free Trade Agreement

The recently concluded Korea-Australia Free Trade Agreement (KAFTA) provides a further institutional variation through the Australian intergovernmental path. The DFAT's invitation for public submissions attracted just two from the states and territories; both were broadly supportive of the negotiating objectives. In terms of bureaucratic consultations, the agreement was on the agenda for both the Senior Trade Officials' Group and the SCOT. State and territory premiers and chief ministers were contacted by the minister for trade in 2009 in relation to Australia's initial services-and-investment offer, which was identified as being particularly important for the states and territories. No state or territory made a submission to the parliamentary JSCOT on KAFTA.

The Commonwealth Government text on the intergovernmental process that appears in the National Interest Analysis consultation annex and in the Regulation Impact Statement for KAFTA are almost identical. It notes the use of the bureaucratic intergovernmental forums, the call for public submissions, and the regular contact through meetings and correspondence. In recent agreements this has become the "standard" Commonwealth Government text attesting to the effectiveness of the process of consultation with the states and territories.[4] In the case of KAFTA, the National Interest Analysis and the Regulation Impact Statement note the high-level (ministerial) consultations on issues of direct relevance to states and territories. The intergovernmental processes for the agreements with Japan and China are similar to the Korean example. Officials' groups are in full use, the JSCOT process has ceased to be used by the states and territories, and more extensive consultations are in evidence where specific interests relating to states and territories can be identified or need to be defined in a schedule or annex.

This latter point is significant. In the variations in intergovernmental relations concerning the different Australian trade agreements, there is a common principle guiding Commonwealth actions: states and territories should be consulted only where there is direct relevance. Otherwise, sub-national governments are kept at arm's length. A transcript of evidence from a senior Commonwealth Government trade official at JSCOT is telling. Responding to Australian Capital Territory complaints about the intergovernmental process relating to the Thailand-Australia Free Trade Agreement, the official argued that "the substance ... of the negotiations was not as relevant to the states and territories," hence the consultation was less (Australia 2004b). From the Commonwealth Government perspective, consultation is to be conducted on a need-to-know rather than a broadly cooperative basis.

Given the institutional variations evident in the intergovernmental processes related to the Australian agreements with New Zealand, the United States, and Korea, it is clear that the governance burden on the Australian federation is greater when international trade obligations stretch further behind borders. As anticipated, states and territories are more involved when trade agreements are more complex. However, the depth of Australian agreements has not followed a linear trajectory; the most comprehensive and far-reaching agreement is arguably Australia's oldest, with New Zealand. It is also the most formally institutionalized.

Many of Australia's newer agreements have not required this level of intergovernmental cooperation, or at least this is the Australian Government's view. Where they do intrude on sub-national areas of competence, the central government consults on a need-to-know basis. The institutional framework for trade-policy cooperation has matured and stabilized since Australian trade agreements were first negotiated. It retains some ad hoc features consistent with Australia's version of pragmatic federalism. However, the consistent use of certain bureaucratic processes is well established. Viewed optimistically, the development of these mechanisms attests to the adaptability of Australian federal institutions and their capacity to meet policy needs as they arise. The downsides are the lack of transparency and public involvement in the process, and the potential for a lack of political commitment at the sub-national level.

The Australia-European Union Trade Agreement

The Australia-European Union trade negotiations –announced in 2017 after scoping on both sides, and launched in mid-2018 – is included here as a prospective example of the possible challenges to multilevel trade policymaking in Australia. Given the recent Canadian experience with the Comprehensive Economic and Trade Agreement (CETA) and the likely content of such an agreement, it is almost certain to test Australian intergovernmental processes (Elijah 2017; see Paquin, and Hederer and Leblond, in this volume). CETA provides some clues for the Australian experience in terms of, first, the institutional process undertaken by Canada and the European Union to reach agreement and, second, content that clearly impinges on state and territory policy authority. Negotiations for CETA were genuinely multilevel. Canadian provinces were represented during the CETA negotiations and have been vocal in evaluating the deal after its signing.

Projected gains from CETA are substantially attributed to behind-borders liberalizing measures and to trade in services in particular. As several chapters in this volume demonstrate, the negotiations underlined the need for effective coordination among the Canadian provinces and territories and with the federal government. If the CETA experience is any indication, the Australian states and territories (and perhaps even local governments) will need to be involved in negotiating the agreement with the European Union. Given what has been established here about the Australian intergovernmental process, this raises a series of questions for the Australian Government. What level of involvement will the European Union seek for Australian states and territories? How will local government be represented? Will the Australian consultations be limited to those chapters that clearly affect states and territories? When negotiations raise politically sensitive issues, will consultations remain at the bureaucratic level or be elevated? With negotiations at an early stage, these questions have yet to be answered. The DFAT has called for public submissions on the forthcoming Australia-European Union trade agreement. At the time of writing, Victoria was the only jurisdiction to respond. The submission welcomed the potential agreement, noted potential benefits for Victoria, summarized Victorian industry consultations, and reminded the Commonwealth Government of the need for close consultation (Victoria 2017).

Two multilevel challenges have already presented themselves to the Australian Government. First, the question of the recognition of the European Union's list of geographic indications (GIs) has arisen as one of the more controversial negotiating points between the parties. Early signs suggest that GIs may be a point of differentiation among the Australian states and territories, depending on their export profiles and sensitivities to European imports of specialty food products. Second, the European Union's commitment to negotiating

trade deals transparently – and insisting that potential trade partners do likewise – runs counter to established Australian practices,
for example the need-to-know principle that operates between the
Commonwealth Government and the states and territories (European
Commission 2015). The DFAT has been obliged to release more information than would usually be the case during the course of the negotiations. The impact of this additional disclosure on the involvement
of the Australian states and territories in trade negotiations is not yet
clear.

Conclusions: Exit, Voice, and Loyalty

As Dowding et al. (2000) have argued, Hirschman's influential "exit,
voice, and loyalty" framework has been usefully employed across disciplines, though without always drawing the analytical distinctions
in ways that do justice to the original work. For present purposes the
framework usefully sets out options for actors in multilevel systems
where those actors are managing the "fundamental dilemma" between
"autonomy and collective problem-solving" (Jachtenfuchs and Kasack
2017, 598).

Following Jachtenfuchs and Kasack's recent treatment, this chapter defines *exit* as a withdrawal from collective policies, and *voice* as
an attempt to influence collective decisions. *Exit* can mean a variety
of things: secession, exit from specific policies, or autonomous application of collective policies. They conceptualize *voice* as a continuum
including three broad types: intergovernmental agreements, veto, and
participation in central decisions (2017, 602–9).

On the face of it, Australian states and territories do not appear to
have many options for exit from Australian trade policy. Commonwealth Government dominance in external affairs is not challenged. In
trade policy the states and territories are included as bit players when
their areas of competence are directly affected. Ultimately the states
and territories cannot expect to dictate the terms of international agreements. The 1996 guidelines on Commonwealth-state consultation on
treaties state explicitly: "these principles and procedures are adopted
subject to their operation not being allowed to result in unreasonable
delays in the negotiating, joining or implementing of treaties by Australia" (New South Wales Government 1997).

Western Australia is the only jurisdiction that sporadically toys with
the idea of secession (and even once voted to leave); however, the main
point of contention here relates to the distribution of tax revenue across
the federation, rather than trade policy per se (Jericho 2015).

The proposition of state or territory exit from Australian trade policy when defined as exit *from specific policies* becomes more compelling. Here the issue of content is paramount. The likelihood that an Australian state or territory would threaten to leave the federation because of a trade agreement is unthinkable; however, it is not impossible that a state or territory could signal unwillingness to implement a particularly controversial agreement or even certain measures in an agreement. Dowding et al.'s link between voice and exit is useful in this context: "voice can be more effective if there is a threat of exit" (2000, 472). Australian states and territories could potentially use the threat of non-compliance to increase their influence over content.

In relation to voice, the links between state and territory multilevel politics and the increased electoral salience of trade politics may yet prove important in the Australian context. Australian states and territories were more active – and louder – during the Australia-United States negotiations. A vocal premier (especially from a larger jurisdiction) can make trade policy much more difficult for the Commonwealth Government, even if the agreement ultimately goes ahead. The role of civil society in animating state and territory participation in Australian trade politics warrants further research.

Australian jurisdictions also have different views and material interests in the prospective agreements undertaken by the Commonwealth Government. The states and territories have significantly different populations, land mass, economic profiles, political traditions, and administrative capacity. The territories in particular rely heavily on the Commonwealth Government in certain policy areas. It is reasonable to expect that voice is therefore exercised differently across the federation. This chapter has shown that some jurisdictions are at the activist end of the spectrum in trade policy. Victorian governments have no qualms about publicly shaming the Commonwealth Government, and the Australian Capital Territory routinely complains, on both policy and process. Other jurisdictions do not appear to exercise voice in this way – at least publicly. It is possible that some jurisdictions are highly engaged in the trade-policy process that occurs bureaucratically, but gauging this version of voice is difficult given the lack of transparency.

Here the Australian approach differs from that outlined in Jachtenfuchs and Kasack, where voice by sub-units is "usually exercised through formal decision rules" (2017, 607–8). Certain principles and procedures apply to Australian intergovernmental relations, especially the institutions of the COAG . In the case of the Australia-New Zealand trade deal, these rules were applied to state and territory involvement in trade policy, even extending to the use of intergovernmental agreements. In general, however, the Australian reality is informal and heavily reliant on officials. Notwithstanding specific examples of sustained collaboration to negotiate, implement, and review deep trade agreements, permanent institutional change to cope with the demands of the new trade agenda has not yet occurred. This bears a striking resemblance to the recent history of trade politics in Canada (see Paquin in this volume). Kukucha describes "a pattern of incremental change, with sporadic bursts of more active consultation in specific benchmark agreements" (2016, 13).

This chapter set out to illustrate the variations in multilevel trade politics in Australia with particular reference to Australia's trade deals with New Zealand, the United States, and Korea. The intergovernmental processes behind these agreements varied significantly. The variation can be explained primarily in terms of the relative depth of the agreements (which in the Australian case is not a linear progression) and the peculiarities of the Australian institutional configuration (which is ad hoc and deeply pragmatic). There is, however, an additional dynamic at work in the Australian case. When a proposed trade agreement attracts significant public attention, sub-national governments are more likely to seek a larger role in negotiations and make greater use of intergovernmental avenues for input. This is evident from the experience of the Australia-United States negotiations for arguably Australia's most controversial trade deal to date. The same dynamic may surface in the course of the Australia-European Union negotiations. It is a live question whether the current institutional landscape and the established modes of intergovernmental cooperation are adequate to meet the challenges of Australian trade policy. A confluence of factors, such as a proposed deep trade agreement with strong state and territory implications and a controversial public profile, could strain the existing mechanisms. Commonwealth Government accounts of the process are detailed and positive, and it is clear that *some* state and territory interests are accounted for. The Commonwealth Government acknowledges the importance of services trade in particular for the states and territories. Yet the extent of state and territory *loyalty* is difficult to estimate. Less visible state and territory representations – for example, the decline in the number of submissions to the Australian parliamentary treaty process – may indicate a level of satisfaction with trade-policy consultations. It could also signal disengagement or apathy as a response to sustained neglect on the part of the Commonwealth Government. Given the centrality of state and territory governments in implementing new-generation trade agreements, and their likely continued importance in Australian trade policy, neglect by the Commonwealth Government would be best avoided.

NOTES

1 See for example the *Guidance on COAG Councils*, in which it stipulates that documents are to be "treated as sensitive, and only distributed on a strict need to know basis" (Australia 2016a); see also Saunders 2002, 73.
2 The report was accompanied by two dissenting opinions. The coalition (government) senators found the criticism of DFAT to be "overblown and borderline insulting" (Australia 2015, 78). The Australian Greens senators argued that the review had not gone nearly far enough: Australia should not enter into any treaty unless it is "fully transparent and democratic" (Australia 2015, 80).
3 For a full set of trans-Tasman documents proceeding from CER up until 2003 see New Zealand Ministry of Foreign Affairs and Trade (2003).
4 The text also matches the process set out in detail by Commonwealth Government official Michael Mugliston in relation to the ASEAN-Australia-New Zealand Free Trade Agreement. See Mugliston (2009).

REFERENCES

ACT (Australian Capital Territory). 2014. Chief Minister. *Submission for the Joint Standing Committee on Treaties*. Australia-United States Free Trade Agreement.
Andre, Pamela, Stephen Payton, and John Mills, eds. 2003. *The Negotiation of the Australia New Zealand Closer Economic Relations Trade Agreement 1983*. Documents on Australian Foreign Policy, Australian Department of Foreign Affairs and Trade and New Zealand Ministry of Foreign Affairs and Trade, Commonwealth of Australia. Canberra.
Australia. 1995. Senate Committee on Legal and Constitutional Affairs. *Trick or Treaty: Commonwealth Power to Make and Implement Treaties*. http://www .aph.gov.au.
– 1997. *Treaties Council Meeting Communiqué*. 7 November. https://www.coag .gov.au/.
– 2004a. Parliament. Joint Standing Committee on Treaties. *Australia-US Free Trade Agreement*. Report 61, 23 June.
– 2004b. Parliament. Joint Standing Committee on Treaties. *Australia-Thailand Free Trade Agreement*. Report 63. http://www.austlii.edu.au.
– 2014. Parliament. *Korea-Australia Free Trade Agreement: National Impact Assessment*. Tabled in the Australian parliament, 13 May.

– 2015. Senate. Foreign Affairs, Defence and Trade References Committee. *Blind Agreement: Reforming Australia's Treaty-Making Process.* https://www .aph.gov.au.

– 2016a. Commonwealth-State Relations Branch, Department of the Prime Minister and Cabinet. *Guidance on COAG Councils.* August. https://www .coag.gov.au/.

– 2016b. Department of Foreign Affairs and Trade. *Australia-New Zealand Closer Economic Relations Trade Agreement.* http://dfat.gov.au.

Broschek, Jorg. 2015. "Pathways of Federal Reform: Australia, Canada, Germany and Switzerland." *Publius* 45 (1): 51–76.

Capling, Ann, and John Ravenhill. 2015. "Australia's Flawed Approach to Trade Negotiations: And Where Do We Sign?" *Australian Journal of International Affairs* 69 (5): 496–512.

Council of Australian Governments. 2017. https://www.coag.gov.au/.

Dowding, Keith, Peter John, Thanos Mergroupis, and Mark Van Gugt. 2000. "Exit, Voice and Loyalty: Analytic and Empirical Developments." *European Journal of Political Research* 37 (4): 469–95.

Elijah, Annmarie. 2017. "Is the CETA a Road Map for Australia and the EU?" In *Australia, the European Union and the New Trade Agenda*, edited by A. Elijah, D. Kenyon, K. Hussey, and P. van der Eng, 55–74. Canberra, Australia: ANU Press.

European Commission. 2015. *Trade for All: Towards a More Responsible Trade and Investment Policy.* Luxembourg: Publication Office of the European Union.

Hirschman, Albert O. 1970. *Exit, Voice, and Loyalty: Responses to Decline in Firms, Organizations and States.* Cambridge, MA: Harvard University Press.

Hollander, Robyn, and Haig Patapan. 2007. "Pragmatic Federalism: Australian Federalism from Hawke to Howard." *Australian Journal of Public Administration* 66 (3): 280–97.

Jachtenfuchs, Markus, and Christiane Kasack. 2017. "Balancing Sub-unit Autonomy and Collective Problem-Solving by Varying Exit and Voice: An Analytical Framework." *Journal of European Public Policy* 24 (4): 598–614.

Jericho, Greg. 2015. "Want to Go It Alone, WA? Good Luck with That." Australian Broadcasting Corporation, 15 April. http://www.abc.net.au.

Kukucha, Christopher J. 2016. "Provincial/Territorial Governments and the Negotiations of International Trade Agreements." *IRPP Insight 10*, 18 October.

Leslie, John, and Annmarie Elijah. 2012. "Does N=2? Trans-Tasman Economic Integration as a Comparator for the Single European Market." *Journal of Common Market Studies* 50 (6): 975–93.

Mugliston, Michael. 2009. "Negotiating the ASEAN–Australia–New Zealand Free Trade Agreement." Paper submitted to the Intergovernmental

Relations 2009 conference, A Practical Approach in a Changing Landscape, 21 July. Accessed 1 November 2019. https://dfat.gov.au.

New South Wales. 1997. Premier and Cabinet. *Principles and Procedures for Commonwealth-State Consultation on Treaties*. Memorandum M1997–01. https://arp.nsw.gov.au.

– 2004. Cabinet Office. *Submission for the Standing Committee on Treaties, Australia–United States Free Trade Agreement*. Sydney: Government of New South Wales.

New Zealand. 2003. Ministry of Foreign Affairs and Trade. *Critical Paths in Trans-Tasman Economic Relations: CER 20th Anniversary*. Wellington, New Zealand: MFAT.

Nicholson, B. 2003. "Bracks Slams State Trade Exclusion." *The Age*, 27 July. https://www.theage.com.au.

Painter, Martin. 1998. *Collaborative Federalism: Economic Reform in Australia in the 1990s*. Cambridge: Cambridge University Press.

– 2008. "Public Sector Reform, Intergovernmental Relations and the Future of Australian Federalism." *Australian Journal of Public Administration* 57 (3): 52–63.

Parker, R.S. 1977. "Political and Administrative Trends in Australian Federalism." *Publius: The Journal of Federalism* 7 (3): 35–52.

Phillimore, John. 2013. "Understanding Intergovernmental Relations: Key Features and Trends." *Australian Journal of Public Administration* 72 (3): 228–38.

Queensland. 2004. Government. *Submission for the Standing Committee on Treaties, Australia–United States Free Trade Agreement*. Brisbane: Queensland Government.

Reid, Gregor S. 1974. "Political Decentralization, Cooperative Federalism and Responsible Government." In *Intergovernmental Relations in Australia*, edited by R.L. Mathews, 23–42. Sydney, Australia: Angus & Robertson.

Saunders, Cheryl. 2002. "Collaborative Federalism." *Australian Journal of Public Administration* 61 (2): 69–77.

South Australia. 2004. Government. *Submission for the Standing Committee on Treaties, Australia-United States Free Trade Agreement*. Adelaide: Government of South Australia.

Thurbon, Elizabeth. 2015. "10 Years after the Australia-US Free Trade Agreement: Where to for Australia's Trade Policy?" *Australian Journal of International Affairs* 69 (5): 463–7.

Victoria. 2017. Government. *Submission: EU-Australia Free Trade Agreement Negotiations*. Melbourne: Government of Victoria.

Walsh, Cliff. 2012. "Australia." In *Internal Markets and Multi-level Governance: The Experience of the European Union, Australia, Canada, Switzerland, and the*

United States, edited by G. Anderson, 10–54. Oxford: Oxford University Press.

Weiss, Linda, Elizabeth Thurbon, and John Mathews. 2005. *How to Kill a Country: Australia's Devastating Trade Deal with the United States*. Sydney, Australia: Allen & Unwin.

Western Australia. 2004. Office of the Premier. *Submission for the Standing Committee on Treaties, Australia–United States Free Trade Agreement*.

Wiltshire, Kenneth. 1992. "Australia's New Federalism: Recipes for Marble Cakes." *Publius* 22 (3): 165–80.

10 From *Nada* to Namur: Sub-federal Parliaments' Involvement in European Union Trade Politics, and the Case of Belgium

YELTER BOLLEN, FERDI DE VILLE, AND NIELS GHEYLE

In October 2016 the Belgian Walloon region made headlines worldwide when it refused to give the authority to the Belgian federal government to sign the European Union-Canada Comprehensive Economic and Trade Agreement (CETA), leading Canadian prime minister Justin Trudeau to postpone his visit to Brussels for the signing ceremony. This was a surprising development, given that the 2009 Lisbon Treaty reforms had been intended to streamline European Union (EU) trade policy by enlarging its scope, thereby transferring the responsibility of controlling trade negotiations from national legislatures to the European Parliament (EP) (cf. Krajewski 2012).[1]

In this chapter we will not go into the legal discussion about the status of CETA and whether or not it should have been considered a "mixed agreement," implying member-state ratification. Rather, we will look at the political dimension and analyse how exceptional the CETA saga was and why sub-federal parliaments have become more involved in EU trade agreements, seemingly in contradiction to the spirit of the Lisbon Treaty (see Garcia in this volume).

Empirically, we look at the Belgian case and at the involvement of parliaments at the national and regional levels in particular. We argue that parliaments have become more involved in EU trade politics – against expectations about what would happen after the Lisbon Treaty reforms – because the expanded scope of EU trade agreements has led civil-society organizations (CSOs) to mobilize more strongly against some provisions in these deals. Their argument that the agreements would limit the policy space of sub-federal parliaments resonated with Members of Parliament (MPs), leading them to spend more time and energy on EU trade policy than they used to. This helps explain the remarkable evolution of the Belgian parliament's involvement in EU trade politics from almost *nada* to one that attracted cameras from all over the world to the Walloon parliament in Namur in October 2016.

In the next section we review the literature on EU trade policymaking after the Lisbon Treaty reforms, with a focus on the role of the parliaments (national and sub-federal) of member states. Subsequently, we discuss the involvement of the Belgian parliaments in trade since the start of the century, based on desk research and twenty interviews with decision makers and stakeholders in Belgium. In the fourth section we elaborate on our explanation of the recent politicization of EU trade policy in Belgium. We conclude with some reflections about the implications of these developments for the future of EU trade policy.

Parliaments in European Union Trade Policy after Lisbon

Although trade policy has been a supranational competence from the outset of European integration, there have always been political and judicial struggles over the exact scope of this competence and the division of labour between the EU and the member-state level (Billiet 2006; Young, Holmes, and Rollo 2000). At its core much of this debate has revolved around the trade-off between efficiency (by increasing supranational authority and European Commission autonomy) and legitimacy (by ensuring control by representatives close to the citizens): how can the EU negotiate and conclude ambitious agreements while respecting citizens' preferences (Meunier 2005)?

The Lisbon Treaty attempted to resolve this trade-off by transcending it (cf. Devuyst 2013; Woolcock 2013; Garcia in this volume). On the one hand, the "efficiency" dimension was strengthened by expanding the scope of supranational trade competence (which now also covers services, intellectual property rights, and foreign direct investment), abandoning the need for national parliamentary ratification. This change was necessary, it was argued, to make the EU a more reliable and efficient negotiating partner. On the other hand, the "legitimacy" of the EU's trade policies was to be bolstered by expanding the role of the European Parliament (EP).[2] Switching control of EU trade policy from member-state parliaments to the EP was seen as an improvement as "most member state parliaments have never been able – or perhaps interested enough – to provide effective scrutiny of EC external trade policy as they are two steps removed from the real negotiations" (Woolcock 2010, 7). Hence, several EU trade-policy observers considered the Lisbon Treaty reforms to be an unequivocal win-win for the effectiveness and legitimacy of EU trade policy, "go[ing] a considerable way to filling the democratic deficit that previously existed with the technocratic decision-making process" (Woolcock 2010,14).

The reforms were not universally welcomed, however. On the one hand, two authorities in the legal discipline of EU external relations, Marc Maresceau and Joseph Weiler, expressed their scepticism about the impact of the EP's new powers on the effectiveness of EU trade policy (cited in Devuyst 2013, 311–12). On the other hand, some scholars pointed out that giving the EP more power in trade might be positive in terms of control at the supranational level, but that this might create new problems. As several policy domains potentially affected by deep trade agreements (e.g., social, health, or education policies) remain member-state competences, and distributive or redistributive consequences of trade agreements have to be mainly dealt with at the member-state level in the EU's overall architecture,[3] the loss of national parliaments' power could weaken the legitimacy of an expanded EU trade policy. Since the EU's new-generation trade agreements go well beyond classic at-the-border instruments such as tariffs, expanding into the deep trade zone of regulatory and normative issues (Young 2007), subsidiarity did not unambiguously favour further Europeanization (Bossuyt 2012; De Ville 2012). Seen from this angle, the Lisbon Treaty changes did not overcome the fundamental trade-governance question: how can we reconcile the benefits of institutionalized open trade with the right of national or subnational authorities to pursue legitimate domestic-policy goals (De Ville 2012; see also Howse and Nicolaïdis 2003; Rodrik 2007)?

This latter question is our starting point to understand the sudden increase in attention to EU trade policy in parliaments in Belgium at the national and regional levels. This development has recently caught the interest of other scholars as well. Rosén (2017) has discussed the disagreement during the Convention on the Future of Europe (2001–3) – leading to the ill-fated Constitutional Treaty that later evolved into the Lisbon Treaty – about the desirability of handing the EP co-decision competence in trade. She concluded that the EP succeeded during these negotiations in convincing the other convention members that this transfer of power was in line with the EU's constitutional principles and the Laeken Declaration's emphasis on legitimacy. Jančič (2017) has studied the involvement of national parliaments in the Transatlantic Trade and Investment Partnership (TTIP), focusing on the United Kingdom and France. His intent was to explain the differences in parliamentary influence over the executive in the negotiations through a comparison of the United Kingdom and France. He finds that "the key factors of parliamentary influence over the executive in EU external trade relations are the nature of the agreement, information access, and the level of fusion between the government and parliamentary majority" (2017, 216). Our aim is to explain why national parliaments have taken up their scrutiny function at a time when they seem to have lost this competence; they neglected this role in the past when they held the formal responsibility.

In the next section we descriptively map the evolution of parliamentary activity in Belgium over the past two decades. Subsequently we offer explanations for this evolution. They have been abductively generated (cf. Friedrichs and Kratochwil 2009). This means that our search for them has been guided by the literature discussed in this section and by our own previous research on Belgian involvement in EU trade policy, on recent EU trade agreements, and on politicization of the policy domain (e.g., Bollen 2018; De Ville and Siles-Brügge 2016; Gheyle 2019). During our empirical analysis of parliamentary debates and interviews we have been open to alternative interpretations.

The Belgian Regions and Communities in EU Trade Policy

Our focus on Belgian parliaments as a case study serves to highlight that the European Union is a multilevel polity (see Bursens and Högenauer 2017 for a discussion of the EU's multilevel parliamentary system), in which the sub-federal level is composed of not only national but also sub-federal (regional) executives and parliaments, which have legislative powers in several member states. Belgium is considered to be a "dual federal system" (Beyers and Bursens 2006), in which the national and the regional level hold exclusive legislative and executive powers. The sub-federal level, which is divided into regions and communities (a division that is unimportant for our chapter), holds exclusive competence for, inter alia, agriculture, education, cultural, and health policy. Through the *in foro interno, in foro externo* principle, they have the competence also to develop external policies, including through participation in EU decision making, for these areas. Their competences for issues that can be affected by international trade agreements means that they have a stake in EU trade policy. But they also hold formal competences for trade policy specifically. The making of trade policy in Belgium is discussed in the next section.

Trade Policymaking in Belgium

Since the late 1980s a series of constitutional reforms have altered the way in which foreign and trade policies are formulated in Belgium. First, the Sint-Michiels Agreement of 1993 granted the subnational governments the ability to sign international agreements in those matters where they hold exclusive competence. Subsequently, in 2001, export policy, along with federal funds and personnel, was fully regionalized.[4] Coordination on Belgian positions in EU trade policy has remained a competence of the Belgian federal level, however. A non-hierarchical system has been set in place, in which the federal level is primarily in charge of coordinating with the other levels to find Belgian positions over EU trade-policy issues. This means that Belgium cannot take any stance unless Wallonia, Brussels, and Flanders (i.e., the community or regional governments) are able to agree on a position. Without consensus Belgium would need to abstain. These transitions were not always very smooth and were often accompanied by inter-institutional struggles (Bollen et al. 2015; Coolsaet 2015).[5]

This devolution has led to the construction of regional trade administrations and export agencies, as well as the growth of an intensive process of coordination between the federal and sub-national levels, organized by the Ministry of Foreign Affairs. This coordinative webbing has also spread to the sub-national levels, in which various parties and departments now have to come to a regional position as well. Flanders has dealt with this by creating institutions that are similar to those at the federal level: with the support of his administration (Department International Flanders) the Flemish minister of foreign trade[6] organizes biweekly consultations in a working group on EU trade; here, Cabinet members and technical personnel from all interested departments discuss policy positions drafted by International Flanders. Wallonia's internal decision making is less institutionalized and relies on informal contacts between the administration of the minister of commerce, the regional and communal heads of government in charge of foreign affairs, and the joint international affairs' administration of the Francophone Community and the Walloon Region, Wallonia-Brussels International.[7]

Parliamentary Involvement

The Belgian parliaments are weak and subjugated players in the Belgian system, which is dominated by the parties in government. The real decisions are made in the sub-federal administrations and at the inter-ministerial level, coordinating across the Belgian strata. There is little reason to expect trade policy to be any different, especially since the "formal" role of the parliaments has always been rather limited in this regard. Apart from ratifying treaties (until the Lisbon Treaty), they could at most vote for non-binding resolutions.

Yet their lack of clear avenues for a strong formal role in the Belgian trade-policy system does not necessarily exclude parliamentary influence through other means. Non-binding resolutions, parliamentary questions and hearings, and reports and interviews in public media can all put pressure on government policies. Individual MPs can also build up expertise and a network of their own, for example within the cabinets or through influential stakeholders, that allow them to exert some control over the Belgian position taken in the European Council. The parliament can also serve as a "bull-horn" or intermediary for societal or interest-group demands.

In the next sections we analyse to what extent Belgian parliaments have been active on EU trade policy, and try to explain the evolution over time.

Trends in Belgian Parliamentary Scrutiny of Trade Issues since 2000

Using the search engines of the Walloon, Flemish, and federal parliaments,[8] we constructed a database of all trade-related questions (written and oral).[9] Although activity on trade, broadly defined, was present before 2009, especially in the sub-federal parliaments, it concentrated on issues such as export promotion, trade performance of regional companies, and weapons export. In figures 10.1 and 10.2, we exclude these topics and focus on activity related to trade politics *sensu stricto*.[10] As can be seen from figure 10.1, in all three parliaments the attention to strictly defined trade issues has generally been low but has increased spectacularly since 2013.

In the federal parliament the attention paid to trade issues was low overall, with a peak in interventions in 2005 (related to the liberalization of textiles and the World Trade Organization's Doha Development Round). The increase since 2013 is unprecedented. This dynamic is not wholly attributable to the increasing zeal of a small number of individual MPs; it is also driven by an increase in the number of MPs who are active in this theme. In the Flemish parliament, activity related to trade issues has been slowly increasing since 2009. As at the federal level, this growing activity is accompanied by an increasing number

10.1 Activity on Trade in the Belgian Federal, Walloon, and Flemish Parliaments

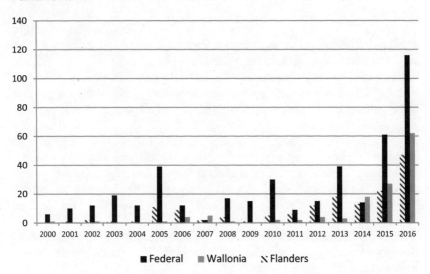

of active MPs. In the Walloon parliament, as in the other ones, there was a steady increase in attention, especially after 2013, which has been accompanied by a rise in the number of active MPs.

The bulk of the extra trade activity has been focused on EU free trade agreements (FTAs) and, within this category, on the European Union-United States TTIP and CETA in particular. Figure 10.2 is especially interesting for the sequence of the growing interest that it highlights. The increase started in 2013 with activity on TTIP in the federal parliament. In 2015, debate on TTIP was still by far the most important category of trade-related activities in the federal and Flemish parliaments, while in Wallonia activity on CETA had already overtaken interest in TTIP. In 2016, finally, CETA was the core trade occupation in all three parliaments. Also remarkable is that the attention to TTIP and CETA has also led to a very recent, significant increase in considerations of other FTAs in all three parliaments. Hence, we find that activity on EU trade policy in Belgian parliaments has increased since 2013, starting with attention to TTIP, spilling over into much commotion around CETA, and resulting, in the final year of our analysis, in a significant spillover to other trade agreements as well. In the next sections we look at what has been behind this surge in activity, based on a substantive analysis of parliamentary debates and interviews with MPs and stakeholders.

10.2 Activity on CETA, TTIP, and Other Free Trade Agreements in the Federal, Walloon, and Flemish Parliaments

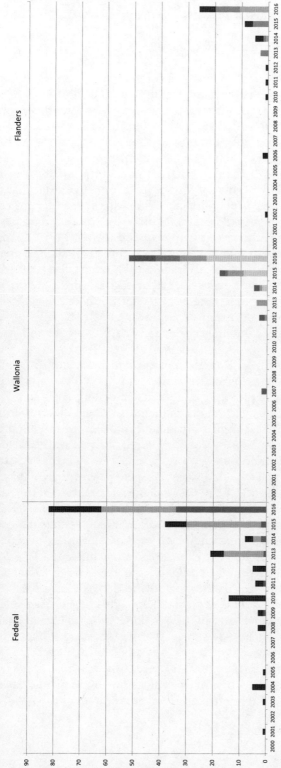

■ CETA   ■ TTIP   ■ TTIP & CETA*   ■ Other Free Trade Agreements

* Some questions explicitly targeted both Free Trade Agreements

Substance of the Parliamentary Trade Debates

Next to composing these general figures on the rough quantitative trends in parliamentary scrutiny, we also conducted a series of interviews with Flemish, Walloon, and federal MPs to substantiate our findings. In addition, we looked at the substance of parliamentary debates, hearings, and resolutions, while using GoPress to perform a cursory analysis of the press coverage of recent events.

Our interviewees confirmed that parliamentary attention to trade policy had generally been very low, at least until TTIP, and that trade had never been a divisive, partisan issue. This is true for all parliaments. In the Flemish parliament, for example, discussion had often been limited to the economic missions undertaken by Belgium and the regions. With the exception of arms trade, there was seldom any discussion or ideological debate on trade policy, which also reflected the lack of real, politically salient cleavages among the parties.[11] As a result, MPs devoted little time to trade policy, which only reinforced the low salience of this policy domain in the parliaments. The MPs we interviewed also admitted that they depended on the expertise and agenda-setting of outside players such as CSOs.

Our interviewees confirmed that parliamentary ratification, still a necessity before the Lisbon Treaty reforms, had always been a pro forma – or rubber-stamping – procedure. One interviewee could recall only one instance in which the parliament had defied the government by refusing to ratify a signed agreement, the European Union-Israel Association Agreement. The conflict here had to do with the Israeli-Palestinian conflict and little with trade policy as such. Even here, the parliament eventually yielded to government pressure and ratified the deal.[12] Generally, the MPs were aware of the constraints that the Belgian system imposed on parliamentary action. They did not believe that the parliamentary debates in themselves had much power to shape policy. By the time these dossiers ended up in the committee, negotiations were often near completion or even already concluded, and the parties in coalition would expect their MPs to vote in favour of a deal. Given the parliament's subservience to the governing coalition's policies and dynamics, any subsequent debate would mostly be for show. Especially for MPs from the governing parties, making use of informal channels to influence decision making at an earlier stage was more likely to bear fruit but rarely happened.[13]

Our interviewees did confirm, in line with the statistics presented, that parliamentary work on trade has picked up tremendously in recent years. Most of this activity has revolved around the controversial deals with the United States and Canada. In Flanders, for example, TTIP has received a rare amount of parliamentary attention: not only have the negotiations been discussed in multiple debates, but they have also been the subject of hearings with academics, stakeholders, and EU and US diplomats and politicians. Even MPs from the left-wing opposition were pleased (and a little surprised) with the amount of space allotted to these deals.[14] Moreover, the passive consensus has made way for ideologically charged divisions. Our respondents from the right echoed the *Economist*'s (2016) observation that old left-right cleavages had been cross-cut by an open-closed divide (already argued in Kriesi et al. 2008). Respondents of the left rejoiced that the doctrine of "there is no alternative" had now been challenged, even though the right-wing majority still tended to support any proposed trade deal and argued that the left was now aligning with right-wing populists.[15]

The same developments were present, *a fortiori*, in Wallonia. With the arrival of the new parliament in May 2014, there was an important shift in the modus operandi of the assembly regarding trade deals. Whereas, before, its committee on European affairs "had not spent resources on scrutinizing the pre-approval phase of the deals," it now took an interest in the ongoing TTIP negotiations, therefore "radically changing the parliament's practices by preoccupying itself, proactively, with a potential future treaty, rather than finding, at the time the agreement is enacted, that certain elements could have taken another form" (Comité d'avis chargé des questions Européennes 2015, 1–2; our translation). The parliament then organized a series of committee and plenary debates, as well as hearings with policymakers, stakeholders, and experts, and also greatly increased the volume of questions directed at the government.[16]

As in Flanders, these debates were ideologically charged, but, contrary to the centre-right majority's general satisfaction with the deals in the north, in Wallonia this led to a revolt against the rubber-stamping of FTAs. This has gone farthest with regard to CETA. On 26 May 2015 the centre-left Parti Socialiste (PS) proposed a resolution outlining a number of significant concerns about CETA, which was adopted, with the support of all parties except for the liberal Mouvement Réformateur, on 7 April 2016. The draft resolution's wording was strong, calling CETA a "Trojan horse" and opposing the deal as it stood, but became even sharper and more detailed in the final version – now openly asking that the government not give the federal level the power to sign the deal. On 14 October 2016 the Walloon parliament again confirmed its resistance – a message condoned by the Walloon government. This triggered an intra-Belgian as well as a European crisis because it meant that Belgium would not be able to sign the treaty. After several days of hard renegotiation by the Walloon government and the other Belgian governments, including facilitation by and pressure from European institutions – and, defying Belgian and EU constitutional practice, even involving direct negotiations between the Walloon government and the Canadian minister of international trade – the parliament did ultimately condone Belgium's signing of the deal on 28 October 2016; only Ecolo and the Parti du Travail de Belgique voted against, while recognizing the efforts made by the coalition in the two weeks of the CETA saga. Whether the parliament will eventually also *ratify* the agreement remains unsure, however, and the ratification is now (according to the intra-Belgian deal) contingent on a series of demands being met. Although it is unclear to what extent this move is indicative of parliamentary "emancipation" from the regional government (the government was critical of the agreement itself, and the resolutions were supported by the governing parties), this nonetheless represents a break from past passivity.

Finally, the politicization of TTIP has also fostered the parliaments' need for expertise and networks in these dossiers. The federal chamber of representatives, as well as all regions, has organized parliamentary hearings about CETA and TTIP and has invited EU trade commissioner Cecilia Malmström to come and explain the deals. The federal parliament has also tried to strengthen its links with the Committee on International Trade, which, as Belgian MPs acknowledge, still houses most trade-related expertise.[17]

Some, but certainly not all, MPs are pessimistic about the durability of this new interest in trade policy, an issue that we will pick up in the concluding section. Still, the break from the past is remarkable and, in light of the diminished formal power of the national parliaments since Lisbon, puzzling. In the next section we offer an analytical explanation for this finding.

Explaining the Shifts in Parliamentary Involvement

In line with the general framework of this edited volume, and in our explanations of the evolution of Belgian parliamentary involvement in EU trade policy, we focus on three factors: the evolution of EU trade policy; civil-society activity; and the federal institutional configuration. We argue that the spectacular increase in parliamentary involvement can be explained by changes in the scope of EU trade agreements and by the way civil society actors have used this to "activate" MPs. While the Belgian federal institutional configuration has not fundamentally changed in the period we studied (the sixth state reform of 2011–12 did not alter competencies or coordination mechanisms relevant to trade policy), characteristics of the Belgian federal system facilitated the parliamentary politicization of TTIP and CETA. Before discussing how the interaction between these three factors help to explain the increased involvement of Belgian parliaments in EU trade policy, we briefly summarize why their attention had been so low previously.

The Lack of Attention before the Lisbon Treaty

The first question we need to consider is why Belgian parliaments dedicated so little attention to EU trade policy before the Lisbon Treaty entered into force, that is, when they still had the power to ratify EU trade agreements. Part of the answer can be found in how Belgian parliaments are organized and relate to the government, as discussed. MPs have an overcrowded agenda and cannot afford to spend many resources on a technical and often low-key issue such as trade policy. The Belgian parliaments do not have the capacity to study these issues in much detail. This lack has been reinforced by government-parliament dynamics in foreign affairs in general. The Belgian constitution stipulates that (as is the case in most countries) foreign policy is the prerogative of the executive branch: the federal government negotiates and signs deals; Parliament ratifies them. No formal procedures (for example, specialized trade policy committees) assured that Parliament was regularly updated in detail about ongoing negotiations. This combination of powerlessness and information asymmetry arguably raised the bar for parliamentary involvement because the follow-up of trade deals was entirely up to the initiative of Parliament, which then would have to "sacrifice" time and resources allocated to the other themes over which it had more immediate control.[18]

Activity on trade issues was also low because public interest was limited, and parliaments are to a certain extent "reactive" institutions. If there is little interest in trade from local constituents, the press, civil society, or business, the incentive to focus on an issue will be small and will then largely depend on specific interests and resources of particular MPs. Of course, this is in some ways a vicious circle because lack of attention and expertise in turn lowers the potential for parliaments to pick up and politicize an issue.

The Shift in Recent Years

The more important question for our chapter is why the Belgian parliaments' passivity has disappeared to a considerable extent in recent years, paradoxically after their competences had been transferred to the EP after the Lisbon Treaty. We argue that this has to do with the interaction of the changed content of EU trade agreements; the increased activity of CSOs and the way they have framed these new-generation trade agreements; and the more idiosyncratic political situation in Belgium in the period of the TTIP and final phases of CETA negotiations, as made possible by the federal institutional configuration.

THE ALTERED SUBSTANCE OF EU TRADE AGREEMENTS

Part of the explanation relates to the nature and substance of the new generation of FTAs. TTIP and CETA are examples of the movement towards deep trade agreements and include provisions that seem to encroach directly on domestic policy space (De Ville 2016; Young 2007). This not only has resulted in renewed discussion about the legal status (exclusive or mixed) of these agreements, and hence about the competence of sub-national parliaments with regard to them, but also has aroused the attention of MPs. After all, activity on CETA preceded the decision by the European Commission to declare the agreement "mixed" in July 2016.

The first of the salient provisions inciting the attention of MPs is *investment protection*, which only became a supranational competence with the Lisbon Treaty, as discussed. Investment-protection provisions and the settlement procedures to adjudicate disputes (better known under the acronym *ISDS*, which stands for investor-state-dispute settlement), through which international investors can sue governments and demand compensation against public measures that offend their treaty-sanctioned rights, are not limited to decisions by the federal or EU level but extend to every government level. Therefore, every government level also has a reason to fear that its policies could become the target of a complaint by an investor that might result in sanctions as well as in a chilling effect in decision making to avoid the risk of being sanctioned. Secondly, TTIP was the first agreement of which the self-proclaimed central objective was regulatory cooperation, precisely to remove regulatory differences between the parties as well as to establish mechanisms to lessen the probability of parties adopting different regulations in the future (see De Ville and Siles-Brügge 2016). The latter should be achieved by adhering to good regulatory practices – procedural requirements that governments should follow when adopting regulations to ensure that they have given sufficient consideration to the trade and investment effects and opinions of stakeholders – and bilateral regulatory cooperation – mandatory consultations on regulations by representatives from both parties. What the critics of this new dimension of trade agreements fear is that these ostensibly innocent provisions will lead (analogous to the concerns about investment protection) to paralysis by analysis and to regulatory chill, in other words to less decision-making autonomy and to lower levels of protection than would have been decided by governments absent these provisions.

These deals might thus further limit parliaments' power to shape society, possibly leading to increased awareness of, and in some cases opposition to, the deals. In the Belgian case there is some evidence that parliamentary attention was triggered by the substance of the agreements. Parliamentary debates have focused primarily on ISDS and regulatory cooperation, as well as on the fear of liberalization of public services. Much less attention has been dedicated to the more traditional elements of the negotiations such as tariffs. The new, intrusive nature of the treaties was also mentioned in some of our interviews as reasons for the increased activity. However, this argument about the content of the latest generation of trade agreements does not explain the different degree of attention that has been given to TTIP and to CETA, only after the conclusion of the negotiations, on the one hand, and to the European Union-Japan and other deep and comprehensive EU trade negotiations on the other, while their substance is very comparable. Our empirical analysis showed that it would be wrong to identify a direct causal link between the changed substance of EU trade agreements and increased parliamentary activity.

The missing link, as we hope to show in the following section, is the wide-scale mobilization against TTIP, and subsequently CETA, by a number of CSOs.

MOBILIZATION BY CIVIL-SOCIETY ORGANIZATIONS
AND PUBLIC SALIENCE

The TTIP and, to a lesser extent, CETA have led to an unprecedented politicization of the EU's trade agenda. Again, this is linked to the substance of the treaties, which raised concerns about the impact on domestic policies and policy space. These worries were probably also exacerbated by the fact that TTIP, which received the brunt of the contestation, was being negotiated with the United States. Not only did it arouse some latent anti-Americanism in parts of the public in some member states like Germany and Austria, but also the risk of deregulation or regulatory chill (for example, related to ISDS cases or the possible lowering of food standards) was far more likely with such a powerful political and economic counterpart.[19] However, it seems unlikely that these elements would have sufficed to bring about the measure of opposition we have witnessed in recent years, without the active, successful, and enduring mobilization and organization by a wide coalition of CSOs and their networks (Gheyle 2019).[20] Civil society has been able to foster a self-feeding cycle of growing press coverage, public awareness, and mobilization, which eventually has led to political, including parliamentary, attention and contestation.

In Belgium, TTIP has led to the emergence of new trade policy coalitions, similar to what happened in other countries such as Germany and Austria (see Broschek, Bußjäger, and Schramek in this volume). Before TTIP there was a small but committed group of Belgian CSO and trade union representatives who regularly worked and campaigned on trade policy, and built up considerable expertise. Their work was mostly related to development and global justice issues. For example, they mobilized against the BLEU (Belgian-Luxembourg Economic Union)-Colombia Investment Treaty because of labour issues in Colombia, and campaigned against the economic partnership agreements because of concerns about the development impact of these deals. Outside of this core group (which includes Centre national de coopération au développement, Oxfam, and Wereldsolidariteit), trade policy was a secondary issue for many other organizations.[21] TTIP, however, has drawn many new organizations to trade politics, given the possible scope of the agreement. A core group of trade unions, north-south organizations, and several environmental groups has sided with less traditional groups, such as consumer, health insurance, and climate organizations, in the self-named 4 May (2015) Coalition (Verenigde Verenigingen 2015). This nationwide coalition has been the main civil-society lobbying organization within Belgium on TTIP and CETA and is coordinated mainly by the Centre national de coopération au développement. In addition, a more broad-based "Stop TTIP" coalition, with a very large membership, was established and acts more as the mobilization pillar of the 4 May Coalition, planning actions or demonstrations, writing letters to ministers, and producing press releases (Verenigde Verenigingen 2015).[22]

These organizations were successful in their attempts to mobilize their membership and parts of the public and also in generating parliamentary scrutiny.[23] The important role of civil society clearly emerges, for example, when parliamentary texts and discussions are analysed. In Wallonia's debates and resolutions, at various times opponents to the deals hailed the work of the CSOs in raising awareness, or mentioned that the democratic stakes had greatly increased now that such a substantial part of civil society and the general public was involved. For example, in the 2015 CETA Resolution the authors state that "*récemment, les négociations entourant [en général TTIP, CETA, et FTAs] ont mobilisé largement la société civile belge et européenne, mais également les parlements européens et nationaux*" (recently, the negotiations surrounding TTIP,

CETA, and FTAs in general have largely mobilized Belgian and European civil society, as well as the European and national parliaments). Civil society's role was also confirmed throughout our interviews.[24]

In the book written by Walloon minister-president Paul Magnette about the whole CETA episode, the first chapter is revealingly entitled "When Civil Society Awakens" (2017). There have been frequent contacts between civil society and especially the parties of the left (greens, socialists, and to a lesser extent Christian democrats), and some of the CSOs claim that a substantial amount of parliamentary questions have been fed by them.[25] Some MPs acknowledged that they did not actively scrutinize the treaties until CSOs made vigorous attempts to raise awareness and foster opposition. At least initially the MPs lacked not only awareness but also expertise, which the CSOs could provide.[26] This claim is bolstered by the fact that the PS, the Centre démocrate humaniste, and Ecolo, which, from late 2014 on, would start opposing these deals fiercely from within the parliaments, had all been part of the Walloon government when CETA was mandated and concluded – and the Socialistische Partij Anders in Flanders and the PS, the Centre démocrate humaniste, and the Socialistische Partij Anders were represented at the federal level.

Party Politics in the Belgian Federal System

There are also some institutional and party politics dynamics at play in the Belgian federal system that help explain the spectacular increase in parliamentary attention on EU trade agreements.[27] These have to do with the presence of asymmetrical coalitions in Belgium after the elections of May 2014. Although elections for the Belgian federal and regional parliaments were held simultaneously, different majorities were formed in the federal and Flemish governments (centre right) on the one hand and in the Walloon regional government (centre left) on the other. In combination with the de facto veto power that regional governments have over Belgium's position on EU trade policy, and the alleged malfunctioning of intra-federal consultation committees (cf. Magnette 2017), the differences provided fertile ground for the politicization of TTIP and CETA in the French-speaking parts of Belgium in particular.

Notably, the fact that the PS was part of the Walloon but not the federal government is seen by many as an important factor in this party's activism on the trade front. Magnette's refusal to sign CETA was perceived as a way both to sabotage the federal government (in which the liberal Mouvement réformateur is the only Walloon party) and to strengthen its profile vis-à-vis the communist Workers' Party, which had been surging in the polls. Had the PS been present in the federal government, the party's stance might have been less confrontational, and this may have also dampened the enthusiasm of its MPs. This counterfactual conditional statement is of course hard to assess. But had the PS been in the federal government, the kind of tightrope politics witnessed in October 2016 would have been less likely. The conflict would probably have been resolved within the coalition, unless the PS was willing to threaten the Cabinet's survival over trade. However, it seems plausible that the difference would have been one of degrees and not of kind. The parliaments could not have turned a blind eye to the strong and persistent campaigning by a broad set of societal groups, and awareness, expertise, and contestation would have increased anyway; however, the immediate political fallout may have been different. This factor echoes findings in the literature that a divided government (Belgium in this period, with different majorities at the federal and sub-federal levels, could be considered a divided federal government) leads to a stronger parliamentary grip over an executive's trade policy (Lohmann and O'Halloran 1994; Maurer 2005, quoted in Jančič 2017).

Conclusion

In recent years we have seen a somewhat paradoxical evolution in EU trade politics. Although the Lisbon Treaty was meant to facilitate the adoption of trade agreements by clarifying the exclusive supranational competence of the EU through updating the scope to the new trade agenda, parliaments below the supranational level have become more involved in trade policy than ever before.

We have investigated the shift in involvement across the Belgian parliaments. In the fifteen years leading up to 2013 the federal, Flemish, and Walloon parliaments paid little attention to EU trade policy. The focus changed thereafter, especially in Wallonia but also in the other assemblies. Several interacting factors fuelled the increase in parliamentary involvement. First, TTIP and CETA contain provisions, most importantly on investment protection and regulatory cooperation, that are perceived to go qualitatively beyond older trade agreements by potentially interfering with sub-national policy choices. Second, TTIP has generated unseen civil-society mobilization that was difficult for MPs (especially those on the left and in the opposition) to ignore. Finally, the asymmetry between the Walloon and federal governing coalitions has favoured a more activist opposition by Wallonia, and the Belgian federal institutional set-up has allowed them to pursue an obstructionist approach.

An important remaining question, which also divided our respondents, is how durable the politicization of trade policy and the consequent attention and involvement of sub-national MPs will eventually be. With the TTIP negotiations being halted (at the time of writing, the European Commission and the Donald Trump administration are considering negotiations on a more limited number of issues, excluding ISDS and horizontal regulatory cooperation), civil-society activism may weaken. In response, attention to EU trade policy in sub-national parliaments might fade out as well. As the European Commission has decided, after a ruling by the Court of Justice of the European Union (Opinion 2/15), to take investment protection out of trade agreements, it might become more difficult for CSOs to mobilize against such deals. However, significant energy and resources have been invested in building expertise and networks by CSOs as well as by sub-national MPs. Such sunk costs might lead them to continue their involvement in EU trade politics, especially if current efforts turn out to be successful in influencing both the outcome of negotiations and the elections.

The recent CETA episode in Belgium has already strengthened the activity of the Walloon parliament. It seems determined to scrutinize further the other trade deals currently being negotiated, most significantly the Trade in Services Agreement. Furthermore, the Namur Declaration, boosted by Walloon minister-president Paul Magnette and signed by the likes of Thomas Piketty and Dani Rodrik, also shows that the opposition is trying to seize the momentum to reform EU trade policy generally (Magnette 2016). In this paper we have described and offered explanations on how we have gone from *nada* to Namur in terms of national parliamentary activity on EU trade policy. What will follow from Namur (and its declaration on trade) is an open question. Paul Magnette seems to believe that the CETA saga could lead to substantial change in EU trade policy: the final chapter of his book is titled "Towards a Different Globalization."

To come back to the perennial discussion about EU trade politics and efficiency and legitimacy: what is the likely effect on this trade-off of the increased sub-federal parliamentary involvement? Against the negative reception of what happened in Belgian parliaments regarding CETA in October 2016, we argue for a positive reading. The saga has generated a welcome debate about a policy domain that affects several competences of parliament at the national and regional levels. Rather than necessarily jeopardizing EU trade policy, the involvement of MPs (and those from other member states) might be enhanced during the negotiations by collaboration between the European Parliament and the national parliaments, as well as by outreach by the European

274   Yelter Bollen, Ferdi De Ville, and Niels Gheyle

Commission. Steps in that direction have already been taken by the Belgian parliaments, the European Parliament, and the European Commission and could be reinforced.

NOTES

1 A third reform of the Lisbon Treaty, bringing trade policy under the foreign-policy umbrella of the treaty (without, however, making the European External Action Service responsible for the policy domain), is of less importance for this paper.
2 The European Parliament was given co-decision powers in trade-policy legislation. With respect to free trade agreements, the Lisbon Treaty stipulates that the EP has to be kept continuously informed by the European Commission about the state and progress of trade negotiations (in contrast to the European Council, it does not have to give the commission the authority to open negotiations) and that EP's consent (by a simple majority of its members) is required for an agreement to enter into force.
3 An exception that was specifically introduced to respond to the dislocation effects of EU trade liberalization is the European Globalisation Adjustment Fund, but this is generally considered to be underfunded and underutilized (cf. Falkner 2016).
4 For example, the Belgian Service for International Trade was transformed into the inter-federal Agency for Foreign Trade and was to operate at the service of the regional export agencies that had been created in the 1990s.
5 Economic diplomacy and export promotion have been the most important bones of contention. Flanders in particular has been suspicious of the federal level clawing back some of its lost prerogatives (Coolsaet 2015). Moreover, there have been persistent concerns that the fragmentation of international trade policy is hampering the coherence and the pursuit of Belgian and sub-national trade interests. For example, minister of development Alexander De Croo recently launched a proposal to reverse some of this devolution in a variety of policy areas, including trade and development.
6 This has almost always been the Flemish head of government, or minister-president.
7 Interviews with Wallonie-Bruxelles International, 23 June 2016; and Departement Internationaal Vlaanderen, 26 April 2016.
8 We decided to focus on the three largest parliaments in Belgium and to exclude the Brussels and German-speaking parliaments. In very general terms, it can be said that they have taken positions that are close to the one of the Walloon parliament.

9 Long lists of keywords were used to search for questions or resolutions that dealt with trade policy. The list is too long to include here but is available from the authors. The number of interventions is not strictly comparable because of differences in the size of the parliaments and the way in which the search engines function, but the differences should be marginal.

10 Activity related to trade politics includes all questions related to anti-dumping, the World Trade Organization, FTAs, market-access issues, trade ethics (e.g., fair trade), and the trade-development nexus. It excludes questions related strictly to investment, arms trade, and economic diplomacy (export promotion, trade missions, and general questions about the commercial performance or trade-promoting institutions of Belgium and the regions).

11 Interviews with Flemish MP (Nieuw-Vlaamse Alliantie), 16 November 2016; Federal MP (Socialistische Partij Anders), 14 July 2016; and Flemish MP (Open Vlaamse Liberalen en Democraten), 25 November 2016.

12 Interview with federal MP (Socialistische Partij Anders), 14 July 2016.

13 Interviews with Flemish MP (Nieuw-Vlaamse Alliantie), 16 November 2016; and federal MP (Socialistische Partij Anders), 14 July 2016.

14 Interview with Flemish MP (Groen Party), 10 November 2016.

15 Interviews with Flemish MP (Groen Party), 10 November 2016; federal MP (Mouvement Réformateur), 27 October 2016; Flemish MP (Nieuw-Vlaamse Alliantie), 16 November 2016; and Flemish MP (Open Vlaamse Liberalen en Democraten), 25 November 2016.

16 Interview with Walloon MP (Ecolo), 12 December 2016.

17 Interview with federal MP (Socialistische Partij Anders), 14 July 2016.

18 Interviews with federal MP (Socialistische Partij Anders), 14 July 2016; federal MP (Groen Party), 16 September 2016; and Flemish MP (Open Vlaamse Liberalen en Democraten), 25 November 2016.

19 In earlier agreements there was no power asymmetry to the disadvantage of the EU, given that the EU mainly conducted trade negotiations with smaller developing, and/or ex-colonial countries. With the United States, the EU was for the first time meeting a partner of at least equal power, heightening the fear that EU organizations and societies might be harmed.

20 Of course, the substantive and the mobilization explanations are related. The CSOs have captured the attention of national parliaments to some extent by arguing that TTIP and CETA threaten the policymaking autonomy of national governments. And these elements of the deal were in turn partially responsible for the mobilization of civil society.

21 Interviews with Christelijke Mutualiteit (CM), 21 April 2016; TestAankoop, 19 April 2016; 11.11.11, 21 March 2016; Algemeen Belgisch Vakverbond / Fédération Générale du Travail de Belgique, 23 May 2016; and Algemeen

Christelijk Vakverbond/Confédération des syndicats chrétiens,
12 May 2016.

22 The "Stop TTIP" coalition is also coordinated by the Centre national de
coopération au développement, which shows that the Belgian civil society
is still a small, but well-connected group of organizations that are able to
mobilize their partner organizations and, subsequently, their members.
The membership of this alliance is evidence of the non-traditional
opposition to trade policy. Here too the question of the durability of the
alliance is prominent. For some, the actions and cooperation in the last
two years were a building block for more to come, while others were more
pessimistic about sustaining the attention of all these organizations for
other trade deals.

23 Interview with Centre national de coopération au développement, 22
February 2017.

24 Interviews with Centre national de coopération au développement,
22 February 2017; Union Wallonne des Entreprises, 24 June 2016;
TestAankoop, 19 April 2016; Christelijke Mutualiteit (CM), 21 April
2016; Algemeen Christelijk Vakverbond / Confédération des syndicats
chrétiens, 12 May 2016; and Verbond van Belgische Ondernemingen, 13
April 2016.

25 Interview with Centre national de coopération au développement, 22
February 2017.

26 Interviews with Flemish MP (Groen Party), 10 November 2016; Walloon
MP (Ecolo), 12 December 2016; and federal MP (Socialistische Partij
Anders), 14 July 2016.

27 One idiosyncratic reason that the debates have received this kind
of attention even in the Flemish parliament has to do with an intra-
parliamentary development: the rejuvenation of the commission for EU
affairs under chairman Rik Daems, and his willingness to make room for
in-depth debates on foreign economic policy. This allowed committee
members to build the requisite expertise, which in turn stimulated
discussions. As we saw before, this was to some extent also true of the
Walloon committee, which decided in 2014 to be more vigilant about
trade negotiations in particular (interview with Walloon MP (Ecolo), 12
December 2016).

REFERENCES

Beyers, Jan, and Peter Bursens. 2006. "The European Rescue of the Federal
State: How Europeanisation Shapes the Belgian State." *West European
Politics* 29 (5): 1057–78.

Billiet, Stijn. 2006. "From GATT to the WTO: The Internal Struggle for External Competences in the EU." *Journal of Common Market Studies* 44 (5): 899–919.

Bollen, Yelter. 2018. "The Domestic Politics of EU Trade Policy: The Political-Economy of CETA and Anti-dumping in Belgium and the Netherlands." PhD diss., Ghent University.

Bollen, Yelter, Marjolein Derous, Ferdi De Ville, Niels Gheyle, Jan Orbie, and Lore Van den Putte. 2015. "Belgium's Role in EU Trade Policy." *Studia Diplomatica* 68 (2): 73–90.

Bossuyt, Fabienne. 2012. "De impact van multilevel governance op de democratische input in het EU-handelsbeleid onder het Verdrag van Lissabon." *Res Publica* 54 (1): 63–84.

Bursens, Peter, and Anna-Lena Högenauer. 2017. "Regional Parliaments in the EU Multilevel Parliamentary System." *Journal of Legislative Studies* 23 (2): 127–43.

Comité d'avis chargé des questions Européennes. 2015. *Projet de Partenariat Transatlantique de Commerce et d'investissement entre l'Union Européenne et les États-Unis (TTIP)*. Brussels: Sénat de Belgique.

Coolsaet, Rik. 2015. *Belgie en zijn buitenlandse politiek: 1830–2015*. Leuven, Belgium: Van Halewyck.

De Ville, Ferdi. 2012. "Subsidiarity and EU Trade Policy: Overview of the (Complex) Discussion, Treaty of Lisbon, and Implications for Flanders." In *Subsidiarity and Multi-level Governance*, edited by J. Loisen and F. De Ville, 125–36. Brussels: Koninklijke Vlaamse Academie van België voor Wetenschappen en Kunsten.

– 2016. "Regulatory Cooperation in TTIP: A Risk for Democratic Policy Making?" Foundation for European Progressive Studies, policy brief. February.

De Ville, Ferdi, and Gabriel Siles-Brügge 2016. *TTIP: The Truth about the Transatlantic Trade and Investment Partnership*. Cambridge, MA: Polity Press.

Devuyst, Youri. 2013. "European Union Law and Practice in the Negotiation and Conclusion of International Trade Agreements." *Journal of International Business & Law* 12 (2): 259–316.

The Economist. 2016. The New Political Divide. 30 July 2016. https://www.economist.com.

Falkner, Gerda. 2016. "The European Union's Social Dimension." In *European Union Politics*. 5th ed., edited by M. Cini and N. Pérez-Solórzano Borragán, 268–80. Oxford: Oxford University Press.

Friedrichs, Jörg, and Friedrich Kratochwil. 2009. "On Acting and Knowing: How Pragmatism Can Advance International Relations Research and Methodology." *International Organization* 63 (4): 701–31.

Gheyle, Niels. 2019. "Trade Policy with the Lights On: The Origins, Dynamics, and Consequences of the Politicization of TTIP." PhD diss., Ghent University.

Howse, Robert, and Kalypso Nicolaïdis. 2003. "Enhancing WTO Legitimacy: Constitutionalization or Global Subsidiarity?" *Governance* 16 (1): 73–94.

Jančič, Davor. 2017. "TTIP and Legislative-Executive Relations in EU Trade Policy." *West European Politics* 40 (1): 202–21.

Krajewski, Markus. 2012. "The Reform of the Common Commercial Policy." In *EU Law after Lisbon*, edited by A. Biondi, P. Eeckhout, and S. Ripley, 292–311. Oxford: Oxford University Press.

Kriesi, Hanspeter, Edgar Grande, Romain Lachat, Martin Dolezal, Simon Bornschier, and Timotheos Frey. 2008. *West European Politics in the Age of Globalization*. Cambridge: Cambridge University Press.

Lohmann, Susanne, and Sharyn O'Halloran. 1994. "Divided Government and U.S. Trade Policy: Theory and Evidence." *International Organization* 48 (4): 595–632.

Magnette, Paul. 2016. *Namur Déclaration*. 5 December 2016. Namur. Accessed 6 November 2019. http://declarationdenamur.eu.

– 2017. *CETA: Quand l'Europe déraille*. Waterloo, Belgium: Éditions Luc Pire.

Meunier, Sophie. 2005. *Trading Voices: The European Union in International Commercial Negotiations*. Princeton, NJ: Princeton University Press.

Rodrik, Dani. 2007. *How to Save Globalization from Its Cheerleaders*. Cambridge, MA: Harvard University Press.

Rosén, Guri. 2017. "The Impact of Norms on Political Decision-Making: How to Account for the European Parliament's Empowerment in EU External Trade Policy." *Journal of European Public Policy* 24 (10): 1450–70.

Verenigde Verenigingen. 2015. Trans-Atlantische handelsakkoorden: Het Belgische middenveld slaat de handen in mekaar tegen deze ondemocratische dereguleringsakkoorden. Accessed 6 November 2019. https://www.epsu.org.

Woolcock, Stephen. 2010. "The Treaty of Lisbon and the European Union as an Actor in International Trade." ECIPE Working Paper, no. 01/2010. Brussels: ECIPE.

– 2013. *European Union Economic Diplomacy: The Role of the EU in External Economic Relations*. Farnham, UK: Ashgate Publishing.

Young, Alasdair. 2007. "Trade Politics Ain't What It Used to Be: The European Union in the Doha Round." *Journal of Common Market Studies* 45 (4): 789–811.

Young, Alasdair, Peter Holmes, and Jim Rollo. 2000. "The European Trade Agenda after Seattle." SEI Working Paper, no. 37. Falmer, UK: University of Sussex. Accessed 6 November 2019. https://www.sussex.ac.uk.

SECTION THREE

The European Union – A Distinct Federation

11 Multilevel Trade Governance in Europe in the Aftermath of the Lisbon Treaty

MARIA GARCIA

The European Union (EU) represents a unique type of organization. Constituted by sovereign and independent states, it nonetheless possesses some of the attributes normally associated with states: legislature, executive, judiciary, territory, and authority over numerous policy areas. Lisbeth Hooghe and Gary Marks (2001) characterized European integration as a polity-creating process in which authority and policy-making influence are shared across multiple levels of governance – subnational, national, and supranational.[1] Trade policy in the EU has been characterized by the interaction of two main levels of governance, the supranational (represented by the European Commission as the EU's trade negotiator) and the national (represented by the member states acting collectively in the European Council to empower the commission). In this domain the EU level could be seen as akin to the federal government in a federal state, and the member states to the sub-federal states or provinces. This chapter assumes this equivalence; however, it retains the terminology pertinent to the EU, referring to the EU level and member states in order to avoid confusion.

Sub-national levels of governance are not explicitly mentioned in the EU treaties with respect to trade and traditionally have had an indirect impact via control of national governments. Their degree of involvement in shaping EU trade policy by means of national governments depends on the particular institutional characteristics in each member state, as several chapters in this volume show. In October 2016, when the regional parliaments of Brussels and Wallonia in Belgium initially refused to grant consent to their federal government to sign the European Union-Canada Comprehensive Economic and Trade Agreement (CETA), the significance of sub-national levels of governance in EU trade policy came into sharp focus. As this chapter argues in the third section, the shift was largely due to both a substantive change in international trade negotiations with the inclusion of a "new trade agenda" (Young and Peterson 2006), including regulatory matters, and, crucially, activism against a separate agreement, the Transatlantic Trade and Investment Partnership (TTIP). Various chapters in this volume (Bollen, De Ville, and Gheyle; Broschek, Bußjäger, and Schramek) highlight the complex societal and party political dynamics and opportunity structures in federal systems that explain the unprecedented level of the sub-national authorities' interest and activism on TTIP in Belgium, Germany, and Austria. Importantly, what these cases brought to the fore was the end of a permissive consensus around EU trade policy, its problematization, and its politicization,[2] and a new degree of salience of trade matters in media and public debates.

Ironically, within the EU context, institutional innovations introduced in the Treaty of Lisbon of 2008 should have facilitated the enactment of EU trade policy and simplified the ratification and implementation of EU trade agreements. Instead, institutional changes set in motion complex dynamics and power plays between different levels of governance (vertically between the EU level, member states, and even sub-federal levels and horizontally between different EU institutions), as they interpreted the new rules of the Lisbon treaty in different ways, each seeking to maximize their own power in trade policy vis-à-vis the others (see Bollen, De Ville, and Gheyle in this volume). James Mahoney and Kathleen Thelen (2010, 11) claim that even once institutional rules have been codified, as they were in the Lisbon treaty, their "guiding expectations often remain ambiguous and always are subject to interpretation, debate, and contestation." For them, this ambiguity is a lasting feature, as "actors with divergent interests will contest the openings this ambiguity provides because matters of interpretation and implementation can have profound consequences for resource allocations (actors' power capabilities) and substantive outcomes." This is especially significant as "the original designers [of the treaty] may be less capable of sustaining control over long-term paths of institutional development" (Pierson 2004, 163), as became apparent with the conflict between the member states and the European Commission regarding EU-level competencies over investment. The intersection of these unintended consequences of the institutional ambiguities of the Lisbon treaty, the nature of new trade agreements that include investor protections, and the potential to impinge on domestic regulation and changing domestic political settings (political and social climate) have resulted in this novel level of contestation of EU trade policy. This chapter traces the institutional dynamics unleashed in the aftermath of the Lisbon treaty, and the power plays across different levels of governance. It does this within the empirical context of the ratification processes of EU trade agreements following the treaty, where member states and sub-federal levels of governance have sought to reshape EU trade policy in response to social pressures and political preferences within their respective jurisdictions.

The second section describes the multilevel structure of EU trade policymaking, paying attention to the competencies and distribution of tasks and powers across actors and territorial jurisdictions, and the changes introduced by the Treaty of Lisbon. The third section undertakes a qualitative comparison of the international-trade-agreement-ratification processes that have taken place to date since the entry into force of the treaty, tracing the particular institutional dynamics in each ratification process. The fourth section draws conclusions from the comparison and establishes that the major problems in ratifications have stemmed from two key sources: (1) the ambiguities in the institutional architecture that enable member states to exert boundary control over the transfer of competences to the EU level in the Lisbon treaty; and (2) the social dimension in which particular interest groups and political parties have strategically used national ratification rules to express their objections to the liberalizing ethos enshrined in EU trade policy.

Multilevel Institutional Architecture of the European Union's Trade Policy

The Common Commercial Policy or trade policy of the original European Community was one of the policy areas with greater delegation of authority to the supranational level, falling under the "community-method" of governance (Wallace, Pollack, and Young 2015). This method is "an inter-institutional process of decision-making premised on the role of the European Commission as the executive instigator of legislative and budgetary initiatives together with the relative roles of the European Parliament and Council as legislative and budgetary authorities tasked with reaching agreement on proposals" (Armstrong 2011, 186). The European Court of Justice (ECJ) has a critical role as the interpreter of the treaties and the arbiter of the system. Its judgments ensure that the system and rules are legally implemented. The interplay between the political and judicial institutions "reinforces a conception of EU governance as dominated by hierarchy as a mode, and by law as an instrument, of governance" (Armstrong 2011, 187).

Article 207 of the Treaty on the Functioning of the European Union (TFEU, or the Treaty of Lisbon of 2008) lays out procedures for the operationalization of trade policy and defines the tasks and competences of the various EU-level institutions: The "European Parliament and the Council, acting by means of regulations in accordance with the ordinary legislative procedure, shall adopt the measures defining the framework for implementing the common commercial policy" on the basis of proposals emanating from the European Commission. Member states have delegated competences over trade matters to the EU level but remain involved collectively through their participation in the European Council, setting guidelines for the commission and legislating on its proposals.

Initially, trade policy was mainly concerned with the setting of tariffs and trade-defence measures, and the European Commission was granted so-called exclusive competencies over these, while matters relating to services remained "mixed" competencies, meaning that the commission could negotiate on these externally but required explicit permission and guidelines from the European Council, and the ratification of any agreement covering mixed competencies needed additional ratification in each member state. Over time, the ambit of exclusive competencies in trade has gradually increased. This followed a functionalist logic arising from changes in the nature of trade negotiations, as international trade negotiations shifted from goods to services, aspects of intellectual property, and non-tariff barriers to trade during the GATT Uruguay Round, which created the World Trade Organization (WTO) in 1995. The European Commission, as the EU's trade negotiator, had to strike deals on a broader set of issues, including some over which it lacked exclusive competence, as such matters remained national prerogatives. As a result, subsequent revisions of the EU treaties culminating in the Treaty of Lisbon increased the trade competences of the EU level to facilitate its effectiveness on the global stage and consolidate a growing body of ECJ jurisprudence reaffirming competence of the EU to enter into international trade agreements (see Gammage 2018; Leczykiewicz 2005).

The treaties also established a specific procedure and clear roles for the negotiation of trade agreements with third parties. Firstly, the European Commission makes recommendations to the council of the European Union, which authorizes it to open the negotiations, by approving a mandate containing broad instructions for the negotiations. During the negotiation stage a trade committee appointed by the council, comprising representatives of the member states, assists the commission, ensuring a high degree of intergovernmental cooperation. Article 207 also mandates that the commission report to the European Parliament's International Trade Committee on the progress of the negotiations.

The European Council can conclude agreements on the basis of a qualified majority vote,[3] but if the agreement includes provisions relating to the following areas, unanimity is required:

- internal EU "trade in services and the commercial aspects of intellectual property, as well as foreign direct investment;
- "trade in cultural and audio-visual services, where these agreements risk prejudicing the EU's cultural and linguistic diversity;
- "trade in social, education, and health services, where these agreements risk seriously disturbing the national organization of such services and prejudicing the responsibility of Member States to deliver them" (TFEU 2008, article 207).

The procedure described in the treaties established three distinct stages in the negotiation of trade agreements: the mandate, the negotiation and conclusion, and the final ratification.

The delegation of powers to the European Commission to negotiate trade agreements mirrors practices at the national level, where trade policy is normally undertaken by the executive branch of the state. Delegating negotiating authority to an executive body or, in the EU's case, a supranational entity (the European Commission) presents a number of advantages. It creates a clear interlocutor for negotiations. Granting specific authorization and guidelines to the negotiators (through the council's mandate) enhances the partner's trust in the negotiations and the fact that outcomes will be respected by EU member states. Moreover, the delegation of trade powers to the commission has been described as a design that purposefully isolates the executive from societal pressures (Meunier 2000),[4] preventing capture by interest groups or member states. Thereby, it grants the commission leeway to fulfil its mandate in trade, which is explicitly outlined in article 206 of the TFEU: "The Union shall contribute, in the common interest, to the harmonious development of world trade, the progressive abolition of restrictions on international trade and on foreign direct investment, and the lowering of customs and other barriers."

Given this delegation of power, relations between the council and the commission in trade policy have often been analysed through the prism of a principal-agent framework (Damro 2007; Elsig 2007; Kerremans 2004; Meunier and Nicolaïdis 1999; Reichert and Jungblut 2007). While delegation may help to solve problems of collective action and enhance the EU's single voice, it gives rise to a set of principal-agent problems that arise because the principal (the

European Council) cannot guarantee that the agent (the European Commission) will perform exactly as the principal wishes (Reichert and Jungblut 2007, 397). Principals, therefore, develop tools to ensure that they can control the agent. The definition of a mandate prior to delegating authority is a key tool because the mandate will constrain the parameters of what the commission can and cannot negotiate with a third party.

Monitoring and reporting requirements are important tools for principals to exert control over agents during the policy process (Dür and Elsig 2011, 329). Through the trade committee, made up of national trade experts and/or members of the national permanent representations to the European Union, the European Council exercises control over its agent. The constant interaction between the European Commission and the council's trade committee exemplifies the negotiated nature of the multilevel polity system in the EU, and the institutionalization of a close partnership between the EU and the levels of governance of the member states (European Council representatives). Changes introduced in the Treaty of Lisbon have resulted in the European Parliament (EP), especially its International Trade Committee, also exercising a monitoring role over the commission throughout negotiations.

Principals can also exercise power and control over their agent at the end of the policy cycle via sanctioning, non-acceptance of negotiated agreements, or termination of mandates (Dür and Elsig 2011, 329). In the case of EU trade agreements, the council must vote in favour of the text negotiated to conclude negotiations. Constant communication and consultation with the council (especially through the trade committee) and with the EP throughout the earlier phases reinforce the strong formal intergovernmental relationships (i.e., between the EU and the member states) and the relationships among member states in the council that characterize the EU system. Close cooperation throughout the process vertically, between EU-level institutions and member-state representation (in the council), and also horizontally among the member states in the council, attests to the high degree of institutionalization of intergovernmental relations in the EU case. It is also designed to prevent a situation in which an agreement negotiated by the European Commission is rejected at the ratification stage by the European Council and the EP as they exercise their legislative functions, particularly because within the EU architecture for international trade agreements, the council (acting as second chamber in its legislative function) possesses strong treaty-guaranteed powers, as detailed previously.

Ratification at the EU level involves a vote in favour in both the European Council and the EP. At this point an agreement can come into effect provisionally, with the exclusion of any provisions covering mixed competences. If an agreement includes mixed competencies, and most modern agreements do,[5] final ratification will require ratification by each member state in its parliament in accordance with its domestic processes for the adoption of international agreements. Typically, national parliaments vote to ratify the agreement, allowing the implementation of all areas of the agreement. In Belgium a positive vote in all regional parliaments is also required to authorize the executive to ratify a treaty.[6] In other member states, regions are involved through their representation in upper chambers. Figure 11.1 summarizes the ratification processes in each member state.

Parliamentary approval is sufficient for ratification in all member states, although some additionally allow for a referendum; France and the Netherlands specifically permit this. In other states there is no specific mention of the possibility of a referendum nor is such a procedure explicitly excluded, except in Belgium and Germany. The possibility in some states (Croatia, Lithuania, Hungary, and the Netherlands) for citizens to instigate a referendum opens the ratification process to horizontal levels of governance outside of the vertically embedded governance hierarchy of sub-federal-national-EU level.

The ratification process described is time consuming and adds to already lengthy trade negotiations. It also shows how, increasingly, the European Commission negotiates on behalf of multiple principals, all of whom have different involvement in the monitoring of negotiations and drafting of a mandate. As Reichert and Jungblut have argued, the commission responds to the council and the EP, the latter deriving its legitimacy from European electorates, yet

> the insulated nature of the Council of Ministers, where the governments meet collectively, makes it more difficult for their principals in the national parliaments to monitor them, and therefore, more difficult for the general publics to exercise control over the policy decisions of the national governments at the European level. (2007, 411)

Gradual enhancement of the commission as a "single voice" in trade policy (Meunier 2000) has improved the EU's collective effectiveness but diluted the ability of each individual member state to determine trade policy. Under these circumstances the ratification of agreements

11.1 Ratification Process of European Union Preferential Trade Agreements That Include Mixed Competences

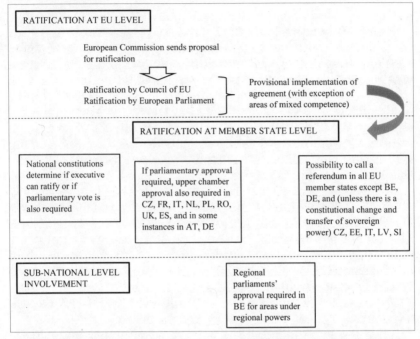

Abbreviations of member states: AT (Austria), BE (Belgium), BG (Bulgaria), CY (Cyprus), CZ (Czech Republic), DE (Germany), DK (Denmark), EE (Estonia), EL (Greece), ES (Spain), FI (Finland), FR (France), HR (Croatia), HU (Hungary), IE (Ireland), IT (Italy), LT (Lithuania), LU (Luxembourg), LV (Latvia), MT (Malta), NL (Netherlands), PL (Poland), PT (Portugal), RO (Romania), SE (Sweden), SI (Slovenia), SK (Slovakia), UK (United Kingdom).

Sources: TFEU (2008) and Grosek and Sabbati (2016).

at the national level opens an opportunity for some principals, who achieved less impact in the previous stages of the negotiations, to exert their control via acceptance or non-acceptance of the agreement, but risks creating veto opportunities.

Increasing the EU's coherence and effectiveness as an external actor was a key ambition of the Lisbon treaty. The institutional changes introduced in trade policy aimed at facilitating trade negotiations, democratizing trade policy through greater involvement of the EP, and limiting potential for national veto opportunities, to improve effective collective action. The Lisbon treaty's novelties in terms of trade policy can be summarized as follows:

- *Transfer of authority in trade matters to the EU level on all trade-related disciplines including foreign direct investment and investment protection.* This is reinforced by the application of qualified majority voting to most of trade policy, with few exceptions requiring a unanimous vote in the European Council.
- *Enhanced role of the European Parliament in trade agreements.* This translated into the EP becoming a co-legislator with the European Council in the adoption of legislation framing trade policy in accordance with the ordinary legislative procedure, and the requirement that international trade agreements receive the consent of the EP.

Together these changes marked a shift towards the consolidation of a European single voice, and empowerment of the EU. While the over-arching architecture remained one of shared rule, ensuring the strong participation of member states via the council, the transfer of competences to the EU level, and the greater role of the EU-level parliament, particularly in trade agreement ratification, as well as extending the use of qualified majority voting, can be interpreted as a shift towards the self-rule pole in the self-rule versus shared-rule spectrum.

In practical terms, the new arrangements should "strengthen the European Union presence in trade and investment" (Woolcock 2010, 25), in the multilevel politics of trade in the EU. They should have relocated scrutiny, adoption, and ratification of EU trade agreements to the EU level, removing the need for national-level ratification of agreements. Of course, participation by member states in the process is preserved through their legislative role in the European Council, with clear and strong powers of surveillance over the European Commission's actions and of decision making (amendment and approval of policies). However, these powers are exercised on a collective basis and under the shadow of qualified majority voting, rather than individually within national jurisdictions.

Lisbon Treaty Fallout: Comparing Post-Treaty Free Trade Agreement Ratifications

In a system where the member states are collectively involved in all stages of the trade negotiation process, and where prior informal practices of extensive consultation with the EP are formalized (Woolcock

2010), the likelihood of conflicts arising at the ratification stage should be greatly reduced. However, trade agreement ratifications in the post–Lisbon treaty era have been fraught with the threat of non-ratification.

Ambiguities at the European Union Level: European Parliament Activism

The first agreement to undergo ratification under Lisbon treaty procedures was the European Union-Republic of Korea Free Trade Agreement, which, having been negotiated prior to the treaty, excluded investment. The ratification process and enhanced role of the EP afforded certain social interests an opportunity to express dissatisfaction with the agreement and attempt to reopen certain issues. The ratification took longer than expected, following the conclusion of the agreement in October 2009. In the Trade Policy Committee the Italian government voiced concerns about greater access for Korean cars, until the end of the ratification process. Small- and medium-sized car producers and the European Automobile Manufacturers' Association lobbied for adjustments to provisions on technical barriers to trade and the use of a special safeguard mechanism in relation to the Korean duty drawback clause (Elsig and Dupont 2012, 498); when the agreement came to the EP for a vote, they lobbied MPs to reject it. At the EP the "newly acquired power allowed the EP to flex its muscles, to push the Commission to review the duty drawback clause, and to negotiate with the different institutions (Council, Commission) on how to design implementation legislation" (Elsig and Dupont 2012, 498). After succeeding in getting the commission to agree to a safeguard clause that would allow the EU to suspend reductions in customs duties (or increase them if lower rates led to an excessive increase in imports), and securing the right for the EP and the auto industry to ask the commission to launch an investigation that could lead to activation of the clause, the EP ratified the free trade agreement in February 2011 (European Parliament 2011). A combination of institutional vying for power (EP), and social pressure (car manufacturers), complicated the ratification.

The ratification of the EU-Colombia/Peru Trade Agreement,[7] negotiated with a pre-Lisbon treaty mandate, was also marred by controversy. In this case, civil society activists rallied against the agreement, voicing concerns over threats to and deaths of trade unionists in Colombia throughout the entire negotiation process. It is worth highlighting that the EU's trade and sustainability chapter in post-2006 trade agreements includes the promotion of social and environmental rights but is exempt from the Lisbon treaty's dispute-settlement mechanism and instead is subject to its own non-binding mechanism for the resolution of disputes.[8] The EP, which has positioned itself as the defender of human rights, threatened to stall the ratification unless tighter mechanisms to ensure respect for human rights were introduced. Divisions within the EP between political groups generally in favour of trade agreements (European People's Party, European Conservatives and Reformists, Alliance of Liberals and Democrats for Europe) and those sceptical of these types of arrangements (Progressive Alliance of Socialists and Democrats, Greens / European Free Alliance, Confederal Group of the European United Left / Nordic Green Left) were magnified by targeted lobbying by civil-society groups.[9] The EP called for Peru and Colombia to establish binding road maps to protect trade unionists, human rights, and the environment. Once this had been accepted by the EU's negotiators and Peruvian and Colombian governments, the EP adopted a resolution on 13 June 2012 in favour of the trade agreement, which was then officially signed on 26 June. The EP ratified the agreement with a 72 per cent majority vote in favour on 11 December 2012 (OneEurope 2013).

In the Korea and Colombia/Peru cases, politicization of the ratification stage came as the new principal, the EP, which had hitherto had a reduced role in these negotiations, exercised its new powers. In both cases, societal interest groups also mobilized to exert pressure on the EP and the European Council at the ratification stage, even though these groups would have been involved in consultations from the early stages of the negotiations.[10] Member-state governments, however, supported negotiations and the ratification processes.

Ambiguities at the Member-State Level: Challenges over Boundary Control

A direct challenge by the member states against the transfer of sovereignty in the Treaty of Lisbon became evident in the ratification of the EU-Singapore Free Trade Agreement. Although the negotiations for the agreement had commenced under a pre-Lisbon treaty mandate, at the end of negotiations the EU negotiated a chapter on investment to be attached to the agreement. Sophie Meunier (2017) argues that the extension of EU-level exclusive competences over trade under the Lisbon treaty resulted from luck and "stealth" on the part of enterprising commission officials. Prior to the year 2000, the European Commission had undertaken, alongside the member states, international negotiations in the area of investment (the Agreement on Trade-Related Investment Measures at the WTO and the ill-fated Multilateral Agreement on Investment); it therefore supported a formal transfer of competencies over these matters. The commission had argued for such a transfer during the intergovernmental conference that led to the Treaty of Amsterdam (1997), but was opposed by member states, particularly France, Germany, and the United Kingdom (Young 2002, 45). During the European Convention (2001–3), trade policy fell under the remit of the working party dealing with the complex and controversial matter of external policies. In one of the meetings of the Praesidium, former Irish prime minister John Bruton suggested that the matter of removing obstacles to foreign direct investment be addressed, which led Michel Barnier, the representative of the European Commission, to include a line adding investment to the common commercial policy (Meunier 2017, 603). Despite opposition by member states and thirty-two amendments to the line, the matter was drowned in the thousands of amendments suggested to the chapters on external policies, which were prioritized by member states. Thus, the inclusion of investment in the common commercial policy remained in the text (Meunier 2017, 604).

Given the opposition of member states to the expansion of EU-level competencies, when the first agreement including chapters on investment came about, member states challenged the commission's authority. On 17 October 2014 the negotiations for a free trade agreement with Singapore were completed, but the commission opted to delay the ratification process. Former trade commissioner Karel De Gucht referred the agreement to the ECJ for an opinion on how the ratification process should proceed (European Commission 2014). The commission argued that, given its new powers over investment and the empowerment of the EP, a ratification at the EU level was sufficient. Member states argued that the area remained a mixed competence, and therefore the agreement would also require national ratification in each member state. They bolstered their arguments by invoking the absence of a definition of *investment* in the Treaty of Lisbon, which did not explicitly differentiate between foreign direct investment in the form of investment flows for business purposes and portfolio investments (buying a non-controlling share in an investment).

Substantiating claims that sub-federal actors would be more willing to relinquish boundary control if they had early influence over the negotiations, the reluctance to accept the transfer of investment competences to the EU level, given their inability to impede its inclusion in the treaties, led member states to attempt to reassert their boundary control on the matter by exploiting institutional ambiguities in the treaty. This was done, firstly and more immediately, by sabotaging implementation and, secondly, by ensuring a voice in the future (and the ability to exert pressure on the commission in the shadow of veto) by establishing that the area remained a mixed competence, and retaining the right to future national ratifications.[11]

On 16 May 2017, the European Court of Justice (2017) delivered its opinion, determining that, although the European Commission had exclusive competence over trade, matters relating to non-direct foreign investment and the regime regulating disputes between investors and states remained areas of mixed competence and therefore required conclusion and ratification by both EU institutions and member states. As Broschek and Goff highlight in the concluding chapter, the allocation of competences is often ambiguous. The ambiguity introduced into the text of the Treaty of Lisbon regarding investment because of the failure to define its scope, combined with the "stealthy" manner of its introduction (Meunier 2017), created a situation in which "the original designers may be less capable of sustaining control over long-term paths of institutional development" (Pierson 2004, 163), and the ECJ has a prominent role in determining the institutional evolution. Rather than ushering in the EU-level trade policy and ratification envisaged in the Treaty of Lisbon, the ECJ solidified a lengthy multilevel ratification process. As the next section argues, the multilevel ratification – particularly of matters relating to investor-state-dispute mechanisms, an area that has been subject to intense politicization in recent years – has the potential of entrenching member states (and sub-national regions) as veto players in the scheme of EU trade policy.

Ambiguities at the Member-State Level: Politicization
and Social Mobilization

The potential for politicization of trade agreements, and for impediments to EU trade policy at the member-state level, was exemplified in 2016 in two cases of national-level challenges to EU trade policy at the ratification stage: the EU-Ukraine Association Agreement and CETA. The opposition to the Ukraine agreement was led by political parties, and various activist groups, later joined by political parties, were the key source of contestation to CETA. In both cases, social opposition and mobilization revolved around the comprehensive nature of modern trade agreements, specifically the inclusion of simplified visa requirements (Ukraine) and contentious regulatory cooperation and investor protections (CETA). Both cases demonstrate the relevance of the social dimension (social mobilization and party politics) in recent trade-agreement politicization.

EU and Canadian officials launched negotiations for CETA in May 2009 and concluded them in September 2014. Negotiations had followed the fate of most trade-agreement negotiations. References to these appeared in the specialized economic press, and in more mainstream media only when milestones in the negotiations were reached (e.g., launch, agreement in principle, formal conclusion). However, in 2014 the situation changed. President Barack Obama and Trade Commissioner Karel De Gucht had announced the launch of the TTIP negotiations in February 2013. One year later, European civil society organizations opposed to the negotiations grouped together under the "Stop TTIP" banner to collect signatures for a citizens' initiative against TTIP and CETA, and collectively and individually organized anti-TTIP and -CETA demonstrations. CETA's notoriety and salience increased exponentially in 2014 as the agreement reached its conclusion, when opponents to trade agreements, and especially opponents to TTIP negotiations, discursively presented CETA as a precursor to TTIP and noticed that the agreement contained some of the provisions to which they objected in TTIP. Thus, in mid-2014 as the movement against TTIP gained force, CETA became embroiled in TTIP debates and a target of mobilization and opposition.

Key among opponents' concerns were the conduct of negotiations behind closed doors, potential dilution of EU health and environmental standards, and the inclusion of investor-state-dispute-arbitration procedures, characterized as a corporate power grab and a threat to future policy space.

The realization that the CETA text also included investor-state arbitration and that, given the similarities in regulatory preferences in Canada and the United States, CETA could be used as a basis upon which to craft an even more ambitious agreement with the United States, led to vocal opposition to CETA. Indeed, aware of how difficult ratification of this matter would be, considering the opposition campaign as well as the fact that member states were also challenging EU jurisdiction in this area (in the Singapore case), the European Commission proceeded to renegotiate fully the investment chapter with Canada. The new iteration abandoned the existing regime of ad hoc dispute tribunals and established a novel investment court system, with permanent arbitrators, appeals procedures, greater transparency, and specific language limiting the application of dispute arbitration and reiterating the ability of states to regulate in the public interest (CETA 2016, chapter 8, section D). With these amendments in place, the ratification process began. In order to facilitate the signature of the agreement and provisional application of the bulk thereof, the commission conceded that the agreement be ratified as a mixed agreement, although it reiterated at the time that the final decision on where the competences lay was in the hands of the ECJ, which had still not deliberated on the Singapore case (Ross 2016).

Ratifying CETA as a mixed agreement required ratification in each member state. Despite support of CETA by the Belgian government, its federal system required that all sub-regional parliaments consent to the prime minister signing an international agreement. The Wallonian parliament's reservations on CETA over investment disputes and agriculture (see Bollen, De Ville, and Gheyle's chapter in this volume) delayed the official signing ceremony in Brussels by several days. The regional parliament enabled the Belgian prime minister to sign CETA after reassurances that the federal government would monitor the impacts of CETA on Wallonian agriculture, that CETA would not prevent states and regions from regulating in the public interest, and that it would refer CETA to the ECJ for a decision on whether the proposed investment court was compatible with EU law and human rights. With the backing of the European Council, CETA began its journey though the ratification process. On 15 February 2017 the EP voted in favour of the ratification of CETA by 408 votes to 254, with 33 abstentions (European Parliament 2017), paving the way for the provisional implementation of most of the agreement, with the exception of investment protection and areas of mixed competence. At the time of writing, votes to ratify CETA were still to take place in most member state parliaments and in the Belgian regional parliaments. In early 2019 the ECJ ruled that CETA's investment provisions were compatible with European law.[12]

Despite the support of CETA by the executive branches of member states, ratification in national parliaments offers political parties and societal groups an opportunity to contest and stymie the process. Concerns over TTIP – which had been instigated in various national parliaments by Green parties and parties on the left of the political spectrum that were opposed to the extension of liberalization in general, and in response to civil-society campaigns (Streinz 2015, 279)[13] – were transferred onto CETA. In France 153 left-wing elected officials, including 53 Members of Parliament, requested that the French Constitutional Court investigate whether CETA was compatible with the French constitution. On 23 March 2017 the Constitutional Court launched a full investigation of whether investor-state arbitration breaches the constitutional principle of equality (because it grants additional rights to foreign investors) and whether national sovereignty was being undermined in CETA (EurActiv 2017). On 31 July 2017 it determined that there was nothing in CETA in breach of French constitutional law (Conseil Constitutionnel 2017). However, the French government opted to postpone ratification until after the EP elections of 2019, mindful of mixed feelings about the agreement, and has insisted on stronger links to the 2015 Paris agreement and environmental rights in the agreement (EurActiv 2018a). In July 2019, France eventually ratified CETA.

In Germany the left-wing party Die Linke, consumer associations, and private citizens referred the case to the German constitutional court, the Bundesverfassungsgericht (see Broschek, Bußjäger, and Schramek in this volume). In December 2016 the German constitutional court ruled in a provisional judgment that a provisional application of the bulk of CETA falling under exclusive EU competence was possible but that until it delivered a final judgment, any decision taken by the joint committees established under CETA should have broad democratic support and that CETA article 30.7(3)(c) had to be interpreted in order to allow Germany to terminate unilaterally the provisional application of CETA (IISD 2016). The decision of the German constitutional court enabled the provisional implementation of trade agreements but also reinforced the separation between exclusive and mixed areas of competence, in a similar way to the ECJ's opinion on the Singapore agreement.

Bulgarian president Rumen Radev, for his part, claimed that he had never welcomed CETA, despite the Bulgarian government's signing of it in October 2016 after Canada gave written guarantees that it would lift visa requirements for Bulgarian and Romanian citizens (Sputnik News 2016). He referred CETA to the Bulgarian constitutional court to determine its compatibility with the Basic Law on 18 July 2017 (Sofia Globe 2017). A new anti-establishment Italian coalition (including the centre-right coalition and the Five Star Movement), resulting from the March 2018 elections, also threatened to reject CETA ratification in July 2018, claiming inadequate protection of Italian products that had protected geographic indications (EurActiv 2018b).

Domestic political parties and activist groups are continuing their campaigns against trade agreements, even once these have been approved by the governments of EU member states (in the European Council) and elected representatives in the EP. The politicization of member-state-ratification processes enables them to challenge the decisions and votes they oppose. By making use of recourse to constitutional courts, activist groups have placed these in a position to determine the future institutional architecture of investor-state arbitration, especially as the ECJ opinion clarified that the EU level does not have sole authority over this matter. In the Netherlands, activists are pursuing another strategy to stymie the ratification process and have started a campaign to gather signatures to invoke a popular referendum on the ratification of CETA.[14] Although these referendums are not binding in their results, they can derail ratification and elicit responses and actions, as the final case, the EU-Ukraine Association Agreement, demonstrates.

Worryingly, in the case of the Ukraine agreement the main driver of the challenge to the ratification process does not appear to stem from a rejection of the trade agreement or of the trade policy system in the EU. The case of the association agreement with Ukraine differs from the other cases in this chapter because the agreement goes beyond the scope of trade agreements and includes a robust political pillar, including military cooperation and visa-free travel within the broader association agreement. Parts of the EU-Ukraine Association Agreement under exclusive EU competence have been in provisional application since 1 November 2014, as have parts of the Deep and Comprehensive Free Trade Agreement since 1 January 2016.

In 2015 both houses of the Dutch parliament voted in favour of an act of approval for the agreement. Under Dutch law, ratification can also be the subject of a popular referendum, and the public can request such a referendum if over 300,000 valid signatures are collected. Anti-EU groups collected 427,939 signatures online, prompting a referendum. In the 6 April 2016 referendum, 61 per cent of voters rejected the act of approval, and 38.2 per cent voted in favour, with a low overall turnout of 32.3 per cent (*The Independent* 2016). Although the referendum had an advisory and non-binding character enabling the government to enact another act of approval, Mark Rutte's government decided to engage in discussions with the EU institutions and the Dutch parliament. After getting a legally binding statement reiterating that the association agreement was not a step towards EU membership for Ukraine, the Dutch lower house of parliament voted in favour of an act of approval in February 2017 (Politico 2017), and on 30 May a positive vote in the Senate finalized the ratification process. Although the inclusion of this statement was deemed by Prime Minister Rutte to address opponents' fears of Ukrainian membership and increased migration (EU Observer 2017), groups behind the referendum have admitted that their concern was not the Ukraine but that their move responded to their anti-EU stance, where the referendum was seen as a way of antagonizing and opposing the EU (NCR Handelsbad 2016). In March 2017 the Dutch election returned Rutte's People's Party for Freedom and Democracy as the most-voted party, with 21.3 per cent of the votes. However, Geert Wilders' Party for Freedom, which had campaigned on an anti-EU and anti-immigration platform, was the second most-voted party, with 13.1 per cent of the votes. Within this broader context of more vocal anti-EU sentiment within the Netherlands, the reaction to the Ukraine agreement can be seen not as a challenge of the member state against the

EU level in terms of trade policies and jurisdictions (indeed the formal institutions of the Dutch state favoured ratification of the deal) but as a symptom of broader societal rejection of multilevel governance, supranational authority, and globalization.

Conclusion

EU trade policy has been determined and regulated by a hierarchical architecture of relations across territorial levels of government (national and EU), akin to intergovernmental relations between government actors of different tiers in a federal state. The member-state governments, represented in the European Council and the European Commission at the EU level, have been the main interlocutors and drivers behind the EU's trade policy. Although the European Commission has been empowered by the treaties to act as the EU's single voice in trade negotiations, it operates in a multilevel system, whereby it engages in constant negotiation with the council (as represented by the International Trade Committee) in the conduct of trade negotiations, through what has often been described as a principal-agent relationship. In practice, the guidance from the council, and the need for it to approve any final agreement, shows that this is an area of shared rule with the strong participation of the representatives of member states in the entire trade-policy process and with a high degree of collaboration between the principal and the agent.

However, trade policy has also been an area of dynamic changes that have affected the institutional balance between member states and the European Commission. Subsequent treaties have expanded the scope of areas falling under the EU's exclusive competence for the purposes of trade policy and diluted the ability of single member states to act as veto players in the council, by extending the use of qualified majority voting. The Treaty of Lisbon, which further enhanced EU-level trade competences, counterbalanced the delegation of authority to the supranational level, with a greater role for the directly elected EP. This should have enhanced EU-level autonomy in trade policy, particularly when it comes to the ratification of international trade agreements, which could, as argued by the European Commission, take place at the EU level only. Of course, this does not represent a shift to commission dominance over trade policy because, in practice, shared rule would remain dominant as the member states in the European Council collectively retained their crucial role in granting trade mandates to the commission, supervising negotiations, and approving final agreements. Moreover, garnering consent from the EP for an agreement negotiated by the commission requires that the commission consult the EP and ensure that it negotiates a text acceptable to the majority of the members of the EP.

In practice, as the cases of ratifications of trade agreements that have occurred since the Treaty of Lisbon reveal, efforts to streamline trade-agreement-ratification procedures by granting a pre-eminent role in this to the EU level have backfired, as societal interests and particular political parties and politicians have sought to reopen issues with which they disagreed. Initial ratifications of agreements negotiated before the Treaty of Lisbon and without investment chapters were the subject of strong debate at the EP as the institution sought to highlight its importance in the new procedures, showing that even an EU-level-only ratification is not without complications. The EP's position led to additional arrangements being put in place by the European Commission and third parties in order to gain the EP's support. In the case of Korea this meant safeguard clauses to protect EU automakers should imports from South Korea reach extremely high volumes. In the case of Peru and Colombia it was the addition of national road maps on human rights.

Having been unable to prevent the linking of investment to trade policy at the EU level during the constitutional convention, and having then forgone the reopening of the matter in the intergovernmental conference leading to the Treaty of Lisbon, member states that oppose the transfer of investment authority to the EU level have attempted to regain boundary control over this matter by rejecting its implementation and challenging the ratification of trade agreements that include investment chapters. Institutional ambiguity in the Lisbon treaty regarding the extent of investment competences being transferred resulted in the ECJ determining that, although the EU had competences to negotiate investment chapters in trade agreements, matters relating to non-foreign direct investment (portfolio investment) and to investor-state-arbitration mechanisms could not be concluded by the EU alone and required explicit consent and ratification by each of the member states. In practice then, new modern trade agreements – which include investment chapters – will continue to be considered mixed agreements and subject to final ratification in national parliaments.[15]

The complexity that this introduces was highlighted in the case of CETA, in which Belgian regional parliaments delayed the signature of the agreement over concerns about the novel investment-court system included in the agreement. Reassurance in the form of a joint interpretation document highlighting the right to regulate in the public interest, as well as promises by the Belgian federal government to assess the impact of CETA and request an opinion from the ECJ on the legality of the investment-court system, enabled the signature to take place and the ratification process to commence. However, the threat of non-ratification remains.

CETA's challenging ratification process is also a consequence of political parties and civil-society organizations that reject trade liberalization and globalization generally. As trade agreements have become more comprehensive in scope, they have begun to include matters that no longer relate to the exchange of goods but increasingly refer to the way in which goods are produced; the allowing of foreign companies to offer services and bid on public authorities' contracts; and the relationship between foreign investors and public authorities, environmental groups, consumer-protection groups, social-justice campaigners, trade unions, and parties on the left of the political spectrum who have vocalized their opposition to this "new trade agenda" (Young 2002). The inclusion of these matters in international trade negotiations has led to a shift from "*distributive* trade conflict (involving competing economic interests) to conflicts centred on civil society groups' *normative* critique of the expansion of the international trade agenda," and of globalization (De Ville and Siles-Brügge 2016, 95).

What made TTIP special and caused such a rallying cry was that it was framed by transatlantic policymakers as an opportunity to "develop global rules" (Obama, Rompuy, and Barroso 2013) and was the first credible bilateral deal that offered a genuine alternative to the WTO regime. Moreover, the bargaining power of Europe was perceived as weaker than that of the United States (Eliasson and García-Duran 2017). Anti-TTIP sentiment was not universal in Europe; it was prevalent in Germany, Austria, France, and Central European states where activist campaigns gained notoriety, but it served to highlight divisions in society regarding normative positions towards globalization and the EU's new trade agenda. Contestation of TTIP also brought CETA out of the realm of technocratic obscurity and into the limelight. The tortuous process to sign CETA stemmed from the fears of setting precedents for TTIP. The politicization of trade policy and polarization around the issue continues to mar CETA's ratification process. The ECJ's confirmation of the mixed character of the investment part of EU trade agreements consigns them to lengthy member-state ratifications in which groups opposing the international trade agenda can attempt to thwart progress, even when their positions have been defeated in other democratic forums (such as the EU-level parliament or the council's national governments).

Politicization of trade policy, and the role played by civil-society organizations in the TTIP and CETA cases, are significant because they reinforce the fact that the EU's multilevel trade policy is not a purely hierarchical system of inter-institutional relations but a complex multilevel governance in which societal actors play an important role. Moreover, societal actors (including political parties) have been shown to use an array of institutional arenas to shape trade policy: national parliaments, national courts (constitutional courts), and the ECJ.

EU trade agreements will never reflect the views of all possible sectors, groups, organizations, and businesses among the EU's population of 545 million. If every group whose preferences are obviated or traded away in an agreement seeks to reopen negotiations or stymie ratification (be it at the EP or at the national parliaments), the EU risks losing its credibility as an international trade actor. From a legal and institutional perspective, under the areas of exclusive competence, the EU will retain its ability to operate and implement treaties. However, the German constitutional court's provisional ruling that reserves space for Germany to back-track on provisional application of the exclusive-competences parts of the agreement opens the door to uncertainty over a policy area in which the multilevel relations among territorial jurisdictions had been thought to have been reconciled.

NOTES

1 This reflects the diffusion of clear lines of demarcation of authority over certain policy areas (relating mostly to the internal market) as the level of integration qualitatively increased with the creation of the EU in the Maastricht Treaty (1992). The Hooghe and Marks model has been popular amongst scholars scrutinizing EU regional and cohesion policy (Bache 2007; Benz and Eberlein 1999; Hooghe 1996) and environmental policies (Jordan 2000; Knill and Liefferink 2007; Newig and Koontz 2014) because these involve cooperation among all three territorial levels of governance, as well as among non-government actors.
2 Trade policy had been subject to interest-group mobilization in the past. In fact, a large body of international political-economy literature represents trade-policy outcomes as the outcomes of varying degrees of political influence by diverse economic sectors (exporting firms, import-competing firms, multinational firms) (see *inter alia* Hillman and Ursprung 1988; Mansfield and Milner 2012; Milner 1988; Rodrik 1995). The negotiations of the GATT Uruguay Round and the initial negotiations under the remit of the World Trade Organization (WTO) in Seattle also fostered politicization

of trade policy and an increased activism around trade. Some of the trade-activism networks created in response to the WTO were also influential in the mobilization against trade agreements, especially the negotiations with the United States, in Europe (see De Ville and Siles-Brügge 2016).

3 Qualified majority vote is a weighted vote whereby a minimum of 55 per cent of member states, jointly representing at least 65 per cent of the total EU population, must vote in favour of a measure for it to be adopted. Although the requirement of a qualified majority vote applies to most trade matters, the norm is for decisions on trade in the European Council to be made on the basis of consensus.

4 Others argue that interest groups, particularly exporters and importers, have an influential role in EU trade policy (see Dür 2008).

5 The European Court of Justice determined in Opinion 2/15 that areas of mixed competences in new trade agreements are non-direct foreign investment and the regime governing dispute settlement between investors and states. Interestingly, in 2017 in the negotiation mandates for trade agreements with Australia and New Zealand the European Commission decided to exclude investment from the negotiation mandate, leading the way towards an agreement covering only exclusive competences.

6 The Belgian regional parliaments represent the regions (Flanders, Wallonia, Brussels Capital) and the communities (French community, German-speaking community, French Community Commission, Common Community Commission). The Flemish parliament encompasses the representation of the Flemish community, the Flemish Community Commission, and the region of Flanders (Grosek and Sabbati 2016, 4).

7 The European Parliament voted in favour of the EU Association Agreement with Central America, also negotiated with a pre-Lisbon treaty mandate. Although there were anti-trade organizations opposing the agreement, it received less attention than the Colombia/Peru one, given the developmental nature of the broader association and also the fact that deaths of trade unionists in Colombia have been a well-documented salient issue.

8 On the sustainability chapter see Orbie et al. 2016.

9 European People's Party (conservatives), European Conservatives and Reformists, Alliance of Liberals and Democrats for Europe, Progressive Alliance of Socialists and Democrats (socialists), European Green Party and European Free Alliance, and European United Left and Nordic Green Alliance. These political divisions were also evident within member states' parties, as is evidenced in the chapter by Broschek, Bußjäger, and Schramek in this volume.

10 Dür and Mateo (2014) also found that the Anti-counterfeit Trade Agreement had been rejected by the EP after a last-minute intense campaign against the agreement by civil-society groups.
11 The timing of this ratification is important. Although the Singapore agreement was not the object of social mobilization or media salience, by the autumn of 2014, mobilization against TTIP and CETA was strong, and the issue of investor-state-dispute settlement was becoming toxic in core European states.
12 As of early 2019, CETA had been endorsed by the Czech Republic, Denmark, Estonia, Spain, Croatia, Lithuania, Latvia, Malta, and Portugal. On 6 September 2017 the Belgian deputy prime minister submitted Belgium's request for an opinion on CETA's investment chapter to the ECJ (Diplomatie 2017).
13 See also the chapter by Bollen, De Ville, and Gheyle in this volume, as well as Eliasson and García-Duran Huet (2018).
14 An actual referendum will have to wait until after Parliament has voted on the matter (Reuters 2016).
15 The mandates that the European Commission proposed and the European Council approved in 2017 for negotiations of trade agreements with Australia and New Zealand do not include investment chapters, paving the way for agreements that could be subject to the EU-level-only ratification envisaged in the Lisbon treaty.

REFERENCES

Armstrong, Kenneth. 2011. "The Character of EU Law and Governance: From 'Community Method'" to New Modes of Governance. *Current Legal Problems* 64 (1): 179–214.
Bache, Ian. 2007. *Europeanization and Multilevel Governance: Cohesion Policy in the European Union and Britain.* Lanham, MD: Rowman & Littlefield.
Benz, Arthur, and Burkard Eberlein. 1999. "The Europeanization of Regional Policies: Patterns of Multi-level Governance." *Journal of European Public Policy* 6 (2): 329–48.
CETA. 2016. *Canada–European Union Comprehensive Economic Trade Agreement.* Accessed 7 November 2019. https://www.international.gc.ca.
Conseil Constitutionnel. 2017. Décision n° 2017–749 DC, Accord économique et commercial global entre le Canada, d'une part, et l'Union européenne et ses États membres, d'autre part. ECLI-FR-CC, 31 July 2017, 2017.749.DC.
Damro, Chad. 2007. "EU Delegation and Agency in International Trade Negotiations: A Cautionary Comparison." *Journal of Common Market Studies* 45 (4): 883–903.

De Ville, Ferdi, and Siles-Brügge, Gabriel. 2016. *TTIP: The Truth about the Transatlantic Trade and Investment Partnership*. Hoboken, NJ: John Wiley & Sons.

Diplomatie. 2017. Minister Reynders Submits Request for Opinion on CETA. 6 September 2017. https://diplomatie.belgium.be.

Dür, Andreas. 2008. "Bringing Economic Interests Back into the Study of EU Trade Policy-Making." *British Journal of Politics and International Relations* 10 (1): 27–45.

Dür, Andreas, and Manfred Elsig. 2011. "Principal-Agent and EU's Foreign Economic Policies." *Journal of European Public Policy* 18 (3): 323–38.

Dür, Andreas, and Gemma Mateo. 2014. "Public Opinion and Interest Group Influence: How Citizen Groups Derailed the Anti-counterfeiting Trade Agreement." *Journal of European Public Policy* 21 (8): 1199–217.

The Economist. 2016. "If the EU Cannot Do Trade, What Can It Do?" 29 October 2016. https://www.economist.com.

Eliasson, Leif J., and Patricia García-Duran. 2017. "Why TTIP is an Unprecedented Geopolitical Game-Changer, but Not a Polanyian Moment." *Journal of European Public Policy* 24 (10): 1522–33.

Eliasson, Leif J., and Patricia García-Duran Huet. 2018. "TTIP Negotiations: Interest Groups, Anti-TTIP Civil Society Campaigns and Public Opinion." *Journal of Transatlantic Studies* 16 (2): 101–16.

Elsig, Manfred. 2007. "The EU's Choice of Regulatory Venues for Trade Negotiations: A Tale of Agency Power?" *Journal of Common Market Studies* 45 (4): 927–48.

Elsig, Manfred, and Cédric Dupont. 2012. "European Union Meets South Korea: Bureaucratic Interests, Exporter Discrimination and the Negotiations of Trade Agreements." *Journal of Common Market Studies* 50 (3): 492–507.

EU Observer. 2017. "Netherlands Ratifies EU-Ukraine Treaty." 30 May 2017. https://euobserver.com/foreign/138060.

EurActiv. 2017. "France's Top Court Questions Constitutionality of CETA." 23 March 2017. https://www.euractiv.com.

– 2018a. "Inclusion of Paris Agreement in CETA at Risk." 8 October 2018. https://www.euractiv.com.

– 2018b. "Italy Threatens to Block CETA Ratification." 1 June 2018. https://www.euractiv.com.

European Commission. 2014. "Singapore: The Commission to Request a Court of Justice Opinion on the Trade Deal." 10 October 2014. http://trade.ec.europa.eu.

European Court of Justice. 2017. "Opinion C-2/15, Opinion Pursuant to Article 218(11) TFEU – Free Trade Agreement between the European Union and

the Republic of Singapore." Accessed 7 November 2019. https://eur-lex
.europa.eu.

European Parliament. 2011. "EU-South Korea Free Trade Agreement Passes
Final Hurdle in Parliament." Press release. http://www.europarl.europa
.eu.

– 2017. "CETA: MEPs Back EU-Canada Trade Agreement." 15 February 2017.
Press release. http://www.europarl.europa.eu.

Gammage, Clair. 2018. "EU International Relations Law: The Power to
Conclude International Trade Agreements." In Handbook on the EU
and International Trade, edited by M. Garcia and S. Khorana, 36–56.
Cheltenham, UK: Edward Elgar.

Grosek, Kristina, and Giulio Sabbati. 2016. "Ratification of International
Agreements by EU Member States." 29 November 2016. European
Parliament briefing, PE 593.513.

Hillman, Arye L., and Heinrich W. Ursprung. 1988. "Domestic Politics,
Foreign Interests, and International Trade Policy." American Economic
Review 78 (4): 729–45.

Hooghe, Liesbet, ed. 1996. Cohesion Policy and European Integration: Building
Multi-level Governance. Oxford: Oxford University Press.

Hooghe, Liesbet, and Gary Marks. 2001. Multi-level Governance and European
Integration. Lanham, MD: Rowman & Littlefield.

IISD (International Institute for Sustainable Development). 2016. "Only a
Brief Pause for Breath: The Judgment of the German Federal Constitutional
Court on CETA." Investment Treaty News. 12 December 2016. https://www
.iisd.org/.

The Independent. 2016. "Dutch Voters Reject EU-Ukraine Deal in Referendum."
7 April 2016. http://www.independent.ie.

Jordan, Andrew. 2000. "The Politics of Multilevel Environmental Governance:
Subsidiarity and Environmental Policy in the European Union."
Environment and Planning A: Economy and Space 32 (7): 1307–24.

Kerremans, Bart. 2004. "What Went Wrong in Cancun? A Principal-Agent
View on the EU's Rationale towards the Doha Development Round."
European Foreign Affairs Review 9 (3): 363–93.

Knill, Christopher, and Duncan Liefferink. 2007. Environmental Politics in the
European Union: Policy-Making, Implementation and Patterns of Multi-level
Governance. Manchester, UK: Manchester University Press.

Leczykiewicz, Dorota. 2005. "Common Commercial Policy: The Expanding
Competence of the European Union in the Area of International Trade."
German Law Journal 6 (11): 1673–86.

Mahoney, James, and Kathleen Thelen. 2010. "A Theory of Gradual
Institutional Change." In Explaining Institutional Change: Ambiguity,

Agency and Power, edited by J. Mahoney and K. Thelen, 1–37. Cambridge: Cambridge University Press.

Mansfield, Edward D., and Helen V. Milner. 2012. *Votes, Vetoes, and the Political Economy of International Trade Agreements.* Princeton, NJ: Princeton University Press.

Meunier, Sophie. 2000. "What Single Voice? European Institutions and EU-US Trade Negotiations." *International Organization* 54 (1): 103–35.

– 2017. "Integration by Stealth: How the European Union Gained Competence over Foreign Direct Investment." *Journal of Common Market Studies* 55 (3): 593–610.

Meunier, Sophie, and Kalypso Nicolaïdis. 1999. "Who Speaks for Europe? The Delegation of Trade Authority in the EU." *Journal of Common Market Studies* 37 (3): 477–501.

Milner, Helen V. 1988. *Resisting Protectionism: Global Industries and the Politics of International Trade.* Princeton, NJ: Princeton University Press.

NCR Handelsblad. 2016. Oekraïne kan ons niets schelen. 31 March 2016. https://www.nrc.nl.

Newig, Jens, and Tomas M. Koontz. 2014. "Multi-level Governance, Policy Implementation and Participation: The EU's Mandated Participatory Planning Approach to Implementing Environmental Policy." *Journal of European Public Policy* 21 (2): 248–67.

Obama, Barack, Herman van Rompuy, and José Manuel Barroso. 2013. "Statement from United States President Barack Obama, European Council President Herman Van Rompuy, and European Commission President José Manuel Barroso." Press release. 13 February 2013. http://europa.eu.

OneEurope. 2013. "The EU-Peru/Colombia FTA: A Controversial Agreement." 2 July 2013. http://one-europe.net.

Orbie, Jan, Deborah Martens, Myriam Oehri, and Lore Van den Putte, L. 2016. "Promoting Sustainable Development or Legitimising Free Trade? Civil Society Mechanisms in EU Trade Agreements." *Third World Thematics: A TWQ Journal* 1 (4): 526–46.

Pierson, Paul. 2004. *Politics in Time: History, Institutions, and Social Analysis.* Princeton, NJ: Princeton University Press.

Politico. 2017. "Dutch Lower House Backs EU-Ukraine Agreement." 22 February 2017. http://www.politico.eu.

Reichert, M. Shawn, and Bernadette M.E. Jungblut. 2007. "European Union External Trade Policy: Multilevel Principal-Agent Relationships." *Policy Studies Journal* 35 (3): 395–418.

Reuters. 2016. "Dutch Activists Amassing Signatures for Referendum on EU-Canada Trade Deal." 4 November 2016. http://www.reuters.com.

Rodrik, Dani. 1995. "Political Economy of Trade Policy." In *Handbook of International Economics*, vol. 3, edited by Gene Grossman and Kenneth Rogoff, 1457–94. Amsterdam: Elsevier.

Ross, Alison. 2016. "Sign CETA as a 'Mixed' Agreement, Urges
European Commission." *Global Arbitration Review*, 7 July 2016. http://
globalarbitrationreview.com.

Sofia Globe. 2017. "Bulgaria Constitutional Court Asked to Make Binding
Interpretation in Relation to CETA." 18 July 2017. https://sofiaglobe.com.

Sputnik News. 2016. "Bulgaria, Romania Endorse CETA in Exchange for Visa-
Free Regime with Canada." 21 October 2016. https://sputniknews.com.

Streinz, Rudolf. 2015. "Disputes on TTIP: Does the Agreement Need the
Consent of the German Parliament?" In *Trade Policy between Law, Diplomacy
and Scholarship*, edited by C. Hermann, B. Simma, and R. Streinz, 271–95.
New York: Springer.

TFEU (Treaty on the Functioning of the European Union). 2008. Consolidated
version. OJ C 326, 26 October 2012. http://eur-lex.europa.eu.

Wallace, Helen, Mark A. Pollack, and Alasdair R. Young, eds. 2015. *Policy-
Making in the European Union*. Oxford: Oxford University Press.

Woolcock, Stephen. 2010. "EU Trade and Investment Policymaking after the
Lisbon Treaty." *Intereconomics* 45 (1): 22–5.

Young, Alasdair R. 2002. *Extending European Cooperation: The European Union
and the "New" International Trade Agenda*. Manchester, UK: Manchester
University Press.

Young, Alasdair R., and John Peterson. 2006. "The EU and the New Trade
Politics." *Journal of European Public Policy* 13 (6): 795–814.

12 Multilevel Party Politics and Trade: The Case of the Social Democrats in the European Parliament and the German Social Democratic Party

MYRIAM MARTINS GISTELINCK

"If we cannot conclude a trade agreement with Canada, with which country will we be able to do so in the future?" For a long time this was the type of sentence one could only hear from trade bureaucrats in Brussels. No one could imagine it would be the topic of conversation among activists at a congress in 2016 of the Social Democratic Party (Sozialdemokratische Partei Deutschlands, SPD) in Germany, one of the largest social democratic parties in Europe. Rarely had there been general party congresses (involving all delegates) on only European politics in Germany. Never before had there been a party congress exclusively on international trade, let alone a congress on a particular trade agreement. It was the most obvious sign that trade policy had changed its nature. It was no longer a policy shaped by technocratic policy interests, but a topic that was suitable for a broad political discussion, capable of mobilizing the private sector, trade unions, environmental groups, consumer organizations, and religious groups alike. It was a topic so controversial that it motivated many ordinary citizens and civil-society groups to make their voice heard by members of political parties, both in the legislative and executive branches at all levels of government in different European countries. Political parties needed to adapt to the new realities of societal mobilization on trade and multilevel politics.

Using the example of the SPD and the Socialists and Democrats Group (S&D) in the European Parliament (EP) during the negotiations for the Transatlantic Trade and Investment Partnership (TTIP) and the ratification process of the European Union-Canada Comprehensive Economic and Trade Agreement (CETA) as a case study, this chapter examines how civil society successfully interacted with parties at the national and European levels and how party members have tried to influence the course of trade negotiations within this multilevel setting. The focus will be the European level and its interaction with the national level. In this sense, it is complementary to the chapter by Garcia on the European Union (EU) after the Lisbon Treaty and the chapter by Broschek, Bußjäger, and Schramek in this volume that analyses the emergence of multilevel trade politics in Austria and Germany, focussing on the federal and the Länder level.

Parliaments and Political Parties in EU Trade Policymaking

The nature of the EU democracy and the role of parliaments is a much-debated topic among scholars of European integration. As argued by Bursens and Hogenauer (2017), different views are rooted in different conceptualizations of the EU. Some argue that the EU has moved beyond being a mere international organization or agency controlled by the member states and that it contains supranational elements. The Union is seen as a proper political system composed of different layers. Indeed, the definition of the EU as a representative democracy in article 10(2) of the Treaty of the European Union raises some expectations when it comes to parliamentary involvement. Yet it is exactly when it comes to the role of parliaments in shaping EU legislation that the EU faces most of its shortcomings. This is also the case for trade policy, certainly as it was before the entry into force of the Lisbon Treaty in 2009, which brought about some important changes (see Garcia in this volume).

Since the Lisbon Treaty the EP must give its consent to all trade agreements before they can enter into force, and Members of the EP have the right to be informed about all trade negotiations, on an equal footing with the Council of Ministers.[1] These changes have certainly shaped the setting in which European parliamentarians follow and monitor trade negotiations directly. However, giving consent or not giving consent to a trade agreement that has been negotiated for months and sometimes even years is quite a blunt instrument of scrutiny. Some scholars compare it to a car in which the European Commission is clearly in the driving seat, the Council sits next to the driver and gives him instructions, and the EP sits in the back and can pull the emergency break (Woolcock 2010).

Authors studying European politics at a more general level stress that even after the implementation of the Lisbon Treaty, the EP has still been deprived of its legislative powers in key domains of EU competence (Corbett, Jacobs, and Neville 2016). Others claim that as a result, parliamentary representation at the EU level is not enough. At least part of the solution to the democratic deficit needs to be found in the

Council of Ministers. Rather than giving an extensive overview of the discussion on the democratic deficit, however, this chapter focuses on the crucial role played by political parties in both representing societal interests and structuring parliamentary and governmental processes. One could even go so far as to say that political parties are the glue between the parliamentary and governmental processes, and also, as I will show below, between different levels of government.

Classical scholarship on political parties has focused primarily on the nation state as the main unit of analysis. However, in recent years a considerable amount of literature has highlighted the multilayered nature of party politics in Europe, which is influenced by both decentralization within the nation state and the creation of the supranational European level. Both processes have generated challenges and opportunities for rallying societal support and creating consensus. According to Detterbeck (2016), comparative research shows that parties across Europe have adopted different strategies to cope with these changes and the reaction at different levels that they entail. While looking at two dimensions – the strength of joint-decision-making structures on the one hand and the autonomy enjoyed by the state branches on the other hand – he created a typology of five different types of parties: consensualist, federalist, confederalist, centralist, and decentralist.

Detterbeck (2016) also analysed the German party system in light of recent changes in the German federal state structure. He concluded that recent changes in the German federal system led to parties making more use of their regional autonomy, but at the same time the incentive for parties to organize in a strong vertically integrated multilevel structure had in essence not declined. He qualified the German parties Christlich Demokratische Union Deutschlands (CDU) and SPD as consensualist parties with a strong tendency towards uniformity and to finding consensus, and their local branches have privileged access to central party decision making.

Building on this conceptual framework, which combines some insights concerning the role of parliaments in a multilevel policy context and the functioning of political parties, the following sections assess how this all applies to the context of trade policymaking, where societal mobilization and politization triggered political party activities at different scales.

Civil-Society Mobilization and the Social Democrats in European Multilevel Trade Politics

For many years the EU's trade policy was considered to be technocratic and far from transparent. As acknowledged by some scholars, the system, based on the two pillars of the European Commission and the Council of Ministers (the Council gives the mandate, and the commission negotiates), facilitated efficiency by keeping trade policy at arm's length from party political and protectionist forces at the national and regional levels (Woolcock 2010).

National and EU negotiation positions were based largely on informal contacts with private sector organizations. In the last decade the surge of integrated supply chains (and therefore the need for more regulatory convergence), the gradual opening of trade in services, ever-increasing investment flows, and the rise of the emerging powers obliged Europe to reflect deeply on the role and nature of trade policy. As a result of increased parliamentary involvement, but also because of the changing nature of trade itself, EU trade policy had to accommodate a wider range of interests. The positions of the member states could generally be described in terms of two main blocs: the post-industrial liberal north and the industrial, more cautious and more defensive south. Over the years more voices joined the debate on international trade and globalization, including trade unions, non-governmental organizations (NGOs), environmental groups, and consumer organizations. The discussion is no longer confined to small groups of civil servants and stakeholders. The rejection of the Anti-counterfeiting Trade Agreement, an agreement aimed at combating counterfeiting, by the EP and by the governments and parliaments of several member states, served as a clear demonstration of this shift: an unprecedented mobilization of activists ultimately resulted in the treaty rejection.

The negotiations of the TTIP took to a higher level the discussion and the need for more transparency. By 2016 a significantly prominent political discussion on trade and globalization had emerged at the European level and at the national or regional level in some member states.

First Came CETA

One can still consider the public debate on trade as a quite recent phenomenon. When the EU and Canada started to negotiate CETA in 2009, the prospect of having an agreement with Canada was considered largely uncontroversial by most national parties, in all national and regional parliaments and in the EP, but not by a minority of Green and extreme-left parties. When it comes to the EP, one can argue that its composition at that time played a large role. In a parliament with 757 seats, the pro-trade centre-right groups (European People's Party, the Alliance of Liberals and Democrats of Europe, and the European Conservative and Reformists) had a comfortable majority of 414 votes.

Therefore, every free trade agreement could almost automatically count on a significant amount of support from parliamentarians and parties across different member states, and it was very difficult to break this pro-free trade consensus. On the centre left of the political spectrum (the S&D group), parliamentarians highlighted some sensitive areas and priorities for different trade agreements, such as the importance of ambitious sustainable-development chapters, but generally spoke in favour of trade and trade agreements. This was not different for an agreement with Canada.

At the level of civil society, attention to CETA was limited to that of a couple of critical NGOs with considerable trade expertise and that of public service unions. Most of the more critical analysis of CETA was brought forward by Canadian, rather than European, civil-society groups and experts. This lack of European civil-society mobilization resulted in a lack of interest and activity by political parties within national and regional parties until roughly 2013. Indeed, Canada was seen as a country with similar values, norms, and standards to those of Europe. An agreement with Canada might bring limited economic benefits and opportunities, but it was seen as important from a political perspective. Only a few sensitive issues stood out: the potential rise of beef imports to the EU, the import of energy from Canadian oil sands, Canada's challenge in the World Trade Organization to the EU's ban on seal products, and the protection of investments and public services.

It was therefore no surprise that the EP expressed support for the conduct of the negotiations by the European Commission (European Parliament 2011). The multilevel character of the new setting of negotiations, in which accountability was needed towards both the Council and the EP, did not seem to have a substantial impact on the negotiation autonomy of the commission, mainly because of the lack of societal mobilization.

Then Came TTIP

When the negotiations on the TTIP started in 2013, the EP had already gained increasing powers when it came to trade agreements. This had certainly created an additional potential layer of accountability for European trade negotiators, which both civil society and political parties across Europe had started to understand. They also understood that access to negotiation texts and the course of negotiations was key because one of the concerns shared by all groups from the beginning had been the lack of transparency.

Since the entry into force of the Lisbon Treaty the EP has been actively looking for cooperation agreements with the Council and the commission, which would ensure access to negotiation documents not only for parliamentarians in the exercise of their parliamentary scrutiny but also for the general public and their constituencies. Through contacts within national party structures between European parliamentarians and national parliamentarians, national and regional parliamentarians were also increasingly equipped and mobilized to claim their rights to increased access to documents within the context of trade negotiations and, in particular, the negotiations on TTIP.

European parliamentarians, just like other parliamentarians, developed several informal and formal tools to influence the course of different trade negotiations and to ensure that their positions were heard and taken into account. Ultimately, a resolution by the EP would include the main parameters, red lines, and must-haves for the agreement to be adopted by this institution. When a resolution on a certain trade agreement is being prepared, the multilevel structure of trade policy-making can be exploited to the fullest because the EP's position will be an additional set of criteria that negotiators will have to take into account, next to the wishes of individual member states and the collective preferences of the Council. These different positions and criteria do not necessarily contradict each other. On the contrary, they often reinforce each other and consequently often narrow down significantly the negotiators' room for manoeuvre and the prospect of a deal. They can also push for certain key changes in trade agreements, as happened in the case of CETA.

Before the formal start of the negotiations and before the final conclusions of the EU-US high-level working group on jobs and growth – which was established with the objective of examining the opportunities of a comprehensive trade agreement between the EU and the United States – the EP had adopted a resolution expressing its strong support for the work of this working group. The same resolution, adopted in 2012, highlighted many of the offensive interests of European businesses in these negotiations and the need for an ambitious approach to TTIP, going beyond the mere reduction of tariffs. The need for greater harmonization of regulatory regimes, something that is considered to be quite new in trade agreements and that would prove to be extremely sensitive for European citizens, is seen as a way to overcome the many obstacles to transatlantic trade.

At the very moment in May 2013 that the Council of Ministers was discussing the mandate to give to the European Commission to negotiate a comprehensive trade agreement with the United States, the EP adopted another resolution. This resolution had the clear objective of influencing the Council's mandate and formulating a set of the EP's own priorities for the negotiations. As the scope and format of the negotiations became clearer, and the negotiations themselves gained more attention among civil-society groups and national parties, slowly the EP's position towards the negotiations became a bit more "defensive," and the protection of standards, labour rights, consumer rights, and the environment gained more attention. By 2013, access to relevant negotiation documents and contacts with negotiators, stakeholders, and civil society groups, had intensified considerably. As civil society was starting to mobilize, political groups from the left and the centre left (e.g., Greens, the United European Left, and the S&D) became vocal on many of the existing concerns among European citizens.

One of the controversial points of the text that political parties drafted together when discussing the resolution in 2013 was investor-state-dispute settlement (ISDS), as they had in the discussion on CETA. As there was no united position on the topic among political groups (centre-right groups were in favour, and centre-left groups were against), no relevant paragraph was included. A broad majority of political parties agreed, however, that the topic of audio-visual services should be excluded from the negotiations, something that was very difficult for the United States to swallow (European Parliament 2013). In the end, because the Council of Ministers had also made a similar request for exclusion in their mandate, the European Commission was obliged to revise its negotiating strategy and not to negotiate on this topic with the United States. This was a clear example of how the multilevel context of trade negotiations had clearly narrowed the room for negotiations for the European Commission.

Both the 2012 and the 2013 resolution were adopted with a broad support among political groups, including the centre-left S&D with the exception of some of its Belgian and French members. This support for the pro-trade text of the resolutions reflected the broad pro-trade consensus among political groups across the political spectrum, except those of the extreme left. However, in 2013, civil-society mobilization, in particular with regard to the controversial ISDS, led to increased interest and attention by parliamentarians in a couple of key member states, such as Germany, Austria, and France. From the moment the trade unions started to pick up the critical campaigns on ISDS and TTIP, social democratic parties across Europe understood that this was a topic that needed to be understood and dealt with within their political campaigns.

European Elections 2014

At the outset of the campaign for the 2014 European elections it was clear that TTIP would become an issue. Campaign groups such as "Stop TTIP" throughout Europe, or Campact in Germany, were pressing potential candidates very hard on their stance on this important trade agreement. As a result, political parties at the national and European levels started to develop their own positions towards TTIP. Within the social democratic family, discussions were particularly difficult because a compromise had to be found between those with a very critical position on TTIP and those who saw an opportunity in the negotiations of a trade agreement with the United States. In the end, social democratic parliamentarians agreed to campaign on the joint platform, reflecting in a way the "consensualist" tradition of the main political parties in Western Europe as defined by Detterbeck and Hepburn (2013).

Although negotiations with the United States on a comprehensive trade agreement were seen as an opportunity, an agreement would only be acceptable if it fulfilled a range of criteria. First, negotiations would have to be conducted in full transparency. Second, an agreement should not lead to lower EU standards in the areas of food, the environment, and consumer protection. The agreement should include the objective of ratification and implementation by the United States and the EU of all International Labour Organization core conventions. Last, but not least, social democratic parties would oppose the inclusion of the controversial ISDS system (which was the S&D's position on TTIP in 2014).

The German Social Democratic Party on TTIP

Awareness of TTIP and hence political mobilization has never been equal across the whole EU. In some member states, such as Lithuania and Estonia, only business groups had a keen interest in the TTIP negotiations, and in general terms trade-related topics were largely absent from the political radar. In other member states, such as Germany and Austria, campaign groups managed to get thousands of people to protest in the streets against a potential trade deal (see Broschek, Bußjäger, and Schramek in this volume). In Germany the relative success of the anti-TTIP campaign was undoubtedly due to the very active role played by Campact, an online platform for public engagement. Through its critical campaign on TTIP many citizens across Germany became engaged with their local councillors, party activists, and members of regional, federal, and European parliaments on many topics related to the partnership. Next to Campact, many other civil-society organizations, development NGOs, consumer and environmental groups, and, last but certainly not least, trade unions became active.

The dynamics of grass-roots campaigning was not limited to civil society; it gradually shifted towards political parties, including the SPD. As local party representatives were questioned by citizens and civil society about their stance on TTIP, local activists pushed the party leadership to promote the discussion within the party and with their most important allies, the trade unions. Civil-society groups realized that the SPD was a very important target for their campaigns. Not only was the party in a coalition government with the CDU, but also the negotiations fell under the direct responsibility of Sigmar Gabriel, the federal minister of economy and energy and the party leader.

It came as no surprise, therefore, that in September 2014 the SPD held a special party congress exclusively on TTIP. As in other social democratic parties throughout Europe, considerable disagreement existed between those who wanted to send a more positive message on TTIP and those who wanted to reflect the very critical stance towards the agreement that was emerging among German civil-society groups and trade unions. Together with the main trade union organization, Deutscher Gewerkschaftsbund, the party adopted an important decision. The decision started from the assumption that concerns raised in the societal debate in Germany by citizens, trade unions, NGOs, and consumer groups needed to be taken seriously. A "good TTIP" would certainly bring many economic opportunities, but the agreement had to fulfil an important list of criteria if it were to be acceptable: TTIP should not lower environmental, health, and consumer-protection standards; it should protect public services and personal data and promote financial stability; democratic procedures should not be circumvented; investment protection was not needed; and, above all, transparency and civil-society involvement in the negotiations should drastically improve (SPD 2014).

The text of the decision became the basis of a series of activities undertaken and supported by SPD members, from numerous internal party discussions at all levels to city council resolutions, to discussions and reports in the Bundestag and the Bundesrat, to initiatives taken for more transparency by the Ministry of Economy. Owing to societal pressure, all parties in Germany, including the centre right, were forced to engage in internal discussions on TTIP and react to the concerns of ordinary citizens as well as those of their usual pro-free-trade constituencies.

Back in the EP, the newly elected chair of the Committee on International Trade, SPD member Bernd Lange, took up his chairmanship when societal mobilization against TTIP was reaching its peak. Within the EP the majorities had shifted after the European elections, and the pro-trade consensus seemed to have disappeared. The centre-right groups Alliance of Liberals and Democrats for Europe, European People's Party, and European Conservatives and Reformists had 358 votes out of 757 and were therefore dependent on the centre-left S&D to obtain a majority. Within the S&D, members had generally also become more critical and active on trade issues as a result of the interaction with national anti-TTIP platforms. Many parliamentarians were keen on having their position on TTIP heard by the public. This was no different for the SPD members. In 2015 the Committee on International Trade decided to draft a resolution that would take stock of the opportunities and concerns related to TTIP after two years of negotiations.

The initial text received three thousand amendments from members of almost all the different committees in the EP, including committees responsible for agriculture and industrial and employment policies, but also those dealing with culture and education, for instance. From the beginning it was clear that adopting a resolution in support of the TTIP negotiations would be a challenge. In the end the EP adopted a resolution with more than fifty detailed recommendations concerning different areas, reflecting the many concerns that had been raised by civil society – the maintenance of standards, the importance of democratic control, the protection of labour rights, and the provision of public services, among many others – while expressing cautious support for the negotiations (European Parliament 2015).

On the thorny issue of ISDS, the resolution included the following clause: "to replace the ISDS system with a *new* system of resolving disputes between investors and states, which is subject to democratic principles and scrutiny, where potential cases are treated in a transparent manner by publicly appointed, independent professional judges in public hearings … , where jurisdiction of courts of the European Union and the Member States is respected" (European Parliament 2015; italics added). The clause, together with some additional pressure and proposals from the German government, supported by other social democrat ministers in the Council, led the European Commission to make a new proposal in the context of TTIP negotiations to replace the ad hoc ISDS system with a more permanent system of dispute settlement, the investment court system.

The resolution of the EP reflected many of the issues highlighted in the SPD's party-convention decision. However, it was particularly the clause on ISDS, a highly sensitive topic, that changed the direction of the TTIP negotiations. The change in the European Commission's negotiation stance was a result of the interaction between several factors in a multilevel setting, including the changes within the commission itself. Nevertheless, the joint push by the Council and the EP, shaped by political dynamics within the SPD as a junior coalition partner in the German government, was definitely the decisive factor.

The German Social Democratic Party and the Ratification of CETA

While discussions on TTIP gained considerable attention in 2013–15, CETA disappeared into the background. After the conclusion of the negotiations in 2014, the text was being legally scrubbed and translated by the European Commission. As the text was published, some civil-society groups and parliamentarians had the opportunity to thoroughly analyse and discuss it, but this happened mostly below the radar. However, already, back in September 2014, SPD minister Sigmar Gabriel had raised concerns about ISDS in CETA and had called for its removal from the agreement. Together with other social democrat ministers in the Council, including those from the Netherlands, Luxembourg, and Sweden, he started working on a possible review of the CETA text with an eye to moving away from the ISDS system towards a more permanent international investment court. For the ministers it was clear from the outset that any innovation in this regard proposed for TTIP would have to be included in CETA too. The European Commission, however, had been very reluctant to reopen the negotiated CETA agreement, fearing that the agreement as a whole would fall apart.

Meanwhile, social mobilization on TTIP had only intensified, and activists started successfully linking TTIP with CETA, which was considered to be "TTIP through the backdoor." In October 2015 more than 100,000 protesters gathered in Berlin to protest against TTIP and CETA. A couple of months later the SPD organized another party congress on CETA and TTIP, possibly when civil-society mobilization against the two agreements was at its peak. SPD members were highly divided on the topic, with the party base being far more critical than the party leadership, which was already unpopular for other reasons outside of CETA. Nevertheless, the adopted decision gave essentially the same message as had the decision in 2014: yes to CETA and TTIP but under certain important conditions. Moreover, the decision expresses its support of Sigmar Gabriel's proposal for an international investment court and called for the inclusion of this system in both TTIP and CETA. An interesting aspect of this party decision is its request for a broad political debate on trade agreements at all levels of government, alluding to the need for national and regional ratification of CETA. This was a clear concession from the party leadership to the regional party branches and a sign that the SPD, as a "consensualist" party, had to adapt to increasingly autonomous regional branches. This approach would prove to be quite controversial in light of the European Commission's claims of exclusive competence over trade matters.

Meanwhile, in Canada the liberal-progressive Trudeau government took office in November 2015. The Canadian international trade minister, Chrystia Freeland, had understood that even though CETA negotiations had already been concluded under the Stephen Harper government, its final ratification process would be lengthy and difficult. Moreover, discussions on the benefits of trade and, to a lesser extent, on ISDS were also very much alive in Canada. The Liberal government seemed to have a keen interest both in concluding CETA as soon as possible and in giving the agreement its own "Canadian-liberal" touch. As soon as the trade minister was nominated, initial contacts were established between Minister Sigmar Gabriel, Chairman Bernd Lange of the EP's Committee on International Trade, President Martin Schulz of the EP, and the Trudeau government. The main objective of these informal contacts was to convince the Canadian government that changes were needed in the agreement in, among others, the investment chapter in order to make it acceptable both to the SPD in Germany and to the EP as a whole. Indeed, in order for there to be a majority in the EP in support of CETA, a significant majority within the S&D would need to vote in favour of the agreement; within the alliance, the twenty-seven SPD members played a leading role. It is interesting to note here that, just like in the Bundestag, the members of the S&D in the EP organize their activities and determine their positions both in thematic working groups (for instance, on international trade) and in national delegations. Party discipline (members all defending the same line) is very high within national delegations, and certainly higher than within thematic working groups.

The European Commission, however, was very cautious about entering into renegotiations with the Canadian government for fear of derailing the process and also because it did not want to be seen as favouring one particular position, which was not shared by other member states or other political groups. The Canadian government shared these concerns to a certain extent. However, it was ready to engage as much as possible with the critical voices in Europe, not only in Germany but also in Austria, Luxembourg, and Belgium. In the end, the pressure was such that by February 2016 Canada and the EU had integrated almost all the elements of the new investment court system into the legally scrubbed text of CETA.

After publication of the text in 2016 the formal signature process could start in the European Council, which would be followed by a consent procedure in the EP. The SPD leadership, however, had promised a thorough and broad discussion on CETA within the party, including its delegation in the EP, as well as the entire party base and the trade unions. Organizing a political discussion on the basis of a legal text of more than a thousand pages of a highly complex trade agreement was definitely not an easy task and took several months. Meanwhile, the German trade unions had also become active. Together with their counterparts in Canada, the Canadian Labour Council, they had also adopted a list of points of criticism of CETA and changes that would need to be incorporated (DGB, 2016). During the discussion inside the SPD the trade unions were highly influential, in particular among those groups inside the party that were traditionally more on the left and had historical ties with the trade unions. Interestingly enough, in those regions where the SPD was weaker and faced more party competition, such as Bavaria, positions on trade were more radical. Here SPD branches saw in their opposition to CETA a way to reconnect to a societal base that they were gradually losing.

In the end a party congress was organized for September 2016 at which the SPD position on CETA would be voted by a group of five hundred delegates. A couple of days before that important party congress, three positions on CETA seemed to emerge: those in favour of CETA, those against, and those who would like to see some additional guarantees and changes. Minister Gabriel and Minister Freeland had issued a joint statement in Canada, which was specially designed to appease the critical branch of the SPD and the trade unions (Gabriel and Freeland, 2016). In the statement, both ministers call upon the European Commission and the Canadian government to agree on further clarifications regarding important aspects of the agreement prior to the European Council's signature, on the topics of investment protection, sustainable development, public services, and public procurement.

The party congress adopted a final decision, which by many in Europe was interpreted as a green light to CETA, but in reality it consisted of a positive appreciation of the agreement and a list of issues that needed to be further clarified during the ratification process: standards of investment protection, adherence to the precautionary principle, enforcement of the sustainable-development chapter, the role and responsibilities of the joint committee responsible for implementing CETA, the exclusion of public services, and the relationship between CETA and the Paris

Agreement on climate change (SPD 2016). The final decision was a result of a compromise amendment between the party leadership (in favour of CETA) and the more critical branches of the party, supported by a couple of key regional party figures, such as Stephan Weil, minister president of Lower Saxony.

The elements of the decision were the result of a long discussion process within the SPD in Germany, but they also reflected the issues that were the object of debate in other European countries. The SPD decision became the basis of the Joint Interpretative Instrument that was attached to CETA in October 2016 after lengthy discussions with the representatives of other member states, and not the least with the government of Wallonia.

After the decision at the party convention the road was clear for the SPD representatives in the EP to vote in favour of CETA. The interpretative declaration had appeased other social democrats in different European countries, and in the end the EP gave its consent, with 416 out of 757 votes in favour, in February 2017.

Conclusion

The changing nature of trade, the enhanced role of parliaments in the scrutiny of international trade agreements, and TTIP as a "game changer" have led to increased civil-society activism in different European countries, first on TTIP and then on CETA. In Germany, civil-society engagement with political parties at all level of governments forced parties, and in particular the SPD, to react and respond to this multilevel reality with both opportunities and risks.

Opportunities are created when political parties function as a unifying force between party members who have different institutional roles. While working together throughout the process in these different roles, social democrat party members (parliamentarians or ministers) were to an extent successful in achieving their political priorities. Precisely because of coordinated party activities at different levels whereby links were made across institutions (Council and EP), across countries (European social democrats, Canadian Liberals, and German SPD), and with civil society (SPD and trade unions), some aspects of the negotiations and the agreement could eventually be changed in accordance with their political preference, as was the case for the ISDS mechanism in TTIP and CETA.

However, the multilevel structure also creates certain challenges. When civil-society activism creates incentives for autonomous behaviour by regional, national, or European party levels, it becomes increasingly difficult to unite the party behind one position. Neverthe-less, the integrated structure of the SPD (and the S&D) and its decision making seem to have led in the end to a consensual outcome. In the case of CETA and TTIP there appear to have been enough incentives within the party for members to rally behind the position of the party leadership.

NOTE

1 The Council of Ministers comprises ministers of member state governments. Accordingly, it convenes in different constellations. It is also known as the Council of the European Union, or simply the Council.

REFERENCES

Bursens, Peter, and Anna-Lena Hogenauer. 2017. "Regional Parliaments in the EU Multilevel Parliamentary System." *Journal of Legislative Studies* 23 (2): 127–43.

Corbett, Richard, Francis Jacobs, and Darren Neville. 2016. *The European Parliament*. 9th ed. London: John Harper.

Detterbeck, Klaus. 2016. "Party Inertia amid Federal Change? Stability and Adaptation in German Parties." *German Politics* 25 (2): 265–85.

Detterbeck, Klaus, and Eve Hepburn. 2013. "Federalism, Regionalism, and the Dynamics of Party Politics." In *Routledge Handbook of Regionalism and Federalism*, edited by J. Loughlin, J. Kincaid, and W. Swenden, 92–108. London: Routledge.

DGB (Deutscher Gewerkschaftsbund). 2016. *Statement of the DGB: Regarding the Updated Version of the EU Free Trade Agreement with Canada (Comprehensive Economic and Trade Agreement, CETA) after the Process of Legal Scrubbing*. 5 April 2016. Berlin. Accessed 8 November 2019. https://www.dgb.de

European Parliament. 2011. *European Parliament Resolution of 8 June 2011 on EU-Canada trade relations*. 2011/2623(RSP). Strasbourg. Accessed 8 November 2019. http://www.europarl.europa.eu.

– 2013. *European Parliament Resolution of 23 May 2013 on EU Trade and Investment Negotiations with the United States of America*. 2013/2558(RSP). Strasbourg. Accessed 8 November 2019. https://www.europarl.europa.eu.

– 2015. *European Parliament Resolution of 8 July 2015 Containing the European Parliament's Recommendations to the European Commission on the Negotiations for the Transatlantic Trade and Investment Partnership (TTIP)*. 2014/2228(INI). Strasbourg. Accessed 8 November 2019. http://www.europarl.europa.eu.

Gabriel, Sigmar, and Chrystia Freeland. 2016. *Gemeinsame Erklärung: Fortschrittliche Handelspolitik – CETA und darüber hinaus.* Berlin: Bundesministerium für Wirtschaft und Energie. Accessed 25 November 2019. https://www.bmwi.de/.
SPD (Sozialdemokratische Partei Deutschlands). 2014. Globalisierung gestalten-fairen Handel ermöglichen-demokratische Grundsätze gewährleisten. Resolution. Berlin.
– 2016. Globaler Handel braucht fortschrittliche Regeln. Resolution, 19 September 2016. Wolfsburg.
Woolcock, Stephen. 2010. "EU Trade and Investment Policymaking after the Lisbon Treaty." *Intereconomics* 45 (1): 22–5.

13 Municipal-Level Trade Contestation: Activists and Local Governments, from the Multilateral Agreement on Investment to the Transatlantic Trade and Investment Partnership

GABRIEL SILES-BRÜGGE AND MICHAEL STRANGE

This chapter considers the increasing instance of municipal governments allying with social movement organizations (SMOs) in order to formally contest global trade governance.[1] In such cases we see a blurring between state and civil society, as governmental actors engage in societal activism targeted at other levels of government. As such, SMOs enter into multilevel trade negotiations between different organs of the state (as charted by other chapters in this volume). Witnessed most recently during contestation around a string of preferential trade negotiations – including on the European Union-United States Transatlantic Trade and Investment Partnership (TTIP), the European Union-Canada Comprehensive Economic and Trade Agreement (CETA), the plurilateral Trade in Services Agreement (TiSA), and the Trans-Pacific Partnership (TPP) – the phenomenon of collaboration between local governmental actors and SMOs has a longer pedigree going back at least to the General Agreement on Trade in Services (GATS) and Multilateral Agreement on Investment (MAI) negotiations (respectively, in the early 2000s and late 1990s). Such actions have included the passing of governmental motions criticizing the negotiations, going as far in some cases as the establishment of "free zones" – formal statements that a municipality is "symbolically" free of TTIP (or other agreement) and/or otherwise exempt from its provisions.

This municipal activism poses a puzzle. While the increasingly "behind-the-border" provisions of trade agreements may affect the autonomy of local government, it is not always clear that those municipalities declared as free zones would be able to avoid compliance with any trade agreement and so exit global trade governance. Even in the case of less ambitious resolutions merely objecting to aspects of trade and investment agreements, it is important to ask why municipal actors would be responsive to SMOs (which usually initiate the process by presenting sample motions), challenging actions being driven by other *state* actors. For one thing, the policy being contested is ultimately decided at higher levels of government and involves a process of international negotiation and compromise with third parties. What is more, municipal activism involves the collaboration of agents that are often seen as opposed, namely governmental actors and SMOs. While in many cases the passing of critical motions requires only limited resources, governmental actors at all levels take seriously the act of stating formal positions. Furthermore, municipalities have the option to ignore SMOs with, it would seem, little consequence. Trade contestation at the municipal level appears misplaced if we examine it through the lens of conventional SMO-state interaction or merely in terms of how the federal institutional configuration of some states or entities empowers some sub-federal governments. However, we suggest that it is evident that we need to reconsider the political space in which global trade governance is or is not contested.

There is already a broad literature of relevance to this chapter, focusing on several related aspects including the multiple strategies adopted by trade justice groups (e.g., Bàndy and Smith 2005; Danaher and Mark 2003; P.J. Smith and Smythe 1999); alliances between local governments and SMOs (e.g., Verhoeven and Duyvendak 2017); and the role of the local level as a means of engaging global politics – so-called glocal politics (Shepard and Hayduk 2002; see also Sperling 2009). The importance of the local level and free zones also has a history going back to the anti-nuclear movement (Ennis and Schreuer 1987; J. Smith 2001). And existing research has traced the growing role played by city and municipal governments in forming networks to achieve more progressive forms of globalization than their national counterparts have, such as in climate-change governance and in providing sanctuary for irregular migrants (e.g., Bulkeley 2010; Lundberg and Strange 2017). However, arguably this has not sufficiently considered the interaction between SMOs and the municipal governments they have targeted, or the new forms of contestation engendered by their collaboration.

The chapter is structured as follows. First, we consider recent work on local "governmental activism" (Verhoeven and Duyvendak 2017) and how it challenges existing dichotomous characterizations of SMOs and governmental actors as the challenger or the challenged. Second, the chapter maps existing patterns of municipal-level trade contestation, focusing on the motions passed by local governments; this began in North America with the MAI but has since become much more prevalent within western Europe. Third, and drawing upon our theoretical

326 Gabriel Siles-Brügge and Michael Strange

discussion, the chapter compares several key moments in which we can observe municipal-level trade contestation from the perspective of governmental actors. Our argument is that rather than municipal-level trade contestation being seen as a purely symbolic act with few practical implications, it represents an interesting field of contestation in its own right. Specifically, it reflects the complex identities of SMOs and governmental actors – multi-scalar in the case of the former, confounding the challenger-challenged distinction in the case of the latter. The interaction of these identities leads to a form of "mimetic challenge" in global trade governance, the use of the language or norms of the dominant as a form of contestation by the comparatively weak (Hobson and Seabrooke 2007). It needs to be made clear from the outset that municipality activism cannot be viewed exclusively in terms of influencing public opinion or discourse, because, even in the case of politicized trade negotiations, there is not always wider societal engagement in contesting trade agreements (see, for example, De Ville and Siles-Brügge 2016, 108–10). As noted by one Austrian activist, an aspect of their campaign against the GATS was to network various organizations and thus turn it into "a topic of conversation amongst politically interested people" (authors' translation of Stopp-GATS Kampagne 2004, 39). Our starting point is therefore the question of how SMOs define themselves and engage with their (often local) membership.

Theorizing Municipal-Level Trade Contestation

Many scholars have noted that during the second half of the twentieth century social movements changed from being based on mass membership to acting increasingly as centralized and professional lobbyists (e.g., Skocpol 2004). This development might well be understood as a rational response to a changing context that determines what it is possible to do in politics, in which activism is explained in terms of when and how groups can mobilize resources (McCarthy and Zald 1977). However, while acknowledging that the focus on resource mobilization and on the subsequent concept of political opportunity structures (Princen and Kerremans 2008) has proven utility, some have warned that it also risks leading us to overlook important developments (Voss and Williams 2012). That is because, as Voss and Williams argue, the assumption that activists only act according to the prevalent political opportunity structure of their time overprivileges dominant institutions. Local forms of contestation with no direct means to have an impact on the institutions in which policy decisions are made are either dismissed or treated as being less significant.

For Voss and Williams, where social movements have shifted away from being based on mass membership, this can be explained as part of a broader societal shift in which the state has retreated from an ever-greater sphere of society, such that individuals' relationship to power feels increasingly alienated (2012, 358–9). The collapse of collective identities serves as an explanation as much as institutional changes do. For example, itinerant work patterns and communities, as well as the post-industrial collapse of class identity, dislocated many of the traditional alliances that had originally fuelled the labour movement. This has led scholarship on activism to focusing, since at least the late 1990s, on the role that identity politics plays in shaping social movements (Della Porta and Diani 1999).

In the matter of global trade governance, many activists are strategically playful with the question of scale in terms of how they organize and of how they express their collective action *and identity* – whether as, for example, a French, European, or global campaign (Routledge 2003). Multiple scales are also utilized alongside one another. For example, as part of articulating and promoting the collective action involved, transnational networks of activists have produced global group petitions (Strange 2011, 2013) in which the network is framed as global or European, but the list of groups is categorized according to nation states.

The multi-scalar playfulness of SMOs is evident where research has traced their engagement with multiple levels of governance, including the supranational, national, and local (Routledge, Cumbers, and Nativel 2007). SMOs have often made use of municipal or local scales of government to initiate formal motions and other regulatory mechanisms. These need not always have a direct impact on the national or supranational level, but that they take place means these actions are significant for SMOs because they require substantial resources. Many of the SMOs involved operate via a decentralized structure in which much of their mobilization takes place at the local scale. Actions targeting local government can be understood in part as helping to develop the identity of the SMO and its membership. How campaigns are framed with respect to scale can be analysed in terms of geographic signifiers – that is, whenever a campaign action is explicitly framed in terms of geography, for example as British, European, or global. Such signifiers provide a visible means through which the collective action necessary for contestation acquires the identity that helps both politicize and unify an often eclectic mix of political demands (Strange 2013). Where those scales are already recognized, they provide existing frames that may be utilized by campaigners to express solidarity with others who feel affinity with that particular geographic signifier.

This brings us to the role of local governments in municipal-level trade contestation. Are they merely an "empty vessel" and tool to be wielded by social movements? Imrat Verhoeven and Jan Willem Duyvendak (2017, 566) bemoan that the existing social-movement literature has given insufficient attention to the role of such actors in their own right. For one thing, as they argue, it often relies on dichotomizing the state and social movements, treating the latter as being challengers to state authority. It is also overly focused on the movements or merely treats the state as a context (a political opportunity structure), ignoring the agency of governmental actors.

One of the central premises of our chapter is that we need to see municipal-level trade contestation as a *joint* action of governments and social movements. In doing so, we draw on the concept of "governmental activism" developed by Verhoeven and Duyvendak. They define it as "politicians, civil servants and governmental players engaging with citizens, SMOs/NGOs and sometimes business in contentious claims-making to alter or redress policies proposed by other governmental players" (2017, 565). Notably, they cite as examples the TTIP-free zones being studied here. Building on Tilly and Tarrow's (2015) classic framework, Verhoeven and Duyvendak (2017, 567) propose that governmental activism can be seen as a form of "contentious governance." Governmental actors are themselves *also* the "initiators" of contentious claim-making, engaged in "strategic interactions" with SMOs and their opponents in government that are marked by "mutual dependencies" (Verhoeven and Duyvendak 2017, 567–8). Sub-national governmental actors may increasingly depend on SMOs in order to strengthen their relative authority but are still in a hierarchical relationship to national governments.

As in the case of states, provinces, and member states, agreements such as the MAI, GATS, TTIP, and CETA have explicitly included municipalities (or foreseen them to be included) within their scope of application – with potential implications for the autonomy of local governments to deliver public services, for example, apply preferential procurement policies, or violate foreign-investor rights as spelled out in investor-protection clauses (see Aspey and Butler 2017, 237; Global Affairs Canada 2017; Koivusalo and Tritter 2014, 103). However, municipalities have access to fewer formal, institutionalized exit and voice options than have a number of the other sub-federal actors considered in this volume (see Hirschmann 1970). In the case of exit, EU member states (and in some cases sub-national parliaments) have had the formal legal power to refuse to sign and/or ratify trade agreements (see Bollen, De Ville, and Gheyle in this volume). Canadian provinces, for their part, have historically been able to resist implementation of certain provisions within their jurisdiction as a result of constitutional ambiguities (Kukucha 2005; see Paquin, and Hederer and Leblond, in this volume). While there is some debate on the matter, a number of scholars would argue that the US constitutional situation is less ambiguous – with no legal ability for states (and less so for municipalities) to avoid federal pre-emption in the area of international trade policy – although there may be important political constraints to such action when it comes to, for example, procurement policy (Egan in this volume; Kukucha 2015, 226, 229).

Municipalities also have fewer opportunities for voice. They do not benefit from the formalized trade-policy-consultation mechanisms that apply to EU member states in the European Council, and thus rely on making their views known either by pressuring their national governments and parliamentarians or Members of the European Parliament (MEPs), or by participating in more informal consultation mechanisms such as the Civil Society Dialogue of the European Commission's Directorate-General for Trade. Although the Federation of Canadian Municipalities is consulted as part of the Federal-Provincial-Territorial Committee on Trade (C-Trade), provinces have tended to play a much more prominent role. More recently (in the CETA negotiations), they even participated in the actual negotiations, which resulted in municipal-level procurement commitments that many local governments had opposed (Aspey and Butler 2017, 237; Trew 2013, 572–3). Although, in the United States, representatives of both states and municipalities participate in the Intergovernmental Policy Advisory Committee of the Office of the United States Trade Representative (USTR), "it has produced limited policy recommendations to the USTR," with US states (which already have a limited institutional capacity for monitoring trade issues, and municipalities even less so) often seeking other means of making their views known (Kukucha 2015, 230–1; see also Freudlsperger 2017; for a list of committee membership see IGPAC 2018).

As a result, and in contrast to the case of some nuclear free zones in the 1980s (see Ennis and Schreuer 1987, 396), the municipalities that pass motions signalling an "exit" from trade and investment agreements are thus doing so on a symbolic basis (although this is in itself not insignificant, as we argue, because of the formal positioning taken vis-à-vis other state actors) and potentially as a means of exercising voice. Collaborating with SMOs provides a means of dealing with the institutional constraints imposed by limited competences in the field of trade policy. Thus, and counter-intuitively to the political-opportunity-structure framework (and chapters in this volume focusing on federal institutional configurations), a lack of formal competences may partly account for the existence of activism at this level.

We therefore find the focus on municipal governmental activism to be a useful addition to the social movement literature. However, we contend that the framework presented is overly *government-centric* and reliant on the categories of traditional social-movement theory (political-opportunity structures and resources). While scholarly authors are careful to state that activism can originate in both governments and SMOs (Verhoeven and Duyvendak 2017, 565), in practice they focus almost entirely on the agency of governments. Moreover, social movements are merely depicted as the recipients of "ample" governmental resources (broadly defined as including not just financial means but also organizational and ideational means of achieving an end). In contrast, we argue that the benefits of collaboration between SMOs and local governments rest on the new forms of contestation engendered as well as on the exchange of resources. In this aspect, we focus on the processes of identity formation to understand the emergence of these new political alliances.

Understanding municipal-level trade contestation thus goes beyond the governmental-activism model discussed because it highlights not only the role played by SMOs but also the way in which, through the interaction, both types of actor move outside the realm of their prior identities, engaging in actions unlike their usual behaviour. The concept of mimetic challenge as discussed within the "everyday" international-political-economy literature may be helpful in this respect. It refers to incidences in which comparatively "weak actors adopt the discourse and/ or characteristics of the dominant to cloak their resistance-challenges to the legitimacy of the dominant" as a means of highlighting the contradictions within such discourses and practices and delegitimizing them (Hobson and Seabrooke 2007, 17). The utilization of local governmental motions and other bureaucratic mechanisms might be such a form of mimetic challenge by SMOs, emphasizing the legal competences accorded to local government actors in order to contest their supposed usurpation by the accession of national governments and supranational entities to international trade and investment agreements. The *governmental* identity of the municipal actors involved in such activities is therefore key and also a means of highlighting the lack of consultation of such actors in the trade policymaking process. The reliance on mimetic challenge, in turn, might be a sign of their comparative weakness vis-à-vis national and other sub-national governments.[2] That SMOs collaborate with governmental actors in such a way also problematizes a common assumption found in Social Movement Studies in which those two actor types are categorized as "challenger" and "challenged" (see Verhoeven and Duyvendak 2017, 566).

Given the mentioned literature, the analysis that follows is sensitive to there being multiple motives that determine why and how governmental actors and SMOs collaborate at the local level. In addition, it is important to acknowledge that these actors play with scales as part of their identity-making process. Although this latter aspect is most obvious when one studies non-institutionalized actors such as social movements, that municipal governmental actors engage with other scales shows that their identities are not as fixed as would otherwise seem to be the case.

Mapping Municipal-Level Trade Contestation

This section starts with an overview of municipal-level trade contestation. Tables 13.1 and 13.2 chart the number of municipalities that have passed motions critical of specific trade and investment agreements. This is based largely on the information provided on their websites by the SMOs coordinating the respective campaigns, with supplementary information garnered via internet searches.[3] The numbers in the tables should be read longitudinally (i.e., as a means of gauging the level of activity over time). Variations in the number and size of municipalities across countries mean that we should avoid inferring too much from national comparisons. We wanted to focus specifically on the motions here (as opposed to other forms of municipal activism, such as submissions to government inquiries) because of the significant resource investment they entailed for certain SMOs (representing the backbone of their engagement with local government), their important symbolic nature, and what this says about the nature of trade contestation. Likewise, we do not consider the actions of other sub-national governments (which were often associated with the same campaigns), although elsewhere in the chapter we do discuss how such actors provided an avenue for municipal governments to act. Finally, this exercise does not tell us anything about the specific content of these motions – and whether we are dealing with free zones that symbolically exempt themselves from the provisions of the relevant agreements – or more modest documents calling for the revision of certain provisions and/or other issues. These caveats aside, the tables do provide us with an approximate sense of the increasing scale and distribution across time of municipal-level trade contestation.

13.1 Municipal-Level Contestation of the Multilateral Agreement on Investment (MAI) and the General Agreement on Trade in Services (GATS)

	Number of municipalities found to have passed motions	Lead organization
MAI (1998–9)*		
Canada	17	Council of Canadians
United States	16	Public Citizen
Australia	1	Stop MAI Coalition
Japan	1	Peoples' Forum 2001
Switzerland	1	Unknown
United Kingdom	"Several UK local authorities" (Wood 2000, 34)	World Development Movement
GATS (2002–6)*		
France	744	ATTAC France
Austria	388	ATTAC Austria
Belgium	171 (Flanders), 6 (Wallonia), and 1 (Brussels)	11.11.11 (Flanders) & ATTAC France (Wallonia)
Switzerland	93	ATTAC Switzerland
Canada	68	Council of Canadians & ATTAC-Québec
United Kingdom	26	World Development Movement
Italy	10	Questo Mondo non è in Vendita
New Zealand	3	ARENA
Australia	3	Australian Services Union
Germany	1	ATTAC Germany
Hungary	1	Védegylet
Spain	Municipalities in Andalusia, Extremadura, and the Basque Country	ATTAC Spain

Notes: Data is triangulated from various sources to arrive at the most complete and up-to-date picture. *Approximate dates of municipal-level trade contestation.

Sources: Adapted from Verger and Bonal (2006, 60–1) and including data from ATTAC France (2004a, 2004b, 2004c, 2006); ATTAC Suisse (2007); Capling and Nossal (2001); Deckwirth, Fette, and Rügemer (2004); Equations (2006); GATSwatch (n.d.); Leichhardt Municipal Council (2006); Public Citizen (1998a, 1999a, 1999b); Redmond City Council (1999); Stopp-GATS Kampagne (2004); Stopp GATS Switzerland (2006); Sussex (2005); Wood (2000).

13.2 Municipal-Level Contestation of the Transatlantic Trade and Investment Partnership (TTIP), the Comprehensive Economic and Trade Agreement (CETA), the Trade in Services Agreement (TiSA), and the Trans-Pacific Partnership (TPP)

	Number of municipalities found to have passed motions	Lead organization
Europe (TTIP-focused) (2014–17)*		
France	760	ATTAC France
Austria	408	ATTAC Austria
Germany**	307	ATTAC Germany
Spain	199	#NoaITTIP Platform
Belgium	168 (Wallonia), 16 (Brussels), and 5 (Flanders)	StopTTIP.be (specifically, Tout Autre Chose/ D19–20, No Transat, Hart Boven Hard, Acteurs des temps présents)
Italy	82	Stop TTIP Italia Platform
Greece	45	Stop TTIP-CETA Greece Platform
United Kingdom	41	Global Justice Now (formerly World Development Movement) & 38 Degrees
The Netherlands	27	TTIP Alarm (TNI, SOMO, Greenpeace, FNV, Milieudefensie, Foodwatch)
Switzerland (TiSA-focused)	13	ATTAC Switzerland (francophone)/Stopp TISA (German-speaking)
Portugal	10	Não aos Tratados TTIP/ CETA/TISA Platform
Slovenia	8	Association of Municipalities and Towns of Slovenia
Bulgaria	6	Zelenite (The Greens) (political party), Friends of the Earth Bulgaria
Ireland	3	Uplift
Hungary	2	Védegylet

(*Continued*)

13.2 Continued

	Number of municipalities found to have passed motions	Lead organization
North America		
Canada (CETA-focused) (2010–13)*	75	Council of Canadians
United States (TPP-focused) (2013–16)*	38	Alliance for Democracy

Notes: Most of the data for Europe is taken from the map on the website of TTIP Free Zones Europe (2017b). Where more up-to-date or complete data on municipal motions is available from national campaign websites, it has been used. The data was largely collected over the summer of 2017, after the main period of trade-policy contestation in Europe had come to an end. *Approximate dates of municipal-level trade contestation. **For Germany, only data for Gemeinde (municipalities) is included, not Kreise (district councils).

Sources: Adapted from the format used in Verger and Bonal (2006, 60–1), with data from Alliance for Democracy (2016); Amis de la Terre (2016); Collectif Stop TAFTA (2017a); Council of Canadians (n.d.); Global Justice Now (2016); No al TTIP (2017); Stop TTIP Italia (n.d.); TTIP Free Zones Europe (2017b); TTIP Stoppen (2017).

The first thing to note is that municipal-level trade contestation has taken place in three specific episodes grouped around specific trade and investment agreements. Its "birth" can be seen in the campaign critical of the MAI, with protestors said to be drawing on the earlier example of nuclear-free zones. Interestingly, the most celebrated MAI-free zone of the period, Seattle (see J. Smith 2001), was not declared until April 1999 (Seattle City Council 1999), four months *after* the MAI negotiations had been suspended at the Organisation for Economic Co-operation and Development (Graham 2000, 11–12). Coinciding with Seattle's being named host city for the 1999 ministerial conference of the World Trade Organization (WTO), activists were clearly seeking continuity between the previous MAI protests and the campaign against the WTO and its new proposed millennium round. Campaigning that was critical of the MAI drew extensively upon the experience of North American groups, and those based in Canada in particular, through the ultimately unsuccessful campaign against the Canada-United States Free Trade Agreement, which had brought the debate on free trade to the centre of a general election (Hurrelman and Schneider 2015, 222). Drawing on the anti-MAI campaign, the next episode in municipal-level trade contestation came with the GATS negotiations in the first decade of the 2000s, which sought to expand the scope of the services-liberalization commitments undertaken at the WTO, and which included discussion of several public services potentially delivered by municipalities (see Strange 2014, 126–30, 143–5).

The latest, and final, episode of municipal-level trade contestation is the one that is most fragmented, in terms of both the time frame and the target of its opposition. The first to mobilize were Canadian activists and municipalities, which passed motions critical of CETA between 2010 and 2013 (on this, see Trew 2013). It was not until the start of these negotiations in July 2013 that activists launched their campaign against TTIP in Europe (De Ville and Siles-Brügge 2016, 102). The first flurry of municipal motions against TTIP did not make their appearance until spring 2014, although activists also sought to link these motions (not always successfully) to CETA and the plurilateral TiSA (in the case of Switzerland, a non-EU state, motions focused on this latter agreement). Although the TTIP negotiations were declared on hiatus following the election of Donald Trump to the US presidency in November 2016, some critical motions were passed into 2017, with much of the focus of the debate now centring on CETA (which is still undergoing the process of national ratification by all EU member states despite most of the agreement having already been "provisionally applied"). Meanwhile, there were also municipal motions focused on the TPP in the United States between 2013 and 2016.

The second dynamic we observe in tables 13.1 and 13.2 is that the geographic distribution of municipal-level trade contestation has also shifted over time. What initially began with a relatively modest number of resolutions concentrated in North America has increased in scale since the GATS episode. Although similar activity has been documented elsewhere, such as in parts of India (where numerous local government leaders wrote to the prime minister to express their discontent over the GATS negotiations in the first decade of the 2000s; see Verger and Bonal 2006, 61), municipal motions appear to emerge mainly in industrialized states. In the southern hemisphere, both Local Government New Zealand and the Australian Local Government Association were active in publicly warning that GATS threatened to undermine the ability of local governmental actors to provide public services – and there were also a handful of documented GATS-focused municipal resolutions (ALGA 2003; LGNZ 2003).

We have also seen the emergence of networks of municipalities and other sub-federal governments focused on trade contestation, reflecting the growth in scale between the MAI and subsequent episodes. These have largely been centred on Europe. Set against the relative lack of influence of sub-federal governments in EU trade policy – compared to the greater political sensitivities involving the division of competences between federal and sub-federal governments in the United States or Canada – this growth may point to the idiosyncrasies of municipal-level trade contestation as an alternative means for local governments to exercise voice in global trade governance. Turning to the case of the GATS, the French Zone hors AGCS (GATS-free zone) campaign led by ATTAC organized a so-called States General for Local Governments in Bobigny in November 2014, leading to a subsequent European Convention of Local Governments for the Promotion of Public Services in the face of the GATS. This gathered over one thousand municipalities and met in Liège (October 2005) and in Geneva (October 2006) (ATTAC Pays d'Aix 2004; Crespy 2016, 171; L'Union des Villes et Communes de Wallonie 2005). During the campaign focused on the TTIP, CETA, and TiSA an April 2016 meeting of municipalities and other sub-federal governments in Barcelona led to the so-called Barcelona Declaration, which sixty European municipalities signed (TTIP Free Zones Europe 2017a), and a second pan-European meeting of TTIP-free zones in Grenoble in February 2017 (Collectif Stop TAFTA 2017b).

Despite these transnational linkages a third insight garnered from our mapping exercise is that municipal-level trade activism has taken place within the context of nationally based campaigning. For one, only a small proportion of the total number of municipalities that passed GATS, TTIP, CETA, or TiSA motions participated in the relevant gatherings or signed the 2016 Barcelona Declaration. Moreover, within the western European "hotbed" of municipal activism a very small number of countries account for the majority of the motions. The two stand-out cases are Austria and France, which accounted for almost three-quarters of the total number of municipal resolutions in the GATS period and around half in the TTIP, CETA, TiSA, and TPP periods. In these two cases there has been continuity in the alliances between certain social movement organizations and municipal-level governmental actors, notably ATTAC in both France and Austria, which accorded a central role to the municipal level in their GATS campaigns (the Zones hors AGCS and Stopp-GATS Gemeinden) and TTIP campaigns (the Zones hors TAFTA and TTIP/CETA/TiSA-freie Gemeinden). Similarly, Canada saw relatively significant numbers of municipalities pass motions in all episodes, with the Council of Canadians playing a coordinating role throughout. In contrast, the United Kingdom has consistently only seen a very small number of motions, despite the quite significant role played by the World Development Movement (Global Justice Now since 2015) in the transnational network of trade-justice campaigning organizations (see Strange 2014, 147–50). But there has not only been continuity. In the latest episode we saw an increase in activity in Spain, and especially in Germany, which went from one documented municipal motion during the MAI and GATS episodes to over three hundred in the case of TTIP. In part, this may reflect the increased contentiousness of TTIP in Europe, and especially Germany, compared to previous episodes of protest on trade policy (see Broschek, Bußjäger, and Schramek in this volume; De Ville and Siles-Brügge 2017). However, in the case of Belgium we have seen not so much a change in the number of motions as the flipping of municipal activism from the Flemish to the Walloon region, which may itself also be a reflection of differing patterns of civil-society mobilization (see Bollen, De Ville, and Gheyle in this volume).

In sum, we have identified the episodic nature of municipal-level trade activism, its shifting geographical focus from North America to Europe (and significant growth in the process), and the important national-campaigning context in which it arises. The analysis now considers how this has reshaped global trade governance, focusing in particular on the understudied role of municipalities.

Reshaping Trade Governance

The differences between the motions eventually passed by municipalities and the sample motions usually provided by SMOs show the most obvious way in which municipalities have not just been passive actors responding to SMO activism but have themselves played an independent role in municipal-level trade contestation. In this section we consider the kinds of positions adopted by municipalities in their resolutions, focusing on the countries that are experiencing the most municipal activism in each period (Canada and the United States in the case of the MAI, and Austria and France in the case of the GATS and TTIP). We focus on how these differed from the position of the SMOs and what this says about the nature of municipal-level trade contestation from a governmental perspective, suggesting that the very nature of the mimetic challenge implied by the resolutions depends on municipalities' *identity* as governmental actors.

As noted, municipal resolutions often took a more hedged position with respect to the various agreements than did the sample SMO resolution text. This was particularly the case in the US campaign against the MAI, where almost none of the local resolutions we studied (see Public Citizen 1999a) voiced the sorts of unequivocal opposition to the agreement found in Public Citizen's sample text (Berkeley, California, was a notable exception, but it also did not declare itself to be exempt from the requirements of the agreement). The much-celebrated Seattle City Council (1999) resolution, for example, *specifically* opposed the provisions of the draft Multilateral Agreement on Investment, or similar provisions in any international agreement, which undermined

> the authority of local governments to regulate within their jurisdiction, pass laws regarding environmental protection and fair labor practices, support local economic development, and decide how to use public procurement dollars. (Seattle City Council 1999)

Even in France and Austria, where there appeared to be more outright opposition to the GATS or TTIP, a number of municipalities also passed alternatives to the templates of the SMOs GATS-free / Stop-GATS and Hors TAFTA/TTIP-frei (for the national-level Austrian template, see Stopp-GATS Kampagne 2004; for examples of local-level templates in France, see ATTAC 45 2005; ATTAC 91 2005). For example, Aix-en-Provence's GATS resolution did not take an official position on the agreement as such, instead drawing on a specific provision of several of the sample resolutions in "rejecting, a priori, any obligation made in the context of this global agreement to privatize French public services" (authors' translation of Conseil Municipal d'Aix en Provence 2003). The Austrian Light Resolution (derisively named by ATTAC) on the GATS (passed by seventy-eight of the around four hundred municipalities with resolutions on the agreement) was entitled "No Stop of the Negotiations, But Clear Definitions and an Exemption for Municipal Services of General Interest in the GATS Agreement" (authors' translation of Gemeinderat Oberschützen 2003, 8). In the case of TTIP, Austria and France also saw a variety of motions in addition to the SMO templates (for these national-level templates, see Collectif Stop TAFTA n.d.; TTIP Stoppen 2014). In France these included "conditional" TTIP-free zones, to be declared if TTIP was adopted as was proposed (e.g., Conseil de Paris 2016), as well as zones *en vigilance* (with demands ranging from calls for greater debate to specific concerns about the agreement; see Collectif Stop TAFTA 2017a). In Austria there were several iterations of a "transparency resolution," calling for a publication of relevant negotiating documents, as well as some resolutions additionally calling for a referendum on the final outcome (see TTIP Stoppen 2017).

What explains this more hedged position with respect to the trade agreements? We suggest that these resolutions should be seen as attempts by municipalities to claim a voice in trade policymaking, rather than just as a means of *halting* the talks. In contrast to the often more cautious position taken on the agreements themselves, throughout the three campaigning periods one fairly consistent feature of municipality resolutions was their call for greater transparency, consultation, and the involvement of municipalities in the negotiating process. The operative clauses of these resolutions, moreover, were often directed at the lobbying of key elected officials (e.g., state congressional delegations, MPs, MEPs, and the government), with Canadian MAI resolutions being sent to the prime minister and other key elected officials (see Public Citizen 1999b). Local government associations – such as the Federation of Canadian Municipalities (in all three periods), the Australian Local Government Association (in the case of the GATS and MAI), or the United States National Association of Counties (in the case of the MAI) – frequently became involved in issuing declarations in order to lobby government, declarations that were themselves also cited in a number of municipal resolutions (Capling and Nossal 2001, 451; Public Citizen 1999b; Trew 2013, 573; Verger and Bonal 2006, 60). While it is not the purpose of this chapter to assess the success or impact of municipal-level trade contestation, it is interesting to note that there have been some specific policy outcomes that appear to reflect municipal concerns. For example, much of the European GATS campaign was focused on water distribution, often a municipal competence (notably in France and Austria), and the end result was its omission from the EU offer in the negotiations (Crespy 2016, 160–2). Similarly, during the TTIP negotiations the European Commission eventually excluded municipalities from the scope of its horizontal (cross-cutting) regulatory cooperation chapter (Meuwese 2015, 164).

Going one step further, we would argue that the resolutions were also evidence of the challenger-challenged distinction breaking down, with municipalities engaging in a form of mimetic challenge. Municipalities were doing what they could as comparatively weak actors usually excluded from the trade-policymaking machinery: adopting the language of domestic law to contest another domain of rule-making, global trade governance. The stressing of their identity as a legitimate *governmental* actor that should be consulted and involved in the trade-policy process could thus be served by the adoption of a more hedged position on the agreements themselves. In this vein, and even in the case of those municipalities adopting a more stringent position on the various trade and investment agreements, the emphasis was on defending municipalities' constitutionally allocated competences.

In the case of the anti-MAI campaign, the US National Association of Counties (1998) passed a resolution (subsequently referenced in a number of municipal resolutions; see Public Citizen 1999b) in which it "urge[d] the Administration not to agree to any provisions in the

MAI draft text or similar provision of any international agreement that would pre-empt local governments' ability to regulate activities within its jurisdiction." This was in reference to the principle of federal pre-emption by which local and state laws may be overridden by federal laws. Similarly, there were frequent references in the preamble of US municipal resolutions to the fact that the MAI's proposed investor-state-dispute-settlement mechanism "would be external to the United States federal court system and, therefore, unrestricted by existing judicial interpretations of the Constitutional principles" (this statement being based on text from a Public Citizen sample motion; see Public Citizen 1998b). In the US context this form of mimetic challenge may tap into important political sensitivities around states' rights. Although lacking the formal legal powers to avoid US federal preemption, American municipalities, and particularly US states, have benefited from these sensitivities when it comes to discriminatory procurement policies or the inability of private parties to bring claims against states or municipalities in US courts on the basis of WTO rules (Guay 2000, 366–7; Hufbauer and Moran 2015, 2; Stumberg and Porterfield 2001, 183).

The fact that subsequent episodes in municipal-level trade contestation have centred on western Europe also points to the importance of looking beyond the formal institutional channels available to municipalities. Despite facing the constraints of a supranational EU trade policy, municipalities have been able to create a new space of contestation, drawing on concepts from both national and EU law. In the case of the GATS campaign the question of local government's competence in basic public service delivery was clearly emphasized in many of the resolutions (note also, as stated, the focus of the broader GATS campaign on water distribution). For example, the ATTAC Austria sample resolution, which was widely adopted by municipalities, spoke of how "the state (at the federal, regional and local level) has the most important function when it comes to providing so-called services of general interest" (authors' translation of Stopp-GATS Kampagne 2004, 78), while even the Light Resolution sought to explicitly carve out municipal basic services from the scope of the agreement (Gemeinderat Oberschützen 2003). In the case of TTIP and CETA, in which the alleged impact of the agreement went beyond public services, there was also an emphasis on legally enshrined local governmental autonomy. In France, for example, a number of municipalities (e.g., Rennes, Collias, and Le Mans) mentioned the "prerogatives of territorial collectivities" (a specific term for elected sub-federal governments, whose autonomy is enshrined in article 72 of the French constitution) – a provision not found in the ATTAC sample resolution (authors' translation of Ville de Rennes 2014;

Collectif Stop TAFTA n.d.; Commune de Collias 2014; Ville du Mans 2014). In Austria, meanwhile, the ATTAC sample motion adopted by a number of municipalities directly invoked the EU's subsidiarity principle and urged national MPs and MEPs to "not conclude any trade or investment agreement that has a negative impact on the autonomy of municipalities to provide services of general interest or limit their ability to regulate" (authors' translation of TTIP Stoppen 2014, 1, 2).

Ultimately, mimetic challenge in which comparatively weak actors rely on formal, bureaucratic structures to challenge the system is possible when municipalities draw on their identities as governmental actors. The legal, technocratic nature of the global trading system is being challenged by the adoption of the legal, technocratic language of constitutional and European law. To refer, as many SMOs did, to "weak" and "strong" resolutions therefore misses part of the complexity and subtlety associated with mimetic challenge. Contestation is not always explicit resistance and, where undertaken by actors nested within the political system, may well be significant even if the demands appear relatively modest.

Conclusion

The collaboration by municipal governments with SMOs in order to challenge national and supranational trade policy – what we term here *municipal-level trade contestation* – has become established as a phenomenon within the politics of global trade governance despite it being relatively under-researched. This chapter is a first attempt to fill that gap, being only a preliminary exploration. However, the three main periods of contestation discussed do provide some initial findings that require further consideration.

First, there has been a clear increase among industrialized states, and particularly within western Europe, in municipal-level trade contestation. Second, although SMOs appear to have significant influence over how municipal governmental actors formally criticize national (and supranational, in the case of the EU) trade policies, the latter actors do not always fully endorse the entire set of demands made by SMOs. Instead, what we see is evidence of a negotiation in which governmental actors are often keen not to contest the fundamental principles of global trade governance but, instead, focus on preserving their own regulatory space. What this ultimately points to is the blurring of the distinction between SMOs challenging the state and local government actors (who themselves are also engaged in activist politics) doing so. As institutional actors, municipal governments are both empowered and constrained in such a way that they are attractive to societal actors such as SMOs seeking greater institutional legitimacy for their critical message. This alliance and the mimetic challenge it produces also allow municipalities to go beyond the limitations of their institutional role in trade and investment negotiations.

When referring to municipal governmental actors in their trade campaigns (e.g., ATTAC Austria 2014), SMOs frame local government as inherently more democratic than the national and supranational levels, as well as an underdog in relation to the more legally authoritative levels. It is interesting to consider how that narrative compares to public attitudes towards the municipal level, to participation within local elections, and to other forms of democratic practice within the provision of public services. It may be that such framing is merely opportunistic, but, given the correlation between municipal actors and the extent to which SMOs have active local groups, there is also reason to see municipal-level trade contestation as part of a wider attempt to develop forms of democracy that are more participatory and that go beyond purely national representative forms. Further research could well benefit from exploring more deeply the deliberative practices, if any, that municipal governments draw upon when engaging with SMOs. Likewise, there is the potential for new knowledge by studying both the way in which governmental actors adopt such motions within their institutional cultures and their relationship to the national level, as a means to better understand the degree of mimetic challenge.

It is easy to dismiss contestation at the municipal-level as irrelevant to global trade governance. It is difficult to discern if such actions have had a direct impact on any of the national or supranational trade negotiations concerned, even if, as noted in the cases of the GATS and TTIP, there were some changes to EU negotiating proposals that appeared to reflect municipal concerns. For that reason, our intervention has focused instead on the collaboration itself – between municipal governmental actors and SMOs. Our overall argument has been that it is important to study the social practices at play in such moments, particularly with respect to the emergence of new social relations and political identities around the question of where global trade governance should be contested or not. That is because these processes clearly go beyond specific trade negotiations to engage with bigger societal issues, such as the relative role of different governmental levels, but also the relationship between society, the state, and market. There is a clear need for further research in this area, to investigate in more depth the practices at play, the potential for mimetic challenge, and the way in which municipal-level trade contestation relates to other political processes. For example, what role do political parties play in this process when they are active at the municipal level, and do we see tensions between municipal and national divisions of parties with respect to trade politics? And within that relationship, what role is played by SMOs? These questions are just some of the issues requiring new research, with this chapter serving as an initial step within the field.

NOTES

1 We would like to thank Jörg Broschek and Patricia Goff as editors of this volume and organizers of the workshop "The Multilevel Politics of Trade in North America, Europe, and Beyond," held from 14 to 15 October 2016 at the Balsillie School of International Affairs, where very stimulating discussions also took place with other participants. In addition, we would like to thank the anonymous reviewers, Tereza Novotná, Dirk De Bièvre, Johan Adriaensen, Oriol Costa, Arlo Poletti, Niels Gheyle, Alvaro Oleart, Alasdair Young, Gunnhildur Lily Magnusdottir, Magnus Ericson, Linda Berg, Anamaria Dutceac Segesten, Elsa Hedlingand, and Jamal Shahin for the helpful feedback on previous drafts of this chapter. Any remaining errors are our sole responsibility.

2 One might argue that certain municipalities should not be considered weak as they are also simultaneously federal states and/or regional actors (e.g., the Stadt/Bundesland of Vienna or the *commune/département* of Paris). Additionally, many of the campaigns studied in this chapter explicitly included federal, regional states, and other entities. However, the vast majority of municipalities do not possess such constitutional powers, nor do they represent larger regional actors. Therefore, as well as for reasons of space, we focus here on the role of municipalities as weak actors when compared to other entities within the state.

3 This information is sadly incomplete, with the degree of confidence that motions have not been omitted decreasing as we move back in time, given that many key campaign websites are no longer available.

REFERENCES

ALGA (Australian Local Government Association). 2003. ALGA Response to the Department of Foreign Affairs and Trade Discussion Paper on GATS. www.aph.gov.au.

Alliance for Democracy. 2016. Create a "TPP-Free Zone" Where You Live. http://www.thealliancefordemocracy.org/tppfreezones.shtml.

Amis de la Terre. 2016. Liste des Communes hors TTIP. 13 November 2016. https://docs.google.com.

Aspey, Eleanor, and Nicolette Butler. 2017. "Public Procurement in TTIP: An Opportunity to Set Global Standards." In *Global Procurement Theories and Practices*, edited by K.V. Thai, 305–26. Cham, Switzerland: Springer.

ATTAC 45 (Association for the Taxation of Financial Transactions and Citizen's Action). 2005. ATTAC 45 – Dossier AGCS: Campagne d'Appel aux Elus. Accessed 18 November 2019. https://local.attac.org.

ATTAC 91. 2005. Courrier Communes. 20 March. Accessed 18 November 2019. https://local.attac.org.

ATTAC Austria. 2014. TTIP-Protest in die GemeindenTragen! 8 November 2014. https://www.ttip-stoppen.at.

ATTAC France. 2004a. Belgique: Les Collectivités hors AGCS. 24 October 2004. https://france.attac.org.

– 2004b. Les Collectivités du Royaume-Uni hors AGCS. 24 October 2004. https://france.attac.org.

– 2004c. Les Collectivités Italiennes hors AGCS. 24 October 2004. https:// france.attac.org.

– 2006. AGCS: Plus de 800 Collectivités Locales contre l'AGCS. 30 May 2006. https://france.attac.org.

ATTAC Pays d'Aix. 2004. Etats Généraux des Collectivités Publiques contre l'AGCS. https://local.attac.org.

ATTAC Suisse. 2007. Les Communes hors AGCS. 3 July 2007. http://archive .wikiwix.com.

Bandy, Joe, and Jackie Smith, eds. 2005. *Coalitions across Borders: Transnational Protest and the Neoliberal Order*. Lanham, MD: Rowman & Littlefield.

Bulkeley, Harriet. 2010. "Cities and the Governing of Climate Change." *Annual Review of Environment and Resources* 35: 229–53.

Capling, Ann, and Kim R. Nossal. 2001. "Death of Distance or Tyranny of Distance? The Internet, Deterritorialization, and the Anti-globalization Movement in Australia." *Pacific Review* 14 (3): 443–65.

Collectif Stop TAFTA. 2017a. Collectivités. https://www.collectifstoptafta .org/collectivites/.

– 2017b. Grenoble's Response. https://www.collectifstoptafta.org.

– n.d. Resolution 2 Finale. Accessed 18 November 2019. https://www .collectifstoptafta.org.

Commune de Collias. 2014. Motion sur le TAFTA (partenariat transatlantique de commerce et d'investissement). 18 November 2014. https://www .collectifstoptafta.org.

Conseil de Paris. 2016. Vœu de l'Exécutif Municipal Relatif au Traité TAFTA. 13–15 June 2016. https://www.collectifstoptafta.org.

Conseil Municipal d'Aix en Provence. 2003. Motion du Conseil Municipal d'Aix-en-Provence du 28 juillet. https://local.attac.org.

Council of Canadians. 2013. Municipal Governments Need a Say on CETA: Pass a CETA Resolution in Your Community Today. https://canadians.org.

Council of Canadians. n.d. *Take Cities out of CETA*. Accessed 18 November 2019. https://www.google.com/maps/.

Crespy, Amandine. 2016. *Welfare Markets in Europe*. London: Palgrave Macmillan.

Danaher, Kevin, and Jason Mark. 2003. *Insurrection: Citizen Challenges to Corporate Power*. London: Routledge.

Deckwirth, Christina, Dominik Fette, and Werner Rügemer. 2004. *GATS Lokal: Privatisierung in der Kommune und die Rolle des GATS*. Bonn: WEED.

Della Porta, Donna, and Mario Diani. 1999. *Social Movements: An Introduction*. Oxford: Blackwell.

De Ville, Ferdi, and Gabriel Siles-Brügge. 2016. *TTIP: The Truth about the Transatlantic Trade and Investment Partnership*. Cambridge: Polity.

– 2017. "Why TTIP is a Game-Changer and Its Critics Have a Point." *Journal of European Public Policy* 24 (10): 1491–505.

Ennis, James G., and Richard Schreuer. 1987. "Mobilizing Weak Support for Social Movements: The Role of Grievance, Efficacy, and Cost." *Social Forces* 66 (2): 390–409.

Equations. 2006. Compilation on GATS-Free Zones. Bangalore, India: Equitable Tourism. http://www.equitabletourism.org.

Freudlsperger, Christian. 2017. "More Voice, Less Exit: Sub-federal Resistance to International Procurement Liberalization in the European Union, the United States and Canada." *Journal of European Public Policy* 25 (11): 1686–705.

GATSwatch. n.d. Stop the GATS Attack: Involving Local and Regional Governments. http://www.gatswatch.org/locgov-list.html.

Gemeinderat Oberschützen. 2003. Niederschrift: Aufgenommen bei der am 31. März 2003 in der Gemeinde Oberschützen stattgefundenen 7. Gemeinderatssitzung. http://www.oberschuetzen.at.

Global Affairs Canada. 2017. *International Trade Agreements and Local Government: A Guide for Canadian Municipalities*. http://international.gc.ca.

Global Justice Now. 2016. "100 TTIP-Free Cities in the UK by the End of 2016." 19 April 2016. https://www.ttip-free-zones.eu/node/36.

Graham, Edward M. 2000. *Fighting the Wrong Enemy: Antiglobal Activists and Multinational Enterprises*. Washington, DC: Institute for International Economics.

Guay, Terrence. 2000. "Local Government and Global Politics: The Implications of Massachusetts' 'Burma Law.'" *Political Science Quarterly* 115 (3): 353–76.

Hirschmann, Albert O. 1970. *Exit, Voice and Loyalty: Responses to Decline in Firms, Organizations, and States.* Cambridge, MA: Harvard University Press.

Hobson, John M., and Leonard Seabrooke, eds. 2007. *Everyday Politics of the World Economy.* Cambridge: Cambridge University Press.

Hufbauer, Gary, and Tyler Moran. 2015. Government Procurement in US Trade Agreements. Robert Schuman Centre for Advanced Study Policy Paper 2015/09. Florence, Italy: EUI.

Hurrelman, Achim, and Steffen Schneider. 2015. *The Legitimacy of Regional Integration in Europe and the Americas.* New York: Springer.

IGPAC (Intergovernmental Policy Advisory Committee). 2018. Intergovernmental Policy Advisory Committee Members. https://ustr.gov.

Koivusalo, Meri, and Jonathan Tritter. 2014. "'Trade Creep' and Implications of the Transatlantic Trade and Investment Partnership Agreement for the United Kingdom National Health Service." *International Journal of Health Services* 44 (1): 93–111.

Kukucha, Christopher J. 2005. "From Kyoto to the WTO: Evaluating the Constitutional Legitimacy of the Provinces in Canadian Foreign Trade and Environmental Policy." *Canadian Journal of Political Science* 38 (1): 129–52.

– 2015. "Federalism Matters: Evaluating the Impact of Sub-federal Government in Canadian and American Foreign Trade Policy." *Canadian Foreign Policy Journal* 21 (3): 224–37.

Leichhardt Municipal Council. 2006. General Agreement on Trade in Services (GATS) for Local Councils. 27 June 2006. https://www.leichhardt.nsw.gov.au.

LGNZ (Local Government New Zealand). 2003. Local Government New Zealand's Submission on NZ's Approach to the WTO Negotiations on Services. February 2003. Originally available from http://library.lgnz.co.nz; copy archived by authors.

Lundberg, Anna, and Michael Strange. 2017. "Who Provides the Conditions for Human Life? Sanctuary Movements in Sweden as Both Contesting and Working with State Agencies." *Politics* 37 (3): 347–62.

McCarthy, John, and Mayer Zald. 1977. "Resource Mobilization and Social Movements: A Partial Theory." *American Journal of Sociology* 82 (6): 1212–41.

Meuwese, Anne. 2015. "Constitutional Aspects of Regulatory Coherence in TTIP: An EU Perspective." *Law and Contemporary Problems* 78 (4): 153–74.

No al TTIP. 2017. Territorios libres de TTIP, CETA, y/o TISA. http://www.noalttip.org/mociones/.

Public Citizen. 1998a. "OECD & Governments Launch 'MAI Charm-Offensive.'" May 1998. https://www.citizen.org.

– 1998b. "Sample Resolution Opposing the MAI & Its Clones." https://www.citizen.org.

– 1999a. "Anti-MAI/WTO Resolutions in the U.S. and around the World." https://www.citizen.org.

– 1999b. "WTO Ministerial Host City Snubs Clinton Trade Agenda." 12 April 1999. https://www.citizen.org.

Princen, Sebastiaan, and Bart Kerremans. 2008. "Opportunity Structures in the EU Multi-Level System." *West European Politics* 31 (6): 1129–46.

Redmond City Council. 1999. "A Resolution of the City Council of the City of Redmond, Washington, Taking a Position of Opposition to Provisions of the Draft Multilateral Agreement on Investment or Similar International Agreements That Could Restrict the City's Ability to Regulate within Its Own Jurisdiction, to Decide How to Spend Its Procurement Funds, and to Support Local Economic Development." 13 October 1999. http://www .redmond.gov.

Routledge, Paul. 2003. "Convergence Space: Process Geographies of Grassroots Globalization Networks." *Transactions* 28 (3): 333–49.

Routledge, Paul, Andrew Cumbers, and Corinne Nativel. 2007. "Grassrooting Network Imaginaries: Relationality, Power, and Mutual Solidarity in Global Justice Networks." *Environment and Planning A* 39 (11): 2575–92.

Seattle City Council. 1999. "A Resolution Expressing the Seattle City Council's Support for Ensuring Seattle's Ability to Regulate within Its Jurisdiction, Decide How to Spend Its Procurement Funds, Support Local Economic Development, and Pass Laws Regarding Environmental Protection and Fair Labor Practices; and Opposition to Provisions of the Proposed Multilateral Agreement on Investment, or Similar International Agreements, That Could Restrict This Ability." 12 April 1999. http:// members.iinet.net.au.

Shepard, Benjamin, and Ronald Hayduk, eds. 2002. *From ACT UP to the WTO: Urban Protest and Community Building in the Era of Globalization.* London: Verso.

Skocpol, Theda. 2004. "Voice and Inequality: The Transformation of American Civic Democracy." *Perspectives on Politics* 2 (1): 3–20.

Smith, Jackie. 2001. "Globalizing Resistance: The Battle of Seattle and the Future of Social Movements." *Mobilization* 6 (1): 1–20.

Smith, Peter J., and Elizabeth Smythe. 1999. "Globalization, Citizenship and Technology: The MAI Meets the Internet." *Canadian Foreign Policy Journal* 7 (2): 83–105.

Sperling, Valerie. 2009. *Altered States: The Globalization of Accountability.* Cambridge: Cambridge University Press.

Stopp-GATS Kampagne. 2004. Wien: STOPP-GATS Kampagne: Analysen, Hintergründe, Perspektiven. Accessed 13 November 2019. https://www .attac.at.

Stopp-GATS Switzerland. 2006. Stopp GATS. 5 May 2006. http://www
    .stoppgats.ch.
Stop TTIP Italia. n.d. Zone No TTIP. https://stop-ttip-italia.net.
Strange, Michael. 2011. "'Act Now and Sign Our Joint Statement!': What
    Role Do Online Global Group Petitions Play in Transnational Movement
    Networks?" *Media, Culture & Society* 33 (8): 1236–53.
– 2013. "A European Identity in Global Campaigning? Activist Groups and
    the 'Seattle to Brussels' (S2B) Network." *Geopolitics* 18 (3): 612–32.
– 2014. *Writing Global Trade Governance: Discourse and the WTO.* Abingdon,
    UK: Routledge.
Stumberg, Robert, and Matthew C. Porterfield. 2001. "Who Preempted the
    Massachusetts Burma Law? Federalism and Political Accountability under
    Global Trade Rules." *Publius: The Journal of Federalism* 31 (3): 173–204.
Sussex, Edward. 2005. Local and Regional Reaction to GATS and Similar
    Trade Rules. Our World Is Not for Sale. 24 January 2005. http://notforsale
    .mayfirst.org.
Tilly, Charles, and Sidney Tarrow. 2015. *Contentious Politics.* 2nd ed. Oxford:
    Oxford University Press.
Trew, Stuart. 2013. "Correcting the Democratic Deficit in the CETA
    Negotiations: Civil Society Engagement in the Provinces, Municipalities,
    and Europe." *International Journal* 68 (4): 568–75.
TTIP Free Zones Europe. 2017a. Barcelona Declaration. https://www.ttip
    -free-zones.eu.
– 2017b. TTIP, CETA, and TiSA Free Zones in Europe. https://map.ttip-free
    -zones.eu/.
TTIP Stoppen. 2014. Resolution: TTIP/CETA/TiSA-freie Gemeinde. November
    2014. https://www.ttip-stoppen.at.
– 2017. Liste der TTIP-freien Gemeinden. 9 March 2017. https://www.ttip
    -stoppen.at.
L'Union des Villes et Communes de Wallonie (UVCW). 2005. Convention
    européenne des collectivités locales pour la promotion des services
    publics. 20 September. Accessed 18 November 2019. http://www.uvcw.be.
Verger, Antoni, and Xavier Bonal. 2006. "Against GATS: The Sense of a Global
    Struggle." *Journal for Critical Education Policy Studies* 4 (1): 48–74.
Verhoeven, Imrat, and Jan W. Duyvendak. 2017. "Understanding
    Governmental Activism." *Social Movement Studies* 16 (5): 564–77.
Ville de Rennes. 2014. Administration générale: Voeu sur le partenariat
    Transatlantique de Commerce et d'investissement (TAFTA) Présenté par
    les Groupes Socialiste, Ecologiste, Communiste, PRG, UDB, Ensemble Front
    de Gauche et Parti de Gauche Front de Gauche. 30 June 2014. https://www
    .collectifstoptafta.org.

Ville du Mans. 2014. Proposition de Vœu au Conseil Municipal de la Ville du Mans du 13 novembre 2014. https://www.collectifstoptafta.org.

Voss, Kim, and Michelle Williams. 2012. "The Local in the Global: Rethinking Social Movements in the New Millennium." *Democratization* 19 (2): 352–77.

Wood, David. 2000. "The International Campaign against the Multilateral Agreement on Investment: A Test Case for the Future of Globalisation?" *Philosophy and Geography* 3 (1): 24–45.

Conclusion

JÖRG BROSCHEK AND PATRICIA GOFF

We opened this volume with a critical observation: sub-federal units in many, though not all, federations are taking on a new role in trade policy and trade-agreement negotiations, displaying considerable variation in the intensity and modes of participation. Perusal of newspapers in the last few years confirms this. Canadian provinces joined their federal counterparts for the first time at the negotiating table of the Comprehensive Economic and Trade Agreement (CETA); Wallonia asserted its interests before approving the Belgian signature on CETA; other European sub-federal actors, notably German and Austrian Länder, expressed their concerns about CETA and the Transatlantic Trade and Investment Partnership (TTIP); municipalities in Europe and North America vowed to resist implementation of CETA and TTIP; and, as renegotiations of the North American Free Trade Agreement accelerated, the Canadian federal government increasingly lobbied US state governors and congressional representatives, and the US states and Canadian provinces engaged one another in an unprecedented way. This is just a representative list of the kind of multilevel politics that is manifesting itself in trade.

This phenomenon led us to pose three questions in our introduction. First, why are sub-federal actors taking or not taking a new role in trade policy? Second, how are sub-federal units participating in trade policy or trade-agreement negotiations once they have been motivated to do so? In other words, why does sub-federal activity take the various forms that it does throughout our cases? Third, what consequences can we expect from this apparent up-tick in sub-federal activity in some places? We asked our contributors to consider these three questions and to explain why, how, and with what consequences sub-federal actors in their respective cases have (or have not) become more active in debates about trade policy and trade-agreement negotiation.

Through this collaborative effort we identified three key factors that provide entry points into a study of the role of sub-federal actors in trade policy-making and agreement negotiation: the distinctive institutional configuration of a federal system; the nature and scope of trade policy and trade agreements; and the extent of social mobilization, in combination with party politics, that accompanies a particular trade-policy conversation. These elements variously appear in all of the cases presented here. In some instances one or two factors will come to the fore while another might recede. In other instances all three factors are in play. Most notably, the chapters suggest that attention to the interaction of these three factors is critical to deepening our understanding of the role of sub-federal actors in trade and to answering our three questions. In our concluding chapter we develop a basic model that captures the key dynamics of this interaction and begins to explain the evolution of multilevel trade politics (see fig. C.1).

We consider this model to be a starting point rather than an endpoint of further research. It draws on two key literatures that intersect and overlap in this discussion: comparative federalism and multilevel governance scholarship, on the one hand; and literature on the evolution of trade agreements, on the other. These literatures offer a number of conceptual anchors for our discussion. The federalism literature provides insight into the institutional variation that we observe across federal systems. In particular, the spectrum from self-rule to shared rule that federalism scholars use to classify federations, grounded in differences in the allocation of competencies; the degree of institutionalization of intergovernmental relations; and the relative strength of the second chamber illuminate the institutional resources and avenues available to sub-federal actors should they be moved to augment their participation in debates about trade. In addition, comparative federalism and multilevel governance scholarship direct our attention to intermediate actors in multilevel politics, most notably interest groups, social movements, and political parties. The trade literature accentuates the proliferation of preferential trade agreements, as well as the notion of "deep" trade agreements, capturing the recent shift in trade-agreement contents away from tariff reduction towards more intrusive "behind-the-border" measures.

Furthermore, the model builds on our analytical elaborations in the introduction and the key findings grounded in comparative analysis of the case studies assembled in this book. Given the lack of comparative work on the role of sub-federal units in trade policy, this volume is necessarily exploratory. Nonetheless, we are confident that this contribution can serve as a springboard for further research.

C.1 A Basic Model of Sub-federal Engagement in Trade Policy

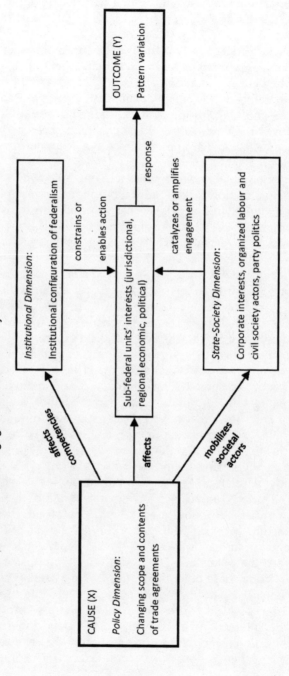

Why Are Sub-federal Actors Taking or Not Taking a New Role in Trade Policy?

Our case studies suggest that trade policy, in its broadest sense, has entered the realm of sub-federal units in all federations, regardless of whether they are strong, moderate, or weak actors in the field (see fig. C.2). We therefore conclude, first of all, that any attempt to explain the evolution of multilevel trade politics needs to start with the changing nature of free trade agreements. The changing scope and contents of these agreements have prompted sub-federal responses because trade-agreement provisions can affect their interests.

We understand sub-federal actors to have three overlapping sets of interests – jurisdictional, economic, and political. *Jurisdictional interests* touch on a sub-federal actor's legislative or administrative authority. Trade-agreement provisions that impinge on the policy competencies of sub-federal governments, like opening up sub-national procurement, constitute jurisdictional interests. Regional *economic interests* arise in debates about trade when policy choices or agreement provisions threaten industries or sectors in a sub-federal jurisdiction. For example, President Donald Trump's threat to place tariffs on foreign auto imports had clear implications for the economic interests of the Canadian province of Ontario, and softwood lumber tariffs would disproportionately affect the economic interests of British Columbia. *Political interests* reflect policy preferences, often tied to key constituencies. European concerns about the import of genetically modified organisms or beef treated with hormones correspond to political interests.

Our volume shows that these types of sub-federal interests come to the fore in varying degrees in our cases studies. The perceived prospective effects of trade-policy developments or trade-agreement provisions (especially behind-the-border provisions in "deep" agreements) on sub-federal interests serve as the main cause for sub-federal engagement in all cases. The answer to our first question, therefore, *mostly* resides on the left side of our model (fig. C.1). However, it is worth noting that the link between trade-policy choices and sub-federal interests can be made in at least two ways. The sub-federal actors themselves may discern the potential effects, and interest groups or civil-society actors can bring these potential effects to the attention of sub-federal governments. Trade policy mobilizes societal and intermediary actors, most notably political parties and interest groups, in different ways. As a result, interaction between the state-society dimension and the trade-policy dimension can be a critical part of the answer to the question posed in this section. Sub-federal actors are taking a new role in trade-policy debates and trade-agreement negotiations because developments in this domain, including the expanding scope of trade agreements, affect their interests in ways that are directly obvious and significant for sub-federal governments or that mobilize key interest groups, political parties, or civil-society actors.

Why Does Sub-federal Engagement Take the Various Forms That It Does throughout Our Cases?

In the following section we summarize key insights of our case studies that advance our understanding of variation in the form and intensity of sub-federal engagement. In accordance with our model, we shift our focus to the dynamic interplay of two key sources of variation: institutions and the larger societal environment represented through political parties, interest groups, and social movements.

The Institutional Dimension

While the increasing number and depth of trade agreements help us understand why many sub-federal actors are moved to intervene in trade-policy debates, often at the behest of interest groups and civil-society actors, there is great variation in the outcomes. Some sub-federal actors are more active than others. As the chapters by Egan, and Schiavon and López-Vallejo, show, compared to their counterparts in Germany and Austria, for example, sub-federal actors in the United States and Mexico are not noticeably more active in trade-policy debates or agreement negotiations. Even *within* federations, sub-federal actors are more active on some trade-policy issues or with regard to some trade-agreement negotiations than others. Paquin's chapter on Canada, as well as Elijah's analysis of Australia, confirms this observation. Elijah argues that institutional mechanisms for intergovernmental co-operation are evolving in Australia, yet states and territories avail themselves of them in different ways depending on domestic political considerations and the nature and complexity of the agreement under negotiation. Her analysis confirms that sub-federal actor participation in trade varies not just from federation to federation but also from agreement to agreement within federal systems, a perspective echoed in chapters by Schram; Bollen, De Ville, and Gheyle; Garcia; and Siles-Brügge and Strange.

In addition, even when the level of sub-federal activity is comparable, the manner in which various sub-federal actors exert their influence varies. Broschek, Bußjäger, and Schramek show that German and Austrian Länder exert their influence through resolutions in the Bundesrat, while chapters by Hederer and Leblond and by Schram show that Canadian provinces exert their influence more directly through intergovernmental mechanisms or through their key role in trade-agreement implementation. Therefore, in order to understand variation in outcomes, we need to specify the intermediate links that operate in between cause (trade-agreement effects on sub-federal interests) and outcome (pattern variation).

One important source of variation emanates from the institutional dimension of our models. We conceptualized federalism as an institutional configuration comprising three core elements: the allocation of competencies, the system of intergovernmental relations, and the second chamber. These elements can promote either institutional autonomy or interdependence between the federal level and constituent units. As a consequence, federal systems align, to various degrees, with either the self-rule or the shared-rule pole.

Where competencies are concerned, the greater the scope of sub-federal legislative and administrative competencies, the more likely trade provisions will impinge on sub-federal spheres of authority. By contrast, if sub-federal units enjoy limited legislative and administrative competencies, there are fewer direct links between trade-agreement provisions and potential constraints on their territorial integrity. For example, more encompassing and deeper free trade agreements have the potential to impinge on the legislative and administrative competencies of the Canadian provinces or the Australian states and territories, and in Austria and Germany new trade-policy provisions are more likely to have an impact on only the Länders' authority to implement federal legislation.

In shared-rule federations, sub-federal units can resort to a highly institutionalized system of intergovernmental relations in order to formulate a common position. The Austrian and German Länder in particular, but also the Swiss cantons, have taken advantage of formalized and differentiated intergovernmental institutions to coordinate among themselves (horizontally) and with the federal level (vertically) on trade-related issues. The lack of highly institutionalized intergovernmental mechanisms, as in the case of the United States, for example, complicates similar efforts in federations that lean towards the self-rule pole. As Michelle Egan's contribution shows, the sheer number of actors involved in intergovernmental institutions hampers effective collective action among the fifty US states. An additional constraint on building intergovernmental capacity in the United States and Mexico results from the combination of federalism and a presidential system of government, in which regional interests are also expressed through elected senators at the federal level rather than by executive actors from the states. Accordingly, the parliamentary systems in self-rule federations like Australia and Canada offer better conditions for the provinces, states, and territories to further the emerging efforts to strengthen intergovernmental coordination or even co-operation in trade policy.

Perhaps even more important, sub-federal entities in these federations derive their power to influence trade-policy formulation indirectly, as trade negotiators anticipate potential non-compliance in the future, meaning once a trade agreement is in effect. The Canadian provinces and the states in Australia and the United States, for example, have the power to disrupt the implementation of trade agreements by deliberately neglecting certain provisions that affect their self-rule competencies. In contrast, the German Länder have a formal role in the ratification of mixed trade agreements through the second chamber, a typical example of shared-rule federalism. This underlines the fact that a narrow conceptualization of federalism that focuses exclusively on competencies fails to acknowledge that regional interests can also find their way into the trade-policy arena through the system of intergovernmental relations or the second chamber. Our chapters reveal how these three institutional aspects of federal systems – competencies, intergovernmental interaction, and the second chamber – variously interact to shape the responses of sub-federal units to trade-policy developments, but also how the institutional configuration may constrain their capacity to act.

Encompassing and deep trade agreements have the potential to impinge on the legislative and administrative competencies of sub-federal units in federations that feature self-rule characteristics, like Australia, Canada, the United States, and Belgium. On the one hand, it seems obvious that the degree of decentralization is important here. The more decentralized a federation is (i.e., the more exclusive competencies there are on the sub-federal level) and the more encompassing a trade agreement is, the more likely it is that sub-federal units will be affected (Broschek and Goff 2018, 13). Indeed, the Canadian provinces and the Belgian regions and communities lend support to this conclusion. Both represent sub-federal units with a comparatively high degree of self-rule, and both sub-federal actors are particularly prominent in trade politics. On the other hand, our case studies demonstrate that the level of involvement is not simply a function of decentralization. Australia, for example, is one of the most centralized federal systems, and yet, as Elijah's study shows, the states and territories have become an integral part of trade politics in many instances. Moreover, US states represent a particularly vexing case because they seem to be active but comparatively weak at the same time. In this respect, one important comparative conclusion from Michelle Egan's case study is that sub-federal units in self-rule federations can only effectively capitalize on the anticipatory threat of non-compliance in the absence of effective federal countervailing measures. In this regard, the federal level in the United States seems to be better equipped to utilize coercive instruments than are its Canadian or Australian counterparts, allowing federal trade authorities to impinge upon or even pre-empt state authority in trade-related matters.

Even if they lack broad legislative competencies, however, sub-federal units are not necessarily powerless. Germany is a case in point. The German Länder have comparatively little legislative autonomy, but they enjoy a certain degree of autonomy in the implementation of federal legislation. If trade-agreement provisions touch on their administrative competencies, the federal government may be required to introduce a trade-agreement-ratification bill as a veto bill (see Broschek, Bußjäger, and Schramek in this volume). Hence, although German federalism is neither markedly centralized nor decentralized, a single trade-agreement provision may trigger a profound involvement of the Länder. Furthermore, Ziegler's study indicates that the Swiss case is particularly interesting for at least two reasons. For one, it combines, in the allocation of competencies, features of self-rule and shared-rule federalism. The cantons not only have considerable legislative autonomy in a number of policy domains but also – similar to Germany and Austria – implement a large bulk of the federal legislation. This is one reason for their comparatively strong role in multilevel trade politics. What is more, and similar to the Belgian case, constitutional provisions further empower the cantons through shared-rule because they enable them to participate in important stages of the negotiation process, such as the formulation of the negotiation mandate under certain circumstances.

Therefore, once sub-federal actors have come to realize that it is in their interest to intervene in trade debates and policy processes, their respective institutional features influence how they will intervene. The European Union (EU) requested the presence of the Canadian provinces at the CETA negotiating table because the dual allocation of competencies gives the provinces direct influence over the implementation of trade-agreement provisions in areas like provincial procurement and patent-life extension, both key EU demands (see Paquin; Hederer and Leblond; and Schram in this volume). Likewise, Belgium's federation gives the regions and communities exclusive legislative powers over trade-related matters, which helps us to understand why Wallonia protested CETA, especially its investor-state-dispute-settlement provisions, by withholding its approval of federal ratification of the agreement.

Building on the model that we have presented and paying special attention to the form that sub-federal activity can take in trade debates, several of our contributors' analyses can be readily understood through the language of *exit* and *voice*. Exit and voice strategies are partially driven by institutional configurations. Again, the self-rule or shared-rule composition of federal systems seems to open up different opportunities for sub-federal governments to entertain exit or voice strategies. Paquin traces the evolution in the mechanisms available to Canadian provinces for ensuring that their voices are heard in trade policy-making. Institutionalized channels mark this collaborative federal model, something that is lacking in the American federal arrangement. Egan shows how US states intervene in the conversation about trade less through intergovernmental channels and more through state-level legislative and regulatory choices. A combination of exit and voice strategies by American states, linked to fragmentation of the internal market, effectively limits federal liberalization efforts.

In most cases the two strategies of exit and voice are closely linked, arguably being two sides of the same coin. In the Belgian case, Bollen, De Ville, and Gheyle demonstrate that Wallonia's threat of exit created an opportunity for the region to voice its concerns about the CETA agreement. Similarly, chapters by Paquin, Schram, and Hederer and Leblond all suggest that the EU's insistence that Canadian provinces be present at the CETA negotiating table was a clear strategy to give voice to Canadian sub-federal actors, in an effort to preclude exit or refusal to implement the agreement at a later date. Interestingly, that similar opportunities were not given to EU member states and their sub-federal governments partly explains why full CETA ratification is in jeopardy. CETA's status as a "mixed agreement" gives European governments at all levels new opportunities for voice and exit.

Indeed, the EU is a fascinating case. As Garcia shows, the Lisbon Treaty was intended to amplify the voice of supranational institutions in trade and investment. The result has been more complex. Backlash against the expanding reach of trade agreements into the policy domains previously reserved for domestic governments mobilized civil society and awakened levels of government that had previously left trade policy and trade-agreement negotiation to their federal counterparts. Chapters by Bollen, De Ville, and Gheyle and by Broschek, Bußjäger, and

Schramek reveal the myriad ways that sub-federal voice and threats of exit materialized across three federal EU member states, Belgium, Austria, and Germany. In all of these cases, voice and exit strategies were activated by the move towards deeper trade agreements, often in response to civil-society mobilization. In effect, however, exit strategies in Austria and Germany have only very limited potential, given the Länders' lack of legislative autonomy. While the Belgian regions are extremely strong, given that they can credibly threaten to deploy exit strategies (having legislative autonomy in trade-related policy sectors) and voice strategies (on ratification), the German Länder are confined to relying on their power to jeopardize the ratification of trade agreements.

The case of Quebec is particularly noteworthy as an example of a sub-federal actor pursuing a voice strategy. While Paquin's chapter outlines how all Canadian provinces have benefited from the evolution of channels for communicating their interests, Schram's study chronicles a proactive effort by the Province of Quebec to mobilize impending external trade negotiations in the service of provincial economic and political objectives. Unlike Wallonia, the Austrian and German Länder, and other sub-federal actors that responded to a perceived loss in regulatory sovereignty or to appeals by civil society, Quebec, Schram argues, initiated a perceived relinquishment of regulatory control to move forward its own economic development and nation-building agenda. In so doing, it played an instrumental agenda-setting role in Canada's negotiations with the EU.

Two other issues surface in the conversation about sub-federal actors' pursuit of the exit or the voice strategy. First, several contributors note that the institutional *capacity* of sub-federal actors to act is critical. The Mexican case is particularly noteworthy. Schiavon and López-Vallejo argue that the institutional structure of Mexican federalism creates openings for states to participate in international affairs. However, a lack of capacity in the form of international affairs budgets and human resources affects the states' ability to do so, even when they are so inclined. Therefore, despite the fact that Mexico is a federation more in line with self-rule that endows Mexican states with the ability to act – for example, through the instrument of inter-institutional agreements – lack of capacity is a constraint. Bollen, De Ville, and Gheyle echo this with respect to the Belgian parliaments that did not see the wisdom of using scarce resources or adding to an already crowded agenda, especially before the Lisbon Treaty reforms. The expanding scope of trade agreements, coupled with civil-society mobilization, changed this calculation after Lisbon.

From another perspective, Siles-Brügge and Strange show how municipalities, typically lacking channels to intervene in discussions about trade-agreement negotiation, enhanced their capacity through joint action with civil society. Likewise, in his analysis of Switzerland, Ziegler notes that federal governments can sometimes augment sub-federal actor activity, empowering them beyond constitutional requirements. This was the case in Swiss negotiations with the EU. Given the enormous economic and political stakes of entering into agreement with this crucial partner, the federal government called for cantonal approval, despite the fact that the prevailing institutional configuration did not require it to do so.

In addition to capacity, *timing* (the stage of the trade-policy cycle at which sub-federal units can intervene) emerges as another key element of sub-federal efforts to pursue exit or voice strategies. Hederer and Leblond hone in on the provincial implementation of trade agreements in the Canadian context. Despite the incremental development of channels for intergovernmental dialogue, the authors argue that implementation mechanisms may not be sufficient to deliver the outcomes identified in ratified deep agreements, like CETA and the Comprehensive and Progressive Trans-Pacific Partnership. This analysis complements other chapters, which focus on earlier stages of the trade policy-making and agreement-negotiation processes. Egan's analysis of the United States, for example, suggests that certain state regulatory initiatives effectively exclude some policy areas from US external trade negotiations. Bollen, De Ville, and Gheyle explore Wallonia's intervention at the ratification stage in CETA. Garcia also examines several examples of trade-agreement ratification in the EU context. Other chapters – including those by Siles-Brügge and Strange; Broschek, Bußjäger, and Schramek; Kukucha; and Gistelinck – all illustrate that sub-federal actors participate in trade discussions at crucial moments throughout the trade-policy and agreement-negotiation processes.

Generally, our case studies fall into three categories (see fig. C.2). The Swiss cantons, the Belgian regions and communities, and the Canadian provinces (and, increasingly, the Canadian territories) represent sub-federal units that play a comparatively strong role in trade policy. On the other side of the spectrum are the Austrian Länder and the Mexican states. These sub-federal actors have been comparatively weak. We can locate the American and Australian states and territories in between, along with the German Länder. The same holds for the member states in the EU. This placement on the spectrum is grounded in institutional features of the respective federations.

C.2 Sub-federal Role in Trade Policy: A Tentative Assessment

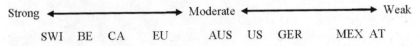

AT (Austria), AUS (Australia), BE (Belgium), CA (Canada), EU (European Union), GER (Germany), MEX (Mexico), SWI (Switzerland), US (United States).

This section has started to unpack one key dynamic in our model, namely the interaction between trade policy and the institutional features of sub-federal actors' respective federations. This dynamic takes us some distance in understanding the variation in outcomes that we observe throughout our cases. However, the explanation is still incomplete. The state-society dimension rounds out our account of sub-federal activity in trade debates.

The State-Society Dimension

The second key source of variation results from the larger social environment. The preferences of sub-federal units cannot be fully understood if they are isolated from the dynamics at the intersection of state and society. This directs our attention to the role of the intermediating collective actors, most notably political parties, interest groups, and social movements. Trade-policy scholarship has demonstrated the importance of organizations representing business interests, labour, or "post-materialist" values. The federalism literature, for its part, has highlighted how the logic of multilevel-party competition shapes institutional and policy dynamics. There is no doubt that trade policy has become increasingly politicized, and, in some countries, highly polarized. Indeed, our case studies support our initial assumption about the causal relevance of the state-society dimension, prompting us to include it into our basic model. Chapters by Bollen, De Ville, and Gheyle and by Siles-Brügge and Strange are particularly noteworthy in this respect. In the former, civil society was instrumental in politicizing CETA provisions and in mobilizing a coalition in response. Institutional shifts in the EU, institutional capacity in Belgium, the politicization of trade-agreement provisions, and civil-society mobilization all combine to explain the activity of Belgian sub-federal actors around trade. In the latter, European municipal actors, which have to date received little attention in discussions of sub-federal activity in trade debates, found new ways to intervene in trade debates. They are institutionally constrained but are able to ally with civil-society actors to amplify their perspective.

These chapters also drive home an important related point. Civil-society mobilization helps us to understand *why* sub-federal actors become involved in debates about trade or trade-agreement negotiations. Social movements or political parties can make salient interests that sub-federal governments might not otherwise pursue in the absence of such pressure. In addition, attention to the state-society dimension illuminates *the form* that sub-federal activity takes. The Gistelinck and Siles-Brügge and Strange chapters show that political party and civil-society involvement influence the manner in which sub-federal actors intervene in trade debates, just as institutional features also influence the form of the activity.

Kukucha's chapter clearly shows that civil-society mobilization is often activated by the nature and scope of trade agreements, and the form it takes in North American federations is linked to institutional arrangements in each context. Gistelinck, for her part, expands this analysis through her attention to party politics and the unique opportunities that exist for their expression post–Lisbon Treaty. Not confined to the national context, German political parties could reach out to their counterparts in the newly empowered European Parliament to influence the debate over specific high-stakes trade agreements. Again, EU institutional developments, alongside the inclusion of controversial provisions in EU trade agreements, led to interesting multilevel party alliances in TTIP and CETA negotiating processes. Ultimately, these case studies show that constellations of the three factors we identify – institutional configuration, evolving trade policy and trade agreements, and state-society linkages – provide robust accounts of the outcomes under consideration in these chapters.

At the same time, however, we consider heightened civil-society mobilization and the polarization between and among political parties as a complementary factor. While institutional characteristics are critical to the understanding of divergent sub-federal responses, the societal context appears to have an amplifying or a catalyzing function in certain instances. In other words, the unprecedented degree of mobilization in European federations like Germany, Austria, and Belgium found its expression in sub-federal activism, but – in isolation – this dimension cannot explain the differences between, for example, the weak Austrian Länder and the strong Belgian regions and communities. Moreover, the Canadian provinces have emerged as comparatively strong sub-federal actors despite the low degree of mobilization and polarization.

This observation opens a rich avenue for future research. Why did tens of thousands of Europeans spill into the streets over CETA and TTIP, while the same agreements received considerably less attention in North America? Under what conditions is civil-society mobilization likely to play a critical role in trade policy or trade-agreement negotiations? On a related front, political-party opposition is a key element of outcomes in the European context. However, although parties in Canada may disagree on finer points, they tend generally to agree about the value of trade and trade agreements. How can we explain this variation in party activity with regard to trade? Some of our contributors open this conversation, but there is ample work remaining to account for this particular current of the conversation.

Implications and Consequences

Formal jurisdiction over trade policy is usually centralized. In most federal systems, including the quasi-federal EU, the federal level enjoys broad, if not exclusive, formal competencies to regulate trade relationships both with other countries and domestically. This is a historical outcome. Economic integration was an important imperative for modern state building (Bartolini 2005; Rokkan 1999). Arguably, nowhere is this more obvious than in the Canadian case. Canada is a federation in which economic nationalism was *the* prime motive for Confederation, as the rich body of scholarship in the tradition of Harold Innis, Donald Creighton, and W.A. Mackintosh has shown. The question, then, is whether the growing importance of sub-federal units in the trade-policy field identified in this volume indicates a major transformative trend. In other words, are we witnessing the reversal of a historically established status quo through the increasing importance of provinces, states, Länder, or cantons in trade policy?

The answer to this question remains necessarily speculative. Trade policy is in flux. At the time of writing this concluding chapter, we are observing a number of events, which may or may not be salient in future years. Donald Trump is in his fourth year as president of the United States. He has pursued an aggressively nationalistic trade policy, which includes real threats of a trade war with China. Negotiations between the United States and the EU towards TTIP have stalled, partly because of Trump's election but also because of developments in European politics. Notably, we await the terms of the United Kingdom's exit from the EU (Brexit), as well as the eventual influence of populist politics throughout Europe and the United States. Negotiations at the World Trade Organization have been long stalled, making preferential trade agreements desirable and common. These are just some relevant observations, but they do suggest that our inquiry may be the product of a particular historical moment, the duration of which we cannot know at this time.

The developments brought to the fore in the case studies of this book reveal profound yet varied political change over time. Whether or not one considers these changes as transformative depends on the scope and durability of change that we will continue to observe in the future. All our contributors emphasize that the role of sub-federal units in trade policy is emerging, regardless of whether their relative role is strong, moderate, or weak. In some cases, like Canada and Switzerland, this process began in the 1980s or 1990s, and in others, like Mexico, Germany, and Austria, it is a more recent phenomenon. The growing involvement of sub-federal actors signifies a general trend if this process becomes self-reproducing. According to Falleti and Mahoney (2015, 220), self-reproducing processes are characterized by "the movement of initial events in a particular direction [inducing] subsequent events that move the process in the same direction." Over time, reversal of the direction of change will be increasingly difficult due to path-dependent dynamics. This holds, in particular, for "self-amplifying" processes, in which the initial event will be expanded and enhanced over time. By contrast, "self-eroding" processes indicate a weakening of initial changes over time, and the direction of change will be more difficult to sustain (Falleti and Mahoney 2015, 220–2).

The burgeoning literature on multilevel governance and, specifically, the "rise of regional authority" (Hooghe and Marks 2016; Hooghe, Marks, and Schakel 2010; Tatham 2016, 2018) suggests that the emergence of multilevel trade politics is part and parcel of a more encompassing transformative trend. Through the lens of this scholarship, we should expect that sub-federal units will most likely consolidate their new role in trade politics. Indeed, the notion of multilevel governance implies that neatly tailored exclusive jurisdictions are the exception. Instead, multilevel governance as a configuration emphasizes that, more often than not, different governmental tiers, often including social actors, are working together in various ways to address collective-action problems that span multiple scales. Moreover, multilevel governance is not only a structure but also a process. This means that multilevel actor configurations are not static, but dynamic and permanently in motion (Behnke, Broschek, and Sonnicksen 2019; Broschek 2015; Piattoni 2010).

As is true of many other policy domains, authority over trade policy is more complex than formal constitutional provisions usually suggest. Often it is ambiguous and potentially contested. Ambiguity and contestation, of course, open up not only opportunities for sub-federal actors to change the status quo but also the possibility of backlash and reversal. We should therefore be careful not to assume a straightforward and uni-directional sequence of change that automatically entrenches sub-federal actors in trade-policy governance. The EU, for example, seems to have learned from debates about the mixed character of trade agreements. In order to avoid the threat of constitutional dead-lock through a complex ratification process that includes member states and, in some cases, sub-federal actors in several member states, the European Commission appears to be deliberately excluding provisions in new trade agreements that would render them mixed agreements (Van der Loo 2018). Such reactive responses have the potential to curtail the nascent efforts of sub-federal actors like the German or Austrian Länder to consolidate their position in trade politics. Moreover, even in federations, like Canada, where sub-federal units have had a longer record of increased participation, their involvement may remain volatile. For example, there is still no institutionalized framework in place that would have perpetuated and clarified the role of provincial and territorial governments in trade policy, thereby leaving it largely to the discretion of the federal government to determine the scope, timing, and intensity of involvement. Accordingly, their participation is ad hoc, varying from trade agreement to trade agreement. Chris Kukucha (2016, 2) concludes that the process lacks the quality of a real transformation but can be better captured by "an uneven pattern of incremental intergovernmentalism."

Against this back-drop, our volume has demonstrated that the emergence of multilevel trade politics opens up a fascinating new research agenda. Trade policy, comparative federalism, and multilevel governance represent important strands of scholarship in political science, but exchange among these literatures is rare. While there is ample preliminary evidence that trade-policy governance is in flux, perhaps even undergoing a major transformation, we lack a deeper understanding of the extent, patterns, causes, and consequences of these trends. Our volume represents the first attempt to address this research gap. We have unravelled the complex relationship among the three dimensions of multilevel trade politics. In doing so, we identified three factors – institutional configuration, trade policy, and state-society linkages – that we suspect carry considerable causal weight for explaining this trend. We hope that this effort will contribute to the development of a larger conversation about the changing nature of trade politics, and multilevel governance generally. These factors can also help us to make some modest predictions about the future.

It is too soon to tell if the phenomenon that we are witnessing – an increase in sub-federal actor activity in trade policy and trade-agreement negotiations in many places – is an enduring shift. However, we suspect that it will continue in places where prospective trade agreements contain provisions that touch on sub-federal regulatory capacity or key economic or political interests. Where this is the case, and where the institutional configuration permits concerted action by sub-federal actors, we expect further instances of enhanced action by sub-federal actors.

We have by no means exhausted the research avenues relating to our three factors. Federal systems represent complex governance configurations. The distinction between self-rule and shared rule can serve as a useful point of entry to reduce empirical complexity, while avoiding the shortcomings of overly abstract and unidimensional classifications. But we also acknowledge that more work needs to be done in order to capture concisely the complex interactions among trade policy, the nature of sub-federal competencies, differences in the systems of intergovernmental relations (and corresponding modes of interaction), and the role of second chambers in the representation of regional interests in different political systems. We also treated the important function of constitutional courts in multilevel environments rather implicitly, just as we had to limit ourselves, for the most part, on the role of sub-federal executives without systematically including parliaments and linkages between parliaments across levels of government in what Crum and Fossum (2009) have called the evolving "multilevel parliamentary field."

Likewise, for the purpose of this book, we conceptualized the state-society dimension as a factor comprising interest groups, social movements, and political parties. We see a huge potential for research that unpacks this dimension to examine more closely the amplifying role of social mobilization or different business interests for sub-federal involvement in trade policy. Moreover, important insights from the growing literature on multilevel party politics – most notably the organizational ties between federal and sub-federal party organizations, or the structure of party systems – need to be included more systematically into this emerging research agenda to understand dynamic pattern variation across cases.

Finally, we would like to emphasize another important avenue for future research. For the purpose of this book we confined ourselves to formal federations in the Western Hemisphere. However, in order to understand how trade politics are becoming truly multilevel, we believe that extending the universe of cases is warranted. As our case studies demonstrate, federalism matters. Most notably, the constitutionally entrenched basis of sub-federal entities is important to understanding why they often emerge as new powerful actors in trade politics, as well as the form this influence takes. Hence, although we think the unitary-federal dichotomy is by no means irrelevant as sub-federal units enjoy constitutional privileges that municipalities or regions in unitary states do not have at their disposal, we also see its limitations. In many unitary states across the world, regions have emerged as powerful actors, if not de jure, then often de facto. Municipalities are often responsible for providing a broad array of public services, ranging from health care to social housing and infrastructure, all areas that have become more deeply affected by recent trade agreements. Big cities may even represent much larger political communities than many less populated sub-federal units in federal states, which gives them considerable weight in multilevel politics. Likewise, Indigenous communities are in the process of raising their concerns more vociferously in the trade arena. They often have a territorial base, adding another layer of complexity. The approach adopted in this volume will hopefully inspire further research on a broader scale and should be considered a starting point rather than an end-point to the study of multilevel trade.

REFERENCES

Bartolini, Stefano. 2005. *Restructuring Europe: Centre Formation, System Building and Political Structuring between the Nation-State and the European Union.* Oxford: Oxford University Press.

Behnke, Nathalie, Jörg Broschek, and Jared Sonnicksen. 2019. "Introduction: The Relevance of Studying Multilevel Governance." In *Configurations, Dynamics, and Mechanisms of Multilevel Governance*, edited by N. Behnke, J. Broschek, and J. Sonnicksen, 1–19. Basingstoke, UK: Palgrave.

Broschek, Jörg. 2015. "Authority Migration in Multilevel Architectures: A Historical-Institutionalist Framework." *Comparative European Politics* 13 (6): 656–81.

Broschek, Jörg, and Patricia Goff. 2018. Federalism and International Trade Policy: The Canadian Provinces in Comparative Perspective. *IRPP Insight* 23. Montreal: Institute for Research on Public Policy.

Crum, Ben, and John Erik Fossum. 2009. "The Multilevel Parliamentary Field: A Framework for Theorizing Representative Democracy in the EU." *European Political Science Review* 1 (2): 249–71.

Falleti, Tulia G., and James Mahoney. 2015. "The Comparative Sequential Method." In *Comparative-Historical Analysis in Contemporary Political Science*, edited by J. Mahoney and K. Thelen, 211–39. New York: Cambridge University Press.

Hooghe, Liesbet, and Gary Marks. 2016. *Community, Scale, and Regional Governance: A Postfunctionalist Theory of Governance, Volume II.* Oxford: Oxford University Press.

Hooghe, Liesbet, Gary Marks, and Arjan H. Schakel. 2010. *The Rise of Regional Authority: A Comparative Study of 42 Democracies*. New York: Routledge.

Kukucha, Christopher J. 2016. Provincial/Territorial Governments and the Negotiation of International Trade Agreements. *IRPP Insight* 10. Montreal: Institute for Research on Public Policy.

Piattoni, Simona. 2010. *The Theory of Multi-level Governance: Conceptual, Empirical, and Normative Challenges*. Oxford: Oxford University Press.

Rokkan, Stein. 1999. *State Formation, Nation-Building, and Mass Politics in Europe: The Theory of Stein Rokkan*. Edited by P. Flora. Oxford: Oxford University Press.

Tatham, Michael. 2016. *With, Without, or Against the State? How European Regions Play the Brussels Game*. Oxford: Oxford University Press.

– 2018. "The Rise of Regional Influence in the EU: From Soft Policy Lobbying to Hard Vetoing." *Journal of Common Market Studies* 56 (3): 672–86.

Van der Loo, Guillaume. 2018. *Less Is More? The Role of National Parliaments in the Inclusion of Mixed (Trade) Agreements*. CLEER Papers 2018/1. The Hague: T.M.C. Asser Institute.

Contributors

Yelter Bollen, Doctor in EU studies, Ghent University, Belgium

Jörg Broschek, Associate Professor and Canada Research Chair in Comparative Federalism and Multilevel Governance, Department of Political Science, Wilfrid Laurier University, Canada

Peter Bußjäger, Professor at the Institute of Public Law, State and Administrative Science at the University of Innsbruck, and Director of the Institute of Federalism in Innsbruck

Ferdi De Ville, Assistant Professor, Centre for EU Studies, Ghent University, Belgium

Michelle Egan, Professor, School of International Service, American University

Annmarie Elijah, Associate Director, Centre for European Studies, Australian National University

Maria Garcia, Senior Lecturer of European Politics, Languages, and International Studies, University of Bath, United Kingdom

Niels Gheyle, Postdoctoral researcher, Ghent University, Belgium

Myriam Martins Gistelinck, Political Advisor to the Chair of the International Trade Committee, European Parliament

Patricia Goff, Associate Professor, Department of Political Science, Wilfrid Laurier University, Canada

Christian Hederer, Professor of Economics and International Economic Policy, Technical University of Applied Sciences, Wildau, Germany

Christopher Kukucha, Professor, Department of Political Science, University of Lethbridge, Canada

Patrick Leblond, Associate Professor and CN–Paul M. Tellier Chair on Business and Public Policy, University of Ottawa, Canada

Marcela López-Vallejo, Professor of International Relations, Department of Pacific Studies-CUCSH, Universidad de Guadalajara, Mexico

Stéphane Paquin, Professor, Ecole nationale d'administration publique, Montreal, Canada

Jorge A. Schiavon, Profesor-Investigador, División de Estudios Internacionales, Centro de Investigacion y Docencia Economicas, Mexico City

Sophie Schram, Boston Consulting Group, Germany

Christoph Schramek, Postdoctoral researcher, Institut für Föderalismus, Innsbruck, Austria

Gabriel Siles-Brügge, Associate Professor in Public Policy, Department of Politics and International Studies, University of Warwick, United Kingdom

Michael Strange, Reader (docent) in International Relations, Department of Global Political Studies, Malmö University, Sweden

Andreas R. Ziegler, Professor, Faculty of Law, Criminal Justice, and Public Administration, University of Lausanne, Switzerland

Index

Newfoundland and Labrador, 38, 40,
  62, 167
Niederösterreich, 216–17
Niedersachsen, 224
Nisga'a Treaty, 167
non-compliance, 60–1, 117, 250,
  357–8
non-tariff trade barriers, 43, 67,
  75, 115
Nordic Green Left, 291
Nordrhein-Westfalen, 219, 221, 224
North American Agreement on
  Labour Cooperation, 166
North American Free Trade
  Agreement (NAFTA): Act, 60–1,
  68; general, 41, 114–16, 137–9,
  160, 164–6, 169; implementation,
  60–2, 64, 67, 117; negotiations,
  44–5, 84, 88, 91, 124, 130, 167, 173;
  renegotiation, 9, 52, 56, 123, 131,
  168, 171, 351
Nova Scotia, 45, 168
Nuevo Leon, 148

Oaxaca, 140, 142, 148
Obama, Barack, 115, 294
Ohio, 170
Ontario, 5, 9, 36, 38, 40, 44, 46–51,
  61–3, 69, 93, 96–7, 166–8, 174, 354
Ontario-Quebec Trade and
  Cooperation Agreement, 97
Open Method of Coordination
  (OMC), 67, 76
Oregon, 169
Oregon Fair Trade Campaign, 170
Oregon Fair Trade Coalition, 169
Organic Law of Federal Public
  Administration, 132
Organization of American States
  (OAS), 159, 166
Österreichische Volkspartei (OVP),
  219

Paris Agreement, 296
Parti du Travail de Belgique, 266
Parti Québécois (PQ), 84, 92, 95, 166,
  168
Parti Socialiste (PS), 265, 271–2
Partido Acción Nacional (PAN), 163,
  173, 176
Partido de la Revolución
  Democrática (PRD), 147, 163, 172,
  176
Partido Revolucionario Institucional
  (PRI), 163, 171–2
Pennsylvania, 169–70
Petriccionne, Mauro, 48
Petróleos Mexicanos, 137
polarization, 20–1, 114, 224, 227,
  300, 363
political opportunity structures,
  326
politicization, 9, 20–1, 26, 121, 209,
  257, 259, 266–7, 269, 271, 273, 282,
  291, 293, 296, 300
precautionary principle, 222, 320
Prince Edward Island, 45
Principles and Procedures
  for Commonwealth-State
  Consultation on Treaties, 240
Pro-Canada Network, 164–5
procurement: CETA, 13, 23, 46, 68–9,
  81; general, 83, 86; Quebec, 83, 85,
  87–9, 93–9; sub-federal, 20, 35, 51,
  56, 81–4, 100–3, 124, 198
Progressive Alliance of Socialists
  and Democrats (Socialists and
  Democrats Group), 291, 308, 312,
  314, 317, 319, 322
protectionism, 112, 160, 173–4
Public Citizen, 169–70, 175, 340
Puebla, 141–3, 148

Quebec, 23, 36–8, 44–51, 61, 63,
  68–70, 81–104, 166–8, 174, 360

Studies in Comparative Political Economy and Public Policy